In the Arms of

AFRICA

Colin Turnbull, on Congolese Independence Day, in the barazza
of the Chef de Poste, Epulu, 1971.
Photograph by Frances C. Train; reprinted courtesy of Frances C. Train.

In the Arms of AFRICA

THE LIFE OF COLIN M. TURNBULL

Roy Richard Grinker

The University of Chicago Press

ROY RICHARD GRINKER is professor of anthropology and international affairs at The George Washington University. He is the author of *Houses in the Rainforest: Ethnicity and Inequality among Farmers and Foragers in Central Africa*; *Perspectives on Africa: A Reader in Culture, History, and Representation*; and *Korea and its Future.*

The University of Chicago Press, Chicago 60637

Originally published 2000
University of Chicago Press edition 2001
Reprinted by arrangement with St. Martin's Press, LLC
Printed in the United States of America
09 08 07 06 05 04 03 02 01 1 2 3 4 5
ISBN: 0-226-30904-5 (paper)

Library of Congress Cataloging-in-Publication Data

Grinker, Roy Richard, 1961–
In the arms of Africa : the life of Colin M. Turnbull / Roy Richard Grinker.
p. cm.
Originally published : New York : St. Martin's Press, 2000.
Includes bibliographical references and index.
ISBN 0-226-30904-5 (pbk. : alk. paper)
1. Turnbull, Colin M. 2. Gay anthropologists—United States—Biography. 3. Gay anthropologists—Africa—Biography. 4. Mbuti (African people) 5. Ik (African people) I. Title.

GN21.T85 G75 2001
301′.092—dc21
[B]

2001027980

⊗The paper used in this publication meets the minimum requirements of the American National Standard for Information Sciences—Permanence of Paper for Printed Library Materials, ANSI Z39.48-1992.

For Joyce

CONTENTS

ACKNOWLEDGEMENTS

When I left for central Africa in 1985 for the first six months of what would ultimately be twenty-two months of fieldwork with the Pygmies and farmers of the Ituri rainforest, I intended to disprove Colin Turnbull. No cultural anthropologist had studied the Pygmies so intensively, and since his classic work in the 1950s no cultural anthropologist had even attempted a follow-up study. Like many other anthropologists, I assumed that his characterizations of Pygmy life were romantic and somewhat fictionalized. When I finished my fieldwork, I accused Turnbull of not knowing the language of the Pygmies, and of ignoring important aspects of Pygmy life that would have led him to construct a different picture of Pygmy society. It was only many years later, after I found myself occupying his former faculty position at George Washington University and became close friends with the executor of his estate, that I stopped seeing him as a scholar I needed to debunk and became aware of the complicated relationship between his work and life.

When I decided to write this book, I remembered that I had corresponded with Colin Turnbull when I was in the field. I located one letter in my files, but even though I was working on the biography, it still took me nearly six weeks to read it. What I found was disturbing, the reason why I had removed the letter from memory: it is one of the kindest professional letters I have ever received. On October 15, 1985, he sent two copies of a long letter, one to Harvard and one to Zaire, of which I reproduce just a portion here:

> Dear Mr. Grinker,
> I have just returned from a few months in Samoa, and heard about your work . . . I hope we can meet. I am sending a copy of this to Africa in case it reaches you there, in case you feel in need of encouragement!
>
> . . . I have no phone here, so be sure to write and let me know when you will be back and if your movements are likely to bring you close to Virginia . . . my own project is to stay right here and get as much writing done as possible for the next six months; but surely we can find time to meet somewhere mutually convenient. Any help I can give, you are

more than welcome, it is really good to know that there is going to be more work done, at last!

I felt terrible not only because of his generosity—indeed, the letter also included much practical advice on working with the Pygmies—but because I never replied to the letter. And when, subsequently, he wrote to me again, suggesting that the Pygmies I was studying were too westernized and that I should go elsewhere, I was too angry to respond. I never heard from him again.

It is difficult to immerse oneself so fully in a single life unless driven to do so by something more than simple curiosity. For me, it was the knowledge that I had failed to meet a remarkable person because I was consumed by youthful narcissism. And because I wanted so much to dismiss his work, I also failed to engage with him intellectually. I want to thank Joyce Chung, who first proposed that I write this book and who helped me see that telling the life story of Colin Turnbull made sense both for anthropology and for me.

This book could not have been written without a remarkable amount of support from many people and institutions. Bob Humphrey, the executor of Colin Turnbull's estate, was at once a colleague, guide, and cheerleader, giving me every possible authorization but keeping most of his opinions to himself for fear of influencing my work. In Bob, Colin Turnbull never had a better friend, and neither have I. I owe my greatest debt to Joyce for her insights and provocations. She is a true partner. And for their love and loyalty, I thank Isabel and Olivia Grinker, and my parents Roy and Florence Grinker.

I have not ceased to be amazed by the generosity, efficiency, and professionalism of the Avery Research Center for African American History and Culture, located at the College of Charleston in Charleston, South Carolina, where the vast majority of Colin Turnbull and Joe Towles's papers are lodged. The Avery's reference archivist, Deborah Wright, gave much of her time and thought to this project. I also thank Boston University's special collections for access to materials from Colin Turnbull's last six years of life, George Washington and Hofstra Universities for releasing documents and letters relating to the professional activities of Colin Turnbull and his partner of twenty-nine years, Joseph Towles, and the National Anthropological Archives at the Smithsonian Institution for materials on James Ford. At Oxford University and Magdalen College at Oxford University, the archivists provided expert assistance on the period from 1941-1956, and Robin Darwall-Smith in particular taught me much about the structure and history of British higher education. In addition, I would not have been able to complete this study without the materials provided by Cumnor House, Westminster School, the American Museum of Natural History,

Michael Korda of Simon & Schuster, Richard Chance, John Enright, Louise Humphreys, Christie McDonald, Michael Radelet, Francie Train, and David Turnbull.

Colin Turnbull's family welcomed me with open arms, gave me their time, ideas, memories, and opened up their homes to me at Christmas, a time when they had many other obligations. I am grateful for their hospitality and interest, and their understanding that I was writing a book that would show the whole Colin Turnbull, warts and all. I am especially grateful to Colin Turnbull's nephew, David Turnbull, and first cousins, Betty Scott, Francis Chapman, and Patrick Gravely.

For their extraordinary passion for this project, I thank my editor Karen Wolny, her assistants, Amy Reading and Ella Pearce, production manager Alan Bradshaw, my agent, Anne Edelstein, and Deborah Baker. Karen and Anne supported this project with more time and attention than I thought possible from an editor and agent. Karen and Anne's enthusiasm and ambition gave this project its momentum. Without both of their editorial talents, their sense of the reading audience, and their constant encouragement to deepen my analysis, this book would have been far less penetrating and coherent. I am especially grateful to Anne for her wise counsel as we negotiated a confusing maze of editors and publishers, each with different ideas and expectations.

Paul Brodwin and Jonathan Higman helped me throughout the writing of this book. They edited, listened attentively to a constant and intrusive stream of updates, ideas, and complaints about the project, and helped me devise strategies to track down hard-to-find sources. I extend special thanks to my research assistants, Beth Pratt, Chris Garces, especially Emily Willis, and the large number of individuals who provided letters, photographs, documents, and anecdotes:

Curtis Abraham, Ram Alexander, Catherine Allen, Kwame Anthony Appiah, Roy Arrons, the estate of Sri Anandamayi Ma, the estate of Sri Aurobindo, Simon Bailey, Odile Bain, Derek Balaam, Frederik Barth, P. T. Baxter, Jim Bell, Nancy Benco, John Berkeley, Paul Brodwin, David Brokensha, Peter Brook, Alison Brooks, John Brooks, Dallas L. Browne, Ken Campbell, Thom Canada, Robert Carneiro, Luigi Cavalli-Sforza, Richard Chance, Howard Chapman, Ven. Tenzin Choephel, Robert Christie, Lance Clawson, Sheila Cosminsky, Clark Cunningham, Richard Curley, Ildiko DeAngelis, John Deschamps, Irven DeVore, David von Drehle, Nick Duffell, G. van Dulken, Jean-Paul Dumont, Eugenia Earle, Dick and Celia Elzay, Joan Fahy, Steven Feld, R. H. Finnegan, Rhoda Fisher, Stan Freed, Pete Gagan, Nathan Garner, Glenn Geelhoed, Gautam Ghosh, John Gillory, Walter R. Goldschmidt, Alma Gottlieb, Karen Gottlieb, Robert Gottlieb, Ruth Gravely, Ted Green, Mathias

Guenther, Philip Gulliver, Lisa Hallstrom, Terese Hart, Kamal Hassan, Tom Headland, James Hendricks, Alf Hiltebeitel, Peter Holmes, Jake Homiak, Nicholas Hopkins, Brian Horton, Valerie W. Hostinsky, Judy Howcroft, Johanna Humphrey, Virginia Humphreys, Ginger Humphreys, Sheila Miyoshi Jager, Horst Jarka, Gordon Johnson, Charles Kaiser, Robin Kennard, Robert Kirkpatrick, Ed Knipe, Igor Kopytoff, Michael V. Korda, Robin Kornman, John Krueger, Ruth Krulfeld, Joel Kuipers, Sheila Lamb, Richard Lannoy, Sam Leff, Don Lehman, Claude Lévi-Strauss, Robert A. Levine, Dan Lieberman, Charles Lindholm, Fred Littleton, Myra Luriano, William Lyon, Richard "Scotty" MacNeish, Jeanette Mageo, Merridy Malin, Maureen Malloy, Girish Mantry, Joan Mark, Phyllis Mayberg, Geeta Mayor, John McGrath, Julio Mercader, John Middleton, Nick Milner-Gulland, Rodney Needham, Michael J. O'Brien, Teresa O'Nell, Natasha Parry, Sheila Patterson, Norbert Peabody, Christopher Pegler, Glenn Petersen, Joe Powell, Cranford Pratt, Steve Raisin, Mary Reinhold-Smith, Zebiya Rigby, Judy Ritter, Alexander Robertson, Enid Schildkrout, Michael Schofield, Ruth Selig, Parker Shipton, John Shore, Geri Ellen Solomon, Jaqueline Solway, Nina Souffy, David Hurst Thomas, Elizabeth Marshall Thomas, Stephen Joel Trachtenberg, Nicholas Treat, Helen Tworkov, Peter VanArsdale, Derek Vereen, Don Vereen, Barry Waddy, Francine Waddy, Mike Wallace, Richard Walker , Raija Warkentin, Jeanine Wedel, Steve Williams, Gordon Willy, Ed Wilmsen, Elizabeth Wood, and John Yellen.

A note on the sources. There are some large gaps in the record I have done my best to fill. Colin Turnbull's World War II service record is a brief listing of his assignment locations. More substantial files from his service are closed to all eyes until 2018. The record of anything he did before 1959, when he met Joe Towles, is further clouded by the fact that Turnbull never said much about it. Because Turnbull wanted to believe that his life began in 1959 when he met Joe Towles and ended when Towles died in 1988, he wrote little about the first thirty-five years of life and even less about the last six years. Despite a wealth of material about Towles and Turnbull's relationship, I was disappointed that, for no reason I can determine, the surviving members of Towles's family—his brother and sister—refused to talk with me.

Adding to the mystery of Colin Turnbull's life's record, he terminated most of his friendships and all of his family ties in 1988 and asked some of his closest friends to destroy copies of their correspondences with him. As far as I know, only one person did. Of those who nonetheless wanted to maintain contact with him, only a handful had the tenacity to keep track of his whereabouts. Even the future executor of his estate, the man handling Turnbull's things while he was abroad in Samoa and later India, frequently had to spend hours on the phone trying to find out if anyone had heard from Turnbull. When Turnbull was ordained a Buddhist monk and changed his name permanently to Lobsong Rigdol, he became even harder to find. I must also add that despite repeated efforts, Thubten Norbu, the eldest brother of the Dalai Lama and Colin's mentor between 1988 and 1992, refused to talk with me for reasons described in the last chapter of this book.

Some of the sources used in this study are highly personal, such as diaries, love letters, and HIV tests, and yet we need to explore them if we are to understand Turnbull both as a writer and as a person. Lytton Strachey, the famed biographer, is reported to have said that "discretion is not the better part of biography." I should point out, however, that most of what I write in this book Colin Turnbull intended for publication. His unpublished and largely unpaginated manuscript, "Lover and Beloved," provides graphic details about his relationship with Joe Towles. In 1991, he scribbled a note on a copy of the manuscript, addressed, I assume, to his agent, Scott Meredith, who rejected the book: "Restricted until deceased. This is a personal, not academic account, entirely factual, and provides, I think, a good look at all that J.A.T. [Joseph Allen Towles] accomplished, and at what cost, from 1959 to 1988. It is highly personal, and though I have no reservations, you may wish to restrict access."

In addition to writing "Lover and Beloved," which is based almost entirely on Joe Towles's diaries, Turnbull later annotated the diaries to assist any future biographer of Towles. The annotations provide important insights into how Turnbull tried to realize his vision of Towles. Colin Turnbull did not intend a biography to be written of him, only of Towles, and then, only logically, of Towles's relationship with him. I thought a lot about his wishes as I was writing this book, and I began to have a recurring dream. Colin Turnbull and I meet on the first floor of an abandoned building. He does not know who I am, but I say proudly, "I know you better than anyone else in the world." He looks at me as if I have said nothing, then smiles as if I have said something grandiose. After an uncomfortable pause, he says, "Don't forget about Joe."

In the end, I was still fighting with Colin Turnbull, only this time it was for his life and legacy. I have turned away his efforts to deflect biography away from himself and toward Joe Towles; those efforts were nothing less than the design and purpose of his life.

In the Arms of

AFRICA

CHAPTER ONE

Pygmalion

ON MOST MORNINGS IN 1957, the Scottish anthropologist Colin Macmillan Turnbull would wake up in his hut next to his young Mbuti assistant, Kenge, their legs and arms intertwined in the way that Mbuti men like to sleep with each other to stay warm. At four foot eight, Kenge was more than a foot and a half shorter than Colin, so Colin could hold him easily with his long legs, arms, and wide hands, keeping them both warm in the damp forest nights.

By daybreak in the Ituri forest of central Africa the temperature often falls below sixty-five degrees, but it feels colder because dew drips incessantly from the forest canopy. Even if you are lucky enough to have a blanket, as Colin and Kenge did, the wool feels heavy and wet. The camp quickly comes alive with the pungent odor of small campfires and the sounds of children singing to welcome the new day. Light enters gently into the small hemispherical huts, made out of thin trees and thatched with *mongongo* leaves, overlapped like tiles. Kenge would emerge first to rekindle the campfire logs, with any luck still smoldering from the night before, for the Mbuti Pygmies do not know how to make fire.

In the afternoons, as thunder rumbled in the distance, Colin and Kenge would rush to the river to bathe. The skies in the Ituri open up, usually within an hour before sunset, releasing a hard and fast rain. When it stops, a few minutes later, the air feels cool and fresh, and black and white magpies and other birds can be seen flying out of their nests to wade in the new streams of rain water. By nightfall, Colin and Kenge had begun to warm themselves by the fire, perhaps eating the smoked meat of a small antelope or water chevrotain, or cassava leaves cooked in palm oil.

Colin spent most of his time with Kenge, who was unusually free to work for him. Kenge had only one blood relative in the area, a half sister, and so he was far less constrained by family obligations than others; because he was an outsider, he had license to be sexually playful with a wide range of people, and he used that freedom in excess. There were also few other Pygmy men willing to be so familiar with a European. Colin relished the nights they spent together, Kenge's sweet body odor, so distinctive to Pygmy men, and the hardness and compactness of Kenge's body, since Mbuti men have virtually no body fat. He would always remember the feeling of Kenge's callused feet rubbing against the soft skin on his legs and feet, protected from the elements by long pants, socks and shoes. Had Kenge commented on Colin, he would likely have talked about the ever-present smell of soap that the Mbuti associate with European bodies, the stark whiteness of his skin, and the enormity of Colin's body as he towered over him during the day, and enveloped and insulated him in the night.

Colin learned quickly that Mbuti men enjoy holding hands and embracing each other at night. The Mbuti have no concept, no word, for sexuality or homosexuality, so physical affection between men does not denote a sexual identity and carries no stigma. Mbuti men can therefore freely express their love for each other. When Colin touched Kenge, he was loving him and making love to him. For Colin also believed that one could make love without sex. One could make love with the rain forest, with music, and with other spiritual phenomena. The Pygmies knew this. They even used the same word for dancing that they used for sexual intercourse. For both Kenge and Colin, love was much more about spiritual ecstasy than about orgasm, more about beholding a universe in the reciprocal gaze and embrace of two men than about mere physical pleasure.

To Colin, Kenge represented the sensuality of the rain forest, and in his 1961 best-selling book, *The Forest People,* he wrote about one evening in particular, when the Pygmies with whom he lived were rejoicing in the forest. Alone in his hut, Colin tried to fall asleep, but the moon was full and shone through. Outside the hut, he heard the Mbuti Pygmies dancing. It was late at night but eventually he felt compelled to get out of his bed, a small black rubber pad and a gray blanket. Anthropologists are, at least at the beginning of their fieldwork, like dogs in a family fight, responding to every stimulus, moving rapidly here and there, but seldom knowing what is really happening around them. They imagine themselves to be human tape recorders, regretting every missed observation or interview for fear it may have contained a revelation. So Colin fought against his fatigue, wrapped the blanket around his back and crawled through the entrance of the hut to watch the festivities. And as he stood up outside the hut, he noticed Kenge.

"There in the tiny clearing," he wrote, "splashed with silver, was the sophisticated Kenge, clad in bark cloth, adorned with leaves, with a flower stuck in his hair. He was all alone, dancing around and singing softly to himself as he gazed up at the treetops.

"Now Kenge was the biggest flirt for miles, so, after watching a while, I came into the clearing and asked, jokingly, why he was dancing alone. He stopped, turned slowly around and looked at me as though I was the biggest fool he had ever seen; and he was plainly surprised by my stupidity.

"'But I'm not dancing alone,' he said. 'I'm dancing with the forest, dancing with the moon.' Then, with the utmost unconcern, he ignored me and continued his dance of love and life."

Turnbull dedicated *The Forest People* to Kenge, for whom, he wrote, the forest was many things, including his lover. Through Kenge, Colin realized a total and consuming passion for both the forest and the Pygmies who lived there, and he would remember the night of that dance as a revelation. For it was on that night, amidst the music and the effervescence, in a momentary vision and a brief conversation, that he became convinced of the human capacity for love and for goodness, which he believed was embodied in the Pygmies. His life and his anthropology were pilgrimages to a beautiful dream world that, in the African rain forest, was inexplicably real. His greatest challenge was to find that same humanity, that same dream, outside the rain forest.

Turnbull looked for it everywhere, and thought he found it in Joseph A. Towles, a young African American man the same age as Kenge, whom he met in New York City two years after he left the Pygmies, in 1959. When Turnbull first laid eyes on him, he thought to himself, "I am back in Africa." Turnbull was thirty-four years old and he would live with Joseph for the next thirty years. In 1959, Towles was an aspiring actor and model but he would soon become an anthropologist. While the Pygmies could be romanticized in writing in words that Colin shaped to fit his own vision, Towles, however, was not so easily fixed.

With the evocative and magical words of *The Forest People,* Colin Turnbull conjured an image of the Pygmies and their world that seized the public imagination and brought him both fame and wealth. Next to Margaret Mead and Louis Leakey, he is perhaps the most well-known anthropologist of the twentieth century. A gifted and persuasive writer, Turnbull used the power of his words and personality to project onto the Pygmies a reflection of his own ideals, altering forever the way that most European and American readers would see the African rain forest and its peoples. Though many anthropologists have disdained the romance and idealism of *The Forest People* as failed science, almost every anthropologist who has ever written about hunter-gatherers anywhere in the world has made use of his work, and what we know about the Pygmies today is derived almost entirely from his work. Many professional anthropologists trace their career decisions to a single reading of *The Forest People,* and the book remains required reading in many high schools and colleges.

If *The Forest People* made his reputation, Turnbull's next major publication, *The Mountain People* (1973) made him controversial. His book told the story of the starving Ik of Uganda, a people on the brink of extinction whose depravity he described in stark detail. In *The Forest People,* he had thanked the Indian guru, Sri Anandamayi Ma, with whom he lived just before he left for central Africa, for giving him his mantra, *Satyam, sivam, sundarm* (truth, goodness, beauty), and for convincing him that those qualities could be found if he looked hard enough; they were the same qualities he had found among the Pygmies and that he believed the Ik had cast aside. If, for Turnbull, the Pygmies showed us the "noble savage" we once were, the Ik, dislocated from their villages to a drought-stricken wasteland, showed us what we might one day become. He portrayed the Ik as a materially and morally impoverished collection of selfish individuals, a people who had abandoned the values of family, love, and altruism for a cutthroat individualism matched only by what he had seen in World War II while serving as a gunnery officer. He watched with horror as Ik men and women attacked each other, even within their own families, to induce vomiting and then eat the vomit; people defecated on each other's doorsteps; expressed joy at the tragedies of others; and having abandoned any effort to cooperate or share, the stronger left the weaker, usually children and the elderly, to die of starvation. "That is the point," he wrote in *The Mountain People,* "at which there is an end to truth, to goodness, and to beauty . . . The Ik have relinquished all luxury in the name of individual survival, and the result is that they live on as a people without life, without passion, beyond humanity."

He proposed to the Ugandan government that the Ik society should be eliminated, that individuals should be rounded up and dispersed over an area wide enough to make sure they never found each other again. The Ugandan government and the anthropological community were outraged. Angered by Turnbull's proposal and what was called a complete lack of objectivity, Fredrik Barth, the anthropologist who led the international attack against him, wrote that *The Mountain People* "deserves both to be sanctioned and to be held up as a warning to us all," that the book was "dishonest," "grossly irresponsible and harmful," threatening to the "hygiene" of the discipline. Turnbull, who had never shared science's devotion to objectivity and had never thought of himself as a conventional scholar, was unmoved.

His life was marked by a heroic piety to such lofty concepts as goodness, perfection, and love—words many people might find sentimental or vague, but which Colin Turnbull elevated to the sacred. For this reason, he decided to write more about experiences and feelings than about scientific facts. He wanted to show the world the goodness he had found among the Pygmies and the evils he had found among the Ik. The truth of the Zairean rain forest or the tragedy of the Ugandan mountains could not be conveyed in an academic publication to be read by a few hundred scholars. It had to reach millions of people and to come from the heart, not through science but through the emotional and spiritual paths for which his anthropology was an ongoing quest.

Despite his popularity, much about Colin Turnbull has remained a mystery, especially the relationship between his own, often tragic life, and the kinds of work he produced. Few people know that he devoted most of his adult life to one partner, with whom he lived openly as a gay, interracial couple in one of the smallest and most conservative rural towns in Virginia, or that despite Turnbull's refined public demeanor and even temper, his relationship with Towles was often cruel and violent. Few know that, in India, Turnbull was one of only a few Europeans ever permitted to live in the ashram of an Indian saint, Sri Anandamayi Ma, that he was fully ordained as a Buddhist monk by the Dalai Lama, that he helped build one of the most famous boats of the twentieth century, *The African Queen,* that he rejected university tenure (lifetime job security) when it was granted to him, or that he had a major influence on anti–death penalty advocacy. Even fewer know of Turnbull's bizarre reaction to Towles's death from AIDS in 1988.

This is a book about Colin Turnbull's public and private lives, and because it is an intimate study it explores some dimensions of experience that biographical subjects or their estates sometimes want to keep confidential. But Turnbull wanted to disclose the full details of his life with Towles, if only because he wanted Towles's life to be widely known. Turnbull believed that Towles was an African American hero, a gay hero, who could model for a younger generation the capacity to overcome oppression. To that end, Turnbull arranged all of his and Joe's papers for Joe Towles's future biographer, and wrote a rambling, unedited, one-thousand-page manuscript he called "Lover and Beloved." Ostensibly a history of his relationship with Towles, it is primarily a transcription of Joe's diaries and a record of Joe's efforts to become a professional anthropologist.

Colin Turnbull donated his private collection of hundreds of African artifacts, ten thousand slides and photographs, tape recordings, videos, and all his field notes to the Avery Center for Research on African American History and Culture at the College of Charleston, South Carolina. He called it the "Joseph A. Towles Collection." Turnbull also gave the Avery the hundreds of greeting cards he and Towles exchanged on holidays over the years, even empty boxes of Valentine's candy. He made sure that if anyone went to the Avery to look through the collections, that person would also find the name of Joseph A. Towles. And any future biographer would have access to everything, from insurance forms and tax returns to sexually playful notes written on scrap paper. The collection had another purpose, to make sure that no one could learn about Turnbull without also learning about Towles, that the life of Colin Turnbull would be visible as a transparency lit only by Joe.

The archive shows Turnbull's extraordinary commitment to Towles. Shortly after they met in 1959, they took wedding vows and considered themselves to be married as husband and wife. Colin called Joe "Josephine" and his love for his wife became a sacred object of worship and devotion. Thirty-five years later, he would pray daily to a shrine consisting of Buddhist and Hindu relics and three photographs, one of his former guru, Sri Anandamayi Ma, who Colin believed was an embodiment of God, the other two of Joe.

The archive and the history Turnbull wrote of his relationship with Towles are both expressions of the way in which Colin sought to merge his life with Joe's. Each took on parts of the other. Towles played out Turnbull's rage and recklessness so that Turnbull appeared to the world as a modest, unassuming and even-tempered man. Towles even fully realized Turnbull's deep-seated wish to be imprisoned, a wish that can be traced to Turnbull's early childhood. On the other side, Towles's imperfections satisfied Turnbull's need to fashion someone born without privilege, wealth or pedigree, and in showing Towles's worth, to prove, by comparison, his sense of his own mediocrity. Turnbull adapted to Towles's own sense of worthlessness—indeed, the very worst of his idea of his blackness—by becoming a stable father figure, one who could give Towles unconditional approval. Turnbull spent much of his life attempting to shape Towles into a world-class scholar. He became convinced that he could single-handedly bring to life the brilliance of Towles's undiscovered and unpolished mind.

Colin Turnbull struggled to create Joseph Towles, but he did so without the arrogance and whimsy of George Bernard Shaw's Pygmalion, Professor Henry Higgins, and he remained largely oblivious to the reasons behind his actions. He was perhaps more like the original Pygmalion, the ancient King of

Cyprus, the noble bachelor and sculptor who crafted and fell in love with an ivory statue of a maiden so beautiful she looked as if she must be a work of nature. The tragedy of Towles was that he tried to comply with Turnbull's need to create him. Turnbull helped make Towles an unsuccessful professor who would never publish or find continuous academic employment and who would continually threaten his ideals with affairs and alcoholism, and later with the psychiatric complications that accompany AIDS. His hope for Joe was a heavy burden for both of them, a burden that no intellectual vigor could lay down.

Both Joseph Towles and the Pygmies were the creations of Colin Turnbull, who was motivated by a deep-seated wish to find goodness, beauty, and power in the oppressed or ridiculed and, by making those qualities known, reveal the evils of western civilization. The vision of the world he summoned was so perfect, so true, so right for him, that it gave all the appearances of being real.

CHAPTER TWO

The Wizard

COLIN MACMILLAN TURNBULL was born at home on November 24, 1924, in a modest house in Harrow, a quiet suburb of London. His mother, Helen Dorothy (Dot) Wellesley Chapman, was a fiery Canadian and Episcopalian woman of Irish descent. She was thirty years old and already the mother of a four-year-old boy named Ian. She named her new son Colin after her former fiancé who had been killed in World War I.

Dot, as she was called, was born in Bray, Ireland, the sixth of seven children. Within a year of her birth, her family moved from Bray to Dublin before returning to Ontario, Canada, where her father's family had already lived for two generations. In the 1860s, her paternal grandfather, George Chapman, and his brother moved to Ontario to start an ice and lumber company at the invitation of an old friend from the British navy who had just completed construction of a large manor house on seven hundred acres of wooded land along the edge of Lake Simcoe. But George's son (Dot's father), Arthur Wellesley Chapman, declined the family business to become an Episcopal priest, first in Needham, Massachusetts and then in Bray, Ireland, where, in 1888, he met his wife, Elizabeth Figgis, and lived for nearly a decade before returning to Ontario.

Dot was raised primarily in Toronto but, as a child, she felt little commitment to Canada and devoted herself instead to Ireland, music, and the Episcopal church. There was talk in the family that she might one day return to Ireland, marry an Epispocal priest, and become a concert pianist.

Her family remembers her as the oddest child of her generation, if not because she had the strongest will and the least patience of all her siblings, then because she looked at the world through a singular lens. Even as a young teenager, she was forceful, outspoken, and passionate. Two of her nieces remember that, as children, they were afraid of the intensity of her feelings, her anger toward children, and her overbearing, theatrical displays of affection. As an adult, she could be hospitable and gracious but was more often unlikable; to her Canadian relatives she was a social climber and a snob. She would never be close with any of her siblings and, in later life, would seldom visit them in Canada.

Dot's brother George loved her for her quirks but recalls that she was "twisted." "No matter what anyone talked about," George says, "she always saw things differently." Dot had the ability to hold firm beliefs that many people found wrong or contradictory, but she had few debating skills and, when at a loss, either folded or lashed out. Like Colin, there was a difference between what she appeared to be and what she was: on the surface, she was privileged and self-assured, but underneath she was a person who felt marginal to the mainstream of society. Often she liked people others despised, and despised those who were the most well liked. Dot would pass on to Colin this capacity to defy common perspectives.

Following World War I, Colin Turnbull's father, John Rutherford Turnbull, was a promising young accountant in England. John, known by his friends and family as Jock, was born in 1884 on the border of Scotland and England, into a Turnbull lineage composed of an uncertain mixture of Campbells, the clan made famous by their massacre of the McDonald clan. It is said that they severed McDonald's head and served it on a platter to his wife, with a napkin in his mouth.

The Turnbull family believes their name can be traced to Robert the Bruce, the fourteenth-century king of Scotland. As the story goes, a bystander turned away a bull that was attacking Robert, and in gratitude the king gave him the name of Turn-bull. Turnbull clan malt whiskey is sold in Scotland today with a label that displays the family crest and the words "I Saved the King." The crest itself is a simple image of a bull's head on a tartan background, but, in accordance with the rules of heraldry, it also shows a sinister bar, a sign that there is a bastard in the family.

Jock and his two sisters were raised by Presbyterian parents in Greenoch, Scotland, where their father was at one time the chief civil engineer for the town. They were devoted Scottish nationalists, and all the Turnbulls, including Colin's two aunts (neither of whom ever married) and his mother, were eventually buried together on the banks of the Clyde river.

Jock left Scotland to fight in World War I where he was decorated with one of the United Kingdom's highest military honors, the Military Cross for Bravery. After the war, he moved to London to advance his career as an accountant, in those days a profession that more closely resembled the portfolio manager or stockbroker of today. From 1918 to 1939, Jock made regular business trips to Canada and met Dot's eldest sister, Lillian Chapman, on one of his early Atlantic crossings. The Chapmans hoped Jock would marry Lillian, but he was more interested in the younger daughters, of whom Dot was the only one willing to leave Canada. She and Jock were married on May 31, 1920, in Montreal, according to the rites and ceremonies of the Church of Ireland.

Jock Turnbull was a cool, quiet, and distant man, utterly devoted to his trade. He was, like many of his fellow Scotsmen, a stolid and stern man who chose his words, actions, and expenditures carefully. His handwriting was deliberate—tiny letters written with a fine-tipped fountain pen forming words clear and uniform enough to be entered into a ledger.

He was not without understanding however. Dot told him about her past love named Colin, and Jock gave her his blessing to name their second son after him. Though remote, he was a loving father who, despite his disapproval of homosexuality in general and his long-held prejudices against blacks, never turned his back on Colin. According to Dot's family, as much as Colin would complain to friends and colleagues about his parents' racism and conservatism, both his mother and father placed their commitment to Colin above their political views and above whatever gossip the neighbors might have whispered about the Turnbulls' queer son.

As an adult, Colin would often talk about himself as a study in contrasts, a combination of stereotypes of the Irish and the Scottish. In him, his parents' attributes met to form a peculiar mixture of the anxious, penny-pinching Scot and the expressive, impulsive Irish. If his mother taught Colin how to cry and show rage, his father taught him the value of detachment and careful study. And if Dot taught him how to revel in moments of happiness, Jock taught him to be withholding and suspicious.

Jock and Dot's marriage was cordial, formal, and stable. They slept in separate rooms and approached sex with ignorance, fear, and no form of birth control. As a young housewife, Colin's mother believed that birth control was a tool the rich wanted to use to stop the poor from reproducing. Colin's father believed that birth control was a hoax and that no one could have sex without also producing a child. Both were convinced that twins resulted from sex during pregnancy and, though she was probably lying, she told Colin just before her death that she and Colin's father had had intercourse only when they wanted a baby. When, as an adult, he learned of his parents' anxiety-ridden sex life, he felt sorry for them. But he was also comforted by the knowledge that he and his brother had been wanted. "I would like to think," he said, "that for my parents the quality of those two acts of intercourse, filled with the intent and longing of which my brother and I were the results, made up for what they lost in quantity."

Jock and Dot seldom argued. In fact, her nieces remember that, in Dot's eyes, Jock could do nothing wrong. When she and Jock did argue, it was almost always about politics. Dot loved politics, and her interest in it intensified after she married and moved to England. For despite her comfortable lifestyle, she faced an unfriendly society; England continually made its Scottish and Irish subjects aware of their place in the kingdom. She and Jock would often be reminded of their heritage, not only by their British hosts but by Jock's family too. Jock's sisters would always remain ambivalent about his marriage to an Irish woman, and Dot was rumored to have rejected the possibility of living in Scotland, thus keeping Jock from his kin and homeland. The Turnbulls never forgave Dot for giving birth to Ian and Colin on English rather than Scottish soil and did not permit her to stay in their home when the family was on vacation in Scotland. On the other side of the Atlantic, Dot's Canadian relatives resented her lack of interest in Canada and criticized her privately for adopting what they called a "phony British accent." As a result, Colin was brought up in a family that was acutely aware of nationality and in which everyday family conflicts could often be traced to long standing political sensitivities.

Colin and his elder brother Ian occupied separate nurseries and each had his own nanny. Jock and Dot each picked a favorite child: Jock chose Ian, Dot chose Colin. The boys for a time slept in the same room until one night, when Colin was about nine years old, Colin jumped into bed with Ian and pulled the covers over their heads so their parents would not hear them. Jock and Dot reacted explosively when they discovered the two boys talking and laughing. Colin believed his father and mother feared they were masturbating, and they argued over which boy was responsible for the disturbance. Predictably, Jock blamed Colin; Dot blamed Ian. The boys were henceforth separated into different bedrooms, even on family vacations. They would forever be isolated from each other emotionally as well as physically, though Colin, in all likelihood jealous of Ian's close relationship with their father, tried to emulate him. Dot and Jock believed that both Ian and Colin were artistic and sensitive, but Ian was the more masculine of the two. Many years later, Jock would recall Ian and Colin's relationship in a letter to Ian's son David:

"[Ian was] . . . at times, extremely naughty, and was the ringleader in many escapades into which he led his little brother—who, I must say, was always very willing indeed to take part! In your uncle Colin's eyes, your father could do no wrong—everything was just perfect, even when it included standing on the roof of the garage to pelt passers-by with crab-apples, or throwing silver-backed brushes and other things from the nursery window."

Jock and Dot paid little attention to the boys, but their neglect was entirely conventional. Dot wanted the best for her children, and that meant the finest nannies and the finest schools. The nanny system depicted in *Mary Poppins,* in which British governesses were drawn from well-bred but bankrupt upper-class families, was in decline, but now there was a new breed of nanny. Many came from Germany, France, Ireland, and the West Indies, and they had considerable power in the upbringing of their charges. Nannies selected the children's toys, clothes, books, food, and companions, and despite their various nationalities, they were intended to teach as much as possible good British and Christian virtues, such as obedience, authority, and the wrongs of self-indulgence.

In his partly autobiographical book about rites of passage, *The Human Cycle* (1983), Colin noted that his earliest childhood memories were of nannies but not of his mother. "I have a hazy but fond recollection of a West Indian nanny," he wrote. "My mother was not allowed to nurse me because of some alleged health hazard, and I have no recollections of her at this time . . . The West Indian nanny [kept] me quiet by feeding me with teaspoons of some liquor. I also vaguely remember suckling at her huge breasts, or at least being held close to them and feeling happy in their warmth, a closeness that I cannot for the life of me recall having had with my mother until I was five or six years old, although I probably did. Then, when I cried, my mother would pick me up and, it seemed, try to smother me in her embrace. I felt much safer with my nanny. But that nanny was also fired, a terrible day I remember well, because my mother, on one of her periodic personal house inspections, discovered an excessive quantity of empty bottles under nanny's bed."

Out of that experience, Colin had a clear sense that, despite the nanny's total involvement with him and her authority within the nursery, ultimate power still rested with his mother. The more distant she was, the more he idealized her; and yet her unexpected intrusions, usually done in order to fire a nanny, caused him more pain than pleasure. Each nanny was fired at the moment they appeared too close to him, too affectionate, too much like a mother, in effect denying Colin any secure attachment. The Turnbull and Chapman families do not recall today that Dot was as possessive of Ian, who was in effect "Jock's son."

As for Colin's father, he was at work much of the time, and was especially distant from the boys when they were young. They would not see his lighter side until years later when he became an animal lover, indulged Dot's two white poodles, kept a donkey named Judy in the backyard, and every morning on the long walk to the train station fed carrots to the horses at a nearby stable.

Colin's most vivid childhood memories concerned two German nannies, Irene Fritzel and Helen Feldman. Irene, who took care of Colin from about age nine to eleven, was large, blonde, pale-skinned, and talkative; she once told Colin that men gave women babies by urinating in their mouths. "Unfortunately, Irene was a Nazi and did not last longer than two years," Colin wrote. "I protested her departure loudly and recounted some of the stories she had told me as evidence of what a good nanny she was." Colin missed Irene so much that he insisted on having another German nanny, Helen Feldman. Helen introduced Colin both to Catholicism, about which he knew virtually nothing, and, through her brother Hans, to Nazism and the Hitler Youth.

"[Hans] used to send me swastika armbands and other paraphernalia that I learned were better kept well concealed. What a way to lose one's innocence. But then came the Munich crisis and Hans sent Helen a letter ordering her to come home at once. My tears were of no avail. Helen left; I lost the last of a succession of mothers and began, at the age of twelve, to know the mother who so undiplomatically gave birth to me in England. Only then did I really begin to know my parents and to exchange the fullness of love with them, to feel secure with them, trusting and understanding."

When *The Forest People* was published, he inscribed a copy to his parents, "To Mom and Dad, with all my deepest love and gratitude for having shown me the really worthwhile things of life. This book, in its way, is a reflection of all you have given me." But at the same time, Colin believed that his love for his parents was more a reasoned relationship than a felt one, and he remained deeply resentful about the distance they had kept. "The feeling of love," he once wrote, "did not develop and begin to truly flourish for another quarter of a century." Letters between Colin and his parents were saccharine, at once both sentimental and superficial, often bordering on the cloying. It was as if his parents had given him the vocabulary for love without the grammar. He knew what to say and when to say it but the underlying principles of love, the most basic structures of feeling were missing.

In 1984, Colin told a friend that, when he was fourteen, he was caught stealing watches at his boarding school, Westminster. Jock was summoned to meet with Colin and the headmaster, but the meeting was delayed for some reason and Jock complained to Colin that he was afraid he might miss an appointment in town with a client. Colin remembered thinking, "Even now, when I am in such trouble, all he can think of is his business." He asked himself then, "Is it silly that a sixty-year-old man should still be sad that his father didn't love him?"

The intensity of the relationships between the children and their parents' servants belied the contrived formality of upper middle class life. The nannies were responsible for and deeply involved with every facet of their charges' lives, and yet they were seen as employees and their influence was seldom acknowledged. They were to be called by first name only and certainly never with a familial term like "Mother" or "Aunt." Colin was permitted to address the gardener only as "Gardener," the chauffeur only as "Mr. Arnold." Inevitably Colin learned that the servants were not of his same status, for acquiescence to the class system was an important part of his training to be a gentleman in British society. Even if he greeted his position with a sense of guilt, it must have been at least partly enjoyable. As a child Colin was always to be addressed as "Master Colin," and later when he lived in the Belgian Congo he was addressed, like all Europeans there, as "Bwana," the Swahili word for master.

Eventually, Colin would interpret his sense of privilege as a duty to help people of color, those with little money or the possibility for social mobility, those who in any way suffered from discrimination. Despite his apparent class comforts, he felt himself to be discriminated against, coerced into living in a society that seemed to value status assigned at birth more than achievement, the individual more than the community, inequality rather than equality. This was not simple white liberal guilt. Loving those who were oppressed was an act of resistance against his society and his parents, neither of whom had given him the emotional stability and nurturing he wanted; in the poor or marginalized he saw himself, and determined to do for them what had not been done for him.

Colin would always remember well the bizarre Struwwelpeter (Peter Strubbel) children's stories his last nanny, Helen, used to read to him in German, because they described people who were different or left out. In one of the Struwwelpeter stories, a wizard admonishes a group of white toys for teasing a black one and ultimately turns the white toys black. "Oh! Blacky, you're as black as ink," says a white toy. The wizard cries out, "Boys, leave the black-a-moor alone! For if he tries with all his might, he cannot change from black to white." The wizard, now enraged, grabs hold of the white toys. "And they may scream and kick and call, into the ink he dips them all; into the inkstand, one, two, three, till they are black as black can be."

Colin Turnbull identified with the black toys in his German nanny's Struwwelpeter stories, but his lifelong efforts to help those he saw as powerless put him more in the position of the wizard. As the wizard, he could distance himself from British society, from his father who appeared not to love him, and from his mother who loved him too much. He longed to be somewhere in the middle, neither white nor black, of no certain nationality or religion. Anthropology helped him imagine that place in the middle, for as an anthropologist he could love the Other, live with the Other, and he could do it all without completely abandoning the station into which he was born. As an anthropologist, he could flirt with the idea of becoming a commoner, of being poor and dependent, but then return to the safety of home and university with a treasure of stories to tell, stories that earned him money and fame. In devoting himself to a love of the Other, he would lead a vicarious existence, one that completed him and helped him reconcile the difference between his public image of himself as a gentleman and his private image as someone perpetually out of place. He justified both his public and private lives by fighting against domination and discrimination. He would love those who accepted his role as wizard, and he would often detest those who resisted him.

Until he joined the Royal Navy in World War II at the age of eighteen, Turnbull had taken only one voyage outside the United Kingdom, a family vacation in France. Yet his fantasies about a life apart from his own world began at an early age. He imagined living in the places the servants had come from, some place far from home, away from his mother's confounding mixture of possessiveness and remoteness, and away from the narrow confines in which he was expected to live. He found people who were from India or East Asia or Africa the most beautiful people of all, not only because they seemed to him to call out for help in a racist world, or simply because he found their physical features aesthetically appealing, but because their beauty spoke to him about a different way of living. And not being able to be with these people made them all the more attractive.

People of color promised him liberation from the isolation of his white world, his nursery, his dependence on his nanny, his mother's authority, and the hopeless fantasies about winning his father's attention and love. On at least one occasion, after his mother cautioned him to stay away from gypsies camping in a nearby field, warning Colin that the gypsies liked to kidnap little boys, Colin promptly ran out to the field and asked to be kidnapped. Where did he imagine the gypsies would take him? Anywhere, perhaps, since home for Colin felt like a place of exile. His nanny caught up with him, took him to the local police station, and asked the police to show Colin the jail cells. Throughout his life, he would try other forms of escape.

"At home my nursery was the safest place," Turnbull wrote in *The Human Cycle,* "for even my mother did not visit there all that often. My bedroom was next, but much more subject to maternal invasion . . . The parts of the house where my parents, brother, or servants lived were all barred to me. Outside the home the Rule Valley [of Scotland] took first place, and I frequently went there in my imagination. Trees and deserted homes came next, then probably the cliffs and rooftops. No wonder one of my childhood fantasies was to become a reclusive monk."

As an anthropologist, Colin would consider the Mbuti Pygmy system of childrearing to be superior to the one in which he was raised. For him, the Mbuti family system was one in which every child was wanted and loved equally whether boy or girl, in which children were taught to respect each other and the environment and were trained to be nonviolent and egalitarian. In his idealized view, no Mbuti child ever searched for sanctuary because the forest was eminently good and safe; few Mbuti ever struggled against their peers because everyone shared and cooperated.

Colin did not question that Mbuti men and women made excellent parents. They held rituals for their children that bestowed upon them community identities rather than individual ones, making virtually no distinctions of hierarchy or status. Children were never pitted against one another. People lived in harmony not because they were coerced to do so by laws, the threat of violence, or other external impositions, but because of an internal desire for unity, reciprocity, and social equality, a desire every Mbuti parent unselfconsciously and automatically fostered in their children. A Mbuti child learned to love others not because love was imposed upon him, but because he had spent at least the first three years of his life, not with nannies, but in his mother's arms, or on her back, and in her bed, in a relationship of constant and selfless giving and receiving. For Colin, that early mother-child bond among the Mbuti was the best model for future relationships with family, friends, and lovers; only when that bond was absent did children and parents find themselves in conflict, with both sides feeling rejected and worthless. Then, in the absence of that bond and when it was already too late, love had to be demanded; then love became the burden Colin knew so well. "What would we lose," he once asked, "if we gave our children something different, something of what the Mbuti have to teach us about motherhood?"

CHAPTER THREE

Hothouse

WHEN HE WAS SIX YEARS OLD, Colin began his education at a school called Downside, where he learned Latin, mathematics, and cruelty to boys. His brother was already a student there, and designated as a "senior boy" (upperclassman) while Colin was a "new boy." Colin remembered that, "In the very first week I was grabbed by other upperclassmen, called 'senior boys,' and brought into their classroom where my hand was held in the sunlight while my brother (I think against his inclination, basically he too was nonviolent) held a magnifying glass over it until my skin began to smoke . . . I do not think I learned anything useful in that school except how to lie with only moderate success, how to cheat, and how to have zero confidence in adults and peers alike. It was another good lesson in the value of isolation, and my own personal survival became very important to me. Being a boys' school it provided no opportunity for getting to know any girls, who remained muggable objects in my estimation, except for my two tomgirl acquaintances."

Within two years, the boys left Downside. Believing that the school did little to limit violence between boys, the Turnbulls enrolled Colin and Ian in what they considered a much better place: a small private, primary day school called

Cumnor House. Colin was one of five pupils admitted in January 1935. Only four years earlier, Martin Wheeler had bravely started the school with six pupils during the Slump, as the Depression was sometimes known in England, when parents were not feeling particularly generous. He named the school after the house he purchased for it in Croyden. By 1934 the enrollment had reached a total of fifty. Wheeler did almost all of the teaching himself, with his wife as matron-housekeeper and cook. By the time Colin and his classmates arrived, there were two additional teachers, Mr. Perry as senior master and Miss Pring. Mr. Perry died tragically of typhoid in 1937; it was Colin's first brush with death.

Colin's classmates remember little about him. He did not keep in touch with them after leaving Cumnor in 1938. What they do remember of Colin is that he had remarkable musical skills, that he almost always needed a haircut and that he occasionally came to school dressed in a kilt. One classmate who used to take the train home with Colin, the 5:38 P.M. Victoria non-stop to Purley, describes Colin as retiring, quiet, and never good at sports. Colin's former classmates are not surprised that Colin had such an extraordinary life but none were especially close to him. Even the classmate reputed to have the best memory could only recall that Colin loved music. The fact that other students did keep in touch with each other suggests that Colin was socially on the margins at Cumnor, or at least that he felt on the margins.

In his 1983 book, *The Human Cycle,* Colin recalled his curiosity about Mr. Perry's sudden death from typhoid: "So were others [curious], but we were all assembled and told that this was what would happen if we played around drains and sewers. I wondered at this, as I had never seen Mr. Perry playing around drains and sewers, but I was merely told, when I voiced my suspicion that something was being concealed from us, that he had 'gone away' (as though he had been dismissed for improper behavior) and 'would not be back.'"

Colin experienced these sorts of masked communication as the ways in which adults in his world kept a hold on their power to indoctrinate him with their own sense of morality. He did not trust his teachers or his parents, all of whom frowned on his inability to merely accept what they told him. He felt isolated both spiritually and intellectually. Even as a schoolboy he wanted to explore religions other than Christianity and the Episcopalian religion taught at his school (he had been baptized Presbyterian), but had no opportunity to do so. Colin's love of music helped him through this time because music was enjoyable in isolation.

Church music quickly became his passion, and for the rest of his life he would play the organ and listen to it in times of need. The sound of the organ brought him to a spiritual place he could not find elsewhere. His fondest memories of childhood were of playing in Westminster Abbey and other cathedrals in England and Scotland. For Colin, there were passages in organ music so strong and full that when he played them his body no longer felt separate from the instrument and, even more, no longer separate from the cathedral. It is not easy to describe such moments as spiritual because they do not require a belief in God or spirits, or as secular because Colin felt the music enter him as deeply as most devout believers would ever expect their religion to do. What is true of the organist is doubtless true for most musicians, including the bassist whose brilliance can sometimes be measured by how inconspicuous he can be in the context of a full orchestra, or the Pygmy vocalist who is nothing without the other singers. But there is something special about the organ in the cathedral because it rests and is played in a house of God. When Colin played at Westminster Abbey, he was enveloped by a feeling that he could only describe as spiritual, as from his fingertips he filled the immense cathedral with sound and instantly felt the sound return to his body, like air leaving him in a moment of exaltation and returning in the next breath.

Colin's teachers and parents disapproved of his reluctance to engage competitively either in sports or in fights with fellow pupils. When he had to choose a sport, at about the age of eight, he chose swimming but refused to compete. Luckily, during soccer one day, a South African teacher, angry that Colin seemed overly intimate with a Chilean pupil, threw a soccer ball into Colin's face. Colin was excused from the sport for the remainder of his stay at Cumnor.

He quickly discerned that the authorities wanted to cultivate a particular kind of man, one not overly creative, sentient, or susceptible. This was a problem for Ian and Colin, both of whom hated school; their father once wrote that both boys were so artistic and sensitive that it was always hard to find the right schools for them. Colin disliked any subject in which he did not excel, and he was dismayed to find that so much of school was devoted to his weaknesses, mathematics and athletics. He was happier when alone, wearing his kilt, walking in the woods or in one of his favorite places, the Rule Water in Scotland, where he would look at his reflection, dip his hand, wet his face, and try to feel the spirits of his paternal ancestors. But he only appeared to be lonely. He anguished more when with others.

Colin had a jeweled soul, a deep, almost melancholic consciousness of the riches that could be found in music, conversation, churches, and the Scottish countryside, a consciousness his teachers seemed to want him to abandon. His report cards complained of a lack of aggression. One read, "Colin cannot stand up in the boxing ring and take his punishment like a man. He must learn to assert himself." In the 1980s, he pondered the question of what his report card would have looked like if it had been written by an Mbuti Pygmy. It would have read, he said, like this: "'Colin is not much good at making other boys' noses bleed, but he has a great gift for telling blindfolded whether the person next to him is a Chilean boy or a South African man by their respective body odors.'"

"And," he added, "they did smell differently. And that report card would probably also have added that I made up for my refusal to accept the dogma delivered to us in religious studies by my ability to detect the presence of Spirit, even in a church filled with smelly people, in the quality of the music. I like to think it might also have said that my resistance to nonrational authority was tempered by my ability to sense order and propriety when I touched the trunk of a sturdy oak tree; and that my parents need not despair of my lack of appreciation of home and family because I would see them all as mine when I looked into my reflection in that shimmering stream that ran through the Rule Valley. What a school that would have been to have written a report like *that.*"

As I read some of Colin's early teacher recommendations in the archive room at Oxford, I wondered aloud why his teachers so seldom mentioned his academics and focused instead on the preparation and performance of the body, especially manners, charm, and solidity. A retired professor from Manchester who was in the same room looked up and said, "You see, in those days, it was more important to be a good chap than an intelligent one."

The so-called public schools—the most elite educational institutions in England—began centuries ago. And for some people, the older the school, the higher the status. St. Peter's York, where Colin's nephew and godson, David Turnbull, went to school was founded in 625. The public schools, many of which are boarding schools, are the descendants of early church-related institutions intended to provide recruits, especially poor boys of high intellect, for the church. But the schools evolved into more secular charitable institutions with scholarships set aside to pay for the education of poor but intelligent children. They were public in the sense that they were sponsored by the state and anyone could apply. But there was nothing in the charter rules to stop the schools from taking on extra pupils if parents were willing to pay for it. And they did pay because the public schools were quickly recognized as the finest schools in England. It was not long before the schools became elite institutions with a few nonpaying boys, called scholars, surrounded by mostly rich, fee-paying students.

Colin's alma mater, Westminster, was established in 1560 under statutes that planned for forty scholars all of whom were to receive a free education. By 1737, there were nearly 450 boys enrolled. Many Westminster graduates became famous in politics, arts, and letters, among them, Ben Jonson, George Herbert, John Dryden, Christopher Wren, John Locke, Edward Gibbon, Jeremy Bentham, A. A. Milne, John Gielgud, and Peter Ustinov. Westminster also produced some famous traitors, including H. A. R. ("Kim") Philby who defected to the USSR in 1963. And it also produced one suspected traitor: Colin Turnbull, who, in 1951, would spend nearly two weeks in a pit in Sudan on charges that he was the famous spy Donald Maclean.

For most of its history, the school has been in one place, adjacent to Westminster Abbey, but on two occasions the school was forced to temporarily relocate—first, during the plague of 1665, and again, during World War II, when Colin was a student at Westminster. Most of the school buildings were destroyed in a German bombing. The students in Colin's house were relocated first to Sussex for a year, then to an eighteenth-century house called Buckenhill in the Herefordshire countryside.

Next to the Abbey but situated so inconspicuously that many Londoners cannot tell you where Westminster School is, the school had its own distinctive dress code. Eton had its collars (broad and stiff and worn outside the jacket), Harrow its boaters (stiff, flat-topped straw hats), and Westminster had knee breeches and stockings until the mid-nineteenth century when they were replaced with top hats, tail coats, and wing collars. In the *Pickwick Papers,* Charles Dickens wrote that the waiters in the White Hart at Bath "in their knee breeches looked like Westminster boys, but the illusion was soon dispelled by their better behavior." For one year, Colin wore the top hat costume. But when the war broke out, the old dress code was abolished in favor of gray suits.

Dress certainly had something to do with Colin's choice of Westminster. He later wrote, "The reason I chose Westminster rather than Eton or Harrow, other than to be separated from my brother [who went to Ottershaw], was that I liked its school uniform. At Eton new boys had to wear an Eton suit, long dark gray or black trousers surmounted by an Eton jacket which is cut off above the waist, leaving both front and rear end totally unprotected; and a huge starched collar unlike anything worn by anyone else. I had been made to wear Eton suits as Sunday dress when I was a quite small child, so I wanted nothing to do with childish dress. Harrow was distinguished, in my mind, by the fact that its uniform was dominated by a ridiculous-looking hat called the boater. I later came to associate the boater with the more vulgar music halls, but I think my prime association was with a lot of uncouth youths of no academic distinction, in hot pursuit of some ugly, unfriendly, and violent sport. There was nothing to attract me there."

At Westminster all new boys had to wear Eton suits, but if you were tall enough, you could be excused from that uncomfortable distinction. And instead of looking like a junior boy you would instantly be seen as a senior. Colin measured himself. Though he was tall for his age, he was still about one half-inch too short to escape the Eton suit. The Turnbulls' gardener suggested that Colin simply pad the heels of his socks.

"With double-thickness soles added to my shoes, I visited the school tailor who measured me and pronounced me ready for tails. There was an uncomfortable moment when he examined my shoes and discovered my real height. But rather than condemn me to Etons he congratulated me on my determination. My family and friends similarly congratulated me on this achievement, more than they did for passing the school's entrance examination. In this way, through my choice of dress, I learned that deceit, if not dishonesty, was an acceptable, even commendable adult value."

There were other ways of distinguishing yourself. The wealthier students wore clothes made of higher quality fabrics. Cliques of boys marked their membership, Colin recalled, "by the angle at which we wore our hats, the way we twirled our umbrellas, the way we adjusted our tails as we sat down." Some sets of friends wore pinstripes, others solid colors. Colin once began wearing a solid stripe to protect himself from a solid-striper who had physically threatened him. Students seeking approval of a certain teacher might also choose to wear his style of pants. Finally, of course, there were private vocabularies, sometimes more than a hundred words, that a particular social set could claim for itself. They ranged from the uninventive ("dead fly pie" for currant pudding) to the ordinary ("Randy" for someone who preferred boys to girls).

Skipping the Eton jacket was like skipping a grade. Yet within the school, one was still a boy. In the early twentieth century, few survived even a year without being whipped, or "tanned," as it was called. By 1923, safeguards were introduced, such as a regulation cane and rules about how many strokes were allowed; but corporal punishment was still common practice during Colin's time.

School life was regimented and restricted, so much so that Evelyn Waugh once wrote that "Anyone who has been to an English public school will always feel comparatively at home in prison." At Westminster, "Courts" were held for various offenses and offered three basic levels of humiliation: punishment by house, school, or headmaster. If you walked along an unauthorized route you could be tanned by the house in which you lived; if you switched off an escalator in the train station during rush hour, you could receive a tanning by the school; if you broke a window or convinced a language assistant to permit the boys to smoke cigarettes, you could receive a public "handing" (sometimes also called "handling") by the headmaster. In such rare cases, the entire school was assembled. "Unlike other ordeals or punishments," Colin observed, handing "was clearly a ritual with high symbolic content. The miscreant was called up to the dais, his offense was made public, and the headmaster then lightly touched him on each hand with one of the birches, and that was that. The effect was powerful; the boy was never again regarded in quite the same way, and the handing carried with it unmistakable ostracism."

During Colin's stay at Westminster, punishment continued to be carried out by whipping and this no doubt made students acutely aware that their bodies were vulnerable to authority. Yet even more acute, perhaps, was the sense of a bond between boys, an awareness that by having violated authority, withstood the punishment, and shown off one's wounds afterward, you became part of the system, a machine for producing discipline and social order. One witness to a public Westminster beating in 1944, two years after Colin had graduated, recalled the excitement the students felt watching it. The historian Gathorne-Hardy, who interviewed the witness, compared the audience's emotional state to the most fundamental bodily functions, thus suggesting that beating was as essential to school life as eating and sleeping. The beating was exciting to watch, sexually stimulating for some, and produced both that sense of collective effervescence so crucial to any ritual's success and a profound sense of belonging. "The corporate emotion after the beating," he wrote, "is like that after an orgasm; perhaps like the release, going even further back, or having done a shit in a nappy [diaper] when very small. And since all members of the community shared these deep subconscious feelings, they were drawn very close together."

For many English men, the subject of British boarding schools brings sexual images to mind: headmasters struggling in vain to quash any expression of their boys' sexual instincts, and boys stimulating themselves, and often each other, in an attempt to relieve their frustrations. For many boys, including Colin, there was a rich sexual underworld that flourished without the stigma of "homosexuality" or "unnatural sex." Public school could be openly, unabashedly homoerotic.

But many boys found that sex in boarding schools was complicated and could have many uses. Sex was a means to gain social status in the school, to display an affected, personal style in those times when homosexuality was most fashionable, or to rebel against the school authorities, who spent a good deal of their time trying to figure out how to prevent the boys from having sex or engaging in "self-abuse," as masturbation was so literally described. There is little evidence to suggest that the schools made anyone become homosexuals. But the boys at the schools did learn how to use sex to acquire and exercise power. It is no surprise, then, that when Colin Turnbull arrived at Westminster, at the age of thirteen, he found a frightening and competitive world. His hopes to get by with his wit and intelligence were not realized.

Whereas sex between boys had been tolerated for the first few hundred years of the public school system, by the end of the nineteenth century, when the category of homosexual became popular as a marker of social and sexual identity, homosexual sex became the main enemy of public school administrations. It meant expulsion. All showers were now equipped with cold water only, to prevent anyone from lingering or luxuriating there too long. Uniforms were cut so they were difficult to remove. Even pockets, it is said, were inspected to make sure they were properly sewn: the school didn't want anyone to secretly masturbate or put his hands into another boy's pants. And when Colin was at Westminster, new boys were called into the headmaster's office to learn the facts of life, facts that included explicit instructions not to urinate in anyone's mouth. For Colin, and certainly for others, those instructions broadened their definition of the facts of life. Paradoxically, the only way to repress homosexuality was to talk about it, and so there flourished a rich discourse on forbidden sex that made homosexuality all the more exciting.

There is no way to know precisely how common homosexual sex was in the schools, but it would be hard to find boys either from the early years or from Colin's day who were unaware of its practice. Despite the public schools' attempts to prohibit friendships between boys of different ages as well as social relationships between boys of different houses, and despite the fact that the schools seldom constructed any public spaces hidden from surveillance, homosexual sex was rampant. Its pleasures as a mode of resistance were enhanced by the lengths the schools took to prevent it. As for sex between the pupils and their headmasters, teachers, and servants, anecdotal evidence in diaries and oral histories suggests it was common but that scandals were usually suppressed by school authorities. Perhaps the most dreadful relationships were between students and prefects, the older boys who were entrusted with authority over the boys at night. Senior boys were known to torture their juniors with adolescent pranks, beat them, and extort sexual favors. Good-looking boys were sometimes given female names and became the "bitches" of older boys. These same older boys were often the school monitors or prefects.

Among the different public schools there was much variation in the kind and frequency of sexual activities that took place, and even within the same school one class of sexually active senior boys could be followed by one more puritan. Some boys loved each other intensely while others used sex as a method of violence; some showed their passion in letters or poetry, and others showed it through physical contact. The schools were, in general, highly sexualized places, where at night, as Gathorne-Hardy has written, "fantasies hovered thick in the darkness above the creaking beds while their physical release poured out in masturbation."

Colin's initiation happened with the gang rape of a close friend. "[He] did not yell for help or scream as I would have done. As he fought silently, he just cried. It was his tears, and mine as I watched, that bound us together and brought a glimmer of beauty and the real meaning of love, by its very absence, to our adolescence. For three long years this was how we learned to deal with our frightening new power, blind to the essential goodness of its nature."

It was a pivotal moment for him. Staring into the eyes of his friend, Colin was not simply learning about the seedier side of humanity or the techniques of male power. That moment signaled his own awareness of an important facet of his identity, that he wanted to be a savior, that he would live to comfort those who were violated and debased, that he would fight against those who used power to harm or even ridicule others. Colin himself was physically unharmed by human cruelty in the public schools or even in the nursery, so far as we know, and that may have been part of his dilemma. He simply could not understand why he remained intact while others were hurt, why he was by nature tall and burly, seemingly self-assured and immovable, while others were weak and vulnerable. He felt guilty about his privileged station in life. Many of the people he and his parents knew bathed in it, but Colin felt forcibly submerged into a sea of privilege, dishonored by it, as it brought him too close to the realm of his friend's persecutors. He was a careful observer, especially of social hierarchy, and his own guilt, however much it may have predated his entry into Westminster, was brought into relief by the events he witnessed. He never actively harmed anyone, not because he had neither the anger nor the inspiration, but because the thought of violence stopped him in his tracks, transforming the anger into either pity or indifference but seldom to aggression.

At night, there was intense competition for sex. Unless one had the reputation for being a Randy, one either fled from sex or sought it out as a way to gain prestige. "There were those," Colin said, "who engaged in entrapment, enjoying the pleasure of a brief encounter and then winning favor by reporting the incident to the authorities. There were those who boasted conquests, real or otherwise, sometimes just to harm some boy who had refused their advances. And of course there were those who acquired another kind of reputation by being willing to give themselves wherever there was advantage, competing for the patronage of other boys . . . "

The significance of the roles played in oral and anal sex between boys resembled those of homosexual sex in many parts of the world past and present. If you were the recipient of oral sex or the penetrator in intercourse, you were powerful, dominant, and male. If, on the other hand, you were the giver of oral sex or the recipient in intercourse, you were weak, subordinate, and female. The implications of these roles prevail today in prisons, and in many parts of Latin America, as they did in ancient Greece. Sex in the boarding schools was certainly about lust for good looking young boys, but sex was also about sadism, older boys' attempts to ensure their place on the social ladder, and younger boys' attempts to climb it.

What Colin did not learn from the other students he learned from his teachers. He was summoned from French class one day to see the housemaster. He recalled:

> My housemaster sat me down in his study and reminded me that I had just turned thirteen . . . His teeth were bad and he smelled of tobacco. He was not wearing his gown, so this was not an academic matter, nor could it have anything to do with the school. It was morning. I was at a loss. My housemaster continued, announcing that my parents had told him that I was uninformed as to the facts of life and had asked him to tell me about them. The brown leather was cold, so I sat on my tails . . . Had I ever had a wet dream . . . and no it was not the same as bedwetting. What about a "nocturnal emission," and that too had to be explained. When I displayed total ignorance of the phenomenon and denied ever having caused it to happen, far from explaining it, let alone its social consequence, he hurriedly ended the ordeal with an abrupt, "Well, don't worry, when it happens, just come and tell me and we'll have another talk." . . . It was 10:30 A.M. . . . He put on his gown as I left, clearly telling me that the facts of life had nothing to do with school and I should forget them at once. So I promptly went to the basement toilet and tried rubbing my legs together and everything else, as he had obligingly specified, and with a curious mixture of fear and delight the appropriate results were achieved . . . There was no time to go and tell the housemaster of my success so I went back to class. "Turnbull," [the teacher] said, "this note says you left your housemaster at ten-thirty. It is now eleven. I presume he was telling you the facts of life and you were delayed on your way back." The class, most of whom were at least one year older than I was, broke into guffaws of laughter, and I was mortified without knowing why.

In addition to masturbation and sex, the most popular behaviors in the underworld of the boarding school were smoking, drinking, climbing onto towers, gambling, and stealing keys. If the boys at Westminster were being taught social techniques, then these were aggression, competitiveness, slyness, and suspicion. They learned how to manipulate and sabotage. They learned how to use their bodies to survive within the school's social system, and they became aware of how their own bodies could be used by others. When a boy at Westminster learned that he could acquire new friends and rise in the school hierarchy by ejaculating in the hallway, splattering his semen on the walls, he also learned a hierarchy of social skills. Sex and the penis were quite literally tools, since in the public schools "tool" was the most common synonym for "penis."

Colin was not a particularly popular boy. He was as little known at Westminster as he was at Cumnor House, with the exception of those interested in music. Westminster made an inquiry about remembrances of Colin on my behalf at a 1998 meeting of the Westminster alumni association, The Elizabethan Club, and put a notice in their newsletter; there were no responses. Class lists did not survive the war nor did most issues of the *College Street Clarion,* the magazine of Busby's, the house of which Colin was a member.

We do know something about life outside the Westminster campus and at Buckenhill in Herefordshire, where Colin lived for his last two years of boarding school. To say that Buckenhill was rundown is perhaps an understatement, but at least it was safe, and Westminster had been completely taken over by the military. Westminster was evacuated in 1939, first to Sussex for a year, and then in 1940 to Buckenhill where, at the request of local officials who feared the local residents might be startled by boys wearing tails and top hats, the school permitted simpler uniforms.

When Colin and his classmates from Busby's House arrived in Herefordshire in the first week of November 1940, they were shocked by what they found. The buildings Westminster occupied in Herefordshire were dilapidated, poorly heated, and cramped, and Buckenhill was in the worst condition of all. An eighteenth-century house, Buckenhill had had no occupants for more than twenty years. The weeds were overgrown, none of the windows had glass, there was no kitchen range, and a tree had sprouted right through the dining room floor. There was no electricity, no heating, and the ninety boys seldom had enough clean water for drinking. Busby's would stay at Buckenhill until August 1945—Colin graduated in 1942—but to the dismay of Westminster's accountants, only a fraction of the boys roughed it out, or were permitted by their anxious parents to rough it out, until their graduation. Colin was one who stayed, and Oxford and the Ituri forest of his later life would seem a paradise in comparison.

Life at Buckenhill was hard but purposeful, and Colin continued to pursue his interests in music, without an organ but with a choir. On June 26, 1942, he wrote to the *College Street Clarion,* in one of the few extant issues, that the Busby's house choir was seriously handicapped by a lack of strong voices and wind instruments. The next month he wrote another letter in an attempt to improve morale: "You have got a standard to keep up now, Busby's, especially in House Choirs. Don't be content with merely keeping it up, do your utmost to improve it. This can only be done by giving every assistance to any enterprise such as carolling or visiting the Blind School.

"The things that call for part singing, such as our informal Mad. Soc. only affect a part of the house, but there is one thing in particular that affects the whole house—House Choirs . . .

"Briefly then, I am asking you all to do what you possibly can for Busby's music. Don't treat it as just one of those things that are only for the initiated; so much can be done by cooperation and general keenness . . . Don't think that just because they are carols that you know and there is no Cup to win for singing them well you can just shout them. Be content with only the best you can do . . . I shall watch your progress with every interest, and I am sure much pride. C. M. Turnbull."

When Colin wrote these words, however, he still had no place to go after Westminster. Even by the end of July 1942, Colin still had not been accepted to any college at Oxford. Although Colin would later suggest that he selected Magdalen, indeed that Magdalen was his first and only choice, the story is not that simple, for his acceptance was late and required the intervention of his father and his cousin, William James Millar Mackenzie, a professor of government, fellow, and tutor at Magdalen College. Mackenzie was loyal to the Turnbulls but he did not think very highly of Colin's academic potential.

Merton College at Oxford, in actuality his first choice, rejected him. Queens also. No other college at Oxford had any vacancies, and so Colin's father decided to write Magdalen and Mackenzie and have Westminster send a recommendation directly to him. In Jock's letter, we have the first evidence that Colin considered a career in the Church of England, a career his mother supported and his father hoped would never happen. Jock wanted Colin to go to work for him at his accounting firm, Gregg and Turnbull, near St. James's Square in London. By August 1 Jock wrote to Magdalen College to beg them for some consideration, if only because Mackenzie was at Magdalen. About Colin, however, he said little: "It may be sufficient to say that the boy's present idea of a career is the Church" and that "he played [organ] at Westminster Abbey, Worcester Cathedral, and many churches in England and Scotland."

Late that week, the college secretary wrote to Jock to say that there were two unexpected vacancies at Magdalen, and that the admissions committee would be willing to look at Colin's application. He wrote, "I hope I am right in assuming that your son is exempt from Responsions." He was not exempt. Responsions was the term for Latin courses required of all incoming students until the early 1960s. Until 1920, ancient Greek had been required as well. Unfortunately, Colin had not taken much Latin, a result of his own failure, not that of Westminster, which encouraged its study. Jock wrote back to say that Colin would be able to pass Latin by the time he arrived at Oxford. There would be last-minute tutoring and outside study to prepare for a Latin exam that Colin would eventually pass.

By August 20, both the recommendations from Westminster and Mackenzie would be in the hands of Bruce McFarlane, the tutor who would eventually interview Colin. Mackenzie, on his way to Washington as the RAF attaché, wrote McFarlane in haste before he departed for the United States, on August 18, 1942:

> Dear Bruce,
> I am told that a young man named Colin Turnbull is trying to get into Magdalen as one of "two unexpected vacancies" after having disappointments at Queens and Merton . . . He is a very decent, quiet sort, who strikes me as having plenty of common sense and good manners, although not likely to have any particular academic distinction; he is, however, very much above the average as a minimum. I believe he has it in mind to go into the Church—a bit odd these days, but he is certainly a cut above the usual run of applications for orders and has the makings of rather a good parson. In other words, he should be at least up to the average run of commoners in time of peace, and I hope you let him in. But if there is strong competition for the places he will obviously have to take his chances on academic gratifications, on which I am not able to advise.

From Buckenhill on August 10, 1942, the dean of Westminster wrote a short note stating that Colin was "an industrious boy and would, I think, benefit from a university course. He is a keen musician, mainly an organist." And, from Herefordshire on August 20, 1942, the headmaster of Westminster elaborated, comparing him to another Westminster student who had been accepted to Magdalen that same year.

"Turnbull: He's not a bad fellow; a point or two below Shenton, I should say. Rather dreamy, fond of playing the organ, and at present means to be ordained. He has considerable charm of manner. I doubt if he would have got highest certificate [but] I should be pleased to vouch for his ability and standard. You may know that Merton turned him down, though they quite liked him, because they were pretty full and because Turnbull still has to take Latin . . . You wouldn't regret him, but I'm not pressing him on you. Good luck to Sir Henry! [Tizard, the newly elected president of Magdalen]. I've known him for some time now and find him downright witty and able."

The next entry in the Magdalen archives tells us, simply, that Colin registered for classes on October 7, 1942, a month and a half before his eighteenth birthday.

CHAPTER FOUR

Class

THE STORY OF HOW TURNBULL FELL IN LOVE with Asia and Africa begins in 1941 when he first visited Oxford.

In stark contrast to Westminster, at Oxford Turnbull felt that he was treated as an adult from the moment he arrived. His tutors assumed he was ready to make decisions independently, and fostered self-discovery and self-expression. Oxford's Magdalen College at least seemed that way to him. He recalled that in his initial interview with McFarlane in 1941, their conversation began with the topics of wine, French and German literature, the music of Benjamin Britten, organs, the deer park and meadow, and ended in an excited discussion of weeds. There was little talk of academics and at the end of the interview McFarlane realized that Colin did not know the name of a single don.

Much of the Magdalen College [pronounced Maud'-lin] that Colin saw that year had been the same since the first foundation stones were laid in 1473. Numerous graduates have written that if they received nothing else from Magdalen, it was a love of architecture and a sense of the spirit of the place, for it is truly one of the most beautiful colleges at Oxford, and has no shortage of famous alumni: Lord Alfred Douglas, Oscar Wilde, C. S. Lewis, and Seamus

Heaney. Although we now know that Colin had wanted to attend either Merton or Queens, he wrote that going to Magdalen was an easy decision, and gave the impression that Magdalen had been his first choice:

> I approached the problem from the vantage point of a sound academic training and total spiritual demoralization. I just took a couple of days off from school and went to Oxford and walked and walked, looking and feeling and sniffing at the air. The moment I saw Magdalen Tower and heard its excruciatingly out-of-tune chimes (I hope they never do anything about that badly diminished seventh) I knew it was for me. The old tower soared into the sky and with it soared my dislocated, earthbound spirit. Directly across the road from the entrance, the botanical gardens filled the air with a fresh scent. The college gate is virtually on the bridge that leads over the Cherwell River and out of Oxford, and being on the edge of the city, Magdalen has by far the largest grounds of any college, including a beautiful deer park. Inside the gate is a quiet yard that leads into the cloisters, on one side of which is the chapel. Through the cloisters is a large expanse of lawn backed by the imposing New Building, in fact, one of the oldest. Behind that is the deer park through which the Cherwell runs, dividing for a time into two streams that encircle a large tree-studded meadow, around which is a path known as Addison's Walk, a place where poetry and music should ever be made. Those were the symbols that I took to be reasons for choosing Magdalen.

Of Oxford during wartime, alumni wrote about their special love of architecture at Magdalen, the look of the buildings in the moonlight, the streets without lights or traffic. More than an education, Oxford remained for Colin a set of sensual memories, always accessible in less lustrous times, when he needed them the most. He wrote, "The ecclesiastical architecture with its inescapable connotations of the sacred jostling together with the pubs and their beery odor of profanity; the great tower clocks which at all of two dozen or more colleges chime every quarter hour at different intervals, reminding one of the constant passage of time; the cathedrals and organs; the secular pealing of belfries full of bells, ringing out Great and Little Toms in a seemingly endless effort never to repeat themselves, all in reality seeming to search for a purity of sound and reminding us of the purity to be found elsewhere."

Oxford graduates often say that Magdalen has always been "the best," by which is meant the best in total. Other colleges excelled in social life, food, intellect, or sports, but Magdalen was the renaissance college, a reputation retained from the sixteenth century. In the seventeenth century, King James

II admonished the Fellows of Magdalen for not supporting his attempts to Catholicize the university by saying, "You have always been a stubborn and turbulent college." Edward Gibbon's time at Magdalen in the mid-eighteenth century is famous among its alumni for the contempt he showed his alma mater. "I spent fourteen months at Magdalen College; they proved the most idle and unprofitable of my whole life." In the next century, Oscar Wilde saw things differently, writing that Magdalen was "the most beautiful thing in England . . . nowhere else are life and art so exquisitely blended."

At the beginning of the twentieth century, however, Magdalen might have lost some of its distinctiveness. A Balliol College student, clearly biased toward Balliol, wrote that "at Magdalen the average man is very pleasant, but he is sadly uniform. There appears to exist a certain repression of the individuality." In the 1930s and 1940s, nonwhite students, especially, thought Magdalen students were homogeneous and close-minded. But even if Magdalen seemed at first a place without diversity—and, after all, it was for "gentlemen" only—Colin soon discovered that Oxford and its environs were not uniform, and he made the best of it by establishing friendships with local Jamaican conductors and Indian students.

The old college system did not facilitate contact with people outside the college, whether in Oxford University or not, unless, of course, the students felt so stifled that they had to escape. Colin wanted relief from the regulations of Oxford, including the low-table–high-table distinctions in which the Senior Common Room members, or Fellows, sat above the rest at a table raised on a dais, and in which strict rules about clothing and appearance applied. Sunday nights required evening dress of tuxedos; when Colin would meet up with old classmates in subsequent years, they would sometimes chat about where one could still find the best top hats in England.

Clearly, after living at the run-down Buckenhill campus of Westminster for his last year of boarding school, he was delighted with Magdalen's better digs. Still wartime promised to be hard at Oxford too, especially if you expected the food, drink, and social life to be as plentiful as many expected from Evelyn Waugh's Oxford of the 1930s. For the purposes of supplying labor and soldiers for the war, students had shortened courses called sections. Students could complete their degrees in as little as two years, and for those intent on training for postgraduate degrees, there was little time for carousing and heavy drinking. The standard of living was generally pretty low with food and luxuries usually scarce. A student might eat one meager lunch at the college and then go into town for a cheap (1 shilling) second one of Spam chop suey, Spam chow mein, or Spam curry.

Students who were twenty-years-old or over were conscripted into the armed forces but those of conscription age who were studying basic science were encouraged to stay in school because they were deemed important for the long-term war effort. Younger men like Colin could volunteer for one of three military training courses: the University Air Squadron, the Army Officer's Training Corps, and the naval unit. Colin chose the navy because he thought that he would be safer there if he ultimately saw the war theater. He had wanted to be a conscientious objector but his parents were strongly opposed to it and Colin acquiesced eventually.

Many Fellows at Magdalen were gone during wartime, but Bruce McFarlane, A. J. P. Taylor, and C. S. Lewis were among those who remained. Colin read with Taylor for the Modern Greats, as distinguished from the greats or classics. If he liked the music of the young composer, Benjamin Britten, McFarlane told him in his application interview, he would be interested in studying with Taylor who was a friend of Britten's and one of Oxford's most prolific historians of modern Europe. Taylor showed Oxford to be remarkably conservative about its faculty when, in 1952, he became the first Oxford don to divorce and still retain his fellowship, though only after a bitter fight with colleagues who assured him their opposition was based on tradition and was "nothing personal."

The tutor-student relationship, something seldom known in the United States, is the hallmark of British higher education. It is conceived as the ideal education in which the tutor and student act together in a relationship of mutual intellectual discovery. At Westminster, Colin had found that "the intimacy of one moment was contradicted by an immeasurable distance the next," but that at Oxford the tutor and student were both adults sharing in an academic adventure. He recalled, "My tutor interrupted my reading of a dreadful essay written in desperation in the small hours of the morning . . . His mind was obviously far away, and he suddenly uttered a thought that had come to him; a new thought. Something had been created, and although it had absolutely nothing to do with what I had written and was reading, I was there when the thought came and was therefore a part of it . . . "

The excitement of the tutorial system did not mean that tutorials were always enjoyable. Colin called them "ordeals," and the so-called Collections ritual was especially frightening. Collections was a public performance, enacted in front of the student body, in which each student donned a cap and gown and, upon hearing his name called aloud, walked the hall to high table and listened as his tutors commented on his qualities or lack of them. To a crowd of laughing students, fellows and tutors, Taylor once said of Turnbull, "He is the most naive student I have ever had and I doubt he will ever make anything of his studies." He added, "But he is quite good at digging my vegetable garden and I recommend we keep him on for another term."

Undergraduates were cared for primarily by their scouts who, it seems, made sure that the promise of wartime hardship was not entirely fulfilled. Scouts cleaned students' rooms, sometimes made their beds, and served food at mealtimes. In Turnbull's day, the relationships between students, scouts, and porters were fairly intimate. Scouts were in charge of individual staircases since the traditional arrangement of rooms was along staircases rather than halls. Still, some rich students brought their own gentleman's gentleman with them. The scouts at Magdalen during Turnbull's stay—Ming, Ing, Mobey, and Perkins or Betnay "the Pearl"—helped as much as they could to arrange private dinners and preserve the sense of dignity of the Magdalen student; they understood just how important food and drink were to these young men.

Inexplicably, scouts had never been addressed with a title and were locally given Asian names, despite the fact that they were nearly all as white and British as one could find. In addition to Ming and Ing, All Souls College had a scout named Tong, though he and all his ancestors were born and bred in the Midlands. Ming had been at Oxford for a long time, first as a junior scout, later as scout. He helped Colin organize his first black tie party, suggesting that four would be too intimate and ten too large. Ming sent Colin to the chef, a man named Butler. Butler and Colin talked at length about the menu, deciding which foods went best with each other, and from there Colin was sent to the wine steward, Bond, for a similar education. Somehow, the war seemed to make no difference when it came to a formal party; everything was available, in or out of season. Once, when Colin gave a party for ten, Butler seemed confused about one of the names: "'A relative perhaps?' he asked. Looking forward to a frown, surprise, or even an outright protest, I said no, he was a Jamaican bus conductor. The chef merely continued to look interested and asked which route. 'Ah!' he said, 'route number two. Yes I think I know the young gentleman. That will make ten.'"

The social atmosphere at Oxford during wartime was unusual. There were more than 17,000 evacuees in town. Magdalen itself housed various government departments, converting science halls into government offices. Some colleges were virtual barracks; Oriel and Brasenose were completely taken over by the army. The Ministry of Food claimed much of St. John's College, housing both the fish and potato controls there. Whether these were brought together because they complemented each other naturally is not known, but according to one historian it did make "this ancient seat of higher learning the biggest fish and chip shop the world has ever seen."

In his memoir, A. L. Rowse wrote of the difference between Oxford during peace and war. He noted that the population had grown by twenty percent and added that, "quite seriously, if there is one town in this country, one town in Europe, which has taken something of the place of Salzburg in pre-Anschluss days, it is Oxford." War entered into scholarship as well so that, paradoxically, a certain intellectual benefit came along with deprivation. Wartime Oxford attracted refugee European academics who injected new forms of scholarship and new perspectives into a sometime stale intellectual environment. Because the population of the town of Oxford increased so dramatically, students like Colin had a chance to meet a more diverse group of people. Moreover, the outward markings of social and economic class were muted. The hierarchical tone of the university gave way to a wartime egalitarianism with less emphasis on career trajectories; the rationing of nearly all consumables meant that people dressed more or less the same and ate the same foods. Later in life, Colin would write that, to his parents' alarm, he was on his way "to becoming a socialist." "And," he added, "Oxford did nothing to cure that . . . on the contrary it was one of the best places in the world for meeting people from all over the world, of every known color and religious persuasion, and from almost every imaginable class." He added: "At Westminster, the natural and healthy urge of the adolescent to find and express 'class' as a general quality was allowed to develop into an assertion of superiority. Oxford began to undo this from the first day under the guise of doing just the opposite."

Years later, when Colin would idealize the egalitarianism of the Mbuti Pygmies, he would reflect on Oxford. For it was at Oxford, ironically, that he learned the value of downplaying competition, though at Oxford this was more likely framed as politesse, especially in the context of eight-man rowing. He wrote, "It used to be said that the Oxford Eight (and they tried to train me for it once) nearly always lost to Cambridge because, since Cambridge so desperately wanted to win, the only gentlemanly thing to do was to let them do so."

The social life at Oxford was active: a fair amount of drinking among some, but the more serious students excused themselves to "sport the oak"—an odd phrase, not currently in fashion at Oxford, that the OED defines as "to shut the outer door of one's rooms as a sign that one is engaged" and traces to at least the late eighteenth century. Oak was the university word for doors since they were made of oak—the older Oxford rooms have two doors, an inner one opening into the room and a thicker outer one opening into the staircase. Sporting the oak was something done with total acceptance by others and without stated reasons, but it was assumed that one would not sport their oak without good reason, certainly not for idle, nonsexual, nonintellectual reasons. It became an almost sacred practice, logically perhaps—it is hard to get through a chapter of Frazer's famous *Golden Bough* on myth, magic, and religion without encountering the spiritual uses of oak. Like his classmates, Colin sported the oak. It did have a sexual connotation, but even more important for Colin, the custom showed a profound respect for privacy.

His early Oxford months were not without excitement. Along with other students, he had his share of fire watching duties, but when there were no enemy planes about they would drink beer and hurl the bottles into the quadrangle. They devised other pranks that showed they were not quite the adults they were assumed to be in tutorials. At one point, Colin and some other students detonated a small explosive in the dean's residence. "The dean was asleep in his bedroom, snoring loudly," he wrote. "We placed the gunpowder under his bed, heaped in a little pile above the bare wires, and led the electric cord into the sitting room, closed the door, pushed the plug into the socket, and fled with the explosion. The next morning the dean appeared, as large and jovial as ever, and not a word was heard of the incident by the rest of the college."

Although Colin does not identify the dean, it was probably his cousin, Bill Mackenzie. Mackenzie kept numerous bottles of 1840 Madeira, a four star vintage, in his bin in the college cellars, "approached by a locked door a child could have picked, let alone one educated at a good Public School." Colin had almost unlimited access to this outstanding drink, magnificent even at one hundred years old and, Colin said, too good for his cousin. In the 1940s, each bottle might have been worth more than a hundred pounds.

In October 1942, at the start of his first term, Colin joined the Royal Navy Volunteer Reserves as an "Ordinary Seaman" with the expectation of being decommissioned only after the "end of present emergency." Although he was now technically part of the navy, at only seventeen years old he was still too young to get his commission. He remained in officer's training, learning basic skills at an Oxford boathouse, in part preparing for war and in part paying the country back for the privilege of staying in school. He did not have to leave Oxford until the following summer to begin formal training for combat at coastal bases and on the cruiser HMS *Cardiff*.

The record of his war years is slim because of issues of confidentiality and in part because many war records simply did not survive. The executor of Colin's estate was able to secure release of a brief service record, but the detailed records are closed until July 21, 2018.

Though Colin was a prolific letter writer, during the war he corresponded infrequently—he explained to his family that he had little opportunity to write or send mail—and many of his friends and relatives waited anxiously for word of his safety. Bruce McFarlane wrote to a friend in May 1945 that he had suddenly received a large batch of letters from the students he cared about the most, among them Colin. "All the strain of waiting for good or bad news is over now—for the moment, at least."

During those years, we do know that Colin strayed as much as possible from the commissioned officers' ward rooms. "I found," he wrote, "that among the ratings on the 'lower deck' I could find young men both closer to my own age and temperament . . . So I learned another irritating truth, about class discrimination this time, namely that like the other forms of discrimination it was equally ridiculous, ill founded and self-serving." But when Colin did find that he wanted to socialize with the officers, he feared that he was affirming the British hierarchy he hated so much and which, to his dismay, was giving him so much pleasure. He felt guilty every time he joined the other officers in their annual Christmas Day ritual of reversal when the servicemen sit at tables and are waited on by the officers. He recognized that the whole point of the reversal is to make everyone aware of the proper hierarchy by showing its opposite.

Colin loved men in the navy, despite the risks, though unfortunately we have no detailed information about those relationships; he dared not write about them in either a diary or in personal letters for fear of prosecution. The navy considered "Buggery and Gross Indecency" to be criminal offenses, and any sailor expressing any sexual interests in men, even without ever having acted or intending to act on those interests, would be immediately sent for examination by a medical officer (to determine if the immoral sailor-criminal had adversely affected the health and security of the unit) and then would be dismissed from the military. The maximum punishment for "buggery" was dismissal and twenty-five lashes, a punishment nearly as severe as that inflicted for mutiny. The laws focused largely on anal intercourse, as if homosexuality and anal intercourse were synonymous; of course, expressions of love between men, and the fulfillment of sexual desires, took many forms. It was hard for Colin not to express his sexual interest in men, usually those in the lower decks, but he was able to do it in ways that, while violating the Navy's laws on indecency, were less likely to get him expelled. He was a passionate snuggler who, though he enjoyed many forms of sex, was more enamored with kissing and caressing.

But this was not a coming out. That would never happen because Colin was what today would be called pre-gay. He loved men without claiming a certain sexual identity and so during the 1940s and 1950s Colin never called himself homosexual, and during the 1960s, when the term "gay" gained popularity, he declined to use that term as well. He was not interested in being gay anymore than he was interested in being British. His perspective on his sexual interests was quite simple, almost certainly too simple to be true: he enjoyed being sexual with people he liked socially, and overall he liked men better than women; consequently, he preferred having sex with men.

Colin performed his duties in the navy responsibly but without enthusiasm or passion, since, as he later recalled, he was not particularly loyal to England

and had a lot of unanswered questions about why people talked so much about the virtues of the military and so little about the greater good. When the navy band played "God Save the King" every morning as hands were called on deck, he would sometimes experience pangs of nationalism, but not always for England. "[God Save the King] always brought a lump to my throat and made me think of goodness and greatness. But then, so did almost every other national anthem, and that of the Germans raised the lump even higher. It was much better music."

He was permitted to choose a commission on the coastal forces in motor launches that held about a dozen sailors. The launches were large open motor boats that sailed low to the surface of the ocean; Colin's crews swept for mines, looked out for torpedoes, and collected dead bodies and dog tags along the shores where the allied forces had invaded. The gruesome scene at the site of the Normandy invasion alienated Colin further from the officers.

"[Getting the name tags] was a disagreeable task for anyone, and most of the seamen, like myself, were in their late teens or early twenties. Some of them found that if the body was sufficiently decomposed a sharp tug at the neck chain with a grappling hook would disconnect the head. If your aim was not good something else might come off, and it became a sort of macabre sport. A lot of tags were lost in the process because the neck was stronger than the chain. When the Germans started attaching explosives to dead bodies and floating them into the anchorage, we were instructed not to make any further attempts to get tags but to blow up all floating bodies on sight. The other two officers on my ship were older than I was. They commented only on the expenditure of the ammunition, which they had to account for, and the quality of the marksmanship. This and other things drew me more and more toward the enlisted men. Most of them were volunteers, as I was, but in many ways they seemed more adult than the officers. It was they who sickened first at poking bloated bodies with grappling hooks and ultimately they just refused to fire at any more bodies, asking if there was not another way of disposing of them. In contrast, the officers on my ship and others seemed to enjoy the target practice and used to swap stories in the wardroom, over their gins and whiskies, about putrid bodies, detached limbs, and burning gasses. In my youthful naiveté this did not seem like adult behavior, it was not even human. Yet there are many who claim that national service, particularly combat duty, 'will make a man of you.'"

There was one event more defining than any other of his passage into adulthood and of a sense of his own mortality. The Germans were sending out unmanned radio-controlled motorboats packed with explosives. They maneuvered these boats into the areas where the allies were anchored, in the hope that they would collide with an allied ship and explode. Colin's goal was to fire on the German boats, exploding them before they got into the anchorage, but one of them got away and struck the ship directly in front of his. In an instant, thirty-three men, one of whom was a close friend from Oxford, died in a massive explosion of metal, fire, and sparks. Colin stood on the bridge with another officer, a fellow Scot named Scouse McBride. "Oblivious to the other explosive motorboats milling around us, he let go of the helm and put his arm around my shoulder and gripped tight, to have something to hold onto as we watched our friends disappear—and with them something of ourselves—to reappear as flotsam the next morning."

There was, in that moment, no time for reflection, talk, or tears, only for a brief recognition that this rush of emotions he felt was something new. It was more than an awareness of his own mortality or the impermanence of the people around him. What was new was the unity he felt with McBride and with his now deceased friend, an urgency to embrace life and connect with others. And when it was all over, and even after many years had passed, Colin would still feel his shoulder as tightly gripped as it was on that night. "I was feeling more alive and more fully than I had ever felt. In contact with this violent display of mortality, I felt at one with my friend from Oxford, sparkling away in the night sky, and at one with the arm still clutching my shoulder. It was a moment of companionship with both of them, the quality of which I had never experienced before. It was a moment of fearful ecstasy, and it took me a long time to understand it. I just wish that I had learned what I learned then some other way . . . "

During those early years in the navy, Colin learned that his brother Ian was dead. On Easter Monday, April 10, 1944, less than a month after Ian's son, David, was born, Ian's spitfire, on a reconnaissance mission to the Belgian border, plunged into the English Channel, and despite an exhaustive search, neither the plane nor Ian's body were ever recovered.

Jock said almost nothing to Colin at the time, and later said little more to his grandson, David, during his childhood. Jock gave financial support to Ian's widow, Margaret, a coal miner's daughter, but he had little need to talk. He felt he had said everything in 1946, when he composed a thirty-five page book addressed to David describing Ian's short life. He wrote, "How proud he was of you when you were born! And how proud of you would he be could he see you now! But you have every reason to be proud of *him;* and (as your Mother will tell you) if you grow up to resemble him in courage and in ideals, you will be travelling in the right direction and as he would wish you to do. In your travels you will certainly visit Greenoch, on the Clyde. Go up to the cemetery there, with its magnificent views over the Highland hills your father loved, and you will see that on our family stone I have had your father's name inscribed. I would have liked to add a few words from John Bunyan: ' . . . And all the trumpets sounded for him on the other side.'

"[But] your father hated all that seemed ostentatious . . . It only remains for me to wish you a long, healthy, happy and successful life; and at the end of it a splendid reunion when the day breaks and shadows fly away."

Colin, who never felt close to his brother, seldom spoke about him after his death to either friends or family, and there is nothing in Colin's papers to suggest how he mourned his death. In his 1983 book, *The Human Cycle,* however, he regretted having never thanked Ian for his friendship; no doubt that regret was one reason he became a devoted godfather to David, who idolized Colin and who would become a successful accountant like his grandfather. David would name his only son Ian.

When the war ended in the spring of 1945, Colin found himself in Germany, where his knowledge of the German language was especially useful. He translated for the Allied Forces at the place where, it was believed, Hitler had last been encamped. He was surprised not by how many German civilians were starving but by how cruelly they were treated by the British officers, who dined along the bay windows of the Officer's Club in open view of many hungry Germans waiting below for some unwanted morsels of food to be thrown out the window.

He wanted desperately to come home, but there was still much work to be done in the waters north of Germany. Colin was also put in a greater position of responsibility, having been promoted to sub-lieutenant and awarded command of a motor launch, the HMS *Pembroke.* In September, he wrote a long letter to Sir Henry Tizard, the president of Magdalen College, in which he expressed his hope to return to Oxford with a newfound determination to complete a degree in Modern Greats. He went on to comment on the war operations.

> *Tuesday, September 4, 1945*
> HMMC 154
> . . . Unfortunately, I have succeeded in getting myself into Age and Service Group 54 which will not be released for some considerable while . . . I should estimate a year and a half to two years . . . One of the great changes that has come over me since joining the Navy has been the acquisition of the desire to work. I must confess that when I was up at Magdalen before I did not make a particularly good attempt at it, though more of an attempt than was generally believed.

> . . . Some of the damage caused by the R.A.F. is almost unbelievable—Heligoland and Eurden [*sic*] are the two worst places we have been to. Heligoland is just flattened completely, it is of little use for anything but bomb practice. Eurden is just a shell, it is obliterated utterly but for part of the outskirts. Such inhabitants as remain live in the vast shelters and wander around the ruins looking for fire wood all day long. They seem to have lost all purpose in life and treat us with complete apathy.

Tizard wrote back in November warning Colin that "many men have difficulty getting back into course work and book learning."

As winter approached, Colin began supervising minesweeping off the Norwegian coast, working his way south into the Baltic Sea, but soon the ice was too thick to permit any real work, and though he was hopeful he would be demobilized by the end of 1946, he became increasingly bored. In February, he wrote Tizard again asking for advice. He recognized that he did not have enough talent to make a profession out of music and for the first and only time in any of his papers he expressed a desire to be a farmer.

"For me the future is rather uncertain—my only real interest, music, has been made impossible as a career and I am faced with the prospect of my father's business, lucrative and quite amusing, but thoroughly distasteful to me. Would it be a misuse of a comparatively useless life to take this job until I was in a position to revert to my second interest, farming? I suppose those are questions I should answer for myself, but some advice from you would be appreciated."

Tizard replied, "You mention your father's business. I don't know what it is, but I don't despise business. The country would soon go downhill if business were generally despised." He suggested that if Colin wanted to pursue his second interest, he would be able to recommend "some agricultural college."

Bill Mackenzie, his cousin, recommended that Colin take a Class B release; Class B was a way for students on scholarship to get out of their military service and return to school. Colin replied to Mackenzie that he was "not a scholar [on scholarship] nor yet an 'exhibitionist' nor even a promising student [a play on 'exhibitioner,' the term for students with scholarships one level below those awarded to scholars]." Mackenzie assured Colin that something could be arranged but Colin insisted that he would only accept the Class B release "provided that it will not be taking a place that might be occupied by a more deserving candidate." Mackenzie confirmed that Colin's release would not have an effect on anyone else, and was able to secure the early release. He was awarded a 1939-1945 Star for service, the France and Germany Star for service in those nations, the War Medal, and the Defence Medal. By August 8, 1946, a year earlier than Colin had expected to leave the navy, Mackenzie had secured a place in a local Oxford garage for Colin's two-seater MG, and he was on his way home.

CHAPTER FIVE

The Flute of Krishna

ONCE BACK AT OXFORD, Colin spent a considerable amount of time with Indian students. Although the number of Indian students peaked in the early 1920s, when the colonial administration was struggling to educate Indians in a British manner, in 1940 there were still plenty of students for Colin to befriend. Unfortunately, Magdalen, like Corpus and University Colleges, had a history of anti-Indian sentiment. Throughout the university, Indians were generally marginalized from many social activities, and increasingly so as Indian nationalism took hold. Indians were less likely to want a British education and the British began to resent Indian elites. By establishing close friendships with Indian students, Colin was expressing his devotion and love of the Other.

His best friend during the immediate post-war years was Satya Paul Mayor, an undergraduate studying engineering at Magdalen. Paul was Punjabi but was born and raised in England. Colin and Paul were close, even more because both of them had served in the navy; Paul wanted to be in the air force but people of Indian descent were not permitted to join. Colin also met Kumari Mayor, Paul's sister. She would become one of the most important women in his life.

But despite having good friends, Colin was unhappy in England. His relationship with his parents, especially his mother, was strained. His father had begun to pressure him to become an accountant, a profession for which Colin had no interest at all, and Dot had become increasingly possessive of him. Her hold on Colin was even more tenacious since, with Ian's death, Colin was her only child.

Dot, in fact, resented Colin's independent spirit and remarkable ability to form personal attachments far more than she would later resent his emerging homosexuality. Even as a teenager, Colin's good looks and social skills exceeded those of his mother. Tall and handsome, with long fingers and enormous hands on which he wore a ring with the Turnbull family crest, he would walk into a room, ethereal and refined, and find all eyes on him. As he got older, he paid less attention to his clothes, but that became part of his charm, a nonchalance that rarely looked contemptuous or stuffy; instead he showed himself to be carefree and affable, exuding a nuanced chic. In comparison to Colin, Dot had few friends and seemed to have little difficulty terminating what friendships she had; Jock's friends were almost exclusively business partners or clients. Colin, in contrast, established friendships like the Pygmies built makeshift huts. They were perfectly good, if impermanent, shelters that could be made quickly, for short or long stays; when they were physically abandoned, they could be revisited and, if not, they were seldom destroyed but simply dried up and faded away, suffering no insult, only the ordinary passage of time.

One way Dot felt she could hold on to Colin was to sabotage his efforts to find a girlfriend or to marry. On a Saturday evening in 1948, a year before he finished his studies, Colin was spending a few days at home on break from Oxford. As he was getting dressed for a date at the opera, in his finest clothes and opera cloak, his mother answered a knock at the door. It was Robin (Robinetta) Roberts, dressed in a ball gown. Robin said she was there to meet Colin, but was told by Dot that Colin was not at home and that she should therefore leave immediately. A few minutes later Dot told Colin that his date had departed, that she had sent Robin away because she disliked her. As his young nephew David watched from the corner of the sitting room, Colin threw whatever breakable objects he could find into the fireplace.

And so, in 1949, when Colin finished his undergraduate studies at Oxford and faced the question of what do with his life, he was decisive. His best friends were Indian. Most of the women he dated were Indian. He was fascinated by Hinduism and even considered studying at Oxford for an advanced degree in Indian religions. Best of all, India was far from England and his parents. He would go to India to study Indian religions at Benares Hindu University, a place recommended by his Indian friends at Oxford. At another level, however, his interests were less academic. He knew that what he really wanted was to follow a spiritual path, simply to be in India, to be away from other Europeans, to break through India's illusions. Like many tourists he was captivated by the mere anticipation of being there. But while other Europeans might stay at luxury hotels and be satisfied by the snake charmers and dancing monkeys performing beneath their balconies, Colin would begin a different journey.

On the way into Bombay from the dock, Colin was thrilled at the sight of the Marine Drive snaking along the bay. The street lights glowed along the drive into the distance, hence it's nickname, "The Queen's Necklace." In the heart of Bombay, and in front of his hotel, he was assailed by an odor so foul it was hard to bear. The smell of feces was everywhere; lepers and other deformed beggars came toward him for money, and polio victims crept along the edges of the crowded streets. The four-star Taj Hotel, where Colin had a reservation, ought to have been a refuge, but he liked it better outside. That was the India of Indians, he thought: poverty, illness, hunger and, within such dire circumstances, a resolute quest for spiritual fulfillment. The magic that attracted tourists was a sleight of hand. India's real magic, Colin believed, was an inner spiritual life accessible only to a special few. He wanted to be one of them.

The record of those two important years in India consists of two accounts separated by more than forty years. The first account is the photo-diary Colin kept and presented to his parents in 1951. The other is a manuscript entitled "The Flute of Krishna," part summary of the 1949-51 diary and part elaboration on it, which he compiled in Samoa in 1991. He was never able to shape "The Flute of Krishna" into a publishable text or one that went beyond a description of the events of those two years. The text offers little information about Hinduism, and in neither account was he particularly introspective in the sense that he looked explicitly at his psychological development at the time. Yet, in his vivid descriptions of events, he does offer some clues to his inner life. The texts suggest that 1949-1951 were crucial years in setting him on the path to becoming an anthropologist. The texts also suggest that his sexual identity was unresolved. That resolution would emerge ten years later.

Neither Colin's parents nor his teachers were enthusiastic about his plans to study for a Ph.D. in religion at Benares Hindu University. His cousin Bill Mackenzie at Magdalen worried that Colin was simply a dilettante—musician, minister, farmer, scholar, and now truth-seeker. In early March 1948, Mackenzie wrote Colin to warn him that the quality of Indian universities was sub-standard, and that religious studies had no practical value. "It seems a pretty desperate project," he wrote. "You would certainly involve yourself in a disaster unless you worked pretty hard under some supervision in London, presumably at the LSE [London School of Economics] . . . I cannot see what you would get out of it either as education or as a qualification for your future career."

Colin wrote back two days later. "I quite understand your lack of enthusiasm for the idea and take heed. As you say, as either an education or a qualification, the value is doubtful, but the point is that now I have decided to pursue an academic career . . . I am well aware that I did not work when up [at Oxford], I didn't shine particularly at what I did do, not for lack of desire, however. I desperately wanted to get to grips with some interesting work, but it was all so utterly pointless—training that I was going to my father's office. The fault was mine, for not training my mind. But now I do know it—at last—beyond any shadow of doubt; and lo! the miracle has happened, believe it or not, and I am working!"

A week later, he wrote again to assure his cousin that he had also begun learning Hindi and Sanskrit, as well as the teaching of English as a foreign language, and that he expected a teaching diploma would "bolster up" his admittedly weak wartime B.A. and increase his chances to qualify for government funding for his education. He added that while he understood that many people at Oxford believed an Indian degree would not be taken seriously, Benares Hindu University was an exception to the "low standards of Indian universities, especially where Hindu Philosophy is concerned." Colin did not tell anyone that he had already decided to look for a guru and would become a vegetarian. With those correspondences and with his stated enthusiasm for study, Colin silenced his critics and was on his way to India.

Within a few days after his arrival, Colin traveled to his friend Paul Mayor's family home, not far from Benares, for a short stay before classes began. From the boat Colin had sent a telegram to Paul's brother Dev saying, "Arriving with empty pockets and loaded machine guns." This caused a stir in the intelligence department; Indian authorities made frequent calls to the Mayor house, eventually inspected it thoroughly, and summoned Colin to the police station on his arrival to lecture him on the dangers of loose talk. Dev's wife, Geeta Mayor, who entertained Colin as well as the intelligence department, recalls that despite his antics "Colin had an elegant presence, soft spoken, one could not help feeling he was made for a special life."

Not long after registering at Benares Hindu University, Colin heard about the great religious teacher Sri Anandamayi Ma whose retreat or ashram was nearby. Sri Anandamayi Ma (1896–1982) was well known in India by 1949, and she is remembered today as one of the most famous of all Indian gurus and certainly the most famous twentieth-century female guru. Colin thought about going to see her, but first he wanted to travel north into the Himalayas where he thought the most holy gurus lived. Colin wrote a friend about his discomfort upon hearing of a famous guru who manufactured lapel buttons with his image on them, made phonograph records, and sold t-shirts. He imagined that Himalayan gurus were different.

He joined two European hikers on a difficult journey into the Himalayas in search of his high-minded and reclusive gurus, and though Colin was in excellent physical condition, he grew weaker and weaker. After reaching one peak on a long ascent, he fell to his knees to catch his breath. His friends went ahead and Colin promised to catch up with them. But he grew dizzy and slightly disoriented, knew he could not go any higher, and ended up crawling halfway down the hill through the thick underbrush until he collapsed. He slept outside that night, continuing down the hill the next morning and along the way eating whatever leaves looked edible in order to get some strength. Finally, he came to a road and collapsed again. A farmer with a two-wheeled cart picked him up and took him to a nearby temple and, as he lay there in the cart, barely conscious, he saw a man coming toward him. The man called out to Colin in a loud voice, "So, you didn't want to come and visit me!" Colin recognized him. He was the man on the lapel buttons and the t-shirts. The guru took him in, diagnosed him with hepatitis, nursed him back to health, and told him to go back to Benares to be with the famous female guru Anandamayi Ma.

Colin found the approach to Anandamayi's ashram far from prepossessing, but when he got into the main courtyard he quickly understood why ashrams were places for enlightenment, peace, and self-discovery. He later remembered, "From the narrow main street leading from the university down to the city center, a series of alleys ran off to the right, down towards the river. These alleys were only a few feet wide, and were as much frequented by cows as by humans. The result was that it was both wet and messy underfoot. And it was quite a long walk to get to this particular ashram. However, once there, stepping through a large but otherwise unimpressive archway, you came into an absolute haven of peace and beauty and cleanliness. A great terrace, lined with flowering trees and shrubs, overlooked the sacred Ganga River, and if Anandamayi was herself in residence—as often as not she was away visiting one of her many other ashrams—the terrace was crowded with people of every class and caste imaginable, the poor jostling the rich, the Sudras the Brahmins, to get close to this famous teacher and hear what she had to say."

Colin went there with two Americans: Judith Tyberg and David Mirer. Judith was from California; she was known in India as Jyotipriya, and had already lived with another famous teacher, Sri Aurobindo. She held a Ph.D. in Sanskrit studies and had published an important book with the Theosophical Society of the United States entitled *Sanskrit Keys to the Wisdom Religion.* David, a conscientious objector during World War II, had already decided to live with a third teacher, Sri Raman Maharshi in Tamil Nadu, southern India. In the courtyard, Colin and his friends searched for Anandamayi Ma but everyone was wearing white and to Colin they looked alike. Colin delighted in the uniformity; after all, he detested the markers of class and status in England. When Colin and his friends finally figured out who she was—a middle-aged Bengali woman sitting on a small carpet with long black hair falling carelessly over her shoulders—they walked toward her and sat down. An hour later Colin would write in his diary that when he saw her face everything vanished from his mind except a profound tranquility.

Colin asked Anandamayi Ma if she believed that by going to India he was rejecting his parents. He clearly believed that there was at least a kernel of truth in this proposition, but she put him at ease. Although one's highest duty, she said, is to one's parents, even that should not come before one's duty to seek truth. With these simple words, Anandamayi Ma perhaps said more than she intended, for Colin not only left his parents physically; by embracing Hinduism, he was also repudiating his parents' religions.

Of the three American visitors, only Colin returned the next day. Nearly fifty women were having a lively discussion with Anandamayi Ma in Bengali, a language Colin did not know. "I thought this was really rather a waste of my time and was about to leave, but some intuition made me stay, telling me that something important was going to happen. Then Anandamayi Ma started singing a lovely little song, still in Bengali, and looking directly at me. I felt a net closing in around me, a net of utter serenity and charm, and resistance was impossible."

Anandamayi Ma was inviting, powerful, and full of love. One of Colin's most salient memories was of her maternal love and, like all her devotees, Colin would call her Ma, or Mataji, meaning mother. He recalled of their first meeting that "A little boy came and curled up beside her, and Anandamayi caressed his long black hair until he fell fast asleep. Sometimes powerful, almost frighteningly so, [she] was now a fragile mother; but a mother with the magic of the moon and the stars and the whole universe within her, and within the child on her lap."

That vision of the boy, perhaps a vision of himself, compelled him to be with her, and in the coming weeks Colin went to the ashram every day. Anandamayi Ma then informed Colin that she had a room ready for him. If he was to live at the ashram, she wanted to know two things. First, what could she call him? Second, what yoga or spiritual path would he like to follow? He answered the second question first—"*Gyana Yog,* the path of the intellect"—and waited for Anandamayi to answer the first.

"What about Shuddhananda? (lover, devotee of purity)?"

"Whatever Mataji says."

"Or Premananda (lover of love)?"
"Whatever comes out of your mouth."
"Premananda!"

All who knew him during this time would in future years call him Premananda.

Anandamayi Ma told Colin he could never become a Hindu, there was no reason for him to change his identity. She argued that everyone in the ashram was identical no matter what they called themselves. In sending this egalitarian message, however, and by allowing Colin to live there, Anandamayi was downplaying one of the most significant features of her ashram; despite her distaste for hierarchy, the ashram was a place exclusively for Brahmins, members of the highest caste in India, and remains so to this day.

In India, generally, Europeans have had an elite status, but within ashrams such as this one they were likened to Untouchables. Europeans followed no caste regulations, would touch anyone and eat with anyone, regardless of their caste, and were therefore polluted and polluting in the eyes of Brahmins. As a result, although there were many Europeans who became devotees of Anandamayi Ma, few Europeans are known to have actually lived at her ashram. A young writer named Lewis Thompson, Colin Turnbull, and an Austrian pianist and school-teacher named Athmananda (whose European name was Blanka Schlamm), lived at the ashram, ate the same foods and wore the same clothing as the other devotees, but by permitting them to live there Anandamayi Ma heard many complaints. Some scholars of India find it curious that she had such great power and such strong convictions about inclusion, yet for the most part she complied with the Brahmins' wishes to exclude nearly everyone else from her temple.

Athmananda had been a devotee of Krishnamurti for three decades before committing herself to Anandamayi for thirty-two more years, until her death in September 1985. She kept a diary during the years Colin was at the ashram, and left it in her will to another devotee, Ram Alexander, of Assisi, Italy. Born in Austria to a Polish father and Czech mother in 1904, Blanka was twenty years older than Colin. She had an extraordinary gift for music and languages. As a young woman, she was organist in Holland for a church associated with the Theosophical Society, which was active in India. She accepted a teaching job at a school in Varanasi, India, and soon came to meet Anandamayi. Athmananda learned to read Sanskrit and, as she was fluent in French, English, German, Bengali, and Hindi, Anandamayi asked her to remain at the ashram as a translator and interpreter, not so much for westerners but for the many Indians who could not speak Hindi or Bengali, the only languages Anandamayi spoke. And yet Anandamayi also knew that if Athmananda stayed there she would be excluded from Brahmin functions and would feel marginalized without a companion. Lewis Thompson had been there before Colin; when he left, Anandamayi saw Colin (now called Premananda or Premanand) as a possible replacement. On December 19, 1949, Athmananda wrote to her diary: "Spent the weekend at the Ashram. [Ma] definitely tries to wean me from being too attached to Her. I asked Her about Premanand who had written to me. She said to tell him: 'That which is most dear to you with that remain always. And this is also for you.' I started crying when I heard this."

Athmananda agreed to look after Colin. She would remain with him during most of his stay at the ashram, and because he spoke neither Hindi nor Bengali she was the interpreter for all of his exchanges with Anandamayi Ma. Yet Colin makes no mention of her in his long manuscript, "Flute of Krishna" or in his other recollections of Anandamayi Ma published in India. Later, in his account of the Pygmies, those who helped Colin would also be erased from the record.

The next month, Athmananda wrote:

> *January 29, 1950*
> . . . No sooner has [Lewis] gone than She provides me with another sensitive young Westerner. She seems to want me to be in touch with at least one other foreigner. I suppose I need that. He is a nice fellow. When he talked to me yesterday, suddenly for a second, I noticed his beautiful blue clear eyes. There was a sudden instantaneous recognition. He told me some incidents from his life that are strangely parallel to mine: How he went fishing, and when seeing the first fish caught with the hook violently stabbed through its mouth, he threw down the rod and ran away in terror. Just like, [with] the chicken I had looked after . . .
>
> *12 February 1950*
> Yesterday translated a private [meeting] for Premananda [and Ma]. I find myself becoming fond of him. It started the other day when he talked to me. Yesterday when he laid his soul bare before Ma I found him delightful, so pure and fresh and sincere and full of joy. He is simple and not at all complicated like Lewis was; he seems much healthier and there is not so much conflict in him. Ma evidently wants me to have some human relationship as She always gives me someone to look after, perhaps to counteract my tendency of being too cut off.

In March, Athmananda wrote about how much she missed Lewis but she comforted herself with the thought of Colin: "Premanand is a charming boy, so balanced and sunny a creature."

At the ashram and with Athmananda's help, Anandamayi Ma taught Colin important lessons about humanity that, he believed, framed his future intellect. Anandamayi Ma taught him that there was a universal humanity but that human beings had the capacity to shape their existence in myriad ways. In future years, Colin would quite consciously try to *become* the people he studied, transcending boundaries most people thought were impassable. She also taught that being born into high status, whether Brahim or Brit, was not necessarily desirable, for we are all humans and therefore subject to the same afflictions. On several occasions, apparently to emphasize her disapproval of social status, she had the Brahmins in her ashram feed everyone else, thus having them act as servants to those who, outside the boundaries of the ashram, would have been their subordinates. The end result of such a reversal of hierarchy was probably similar to that of the Royal Navy's annual ritual reversal—momentary reversals of hierarchy that actually reaffirm the status quo. Colin did not let himself see the reaffirmation of entrenched hierarchy at the ashram as he had on the Navy boats.

Once Ma showed Athmananda and Premananda a door leading from the terrace to her room made especially for them, all the while insisting that there was not a hair's difference between them and the other, Indian devotees. But beyond this, she did little to change the ashram's attention to hierarchy, and one could well argue that by constructing the special door she was acknowledging the need to isolate her relationship with Colin and Athmananda from the rest of the ashram.

When Colin first arrived at the ashram, Anandamayi Ma conveyed her sentiments about the Indian caste system to him in a well-known story about a saint's quest for *moksha,* freedom from the wheel of life and reincarnations, and release from the pains of desire in the external world.

"There was once a famous Brahmin saint who attracted many Brahmin disciples who lived with him and looked after the old man, and learned from him. But eventually the time came for him to die, for even saints must die. His disciples were in despair at the thought of losing their beloved Guru, and finally asked him to give them some sign, after he had died, that his teachings were true, that there really was some form of afterlife. At first the old saint refused, knowing that the most valuable possession they had was their faith, which could never be equaled by mere knowledge. However, they kept urging him so he finally gave in.

"He said to them, 'When you cremate my body, my soul will ascend to heaven, and as a sign that I have won release from his world, I will cause drums to sound. You will hear, and you will know.'

"He then had his bed carried outside and placed under a tree, where he promptly died. His disciples cremated his body according to custom and waited for the expected rolling of the drums. Not a sound was heard. And finally it was plain, either there was no after life, or else their master had been a fraud, and had not won his way to *moksha,* or release.

"However, the disciples did not disband. The teachings they had received were as valid as ever. But they were despondent. Then one day they were visited by a great sage who asked them why they were so unhappy, living in this lovely ashram, with such a heritage of wisdom. They told him what their teacher had said and how there had been no rolling of drums. The sage asked for details. Then he asked to be carried outside just as the Brahmin disciples had carried their Brahmin Guru. The disciples did so, and placed the sage under the same tree where their master had died. The sage looked up and saw an apple. He told the disciples to pick it and cut it open. They did so, and inside was a dead worm, having eaten its way to death. The sage said it too had been a living creature and to cremate it properly. So the disciples did so, and as soon as the fire consumed the body of the dead worm there was a massive thundering of drums."

The lesson of the story, Anandamayi said, laughing to Colin, was that it might have been better to be a worm, or even a cockroach or a cricket, than a Brahmin. The joke had a special meaning since Anandamayi was herself a Brahmin. The old saint had seen the apple before he died and must have had the desire to eat it. Had he been reborn as a human he would have come back with all the desires he had battled so long to overcome so that he could reach nirvana. But he was reborn, instead, as a worm and with just one desire, to eat the apple. And when he had finished and had no desires left, he was at last free.

From late 1949 through 1950, Colin still went to classes at Benares Hindu University but his relationship with Anandamayi Ma took precedence over his studies. He took every opportunity to be with her, especially when she was traveling, and she said it would be good for him to accompany her to Dehra Dun, near the city of Mussoorie in northern India. It was autumn, the time when the Durga puja is performed, the most important annual Bengali Hindu festival. Throughout India a similar set of mythical and ritual elements is incorporated into a reenactment of the day of victory. In Bengal, the goddess Durga is worshipped on behalf of the ancient King Ram and all his subjects.

Although Anandamayi did not predict misfortune if Colin stayed in Benares, he took her invitation as both an order and a threat. Once, he was told, she asked a businessman not to return to Calcutta on a certain day, but he was an important lawyer and said he had to be there to meet a client. He was violently murdered at the railway station en route to this meeting. Colin also heard, and believed, that Anandamayi had once blessed a young couple's marriage, but had disagreed with their preferred wedding date. They went ahead with their own plans, and on the first night of the wedding the bride died of a heart attack; within a few hours, the groom committed suicide.

When he arrived in Dehra Dun, the three-day-long puja was already under way, and it was an extraordinary sight. The image of the goddess Durga was hung with garlands of jasmine and gardenias, and sweets and other foods rested at her feet. Colin wrote in his diary on October 2, 1949 that at the Durga puja he felt a need to surrender to the moment: "Primitive? I couldn't even say that, I was so bewildered by the strangeness of it all. There was only one thing to be done, and that was to sit down with the rest of them. This I did and I occasionally gave a half-hearted clap of my hands, or lurched to one side and mumbled to myself—but for all the notice that anyone took of me I might have been standing on my head and singing 'God save the King,' so I relaxed and allowed my thoughts to collect themselves."

Durga is a goddess known by many names throughout India. She has two primary characteristics, one mild and one fierce. In the same diary entry, he explained Durga's qualities in terms that would make sense to the recipients of the diary, his mother and father. "In her mild form she is worshipped for all the good and feminine qualities, in her fierce form she is worshipped as the destroyer of the evil force. Durga the Good and Beautiful, but also Durga the stern and just—the Divine mother who can love and through her love can fight to protect. It is the same in every religion: there is the great Buddha of compassion, and the stern Buddha who would not tolerate any weakness; there is the Prophet of mercy, but there is also the Mohammet [*sic*] who fought bitterly for his belief. There is the Christ of infinite love, there is still the Christ who could overturn tables and turn money-makers out of the temple."

The drums were loud, the cymbals piercing, and throngs of worshipers clapped out complicated rhythms. Colin looked at Anandamayi Ma who was sitting calmly with her eyes half closed. Many were swaying in front of the six-foot-high idol, and the sight of them reminded Colin of revivalist meetings he had attended in England. But while he viewed those meetings as new inventions, fabricated and forced, this ritual seemed as old as time. The worshipers did not even seem conscious of the idol as a concrete object constructed for the festival. Instead, he wrote, "They looked beyond the symbol to the symbolized." He believed that the devotees were focused on love rather than the goddess of love, on the power of good over evil rather than the realities of death and destruction.

Neither Colin nor anyone else got much sleep during the three days of the festival. Afterward, Colin discovered that Durga had been celebrated in a large number of places in and around Dehra Dun and that all the images were being carried to a nearby lake. He rushed to see a procession led by elephants and every kind of musician. Priests and their assistants threw image after image into the lake. Colin moved toward a rickety wooden bridge from which he could get a clear view of a makeshift island, called Lanka, floating at one end of the lake. In the epic of Ramayana, Lanka is the place where evil is destroyed. So to reenact the victory, the float was jammed with fireworks and set on fire. But things did not go as planned. The mooring ropes burned first, and the island, now free, drifted toward the bridge. The spectators panicked, the bridge collapsed, and everyone, including Colin, fell into the water as they rushed to the shore. With a huge explosion, Lanka disappeared.

We do not know what Anandamayi Ma saw in Colin. He does not even hazard a guess as to why someone in such demand would spend so much time with him. It may have been because he was British. It may have also been the strength of Colin's desire to learn her art, or even perhaps his willingness to see her as a mother and her ashram as the site of a second adolescence. But it may also have been all of these reasons combined with Anandamayi Ma's desire for Athmananda to have a western, male companion. She believed in marriage, and she herself was married, though she also believed in complete celibacy.

Like her other students, Colin found his own way. India, she said, was about *self* discovery. There was no real Anandamayi or Durga or Colin Turnbull. Anandamayi Ma taught him that there was only that which Colin made real for himself. She also taught him that something beautiful and pure can emerge from something ordinary, inconspicuous, or ugly, like a lotus growing up from the mud, its beauty and purity unsullied by its origin. Truth could be found in the most unexpected places, in the mountaintops of India or in temples and ashrams, but perhaps just as likely on a river bank, a city slum, or a farmer's field. It might even be found in one person—someone who Colin might someday meet—in whom, deep inside, there was a brilliant light, an inner truth, struggling to blossom.

Colin would keep a photograph of Anandamayi framed on the nightstand in his bedroom until his death. It stood right next to a photograph of his mother. In 1989, nearly four decades after he left India, he would place a second photograph of Anandamayi Ma in a Hindu shrine he constructed in his living room, amid icons and relics and silk, in between two photographs of his partner, Joseph Towles.

Between 1949 and 1951, Colin spent brief periods of time with other teachers, such as Swami Sivananda, Krishnamurti, and Sri Aurobindo, but none influenced him as powerfully as Anandamayi Ma. He felt that his relationship with Anandamayi Ma was intimate, as it is supposed to be between teacher and disciple. The ultimate goal of the disciple is to put himself in the hands of a single guide, to find one's self through the being of the other. This process informed his later work as an anthropologist. His relationships with the societies he studied, whose members he viewed as his teachers, were patterned on his earlier relationships with people like Anandamayi Ma or his Oxford tutor, A. J. P. Taylor. Reflecting on his teachers, Colin wrote: "The relationship and the conscious effort to dispel the duality [between teacher and student], is all the more powerful when there is only one teacher and one student. In the tradition of the guru-student relationship, it is felt to be essential for those who in childhood or early adolescence have consecrated themselves directly and entirely in the hands of one spiritual teacher who can, it is believed, teach the adolescent how to transform his growing sexual energy into pure spiritual energy."

Colin spent two months living in the ashram of Sri Aurobindo, a teacher who Anandamayi suggested Colin visit. He taught Colin that the sacred and the secular could be joined together and that scientific explanations of human experience had their limits. Aurobindo's ashram was in Pondicherry which, in 1949, was still under French control. Born in 1872, Aurobindo spent most of his early life as a student of classics. After studying at Cambridge University, he returned to India to take the civil service exam and passed everything except horseback riding, a failure that disqualified him from playing polo and therefore of gaining much status within the British colonial empire. He became an Indian nationalist and was frequently jailed by the British as a dissident. In Pondicherry, the French left him alone.

Most ashrams were places for personal spiritual growth where people sought tranquility, sanctuary, a time for self-reflection as they prepared to return, changed, to their everyday lives. But Aurobindo did not want to perfect the individual; he wanted to perfect all of humanity. Aurobindo argued that the Divine could be brought down into this world, blending the secular and the sacred and thereby saving entire communities. He believed that no fundamental transformations in society could be made until humanity altered its consciousness through the Divine and he described the descent of the Divine into the human world in his book *The Human Cycle.* Colin would later use the identical title for his own 1983 book on rites of passage in England, India, and Africa.

Sri Aurobindo's ashram consisted of offices, a library, a meditation hall, dining area, guest quarters, and a private residence for the guru and an elderly French woman called Mother. With wild hair and a dictatorial style, she ran the place. All communication with Aurobindo had to go directly through her. Few others ever saw the great sage. Each morning the residents of the ashram would gather beneath Aurobindo's balcony. Mother would appear first and then the sage would appear to give his blessing through her. Later in the day, she distributed flowers as another blessing. And though she seemed to have little affection for Colin, or so Colin thought, on his twenty-fifth birthday she delivered birthday wishes and new bouquets of fresh flowers to him four times. He never discovered how she knew his birthdate.

Mother, originally named Mirra Alfassa, was born in Paris in 1878, just six years before Aurobindo's birth in Calcutta. She was a talented painter, knew Monet, Rodin, and other notable artists, but found her greatest inspiration in the occult. As Mirra's spiritual power began to reveal itself, she gathered disciples and traveled to India in early 1914 to meet with the unusual man she had heard of in France, Sri Aurobindo. Mirra and the sage corresponded for the next six years, during which time Aurobindo's wife, Mrinalini Bose died in Calcutta and Mirra divorced her second husband. In 1920, Mirra went to Pondicherry to stay. Aurobindo secluded himself at the ashram in 1926 and asked Mirra, now simply called Mother, to manage the day-to-day operations of the ashram, look after their disciples, and grade them on their progress.

Mother was frightening and spellbinding. Despite her age, she played a good game of tennis and encouraged everyone to exercise. She failed Colin in calisthenics and suggested he did not have the physical strength to withstand the power of the Divine when it descended. In a strange way she completed Aurobindo, for in her extraordinary strength as a presence, as an administrator, as an athlete, she was the secular and worldly manifestation of his sacred, spiritual power.

Aurobindo died in 1950 while Colin was still in India. According to his devotees the sage believed that it was time to work in more subtle dimensions of reality and so he willed himself to death. As he left his body in this world, he entrusted Mother to carry on. Mother died in 1973 when she decided that her own work on earth was complete.

Today, Sri Aurobindo and Mother are buried side by side in the central courtyard of the Pondicherry ashram. The tomb is marked by a simple marble table that his devotees perpetually cover with fresh flowers. Their work continues in India and the ashram, at a new and larger site founded by Mother in 1968 about six miles north of Pondicherry, is now called Auroville and the ashram accommodates nearly 800 families. Auroville has administrative offices throughout the world and maintains an elaborate website. It is also engaged in a wide range of large-scale projects, including environmental regeneration, renewable energy, health care, and building technology. In 1999, a reporter for the *New York Times* recommended the ashram as a primary destination for tourists to India.

In 1983 when Colin recalled Aurobindo and Mother, he suggested that they challenged any scientific models of bodily experience he may still have clung to at the time. He wrote,

"To be with either of them for more than a minute was enough to give me a violent headache. A headache is hardly a spiritual experience, you might say, but it was certainly evidence of some kind of power. [At his daily public appearance] Sri Aurobindo did not speak to anyone, he just sat there. It was when his eyes caught mine that my worst headache began, a pressure that at first was not painful, but which grew stronger the closer I got to the man. We had all been shepherded into the audience room in a long, orderly line, as though we were queuing for admission to a movie, and we were presented with a small flower each to put on the ground in front of Sri Aurobindo when we got to the head of the queue, with instructions not to pause or try to look or say anything, but to pass right on. I thought it was going to be a rather bad movie until I finally got up to the top of the stairs and into the far end of the room. It was more than the absolute silence as the long line steadily and slowly inched its way forward . . . There was nothing designated to create any kind of visual effect, no exotic music, no chanting, nothing to tell the senses that anything unusual was happening . . .

"Then, although I had intended to behave according to the rules and regulations, my curiosity got the better of me and I moved my head slightly to one side to look ahead . . . that was when my eyes met those of Sri Aurobindo. The gentle flow, which I can best describe as being like what I feel when I sink into a deep hot bath, stopped for a frightening instant, then, instead of the whole body being gently warmed, my head suddenly started to boil. The flow came through his eyes, but the power, like the heat of an open furnace, came from his whole body and being. I was right in front of the man. My head wanted to burst from a pressure that seemed to come from both inside and outside at the same time. And once I got out I went straight to my room with a violent, painful headache that lasted twenty-four hours. I even took my temperature; it was perfectly normal."

Colin also embarked on a number of pilgrimages, trying to see as much of India as he could before he returned to England. Though Colin had no strict timeline, his companion on many of his trips, a fellow student at Benares Hindu University named Newton Beal, was due back in Ohio by the end of the year. Despite his stated desire to remain solitary for much of his time in India, Colin spent increasingly long periods with Newton, who would figure prominently in Colin's future fieldwork in central Africa. Newton was a high school music teacher from Ohio who, for almost a decade, would accompany Colin on all of his travels in India and in Africa. They were also almost certainly lovers but perhaps not until they arrived in Africa. For in India, Colin tried to remain celibate as a way to honor Anandamayi Ma's belief—a conventional Hindu belief—that the chaste are more likely to achieve a higher state of consciousness or self-realization.

On one trip, Colin's train stopped at Agra, the site of the Taj Mahal. Colin was averse to anything that resembled tourism and was against even getting out of the train. But a friend on the train with him—most likely Newton Beal—insisted on going to the great mausoleum and Colin gave in. It was truly beautiful and Colin marveled at the love that Shah Jahan must have had to build something so extraordinary for his wife. In spite of the fog and rain that day, Colin and his friend decided to go in just as the gates were about to close for the night.

"And just as we got to the end of that long reflecting pool, the moon broke through the clouds, and there was a shimmering white mass of marble, directly ahead of us. But inside it was even more beautiful, and even the guard was content to sit on the floor and just look at it all, and wanted us to do the same. Here was a Muslim saying the same thing as a Hindu—'be a receptacle, let yourself be filled with the Divine.' But finally he took us down to the actual tomb, and while we were there something else happened. From the main shrine above came the sound of a flute. It was the guard's co-worker, he said, saying he wanted to go home. That may well have been all it was. But the flute, to me, was played as though it were played by one of India's greatest masters, and it was a perfect complement to the shadowy moonlight shining through the lattice and the soft glow of the very marble itself. And, I swear, it was more than just beauty, it was a touch of the sacred, of the holy, that gently filled that huge tomb."

On that same trip, as they approached Kailas in the Himalayas, Colin was sitting alone in the early evening on a blanket beside a pilgrim trail, heating up some soup for himself, when he heard the flute again.

"The trail ran along a ridge, with beautifully terraced fields dropping down into the valley about a thousand feet below. And from somewhere down there I heard the flute, as some shepherd boy was lazily waiting for his flock of sheep to return to him so he could drive them home for the night. I have no way of knowing what was in his mind. Rather like the guard at the Taj Mahal he may have been thinking only of getting home to a good hot meal. But beauty seems to have an insidious power of its own, and just as the guard was affected by the moonlight which somehow filled the empty vastness of that marble tomb, so this boy was perhaps affected by the natural beauty of the world around him, and transformed that beauty into the sound of his flute. His song was a song of love, and the yearning was so unmistakable the beauty was almost painful."

The title of Turnbull's unpublished account of his time in India, "The Flute of Krishna," is intriguing. The manuscript contains little that is sexual or erotic and yet Krishna is among the most erotic of gods. An incarnation of Vishnu, Krishna is the Hindu god of love. The young Krishna, disguised as a cowherd, is often depicted with a flute, which he plays so beautifully that few can resist it. The flute has often been interpreted as a metaphor for the irresistibility of the Divine and as a phallic symbol. Krishna's Sanskrit name is Venu, which means flute, and he is sometimes called Venugopala, "the cowherd with the flute." There are countless songs and icons portraying his efforts to steal the hearts of the Gopis, cowherd women. He also reproduced himself so that he could make love with many at the same time and even seduced his eldest aunt, Radha. Male devotees of Krishna will sometimes dress as women as a way of approaching Krishna as a Gopi. The name of Krishna thus evokes potent sexual imagery. (The British thought of him as something of a rake because he used his flute to entice women; the British even launched a court case against Krishna.)

For Turnbull, India was a siren song, beyond both the erotic or divine. It was intoxicating and seductive. It was all-encompassing and irresistible. It may have been an unavoidable spirit filling the void left by Christianity. Though he imagined he had left England and his domineering mother far behind, he found distinct echoes of them in the ashram of Anandamayi Ma, a new loving mother before whom he was willing to fall to his knees whenever she called, and in Aurobindo's awesome Mother who was both cool and caring, as ambivalent about Colin as any real mother might have been.

The flutes he heard reminded him of an old Sufi poem, and that, in turn, reminded him of the possibility that spirituality, as Ma had told him, transcended the boundaries of different religions.

Hearken to this reed forlorn
Breathing ever since 'twas torn
From its rushy bed a strain
Of impassioned love and pain.

The secret of my son, though near,
None can see and none can hear.
Oh, for a friend to know the sign
And mingle all his soul with mine.

'Tis the flame of love that fired me:
'Tis the wine of love inspired me.
Would'st thou learn how lovers bleed?
Hearken, hearken to the reed.

"Was [this] the flute of Krishna that I heard in that high Himalayan valley?" Colin asked himself. "The flute knows no barrier of religion. It may not even be a flute whose sound we hear. It can be a distant yodel of a lover calling to his beloved across the hills; it can be a turbanned patriarch of a music teacher, sitting serenely among all his cushions in a marble hall as snotty students bow and pay their respects to him, then breaking into smiles and song. Or an old man sitting up all night in an ashram hall, looking out over the River Ganges, waiting to greet the rising sun with the holy Gayatri on his lips. Or it can be an aged Abbot, smiling indulgently at the monks below him, chanting their hearts out, knowing that one day they too will stop and listen with wonder to the song they sing.

As he prepared to leave India, he spoke with Anandamayi Ma about his return. Athmananda interpreted and added her own commentary in her diary.

> QUESTIONER [TURNBULL]: I am going back to avoid pain to my parents. But how far should I comply with their wishes? They expect me to settle down and get married.
>
> MOTHER: If you wish to get married you may do so though you may get caught in the movement of the world; but remember that all the Rishis [seers, to whom mantras are revealed] of old were married. Together with your wife go on aspiring towards the Divine. But if you do not wish to get married no one can force you. If you can keep your mind pure without marriage, so much the better.
>
> TURNBULL: Should I take up work for my father's estate and property or welfare work for Indians and Africans?
>
> MOTHER: As you are going back, there is no harm in working. But don't take up work that will bind you.

Athmananda, his dutiful and forgotten translator and companion, would write: "I feel that Premananda will work in England; and though he may come here many times, it will only be to take with him Her light to the West. Suddenly I got a glimpse of how Europe will be influenced through people like Premananda, who is utterly devoted to Her. She told him to regard me as his 'Didi' [older sister]. I am indeed lucky to have a brother like this and to get all Her teaching now in such abundance after having been kicked about and in everyone's way for so long."

On February 20, 1951, on his last day in India, Colin wrote: "The stars shimmered through the tree tops, and they seemed to shed minute tears. The moon was shrouded in mist, and I felt sad and content. The whole of the past two years seemed to unfold before me, and the night around me was peopled with the spirits of glorious Kashi [Benares] . . . For a brief moment I saw Anandamayi sitting on a moonlit terrace, a small boy curled up beside her, head in her lap. The Buddha sat in impassive contemplation beneath the mighty Bo tree. Time and space were empty things, and I felt the inexpressible silence of the northern snows. From the unfathomable mass of the Himalayas came the strains of Krishna's flute, calling its wistful song, asking the eternal question. It penetrates deep into the souls of all who listen, touching them with a magic wand of love and brotherhood. The night was thronged with gods and demigods, and when I faltered at the thought of trying to live even a fraction of what I had learned, the gods took me in their arms. On all sides the unconquerable soul of India came flooding in upon me; challenging, encouraging, and drowning me in an ocean of utter bliss."

And when it was time to leave, Colin and Newton went by boat to the eastern coast of Africa. Quite unintentionally Colin would find himself in the Congo in the heart of the rain forest with the Mbuti Pygmies. There he would hear another resounding call, the *molimo* trumpet, and it would call to him like the flute of Krishna. It would sing of truth and beauty and goodness, not just for him but for anyone willing to surrender to the song and spirit of the forest, a place that both Colin and the Pygmies called mother. Colin had discovered something in India that would be his gift to Africa and anthropology, a lasting faith in emotional, spiritual paths to truth.

CHAPTER SIX

The Rain Forest

WHEN COLIN TURNBULL first entered the rain forest, he found the unexpected. He had envisioned a place where the humidity was overbearing. He was certain it would be untamed jungle through which he would have to forge a path with machete and ax. It would be a place where the heat was overwhelming, the mosquitoes vicious, and the water undrinkable. It would be a place he might last a day or two, but not more.

He also imagined that the rain forest would be a visual celebration of life. It would be teeming with exciting and beautiful species of insects, birds, and mammals. It would be tranquil and, in its isolation, frighteningly silent.

It was none of these things.

The rain forest he had seen in old movies was nowhere to be found. The Ituri rain forest of central Africa was higher in elevation than he had realized, a far cry from the boggy bug-infested swamps in which Albert Schweitzer had lived. In fact, the deeper Colin went into the forest, the farther he could see. The trees were tall and far apart, it was like traveling in a free and open space. And because the trees blocked out the sunlight, it was cool and was protected, rather than besieged, by nature. The temperature fluctuation was remarkably predictable. Even if he found himself unexpectedly under direct sunlight, the temperature was never higher than 90° F. And at night, the forest temperature bottomed out consistently at a cool 65° F.

Shallow rivers and streams captured the bits of light that broke through the treetops, and through the cold, clear, rushing water there were clean floors of sand and quartz. This was not stagnant water with muddy bottoms in which parasitic worms or blood flukes could live. It was pure and quenching. Turnbull would travel along these streams and drink the water with impunity. There were insects here and there, of course, but the mosquitoes stayed up high in the canopy of the forest, feeding on the monkeys and other arboreal mammals. Only when the villagers cut down the trees did the mosquitoes descend in search of blood and transmit malaria to humans.

To Colin's surprise, there was no exciting display of life to be found. Rain forests, he quickly realized, may contain the vast majority of all species of plants and animals on earth, but they also have the lowest density. Unless he was actively hunting, he might see a wild boar, an elephant, a leopard, or the many different kinds of small rain forest antelopes only once or twice a month, and even then he was probably seeing it dead, caught in a hunter's net or trap. In most of the forest too there was little need for a machete. The forest only became dense with undergrowth when people cut down the trees for farming. Ecologists refer to the kind of forest depicted in Tarzan movies as secondary growth, as it spreads only where humans have already made their mark on the land.

While the diversity of life did not advertise itself visually, sound was another matter. The forest was anything but quiet, with coughing, whining animals sounding throughout the day, mournful screams of tree hyraxes filling the night, and the long low creaky sound of the black and white colobus monkey awakening Colin every morning, as if a large, unoiled door was continuously being opened and shut.

But the most extraordinary sound, Colin wrote, was "the sound of the voices of the forest people as they sing a lusty chorus of praise to this wonderful world of theirs—a world that gives them everything they want." These voices reminded Colin of the three-word mantra that would dot his writings for thirty years, words that he used to describe Anandamayi Ma, and that he would have etched on his own gravestone: "This cascade of sounds," he wrote in *The Forest People*, "echoes among the giant trees until it seems to come at you from all sides in sheer *beauty* and *truth* and *goodness*, full of the joy of living."

In 1951, when Colin was preparing to leave India, he did not know for certain that he would go to Africa. But he wanted to delay the return home. Though he was twenty-eight years old, his war service and two years of study in India had not prepared him to make the weighty career decisions his father would demand of him. At Benares Hindu University, Colin had met a thirty-six year-old music teacher from Ohio named C. Newton Beal who was on a leave of absence from his job in the Lancaster City school system to study music. Newton was balding but handsome, lean and muscular. He was energetic enough to keep up with Colin on their various trips into the Indian countryside and contemplative enough to share in Colin's late-night reflections on spirituality. But what they shared the most was a love of sound, and they talked often about harmony, melody, rhythm, and tone. They decided to travel together to Africa in the hopes that they might discover some remarkable music there.

Beal was born in 1914 in Versailles, Ohio, and went on to study music at Capital University in Columbus and Northwestern University in Chicago. In 1941, he became the Lancaster City school's director of vocal music. In 1950 he went to India and then, with Colin, to Africa in 1951. Six years later he would be granted a second leave of absence to go to the Belgian Congo with Colin.

Both wanted to start in Kenya and travel west and north by car or motorcycle until they reached the Mediterranean. They left India by boat at the end of February, disembarking at the Kenyan port of Mombasa. Colin carried just one trunk he had taken from his father, a trunk that his father had borrowed from his friend, a former cabinet minister named Sir Donald Maclean. On its side, Maclean's full name was printed in large letters. Colin would not know the significance of the name Maclean until he tried to leave Africa.

When they arrived in Kenya at the beginning of March, Newton and Colin made their way to Nairobi to stay with a friend and client of Colin's father, Sir Charles Markham. Until some major business setbacks in 1939, Markham had been fabulously wealthy, and his family was well known in the British empire. Beryl Markham, the famous aviator, was related to the Markhams by marriage. The family figured in the 1987 film *White Mischief*, about the unchecked passions of British expatriates in Kenya in 1940. Colin and Newton stayed at the Markhams' for several days and soon realized, with Markham's encouragement, that Kenya would not be safe for long, especially for whites. Most whites in Kenya and England accepted the colonial myth that the so-called Mau Mau, an anti-colonial resistance movement, was a religious cult whose goal was to murder whites. Markham was disturbed by how much time Colin wanted to spend with Africans, and he was worried that Colin's life was in danger.

Colin took Markham's warning about involving himself with Africans seriously, but his fears of being executed were unwarranted. Mau Mau was, in fact, both a religious movement (though by no means either cult-like or unified) and an armed uprising by Kikuyu peasants against the colonial state in Kenya; but it would play out as a conflict between loyalists and liberationists from the

Kikuyu tribe. Contrary to popular opinion during the 1950s, few whites were killed. But because they feared for their safety, Colin and Newton shopped for a motorcycle and decided to leave Kenya. Markham recommended that they travel to see a man named Patrick Putnam, whom he had met many years earlier and who, according to Markham, kept a small hotel in the rain forest of the Belgian Congo; the hotel was, in fact, a glorified mud hut with rooms for European travelers. Colin bought plenty of pens and paper so he could keep a diary of the trip. He assumed he could sell the story when he got back to England, and he did. The voyage was published in two parts by *The Motorcycle* magazine in January 1952.

Neither Colin nor Newton knew much about motorcycles, and Newton refused to learn. With Markham's advice and a small loan, Colin bought a new red motorcycle that he called Ruddi Muddi. It was an AJS 500 sport, a British-made motorcycle used in off-road competitions. Colin took the bike out of the shop and blushed with embarrassment as a curious crowd waited outside to watch him ride away. "Least said about the first few yards the better," he wrote. He would never like motorcycles.

"A small boy pointed out that, until I took my foot off the brake pedal, I couldn't hope for much success; another innocently asked if I knew how to stop . . . To my delight, yet also to my horror, I was careening unevenly away from the jeering crowd, heading for a good-natured Nairobi constable. He sized up the situation pretty well, hurriedly held up all traffic and leapt aside. So far, so good, but with some 18 miles to cover I had obviously got to change gear. It happened accidentally when I mistook left and right and stamped on the gear change instead of the brake pedal."

They crossed Uganda, traveling through the Katwe game reserve and through the famed Ruwenzori mountains, popularly known as the Mountains of the Moon. Now they were on a direct route to Stanleyville in the Belgian Congo, but it was two months before they arrived there. They found something better: Camp Putnam, on the Epulu river. Patrick Putnam, a former Ph.D. candidate at Harvard University's Department of Anthropology, had built several mud huts for tourists who wanted to see the Pygmies.

As a favor to Markham, Patrick invited Colin and Newton to stay at Camp Putnam, with room and board free of charge, for several weeks. Putnam took an instant liking to Colin and tried to find a way for him to stay even longer. At the same time, the Hollywood producer Sam Spiegel was making the famous Katherine Hepburn and Humphrey Bogart film *The African Queen.* Spiegel had to ship the boat, *The African Queen,* and spare parts through the forest and needed considerable help with the transport. Patrick made sure that Colin and Newton got the job. Their primary responsibility was finding a boiler large enough for the thirty-foot boat. They found one in good condition, but when they failed to hitch it properly to their truck, it tumbled out and suffered badly. There were large dents all across one side. When they arrived at Speigel's camp with the boiler, Colin and Newton thought Spiegel was going to be furious and they were contrite; to their surprise, Spiegel said, "Actually, it's a nice touch." The dents are visible in the opening scenes of the film.

Patrick Tracy Lowell Putnam, the son of a Boston surgeon, first went to Africa in 1927 on a two-month Harvard expedition. When he got to the Ituri forest, he did not want to come back. In 1928, his father traveled to Africa to retrieve him and found Patrick living with a native female companion in a rain forest village called Epulu. But by 1929, he was back in the Ituri forest. With only a handful of trips back to the United States, including one failed attempt to earn a Ph.D., and three trips in search of American wives, he would stay in Epulu until his death. He earned some funds from his hotel, but was supported financially by his father and his first two American wives, neither of whom were able to tolerate living in the Ituri forest for very long. When Patrick married his third wife, Anne Eisner, in the summer of 1948, he still owed his second wife yearly divorce and settlement payments that almost entirely ate up his trust fund. For some time, Patrick's father, Charles, had given him all the funds he desired, but when Charles remarried, his new wife curtailed the payments. Subsequently, Patrick received only $2,000 per year and was therefore compelled to look for more income from the hotel. With Anne's help, the hotel became a favorite attraction for European visitors. Unlike the rain forest of today, which is hard to reach even from within the Democratic Republic of the Congo, at that time visitors had easy access along heavily trafficked tarmac roads up to forty feet wide. Today, the main roads leading to Epulu are narrow dirt roads so muddy that often only motorcycles can get through.

Anne Eisner Putnam was a talented painter who had largely abandoned her promising career for Patrick. Born in 1911 into a secular Jewish family, Anne was raised in New York and trained as a painter during the American realist revival. She was politically active on the left, but in politics, as in art, Anne believed there were strict limits to what a woman could hope to achieve. When she met Patrick during one of his rare trips to Boston and decided to follow him to the Ituri without any promise of marriage, she intended to spend her time painting. As it turned out, she needed to paint to stay mentally healthy, for she paid a high cost for life in the Ituri, for *married* life in the Ituri. Only after arriving in the Ituri in 1946 did she become aware that Patrick had African wives. But knowing this, she still decided to marry him in 1948. She seldom spoke or wrote about the other wives. Despite the fact that her whole life was unconventional, she believed in the traditional ideals of commitment in marriage.

Their mud house, affectionately called Le Palais, was large by local standards but, like other dwellings in the rain forest, had no plumbing, telephone, or electricity. The roof was thatched like all of the farmers' huts, but there were shutters for windows. What it lacked in some amenities, it made up for in service. As many as forty men from several different ethnic groups worked at the camp, taking care of the hotel management, food, firewood, water, and landscaping. Workers lived with their wives and children a few minutes walk from the camp. Several Pygmy families lived next to the camp and provided Putnam with meat, honey, and any other food they could gather, such as wild tubers, mushrooms, and edible termites. Putnam was committed to them because they made his hotel famous and desirable. Even more important than the foods they supplied, up to seventy-five Pygmies provided evening entertainment for hotel guests in return for salt or cigarettes. Putnam's biographer writes that the Pygmies also became experienced at acting in movies for the directors who stayed at the hotel and who brought film equipment with them. Guests would also be treated to the sight of a captured okapi, a beautiful animal found only in central Africa (much like its cousin the giraffe, but smaller, with a shorter neck and with white stripes on its hind legs).

The hotel workers also managed a medical clinic and dispensary, a much needed institution in the rain forest, for the other clinics in the area had agendas other than providing health care. Mission hospitals tried to convert the sick and government hospitals tried to tax the sick or recruit them for work in mines or plantations. Patrick also offered an incentive for people to seek medical care: he promised every sick person a cigarette. Putnam's biographer, Joan Mark, says that he was not trying to be Albert Schweitzer. "Africa was not a purgatory but a virtual paradise. His Africa was not the low, hot coastlands where [Schweitzer] was located but the astonishingly beautiful world of the Ituri forest, where the local people, when they were not harassed by outsiders, lived relaxed and even indolent lives. It was the one place on earth where [Patrick] wanted to live."

Like Colin, Patrick was tall and thin, with hands even larger than Colin's. He had a long beard that hid his emotions, and which made him at times resemble Abraham Lincoln. He spoke English like the Boston Brahmin he was, but seemed to prefer Swahili, which he spoke abruptly and imperiously. Colin found Patrick charismatic and engaging. The Pygmies and villagers alike seemed to love Patrick, obey him, and do whatever they could to make him comfortable. Colin must have envied Patrick's high status, as he appeared to hold it without any negative sense of superiority. At least from what Colin could see, Patrick respected and cared for the Pygmies, and the villagers and Pygmies throughout the forest seemed to respect Patrick in turn. Patrice Lumumba, the first prime minister of the newly independent Congo, whom Colin befriended in the early 1950s, later told Colin that he considered Patrick to be an African, since this was the only way that Lumumba could explain Patrick's affection for Africans. Colin later heard that Lumumba considered him an African as well and that if he had been in the Ituri during the violent Simba rebellion of the early sixties, he might have been spared execution. But this air of respect would not last long. By 1953, Patrick would be so disabled by mental illness that he could no longer maintain any affectionate relationships; he would become obsessed with power and control, as if he were playing out a scene from Joseph Conrad's *The Heart of Darkness* or the film *Apocalypse Now.*

Colin enjoyed his stay immensely. He idolized Patrick and he initially saw Anne as a warm maternal figure, as she was helping to raise three Mbuti children who had recently been orphaned or abandoned. Only later would he begin to see in Anne aspects of his own mother. He quickly became proficient in Swahili—the lingua franca and trade language of east Africa, a language that is generally very easy to learn and even easier to learn in the Ituri forest where it is spoken quite crudely and with a good deal of French mixed in—and seriously considered the idea of becoming an expert on the Pygmies. He decided that on his return to England he would find a way to come back, perhaps as a scholar, but also perhaps as a film maker or journalist.

There were, of course, occasional annoyances, such as army ants that attacked the village, but all anyone needed to do was to vacate the village, let the ants clean up, and return a few hours later when the ants were gone. There were also the "funzas," chiggers that lodged in one's feet, laying their eggs and creating a terrible itch; but the local residents were experts at taking out the funzas without breaking the egg sacs. So Colin only had to worry about malaria and filaria, both of which he inevitably contracted. Malaria can be life threatening, of course, but most types of malaria are easy enough to treat provided treatment is accessible. Filaria on the other hand, a generic term for the many parasitic worms introduced through insect bites, can cause river blindness and elephantiasis, and so Colin had good reason to fear the possibility that his limbs or scrotum might swell to an enormous size. Most anthropologists who have worked for extended periods of time in the Ituri have had some form of filaria, suffering swollen joints and severe itching, and sometimes seeing the worms swim right across their eyes. There are drugs to treat filaria, but the treatment is dangerous, especially for Europeans who seem to react much more severely to both the illness and cure than the Africans who have been exposed to filaria all their lives.

What thrilled him the most about the Pygmies during his two months at Camp Putnam was their unique vocal music. Colin told Putnam's biographer,

"The first night out my mind was blown by what I heard! The comparison that came to my mind was some of the really great organ music that you hear in some of the better cathedrals in England." The only European who had spent any length of time with the Pygmies, a missionary named Paul Schebesta, thought the Pygmies had, at best, a simple grasp of melody. Yet Colin found that their music was not only complex but unusually produced. In Pygmy vocal music, there may be several singers each of whom sings only one note of a repetitive melody line. In medieval music this was called hocketing. Hocketing sounds spasmodic because each voice part so abruptly stops as another takes over. The singers may then switch to singing two notes apiece, thus making it difficult to determine the start and finish of the melody.

Turnbull was equally impressed by the Pygmies' resistance to the neighboring farmers and to outside modernizing forces. Having entered the forest, he believed, the farmers tried unsuccessfully to dominate the Pygmies and were forced to compromise by establishing a symbiotic relationship of mutual convenience. Colin saw the Pygmies resisting other attempts at domination too. Despite efforts by missionaries and government authorities to integrate the Pygmies into plantation work, industry, and the churches, the Pygmies seemed to have remained independent. Indeed, they seemed to live a life of relative leisure, acquiring only as much as they needed to survive.

This first visit to Epulu was the beginning of a long relationship with the Pygmies, and a longstanding commitment to the notion that Pygmy culture was the ideal opposite of western civilization. He was determined to earn enough money not only for a second trip but one for which he would be equipped with high quality tape recorders and movie cameras. There was a sense of urgency to his plan because the Mbuti appeared to be one of the few societies still in existence that lived exclusively as nomadic hunters and gatherers. Colin wanted to record their way of life before it disappeared, but first he had to get out of Africa.

Filthy and unshaven, Colin and Newton headed north into miserable desert heat, but they could not hope to travel through the Sudanese desert on their bike. Even if they could brave the heat of the day, the cold of the nights, and the sandstorms, they would never have enough fuel. They managed to secure a first class passage on a barge along the Nile for themselves and Ruddi Muddi. Afterward, Colin, Newton, and their bike traveled by train from Khartoum into Egypt. The ride was uncomfortable because the only space available was a wooden bench in third class. They traveled north for more than six hours at slow speeds, but after all that time the train returned to Khartoum because a dam had broken along the route and, without water, the steam engine could not run. After twelve hours on the train, they were exhausted. Back in Khartoum, someone told them they could rent a boat to take them further north. They shipped Ruddi Muddi ahead to Aswan and boarded a boat, a small dhow, on which they lived for six days, eating tinned cheese and fruit and dipping the emptied tins into the Nile for drinking water.

Near Aswan, they began riding the bike again in an attempt to get to Luxor, a hundred miles northeast. They found a beautiful tarmac road that looked too good not to take. But that wrong turn took them much further east until they found themselves at the Red Sea. As the sun set, Colin and Newton ran out of gas. They started to walk in search of petrol, but when they reached the nearest town, they were promptly detained because they had no passes for travel. The authorities, to their great surprise, found Colin's trunk bearing the name of the person everyone in the western intelligence community was looking for, the Soviet spy Donald Maclean.

It was now the end of May 1951, the same month Donald Maclean, the son of Jock's old friend, Donald Maclean, Sr., and Guy Burgess fled England in response to warnings from Moscow that British intelligence was closing in on them. Both men were from privileged backgrounds: Maclean had attended Gresham's and Cambridge; Burgess, Eton and Cambridge. Maclean went on to work in the foreign office; Burgess became a journalist for the BBC. Both hated capitalism, were devoted students of Marxism, and had faith in communism. And here, near Aswan, were two men who not only looked like Burgess and Maclean—they were white and by all appearances they were fugitives—but had a personalized trunk to prove it. Colin and Newton were arrested and placed in a pit in the ground while the Egyptian authorities contacted British intelligence. It was two weeks before they were released.

This was not a story Colin told many people—few outside of his family knew about it—but perhaps this was not so odd since, as we shall see, Colin made sure that the anthropological community knew nothing about Newton. Colin wanted to give the impression that he had been alone in Africa, broke, isolated, without western influences, as integrated as possible into Pygmy culture. Newton returned to the United States and does not appear again in Colin's life until 1957, when they would travel together again to Epulu. But much happened before that trip.

By the time Patrick Putnam became interested in the Pygmies, they were already famous in European travel writing about Africa. Yet only two scholars—neither of whom had much training in anthropology—had ever studied them: Father Paul Schebesta (an Austrian scholar and missionary from the William Schmidt School of Austrian White Fathers, sent by the Vatican to find a religion supposedly revealed to primitives) and his linguist-colleague Anton Vorbichler. Though he lived with the Pygmies for twenty-five years, Putnam penned only one small article about them, and even that was a struggle to finish. When Colin decided to work with the Pygmies, there was a huge public thirst for information and he had virtually no scholarly competitors in any discipline. Indeed, when Anne returned to her home in New York in 1954, she found an eager audience, and quickly published a commercially successful autobiographical account of her years with the Pygmies entitled *Madami.*

Pygmies offered a special excitement to readers, many of whom imagined them to be living fossils, a people who had somehow remained pure and unchanged after the fall of the rest of the world into civilization. That notion of purity is a thread that runs through Turnbull's work as well. He would make their purity seem more real than ever before. But while Anne would always be viewed as an amateur, and a female amateur no less, Colin would have the authority of being male, a curator, a trained anthropologist, and a scholar. His name would be forever associated within and outside of academia with the Pygmies.

The earliest reference to the Pygmies, or at least to a people who seem to have looked like contemporary Pygmies, dates to the sixth dynasty in Egypt (2200 B.C.), when King Nferkare Pepy II's commander, Harkhuf, went on a trading expedition that turned into a pacification effort between Libyan tribes and the people of Yam. Among the goods Harkhuf brought back for the king was, it seems, a Pygmy man, to dance for rituals honoring the gods. Harkhuf's tomb inscription quotes the young Pepy II's letter asking him to take special care of this musical gift. The name of the Pygmy mentioned in the tomb can be read as "Aka." Aka is the name of a group of Pygmies living today in the northwest Congo basin.

In *The Iliad,* Homer described the Pygmies standing battle with Cranes; Aristotle wrote in his *Historia Animalium* that there were Pygmies who lived in the land "from which flows the Nile" and that they were real beings, not mythological creatures. The thirteenth-century cartographer of the Mappa Mundi, lodged at Hereford Cathedral in England, depicted the Pygmies as cave-dwelling monsters who resembled humans only slightly. When Colin died, he still possessed a 1956 letter from D. D. di Thiene, the Italian consulate general in London, stating that a Professor Maiuri had written about Pygmy images in Pompeian mosaics. The earliest literary references are from the end of the fourteenth century and derive from Homer: "Pigmea is a countree in Ynde toward the eest in mountaynes afore the occean. Therein dwelled the Pygmeis: men lytyll of body: vneth two cubytes longe, they gendre in the fourth yere and aege in the seventh. Thyse . . . fyghte wyth cranes and destroyen theyr nests, and breke theyr eggs, that theyr enmyes be not multyplyed."

In the seventeenth century, the British physician Edward Tyson placed the Pygmies squarely in the animal world by presenting a skeleton of a chimpanzee as that of a Pygmy man. Chimpanzees were not named until 1816, so Tyson firmly believed his specimen was an ancient dwarf, not quite monkey, not quite human. Tyson entitled his work *The Anatomy of a Pygmy Compared with that of a Monkey, an Ape, and a Man, with an Essay concerning the Pygmies of the Ancients. Wherein it will appear that they are all either Apes or Monkies, and not Men, as formerly pretended, to which is added the Anatomy and Description of a Rattlesnake: also of the Musk-hog. With a Discourse upon the Jointed and Round-worm* (1699). As evolutionary thought took hold in the late nineteenth century, Pygmies were increasingly seen as missing links or at least evidence of what humankind might have looked like during the Stone Age. When Henry Morton Stanley first saw a Pygmy man and his wife in the Ituri forest toward the end of the nineteenth century, he idealized them as the most ancient of human ancestors: "The pair were undoubtedly man and woman. In him was a mimicked dignity, as of Adam; in her the womanliness of a miniature Eve."

Stanley's work was part of a general pattern of idealizing the Pygmies that changed the lives of many of them. In 1956, Colin corresponded with an Italian count from Verona, Mario Miniscalchi Erizzo, the grandson of Count Francesco. His more informal title was Senator of the Realm. He told Colin that on April 26, 1874, Count Francesco, an active member of the Italian Geographical Society, accepted two Pygmy children, aged twelve and fourteen, from the Royal Geographical Society. They had been transported by the Italian explorer Miani. The two moved into his villa at Cola, near Peschiera, and began instruction for some years in Italian language and basic academics. Count Miniscalchi sent Colin some newspaper articles from the time that described the Pygmy boys strolling arm in arm with Italian friends, conversing easily in Italian. The first, a boy named Tibo, died in 1883 at the age of twenty-one; the second, Cheirallah, had a long life. Cheirallah wrote to the count's family as late as 1940 saying that he was employed as a saddler for Eritrean troops.

Many other Pygmies were taken to Europe for public display. At times, museologists and other academics in England and the United States seemed nearly obsessed with creating a sense of the exotic and displaying it in freak shows where the demonstration of white dominance and racism masqueraded as science. For the producers of these shows, the displays were tools for personal and financial gain.

In London on June 10, 1905, Hippodrome opened an exhibition that would draw more than a million viewers: a group of six Pygmies, four men and two women, from central Africa. "The curtain rose upon a scene which represented a tropical forest," wrote a reporter for the British newspaper *The Era,* "in the midst of which is an opening, containing four wigwams of small dimensions. Outside were the group of little people who will for some time be objects of curiosity to amusement-seeking Londoners . . . the scene represented a fairly exact picture of the pigmies homes in the Ituri forest of Central Africa."

On the other side of the Atlantic, another showman, Dr. Samuel P. Verner, brought a Pygmy man named Ota Benga from Kasai, Congo Free State, in 1904 to display at the World's Fair in St. Louis. After the grueling exhibition, which extended for some months, Verner told Benga that there was a janitorial job for him at the Bronx Zoo in New York City. When Benga arrived, he found that he was to be displayed in the monkey house, in a cage next to the other primates. Benga never made it back home. Not long after he arrived in New York, he relocated to Lynchurg, Virginia, where he hanged himself.

By the time Colin first entered the Ituri forest in 1951, there were only a handful of scholars who had paid any attention to the Pygmies as a contemporary society. And by the end of the millennium, that number would not increase dramatically. The vast majority of scholars interested in the Pygmies were decidedly not interested in the contemporary society, culture, and language of any group. Rather, they viewed the Pygmies through the lenses of evolutionary biology: if 99 percent of human existence was spent hunting and gathering (agriculture is only 10,000 years old), hunter-gatherers, they argued, or in most cases assumed, provide us with a window, albeit an imperfect one, into our past. Similarly, some scholars in art history and music have looked to the Pygmies as a fountainhead of human culture, seeing their bark cloth designs and music as a primordial human art form untainted by the complexity and materialism of civilization.

There was a wider audience for the Pygmies also: people who read *National Geographic* and other popular magazines. Martin and Asa Johnson, two independently wealthy film makers from Kansas who loved to travel, made a popular movie, *Congorilla,* depicting the Pygmies as childlike creatures who will do anything for cigarettes and who, in adulthood, have the mental capacities of typical American third-graders. One scene shows Martin Johnson holding out a cigarette and beckoning an elderly Pygmy man in English— "Come on, little fella."

The idealization of the unspoiled primitive had begun in earnest by the 1960s and the Pygmies idealized in Colin's work would also capture many American hearts. *The Forest People* would become a best-seller and Colin Turnbull would for years be featured on television's the *Today Show,* the *Dick Cavett Show,* and *Merv Griffin.* The anthropologist Jean-Paul Dumont once suggested, in a seminar at Harvard University, that the American fascination with the Pygmies might have been due to the Vietnam War. While American men and women were dying violently in the jungles of southeast Asia, Americans longed to hear about a peaceful forest-dwelling people.

The same could be said about the "stone-age" Tasaday of the Philippines whom the biographer A. Scott Berg, in a 1999 Pulitzer-prize-winning study, mistakenly claims aviator Charles Lindbergh helped to "discover." The Tasaday, clearly unbeknownst to Berg, are a famous hoax, a contemporary version of Piltdown man. But the fact that people, even today, persist in believing that the Tasaday existed and were "discovered" in isolation from the rest of the world, says something important: there is a longstanding desire in the West to draw a distinction between the primitive and the modern.

Africans also viewed the Pygmies as primordial. The Pygmies have long been called *premier citoyens* (first citizens) in the Democratic Republic of the Congo, a title that not only assumes their primordial existence in the forest but also accords them the privilege of not paying taxes. If the Pygmies are the original inhabitants of the rain forest, then the various farmers that live in the rain forest must be seen as recent arrivals, and indeed most evidence suggests that the farmers have been in the Ituri less than a thousand years. Turnbull never questioned this assumption. Still, there are virtually no data to suggest that the Pygmies who now occupy the Ituri forest have ever lived in the rain forest apart from the farmers. They are indeed an age-old population—geneticists believe it would have taken up to twenty thousand years for the Pygmies to develop their distinctive physical features—but no one knows exactly how ancient.

Many scientists have argued that the rain forests simply do not contain enough food for humans to survive without agricultural supplements, and thus the Pygmies could not have ever lived in the rain forest without farmers. But archaeologists are now beginning to find data that contradict these arguments. New evidence suggests that humans occupied Old World rain forests more than 50,000 years ago, at least 40,000 years before the advent of agriculture. Still, even though humans may have lived in the rain forest at that time, there is no way of knowing whether these inhabitants were related in any way to contemporary Pygmies.

The problem for any anthropologist, therefore, is how to think about the relationship between the farmer and hunter-gatherer. And this is the central problem that Colin and those who preceded him tried to resolve. Are farmer communities and the Pygmy communities that live alongside them separate societies, or ethnic groups in a single multiethnic community? Do the farmers dominate the Pygmies or do the Pygmies dominate the farmers?

There are perhaps 200,000 people living in the Ituri forest who are commonly referred to in the scientific literature as Pygmies. They are almost exclusively hunter-gatherers, though a few may raise one or two crops on small plots. They are all shorter in height than their farmer neighbors. Some Pygmy men may reach a height of five feet, but the vast majority of men and women do not exceed four feet ten inches. Their various farmer neighbors are slightly taller, usually reaching over five feet, but then every living thing in the rain forest is smaller. In a desert, sweat cools the body and immediately evaporates whereas in the rain forest the sweat remains. In a high humidity environment, therefore, organisms have to cool their bodies by radiating heat through the surface area of the body rather than by sweating. The Pygmies radiate heat efficiently because they are so small; smaller bodies will always have more surface area per volume than larger ones because, in mathematical language, volume cubes as mass squares.

All of the central African Pygmy groups have distinguishing features, some of which are more noticeable to their farmer neighbors than height. One farmer group called the Lese says that the Pygmies have much less fat, have redder skin, fuller eyebrows, and much more body hair, especially the women. In fact, the one physical attribute that the Lese say is the most distinctive is *torumbaka,* literally "hair from the crotch," a term used specifically for hair around the navel or between the breasts; Lese men say that it is unique to the Pygmies and that it is the most sexually attractive part of a woman's body.

Pygmy camps vary considerably in size, depending on how well families are getting along at any moment and on the kind of hunting they are doing. Net hunters live in larger camps than archers because they need more people to man the nets. Generally speaking, the camps contain only a few families living in hemispherical huts with frames made of saplings and covered with leaves. Pygmies also build additional settlements in caves, going so far as to build huts within caves when a large group of ten or more people plans to stay for a month or more.

The villages of the farmers who live adjacent to the Pygmies are usually only a bit larger but they are visually very different. The villagers cut down the forest whereas the Pygmies leave it standing. The villagers generally believe that the forest is where evil spirits dwell. And, whereas the borders of the Pygmy camps and the huts themselves are circular in form, the villages contain rectangular houses placed symmetrically in relation to other houses. By all appearances, the village and the forest are diametric opposites.

Throughout the Ituri forest, villagers depict the Pygmies as having unrestrained and uncontrollable desires, mainly for alcohol, marijuana, sex, and violence. They are said to act without planning or meditation, to have no ability to husband their resources (including the money they earn by working at plantations), to speak logically or coherently. Pygmy men are said to require sexual intercourse at least once a day. In contrast, the villagers depict themselves as able to mediate between their drives and the exigencies of a proper and ordered social life; they represent rationality whereas the Pygmies stand for untamed passions. The Pygmies themselves will generally agree with these characterizations with great laughter and poke fun at the villagers who claim to represent them.

Despite the fact that they are most well known as "Pygmies," they call themselves by very different names. The word Pygmy is of Greek origin (from *pygmaiôs*), meaning a measure of length from the elbow to the knuckles), but in addition to being a foreign word, the term has a pejorative connotation. After all, it has been used primarily by people attempting to subordinate them. In Swahili, the Pygmies of the Ituri forest are collectively called either BaMbuti or WaMbuti.

There are four groups of BaMbuti. They call themselves the Mbuti, the Efe, the Sua, and the Aka. Each of these groups lives in association with non-Pygmy groups of farmers and speaks a dialect of the farmer language. When, for example, an Mbuti and an Efe meet, they have to communicate in Swahili or another trade language, Lingala. There does not appear to be a Pygmy language, though remarkably each of the BaMbuti societies speaks their farmer neighbors' languages with similar alterations. For example, although the Sua and Efe languages are radically different, they both drop the sound "k" in favor of a guttural sound; "aka" as spoken by the farmers would then become "a'a" in Sua or Efe, or "impaka" would become "impa'a." Paul Schebesta believed that this similarity of alteration suggested there was once an original Pygmy language, and Patrick Putnam, who had long believed there was never a single Pygmy language, eventually found Schebesta's arguments convincing.

In addition to their striking physical similarities, there are also many cultural similarities between the different groups of BaMbuti. All maintain hereditary exchange partnerships with their farmer neighbors. Ideally, a farmer man will inherit (as one inherits wealth or property) the son of his father's Pygmy trading partner as his own. Nearly everyone has a partner, and often it is said that a "true man" must have a partner. If you ask the partners to describe their relationship they will almost always say that it is economic in nature, that the farmers give vegetables and iron to the BaMbuti, who never farm, and the BaMbuti give meat and honey and other forest goods to the farmers, who seldom hunt or forage.

Farmers sometimes marry Pygmy women, and the children of these marriages are considered by both groups to be members of the farmer group. Pygmy men, however, cannot marry farmer women nor even engage in sexual intercourse with them. Although it undoubtedly happens, any knowledge of it is presumably quickly suppressed, for it is as taboo as incest. (This one-way intermarriage means that, over time, the farmer groups have been getting shorter). The Pygmies provide music and dancing at farmer rituals, serve as chief mourners at farmer funerals, and protect the farmers from their own evil spirits, which the Pygmies generally believe do not exist.

The intensity and intimacy of Pygmy-farmer relationships make it very difficult to talk about the Pygmy groups as Colin Turnbull would, as societies wholly distinct from their farmer neighbors. Patrick Putnam did not believe that the Pygmies had ever lived alone in the rain forest; indeed, he thought that they were incapable of it because they needed the farmer's vegetables, iron arrows, and hunting nets to survive. In the only article Putnam ever published, he wrote that the Pygmies were "a genetically and occupationally segregated segment of a larger economic entity." He initially described the Pygmy-farmer relationships as "symbiotic." Later, he abandoned the use of this term because he felt the farmers actually benefited very little from the relationship.

On the subject of Pygmy-farmer relationships, Putnam and Schebesta, who corresponded often but met only once, had several disagreements. Whereas Putnam believed the Pygmies profited from the exchange partnerships, Schebesta thought the Pygmies were oppressed. And whereas Putnam viewed each Pygmy group and the farmers with whom they lived as distinct, multiethnic groups, Schebesta believed in the existence of the Pygmies as a single cultural unit. Schebesta eventually wrote to Turnbull, "All the Ituri-Bambuti constitute a homogene unity, coloured in different ways by the contact of different negro tribes and languages." Schebesta even argued that there were Pygmies who were unattached to farmers, a point on which, Anne Putnam reported, "Pat disagreed violently with." Finally, whereas Putnam did not believe that the Pygmies had an active spiritual life or cosmology, Schebesta maintained that the Pygmies had concepts of the soul and of a single god. Turnbull would also disagree with Schebesta, arguing against both the notion of a larger Pygmy homogeneity and the notion that the Pygmies worshipped a single god. Turnbull attributed Schebesta's idea about a single god not to any direct evidence but to Schebesta's directive from the Vatican to find a revealed monotheistic religion among "primitives." Turnbull would find little agreement with either of these men on the subject of the Pygmies, though he did find, with Putnam, that the Pygmies profited greatly from the farmers. Turnbull was convinced that the Pygmies only appeared to be oppressed. In fact, he argued, they were play-acting oppression in order to exploit the farmers.

Here was the essence of the intellectual challenge that Turnbull confronted in the 1950s, one which would launch his career as an anthropologist. He would live with the Pygmies in 1951, 1954, and 1957 in an attempt to solve what was fundamentally a problem of domination and resistance, a problem that resonated with much that had come before in his life. If anyone could locate real oppression, Colin believed, it would be him. His two years in India, he believed, had prepared him to discern the most subtle and elusive truths. And if the Pygmies did have a spiritual life, he would be able to find that too.

CHAPTER SEVEN

Magical Sounds

AFTER HE RETURNED TO ENGLAND in October 1951, at the age of twenty-three, Colin moved in with his parents outside of London. He quickly wrote a 120-page book outline called "Pigmies of the Congo," sending it to Patrick and Anne Putnam by January of 1952. (Colin spelled "Pygmies" with a "y" only after 1957). The outline contained the essence of *The Forest People,* the romantic love affair with the rain forest and its people. It had the same fluid prose, the same idealized vision of Pygmy life juxtaposed with a depiction of the hardships of village life as did the finished, polished *The Forest People.*

At the same time, he accepted a position as general secretary of Racial Unity, a new organization founded by Mary Attlee (the sister of Clement Attlee, Prime Minister of England from 1945 to 1951), to collect and distribute information on colonial and racial problems. He told a Canadian newspaper, "[Racial Unity] has the support of Churchill, Attlee and Clement Davies. I'm thinking of settling in Canada, but first I plan to return to Africa in a few months to make a series of documentaries on the central and eastern regions, and to say hello again to my friends, the pygmies."

There is no evidence that Colin actually did anything for the organization and the precise reasons for the failure of the Racial Unity group are unknown.

Newspaper articles from the early 1950s mention only that the group held small conferences about racial tensions, including one with two expert speakers on colonial affairs: Dingle Foot, High Commissioner for India, and Colin Turnbull, a student who, the *Daily Telegraph* noted, had been arrested both as a Jewish spy and as Donald Maclean. In a letter sent to Colin in the Ituri forest, his friend Peggy Appiah told him about the organization's decline. "Did you see Racial Unity was closing down," she wrote, "and the remains amalgamating with Movement for Colonial Freedom (Breakaway!)? I think I shall probably withdraw support though I have not gone into it fully yet." Peggy and Colin had become close friends at Oxford. Her father was Sir Stafford Cripps, a member of the British cabinet and an important influence on British policy in India, about whom Winston Churchill made one of his most quoted comments: "He has all of the virtues I dislike and none of the vices I admire." Peggy had married Joe Appiah, a successful Ghanaian politician (and brother-in-law of the Ashanti king) and lived in Kumasi, Ghana. Her son, Kwame Anthony Appiah, became an illustrious professor of African and African American studies at Harvard; he believes that without Colin's friendship and influence, his mother might never have agreed to marry his father.

In England, Colin reunited with his old friend, Paul Mayor, who reintroduced him to his sister Kumari, a striking Punjabi woman who was enrolled at a nearby women's college. According to Colin, she had once won a beauty contest. Colin began to invite Kumari to coffees and meals, and they quickly became attached. He had, in the course of his travels, realized how attracted he was to non-westerners, people who were oppressed or marginalized from the mainstream, people he believed were free of the constraints and pretensions of British elitism. Colin fell deeply in love with Kumari, not only because she was an Indian woman with beautiful long black hair that reminded him of his guru, Anandamayi Ma, but because, like Colin, she also felt out of place. She was Indian but had been raised almost entirely in England; she felt more at ease socially among her British friends, but soon realized that, despite her involvement with Colin in England, her destiny was to live in India.

As the relationship became more public, however, some difficulties arose. Colin invited Kumari to the Flower Ball, an important gala attended by the young princesses, Elizabeth and Margaret. Kumari was thrilled. Colin recalled, "The Ball Committee was horrified to find that my partner was 'a dark lady.' I was even reprimanded, right then and there, and was only not ejected with my 'dark' companion because of the commotion it would have caused." More disturbing, however, was an event later that year in the south country hunting territory. At a debutante ball for the Duke of Norfolk's daughter, held at Arundel

Castle, a servant referred to Kumari as "that black woman," and she and Colin were escorted to an isolated table.

Colin and Kumari withstood the stares, the discrimination, and the whispers about their relationship. They even thought they could endure Colin's mother's anger that he was with an Indian woman.

In the early summer of 1953 Colin left England to visit his mother's aunt, "Kitty" Gravely, and her children in Toronto. He promised Kumari he would stay in Canada for about three months, but he ended up staying nearly a year.

Most of his other aunts, uncles, and cousins on his mother's side were also in Toronto. Colin's brother Ian had met his cousins only once, when Dorothy and Ian traveled to Canada in 1937 for her mother's funeral, but Colin had never met them. He had never been to Canada and they had never been to England. Colin liked his Canadian family instantly, especially Kitty's son Pat and another cousin, Francis Chapman. Francis was working on the stage crew at the Canadian Broadcasting Company (CBC), which had just been established, and he put Colin in contact with the right people at the CBC. During the winter of 1953-1954, Colin appeared on *Our Special Speaker* to talk about the Mau Mau situation in Kenya. In a long commentary on his own feelings of helplessness in Africa, he compared black Kenyans to black South Africans and to Jews in Nazi Germany. There was, he said, "a stone wall between the races." He would also talk about his voyage to the Himalayas and the flight of the Dalai Lama from Lhasa.

Colin and his cousin Pat Gravely decided to spend that summer at Giant Mine in Yellowknife in the Northwest Territories. Colin planned to go to Africa again as soon as possible and needed money to finance the return trip to the rain forest. He had convinced the mine to hire him to make a film about both the gold mine in Canada and its foreign operation in central Africa. Both Colin and Pat found Yellowknife exhilarating because it was frontier territory with no road access and a local community reminiscent of the Yukon gold rush of the late 1800s. Colin and his much younger cousin lived in dormitories with the other men, mostly professional miners, some of whom, Colin and Pat suspected, were on the run. One of the diggers charmed everyone by producing a boiled egg everyday for lunch from his bottom while cackling like a chicken. He kept a gun in his room and confided to Pat and Colin that, as soon as he earned enough money at Yellowknife, he was heading south to shoot his wife who had taken a lover. "Colin loved it there," Pat recalled. Yellowknife was lush with grit and hope, and the social life—unconstrained, hedonistic, and masculine in the extreme—contrasted sharply with the precision and order of Great Britain at tea time. "The thing about Colin," Pat recalled, "is that he could talk to anyone."

Pat had a harder time with miners—not knowing exactly what to expect, he had brought his tennis racket with him—but, as Pat said, "Colin just blended in and became one of them. It amazed me."

At the mine, Colin worked as an underground sampler while he worked on the film, and Pat worked on the surface bull gang and in the assay department. During their free time, Pat and Colin made expeditions to the encampments of the Dogrib Indians, at that time still living in teepees, and traveled by canoe where it was possible. They had long talks about race relations in South Africa and Rhodesia. Pat remembered: "We both agreed that South Africa was awful and dreadfully repressive, but I thought Rhodesia had set up a more acceptable way of integrating blacks and whites. He disagreed vehemently. He said Rhodesia was worse than South Africa because it was all pretence there, trying to look as if they were being fair and understanding. Many years later, I agreed with Colin that this was just the way to try and hold back the tide. He thought the Rhodesians were ten times slimier than the South Africans."

While at Yellowknife, Colin received a letter from Robin ("Robinetta") Roberts, a woman he had dated regularly in England who was desperately in love with him. Her parents were wealthy and promised Colin a handsome dowry, including land and about 5,000 pounds a year allowance. Late in his life, he recalled the story in a letter to a friend.

> She was wealthy. Moderately acceptable in looks, always trying to make herself look pretty and always impeccably dressed, even when gardening. Tolerably musical . . . Her papa was Master of the Hounds, but she put up with my non-hunting principles nobly, so long as I attended the meet, on foot, and drank the stirrup cups with all the others . . . Her parents offered me a huge farm in Devon . . . That actually was the final straw. Up to that point I had given the idea serious contemplation. So serious she wrote me when I was in Canada asking in what papers did I want her to put the announcement of our engagement. Pat Gravely was with me in Yellowknife at the time, so I got him, a law student, to draft a cagey legal reply to get me off the hook without danger of any breach of promise suit. He should remember that. It worked and I fled to Kumari, of whom I was really fond . . . Robinetta I merely liked, sort of, in small doses. I doubt if you want to know more. It just gets yuckier and yuckier. Particularly when she objected to some of my Indian friends, saying she did not mind meeting them so long as she didn't have to shake hands or actually touch them. "Sorry, that's just the way I am." She felt the same way about spiders. I felt the same way about her . . . The spiders didn't like either of us.

Colin's cousin does remember writing a letter for Colin, but says it wasn't legalistic. Pat simply wrote a letter to Robin saying that he, "Colin," did not love her. But Pat certainly found Colin's difficulties amusing. Here was a budding anthropologist who could live anywhere in the world and write just about anything, but he couldn't figure out how to break up. This was a personal limitation Turnbull confronted many times during his life, one that would lead some of his friends to refer to him privately as a "man-child."

In subsequent years, in England, Colin would sometimes show up at staid garden parties in his Yellowknife sweatshirt, on which was written the Yellowknife motto: "Where the ice worms nest again." His experience at the gold mines was, in its own way, profound; it convinced him of the beauty of manual labor, and his respect for the miners motivated him to work hard with his hands. He would become an indefatigable worker in this cousins' gardens and, in later years, in his own garden and that of the Buddhist centers in which he lived. That respect for work echoed a fellow Magdalen graduate's fascination with the Colorado silver miners on *his* first trip to North America: "The most graceful thing I ever beheld," Oscar Wilde once wrote, "was a miner in a Colorado silver mine driving a new shaft with a hammer; at any moment he might have been transformed into marble or bronze and become noble in art forever." One can only speculate whether Colin, like Oscar Wilde, both of Irish heritage, identified with the miners as outsiders; in Canada with his mother's family, Colin felt distinctly Irish, and in the United Kingdom born and bred Englishmen likened the Irish, at best, to uninvited guests and, at worst, to blacks.

After the summer at Yellowknife, Colin stayed on with Pat in Toronto, working odd jobs with the CBC. Pat and his other cousins grew to love Colin, the favorite cousin who seemed to have fallen into their laps by chance. He was interesting, free, and colorful. When he talked to his cousins, they were absorbed not only by the stories he could tell, but by his gaze, so focused and engaging that when he talked to them it seemed there was no one else that mattered. It was this ability to so intensely connect with his conversation partners that made them feel flattered and favored at no one's expense. Pat probably speaks for most of his relatives when he says that he regretted knowing Colin for only eight years before Colin became involved with Joseph Towles. They would never again have the opportunity to be with Colin alone.

Although Colin recalled fleeing back to Kumari after his year in Canada, when he did return to England in the spring of 1954, he spent virtually no time with her before leaving for Africa. Kumari was very disappointed but resolved to wait for him. Colin's cousin, Christopher (Kit) Chapman, a budding filmmaker, declined Colin's invitation to come to Africa for the five-month-long stay, but his twin brother Francis, who knew almost nothing about film, accepted gladly. Colin insisted that instead of sailing to Africa, they sail to England first and then drive; he thought he could get some money from a motor magazine if he agreed to publish a diary of an overland trip. They would also make sound and film recordings for the CBC. As it turned out, although Colin and Francis each had a Bolex camera, Colin would sell his camera to a British priest living in North Africa, and leave all the filming to Francis.

Together, they would drive a cream and dark blue Kenex-converted Bedford light van from England, across the Sahara, first to Ghana, to do a CBC interview with Kwame Nkrumah, who would become the first president of Ghana, and then to the Ituri forest. The van was fitted with a roof vent and heater to help them adjust to large fluctuations in temperature, a roof rack, reinforced rear springs, and heavy-duty tires. They brought 3,000 feet of film, two tape recorders and 25,000 feet of tape, five jerry cans for fuel, heavy duty batteries and chargers, camping and cooking gear, and equipment for digging the car out of snow, sand, or mud. They also ended up transporting an overweight American journalist named Joachim (Joe) Joesten from Paris to Marrakesh, a favor that put the already overweight Bedford at some risk and damaged the shock absorber directly underneath him. Joesten, who would eventually become an expert on the assassinations of Robert and John F. Kennedy, had just published a book on the Mafia figure Lucky Luciano and, fearing reprisals, anxiously wanted to get lost in North Africa for a while.

When Francis and Colin finally reached the Ituri forest in May 1954, they were given a warm reception by the Pygmies. This should have pleased Colin, but they were met by Anne Putnam who reported that Patrick had recently died of emphysema. She was just forty-three years old and suddenly quite alone. Colin was devastated. He had begun to idolize Patrick during his 1951 trip and felt that, without him, his ability to learn about the Pygmies would be severely limited.

When Patrick became ill, not only with respiratory problems but also with symptoms that might today be described as dementia—according to Anne, Patrick "went crazy in April of '53"—he became self-destructive and threatened all of his relationships. When he died later that year, ostensibly from emphysema though privately many suspected syphilis, Anne must have felt liberated as well as lonely. The European traders and plantation owners living in the Ituri told stories about Patrick's erratic behavior: that he had fashioned a throne for himself, insisting his subjects crawl before him, and that he had once demanded that a local villager handle hot coals with his bare hands to show his respect to Putnam, the king of the forest and a character out of Conrad.

During his stay at Camp Putnam, Colin had received increasingly disturbing signals from Anne. At the end of his five months in the Ituri, Colin believed Anne wanted him to replace Patrick, if not as the heir to Camp Putnam then as her husband. Patrick Putnam's biographer wrote of Colin and Francis' arrival: "Anne was worn out, tense and exhausted, when they arrived, and their presence seemed at first a virtual godsend. Turnbull immediately launched a music festival, and people came from miles around to perform: Bilas, Ndakas, Budos, Ngwanas, and even some Azandes who were working at the elephant training station. 'I can't tell you how nice it is having Colin,' Anne wrote her parents, and two weeks later she added, 'It's incredible how much the natives love him and everyone wants him to have the best.' She added that she hoped he would not rush off to study the Pygmies so that someone would, finally, learn something about the much ignored villagers. She said, 'The pigmies will come later which is good because he is about the only person who has come through who is interested in the real people' [villagers]."

But Anne's idealization was shaken when she began to realize that Colin would not replace Patrick, that he was not interested in the villagers, and that he did not intend to stay any longer than his research warranted. Colin continually tried to free himself from any obligations to the farmers or to Camp Putnam. He had begun to detest the villagers because they felt so superior to the Mbuti, and the villagers in turn began to resent Colin for refusing to pay attention to them or to rebuild Camp Putnam. Colin and Anne fought often during that time. She felt that since she and Patrick had made his experience in the Ituri possible and fruitful, Colin owed her greater respect than he showed. According to Francis, on one occasion the argument was so heated that Anne became hysterical, and began to laugh madly and uncontrollably. She begged Francis to pour cold water over her head to shake her out of the hysteria, which he did.

Colin and Francis spent much of their time exploring the relationship between the Pygmies and the farmers and studying an important ritual of manhood called the *nkumbi,* which Francis filmed. Anne made sure the villagers delayed this ritual, one of the most important events for the Bira in years, pending Colin's arrival. Those films today constitute an important part of the Human Studies Film Archive at the Smithsonian Institution.

Initially, Colin was astonished by the complexity of the Pygmy-farmer relationship, but he would eventually discount its importance. Living in a Pygmy camp or in a farmer village, Colin was confronted everyday with Pygmy-farmer interactions; yet his academic book about the pygmies and farmers, *Wayward Servants,* can be read as a study of their separateness. The nkumbi ritual would provide Colin with much of the data he needed to support an argument for Mbuti autonomy. Among the most important aspects of the nkumbi, for Colin, was the three-month initiation he attended in an Mbuti camp. Colin stayed there for most of that time while Francis and Anne lived at Camp Putnam. The nkumbi is an important rite of passage among the Bira farmers who live in villages near to the Mbuti. For Bira and Mbuti boys between the ages of nine and eleven, the nkumbi marks the distinction between boyhood and manhood, but it is also a method for integrating the Mbuti into village life. Hence, the villagers demand that Mbuti boys participate in the rites of passage through which the villagers can exert supernatural control over them. Colin did not overstate the importance of the nkumbi to the welfare of the village communities; they believed in it so strongly that once, when a village boy died just before his circumcision, he was circumcised and fully initiated just as if he had been alive.

Colin was interested in the nkumbi because, by all appearances, the Mbuti seemed to embrace the nkumbi; and yet, Colin could not reconcile those appearances with his sense that the Mbuti were an independent, autonomous society subordinate to no neighbor or outside power. From his earliest contacts with the Mbuti, Colin wanted to explore the question of whether the Pygmies were truly integrated into village life or whether the Pygmies just went along with the villagers to exploit them for food and iron.

Nkumbi preparations take a long time. A month of various small rites cleanse the village of evil, and there is food and palm wine to collect. Bira and Mbuti mothers shave their sons' heads to signify that their boyhood is over and then shave their own heads as a symbol of mourning. Although nkumbi initiates know that they have been selected, the nkumbi specialists, all of them Bira villagers, try to abduct the boys when they least expect it. They are taken into the forest where they are immediately circumcised. The specialists wrap each boy's penis in a leaf anointed with an anesthetic mixture of herbs, after which the boys are asked to sing special nkumbi songs. The songs inevitably fail to please and so the boys must be trained to sing. As a result of their failure, the priests beat them with a switch, and this, the Mbuti say, takes the boys' minds off the pain of circumcision. No part of the nkumbi ever appeared cruel to Colin; every boy understands what is happening and is eager to become an adult. Even more important, the boys are grateful that they will not become women. For many weeks the boys remain at the nkumbi camp, painted with white clay as if dead because, until they emerge from the camp as adults, they are socially dead. When, after nearly three months in the nkumbi camp, the boys emerge, there is a large procession of celebrants. As the boys lie flat on the ground, everything in the camp is burned completely, a sign that their childhood is a thing of the past.

In 1954, there were no Bira boys the right age for circumcision yet the Bira felt that not to have the nkumbi would be dangerous, bringing illness and death to the village. In fact, the Mbuti had not held an nkumbi since 1951. But there were several uncircumcised Mbuti boys, and so the Bira told the Mbuti to carry out the ritual, even without any Bira men or boys present. The nkumbi would last three months and take place in an initiation camp in the forest, just a short walk from the villages.

"There could be no question of not holding the nkumbi," Colin wrote, "as this would offend the ancestors. And in any case the villagers decided it was worthwhile as it helped to assert their authority over the Pygmies. I heard speculative talk more than once about how an initiated Pygmy, when he dies, goes to serve the tribal ancestors just as he served the villagers during his life."

Colin slept with the boys and their male relatives in the initiation camp, and since the forest camp was only just beyond the village gardens, Francis visited everyday to film. But for much of the time there were no villagers. The rule was that only fathers of nkumbi boys were allowed to sleep in the camp, and since there were only Pygmy boys, only Pygmy men were permitted to stay; Colin and Francis, as outsiders, neither Pygmy nor villager, were the only exceptions. Anne, as a woman, was not permitted to attend the ritual, and this irked her; not only had she begun to feel that Colin was "stealing the Pygmies from her," but the ritual she had worked so hard to delay for Colin's benefit was within earshot.

Some villager men were present at the ritual for brief periods of time during the day, at which time the Pygmies obeyed all of the rules, especially the rigid restrictions on what food they could eat and the methods for preparing and eating it. During the villagers' visits the Pygmies acted subservient to the farmers, but when the farmers left to return to the villages, the Pygmies seemed to Colin an almost entirely different people. In order to make the ritual pleasing to the spirits, the farmers had ordered the boys to remain in bed, to eat only a small number of carefully selected foods, never to bathe, and never to touch or even look at any of the sacred ritual paraphernalia, such as the bull-roarer (a wooden slat attached to a string that makes a loud noise when swung overhead). When the farmers had gone, the Pygmies immediately violated every rule.

He wrote, "So from the first day to the last I was with the nkumbi, day and night; and at night, when all the villagers had left, the boys leaped from the bed where they were supposed to be sleeping and joined their fathers around the fire, eating forbidden foods in forbidden company and in a forbidden manner, using their fingers. One boy jumped onto a log and swung his arms around in imitation of someone swinging a bull-roarer, which of course he should have never seen. Others played their favorite game of punch-ball with the sacred banana. A shower of rain was an invitation to run outside and wash off all the dirt that had accumulated during the day . . . Both the boys and their fathers enjoyed the chance to make fun, in a friendly way, of the villagers, but that was not their sole reason for deliberately breaking all the taboos. They behaved as they did because to them the restrictions were not only meaningless but belonged to a hostile world."

By participating so fully in the nkumbi and attaching himself so closely to the Pygmies, Colin was seeing the Pygmies offstage, something no other visitor had been able to do. Colin found that the Pygmies shared none of the villagers' supernatural beliefs. And the way in which the Pygmies privately flaunted their rejection of village supernatural fears led Colin to wonder why the Pygmies adhered to village customs at all, or why, in this case, the Pygmies permitted their boys to be circumcised. Turnbull concluded that the Pygmies wanted to live peaceably with the villagers, not only because they occupied the same general area, and would thus necessarily be in contact, but also because the villages offered the Pygmies additional places to find food, almost as if the villages were another hunting ground. The only way the Pygmies could enter into adult activities with the villagers was to be regarded by the villagers as adults and, for the Bira, the transition from childhood to adulthood could not take place without an nkumbi. The nkumbi affirmed the tie between the Pygmies, their trading partners, and their partners' extended families. The Mbuti therefore pretended to be subordinate to the Bira when, in fact, they were exploiting them. According to Colin, the Mbuti quite consciously knew what they needed to do to live well, and they were willing to feign inferiority in exchange for it. Colin believed he was now seeing the Pygmies as they really were, although he would later say more accurately that the Pygmies were both empowered and subservient, that they acted differently in different contexts. By describing the difference between the way the Pygmies behaved among the villagers and away from the villagers, he was be able to understand the role of power, authority, and politics in the rain forest. This would be an important contribution to the anthropological study of politics. But he did not go far enough. He continued to believe that the Mbuti could be fruitfully analyzed in isolation from the farmers, a belief that later anthropologists thought was tantamount to analyzing a segment of American society, such as African or Hispanic Americans, without taking into account their relationships with the larger social systems of which they are a part.

The remarkable 1954 footage of the nkumbi has been incorporated in a number of educational films that have appeared on television, but the film maker's name is seldom mentioned. Chapman has had no control over the publication and distribution of his films or recordings and has never received any royalties. This omission is especially troubling in light of the major influence his sound recordings had on western music. It is worth a brief detour to note what happened to the 1954 audio tapes.

The anthropologist Steven Feld was on a ferry crossing Hong Kong Harbor when he noticed a passage in a newspaper review of Madonna's 1994 CD "Bedtime Stories" that read, "In 'Sanctuary' pygmy-like hoots and throbbing low bass notes frame Madonna's declaration 'It's here in your heart I want to be carried.'" Madonna's use of Pygmy music is credited to Herbie Hancock who, in 1992, remade his famous "Watermelon Man" with an introduction copied from a 1966 LP by Simha Arom and Genevieve Taurell's "The Music of the Ba-Benzele Pygmies." Feld investigated and found that a large number of musicians had adapted styles, riffs, chord changes, and arrangements from Pygmy music. Yet for a decade the only source of Pygmy music was Colin and Francis's tapes, which preceded Arom and Taurell's.

Feld, who now teaches at New York University, was a student of Turnbull's at Hofstra University and is also a musician. (He used to perform under the stage name Rufus.) Like Turnbull, his interest in human society was rooted in his love of music. Feld decided to study how Pygmy music became part of contemporary rock and jazz and discovered that Colin figured prominently. Most of the world never encountered Pygmies at the fair or at the zoo; they encountered them far more indirectly through writings and music. He learned that, in addition to Hancock and Madonna, many other musicians adapted Pygmy songs: in the early 1960s, Leon Thomas used Pygmy yodel techniques that he said he listened to with John Coltrane, when Colin and Francis's tapes of the Pygmies, published by the Smithsonian Institution, were the only ones available. John Hassell and Brian Eno's 1979 Fourth World "Volume 1, Possible Musics," has a song entitled "Ba-Benzele" (the name of the Pygmy group Arom recorded in the sixties), and perhaps the best-selling adaptation is the disco CD "Deep Forest," which sold several million copies worldwide, featuring music from the Pygmies and a bass narration about the ancestral wisdom that lies deep in the forest with them. Turnbull and Chapman's recordings are still considered the best, if not because of their excellent sound quality, then because of the quality of the music. Anyone Thomas or Coltrane might have influenced with their Pygmy adaptations was thus indirectly influenced by Colin and Francis.

But Europeans and Americans are not the only ones who adapt the music of other continents. In the collection entitled "Music of the Rain Forest Pygmies of Northeast Congo," Turnbull selected one song (originally the last track on the tape and now repositioned by the Smithsonian as the sixth track, side B) that pokes fun at the Pygmies. He had found a group of Pygmies he had never met before and asked them to sing the oldest song they knew. In a quintessential Pygmy style and arrangement, they sang "Clementine."

At the end of their 1954 field season, Colin, Francis, and Anne decided to return overland to Europe. They would travel together to Makerere University in Uganda for a few days, and then leave Africa through the port of Mombasa, Kenya. The night before they left, and just after Colin had been introduced to the sacred ritual songs called *molimo,* the Pygmies took Colin into the forest and did something to make sure that he would fulfill his promise to return to them. They initiated him with the marks of a Pygmy hunter.

"Kolongo held my head and Njobo casually took a rusty arrow blade and cut tiny deep vertical slits in the center of my forehead and above each eye. He then gouged out a little flesh from each slit and asked Kolongo for the medicine to put in. But Kolongo had forgotten to bring it . . ."

Colin sat on a log and waited while Kolongo went to get the medicine. Blood was dripping from his head. Kolongo rubbed a black ash paste into the cuts until the blood stopped flowing. "And there it is today, ash made from the plants of the forest, a part of the forest that is a part of the flesh, carried by every self-respecting Pygmy male. And as long as it is with me it will always call me back."

The markings on Colin's forehead were visible for the rest of his life.

Anne's departure from Africa marked the end of Camp Putnam. She would return to the Ituri once more, in 1957, but the memory of the rain forest stayed alive through her memoir of her life in the Ituri, *Madami,* which was received well. Anne's father-in-law, however, was not pleased. He resented its publication because his son, who he believed was the true expert, had never completed his own work. But he knew as well as anyone that Anne had tried hard to get Patrick to publish. Anne had told Colin that Patrick would always say, "What's the sense, Schebesta's done it." She would reply, "You don't agree and it would make both your works more valuable . . . Result, no book."

Colin was glad to go to Uganda because he wanted to see Makerere University. Its East African Institute was the intellectual center for African studies in those days. P. T. Baxter, a fellow Oxford student, was attending the 1954 seminars of one of the earliest and most respected Africanists, Audrey Richards. After one seminar meeting, Richards approached Baxter with an urgent request. Colin had written her to say he would be calling on her on a certain afternoon to discuss ways to publish his Mbuti materials. Richards, who was feeling harassed by self-invited visitors, begged Baxter to see him in her place. Baxter recognized quickly that Colin was not a rigorous scientist, an easy judgment since Colin had yet to begin graduate school and until now had been more interested in music than anything else. Nonetheless, he said, "I was impressed by his energy and obvious talents but underwhelmed about him, he seemed a bit over full of himself. I, rather priggishly, told him there was more to anthro' than journalistic observations, and that there was not a simple guide which enabled one to turn layman's impressions into anthro' data. I urged him to go to Oxford and do a course. Which he did. I urged him to go to Oxford, rather than UCL [University College, London] or LSE [London School of Economics] because there was less orthodoxy there about being 'scientific.' I suppose local patriotism played a part. He asked me to write a letter to E-P [E. Edward Evans-Pritchard] on his behalf which I did."

When Colin got back to England at the beginning of 1955, he wrote E. Edward Evans-Pritchard to formally express his interest in pursuing a doctorate in anthropology in general and writing about the relations between Indians and Africans in particular.

> Briefly, the point is whether or not you feel it worthwhile my coming to take a course at the Institute with a view to becoming a professional anthropologist. My qualifications as regards degrees are shaky. I have an Oxford M.A. [a formality, awarded for a fee of ten pounds after completion of the B.A.] but it was taken half at the beginning of the war and half at the end in Modern Greats; those war time degrees were not very satisfactory . . . However, the degrees are there, and I have since been finding myself drawn closer and closer into the realm of social anthropology, and have had the good luck to amass a fairly considerable amount of material on the Pigmies of the Epulu district in the Ituri forest. I also have some reasonable photographs, slides, 16 mm. film and recordings, all of which need to be worked on more systematically and scientifically than I am capable of doing at the moment.
>
> One reason for my wanting to take the course is to enable me to get the material I already have into shape . . . The other reason is that my personal interests arising from two years' study in India and over a year's wandering about central and east Africa seem to be centered pretty definitely in east Africa, where the Indian-African relationship is of such vital interest and importance. So I hope to find a place at Makerere, or to find some other means of working out there in the field of social anthropology.
>
> . . . I also have some notes on the negro-master [Bira-Mbuti] relationship in this district, and I am most anxious to follow all this material up, first having ordered it, as owing to certain administrative changes the whole economy of the pigmies may be altered, and this in turn will lead to a break up of the negro-pigmy relationship.

Evans-Pritchard's reply has not survived but he must have sent encouraging words. For although Colin spent some time in England lecturing on Pygmy music and rituals, he spent most of 1955 and 1956 completing a Diploma in Social Anthropology.

At this time, there were still only four centers of anthropology in England, the three mentioned by Baxter, and Cambridge University. When Colin was first at Oxford, the LSE was the clear leader dominated by experts on the region of Oceania.

But by the time Colin pursued his graduate training in the fifties, Oceania had given way to Africa as the main source of data for new theoretical advances, and the best Africanists were at Oxford. Whereas, before the war, there were never more than ten students in any academic year enrolled in anthropology at Oxford, by 1951, there were fifty, thirty-seven of whom were graduate students. At mid-century, then, Oxford had the most illustrious history among the four centers, since the three fathers of social anthropology, A. R. Radcliffe-Brown, E. Edward Evans-Pritchard, and Meyer Fortes, had all taught there during the 1940s and had produced some of the most influential studies of African kinship and politics. Their persuasive analyses of social structure, based primarily on data collected from African societies, helped establish a new paradigm in social anthropology, one focused on politics and the development of more abstract conceptual models of society.

Simply put, they located political organizations within social systems, such as the family, marriage, and everyday work-life that had previously been seen as operating in isolation. In societies that appeared to have no discernible political system, such as the Nuer of Sudan, these authors saw political systems hidden within kinship systems. In societies that had very obvious political systems, such as the kingdoms of the Zulu or the Swazi of southern Africa, these authors found that politics and law were integral to systems of kinship and marriage. They looked at societies to find an internal structure, almost like a grammar of culture, that shaped both ideas and behavior. Audrey Richards and P. T. Baxter were proponents of this new paradigm. Any thesis on the Pygmies presented at Oxford would almost certainly be pushed in this direction. The Pygmies could not simply be described or explained away as representatives of a stage of cultural evolution; a model of political and social behavior had to be found, something that integrated the Pygmies into a bounded, coherent society.

Back on campus between 1955 and 1957, Turnbull worked on a B.Litt. (Bachelor of Letters) in Social Anthropology (equivalent to a masters degree in the United States and at other British universities) as the first step toward earning his D.Phil., as the Ph.D. degree has long been called at Oxford. His application to write a B.Litt. thesis entitled "The Bambuti of the Ituri Forest" would be accepted in October 1956, months later than it should have been since the application was mislaid in the Oxford administrative offices. But Colin was not entirely sure what was expected of him. The same month that he applied for the B.Litt., he wrote the Anthropology secretary, Phyllis Puckle, to say that he would be up for a visit with the department in mid-July and hoped "someone will be around on Monday to tell me what a B.Litt. is."

He began to visit his old teacher Bruce MacFarlane, who first interviewed Turnbull when he applied to Magdalen and who, in letters to a friend, gives us a glimpse into Colin's behavior at Oxford.

"On Wednesday I was host in Hall to Colin Turnbull. Do you remember him? . . . In his Indian period he became a vegetarian and grew a beard a foot long; I once had to give him a breakfast of oranges and white burgundy; that scandalized the colleagues. When I first knew him he was a Scottish nationalist and wore the kilt. Then an Indian undergraduate called Paul Mayor persuaded him to become a Hindu and go to Benares . . . Now he is veering toward the West Indies and the beard has disappeared (the vegetarianism and the alcohol remain). This follows his getting to know the Jamaican conductors on the Oxford buses. Colin is so impressionable that he now speaks in the cooing voice of a West Indian negro and hums calypso music. He wants a job as lecturer at the University at Kingston in Jamaica. There's an eccentric for you; I must say he entertains me hugely."

Within a few months, Colin came to mind again while MacFarlane was reading a novel about Africans and Jamaicans in England and the white British men and women who tried to befriend them. He wrote to a friend, "My only new reading has been Colin McInnes's *City of Spades;* over-praised by the reviewers but rather a revelation of African Jamaican society in London. Can one never trust novel-reviewers? But it made me think of another Colin who has disappeared since he visited me at Stonor last summer: Colin Turnbull. I think he's in the West Indies." The book, as much a social documentary of post-war London as a novel, shows how many whites in London, far more privileged than blacks, sought close friendship or romance with Africans and Jamaicans, partly because they were fascinated by the exotic and partly because they themselves felt marginalized from British society. The whites depicted by MacInnes were convinced that they could truly understand the experience of racism in England and were, as a consequence, oblivious to how ambivalently their black friends received their interest, friendship, generosity, and pretensions of empathic understanding.

MacFarlane wrote a third letter about Colin to a friend:

"This morning while I was out Colin Turnbull called and left a note. You remember who he is . . . Tall, fair and handsome; inconsequent, impulsive and elusive; all his screws are loose. The lodge has given me his address, 77 St. Aldate's, and I shall go and call on him later this afternoon . . . Norman [Scarfe, another MacFarlane student] always said that Colin was 'untrustworthy' but I never quite understood what he meant. I'd have used your word 'coot' to describe him . . . In fact, though I've 'known' him, for years, I don't feel that I really know him at all. Real communication with him seems impossible."

It is indeed remarkable that McFarlane spilled so much ink on someone he found so inconsequential. He goes on to make an ethnocentric comment that Colin would have taken as an enormous compliment.

"Perhaps one has to belong to one of the 'backward races' in order to get his wavelength. The inconsequence of his conversation and letters reminds me of my various Indian pupils and E. M. Forster's Indians also. He usually hums West Indian tunes in an abstracted fashion when one is talking to him. He has whiskery, improbable handwriting which must mean something odd too."

McFarlane was right on at least two counts. Nearly everyone to ever correspond with Colin would at some point complain about his handwriting; it is almost impossible to read. And if Oxford did anything for Colin, it was to crystallize his attraction to the exotic, already partly formed during his childhood, his profound need to discover his self and self-worth through the Other.

In the summer of 1956, Turnbull traveled to New York City to plan future writing projects with Anne. Colin toyed with the idea of writing a biography of Patrick Putnam and also writing up Patrick and Anne's own notes into a book. The goal was to make Patrick look like a professional anthropologist. On June 24, he wrote Evans-Pritchard to say "I hope I can produce something good for you from N.Y." Anne introduced Colin to the staff of the American Museum of Natural History, in particular, its chair of anthropology, Harry Shapiro, who gave Colin some working space, encouragement, and access to its papers. She would subsequently recommend him strongly for a position as curator of African ethnology at the museum. Anne had given the museum nearly all of Patrick's papers, including his field notes. She also gave Colin the folk tales she had collected over the years, as well as her notes on the *elima* ritual, a ritual of puberty for girls from which all men, including Colin, were excluded.

Colin did not believe there were enough materials to write a complete biography of Putnam and he was also concerned that Patrick's notes were too unscientific to make a contribution to the scholarly literature. Indeed the significance of Putnam's life and legacy was uncertain. In her biography of Putnam, Joan Mark wrote, "Patrick Putnam did not write a great book in anthropology. However, he made it possible for someone else to do so. That is contribution enough."

Colin and Anne had a blow-up over Colin's reluctance to do a biography. She felt that she had given Colin everything and that he had given her little in return. Now that he seemed reluctant to do anything on behalf of Patrick's memory, she was suspicious of his overall intentions. Despite those suspicions she continued to give Colin her and Patrick's materials, expecting that at least their contribution would be credited in any of Colin's future publications.

Leaving Anne on poor terms, Turnbull returned to Oxford to complete his B. Litt. When he arrived home, there was good news. Kumari was still waiting and the Emslie Horniman Anthropological Scholarship Fund had awarded him one thousand pounds for two years' study at Oxford. Although he was delighted with the money, Colin did not think it was possible to complete his B.Litt. and D. Phil. in two years unless he relied heavily on the notes of other writers, including Putnam's. In his application to register for the B. Litt., he noted that his thesis would be based on the existing literature as well as his own fieldwork, and that the thesis was necessary to African studies because "Schebesta's material is unsatisfactory in several respects, notably in that it fails to give an accurate, detailed account of any one specific group of Bambuti."

Colin continued to find cause to disagree with Schebesta. Schebesta said the Pygmies had chiefs, but Colin found they had none; Schebesta wrote that Pygmy music was entirely instrumental, but Colin found a rich repertoire of vocal music. Colin also found Schebesta's beliefs that the Pygmies could be studied solely from the perspective of the villagers nonsensical. Eventually, Colin and Schebesta would meet in Vienna, but they never reconciled their differences.

Colin continued to see Kumari but she was getting impatient. His family, ordinary in their attitudes for mid-twentieth century England, but perhaps racist by turn-of-the-millenium sensibilities, did not support the relationship; Colin's mother, possessive and fearful of losing him, took the stronger position. She repeatedly pointed out to Colin and Kumari that if they remained together they would face enormous social problems and their children would have an uncertain identity. She even did so immediately after the event at Arundel Castle at which they felt so ostracized.

In contrast, Kumari's parents' attitudes were promising. Her family, almost all of whom had lived in England for more than a decade and saw themselves as progressive and open-minded, left the matter largely up to her but did actively encourage Colin to pursue the marriage. Not only did they give her the freedom to make her own marriage decision, but when she finally returned to Benares in 1957, she lived alone in a flat in the city center, something most Indian women were never permitted to do. Despite the social and family problems they encountered or expected to encounter in England, and perhaps emboldened by them, Colin and Kumari promised to get married when either he or she became economically self-sufficient.

Throughout the 1950s, though Colin had enough money to support himself in school, he seldom had enough to afford material luxuries. One day he noticed a unique and expensive tie clip in a store window, went inside to look at it, and became nearly obsessed with owning it. He saved money here and there until he decided finally that it was something he had to have, but on the afternoon he went to buy it the storekeeper reported that another customer had purchased it the previous day. That night Colin met Kumari for dinner and apologized for his depressed mood, even saying that he was embarrassed by his obsession with the tie clip. Kumari reached out to Colin's hand in friendship, placed a small box in it, and said smiling, "I'm the other customer who bought the tie clip yesterday."

In the spring of 1957, when Kumari finished her undergraduate degree in London, she went to Bombay to work for the American advertising firm J. Walter Thompson with vague hopes that Colin would come after her. But within a few months Colin would go to Africa for another year among the Pygmies. Though they tried to intensify their relationship through correspondence, their relationship had suffered from too many long breaks in communication. During the roughly six years they had known each other, Colin had spent more than two years abroad.

On June 14, 1957, Colin handed his complete B. Litt. thesis to Rodney Needham before his oral exam the following month and was approved for D. Phil. Status. However, the two examiners, Rodney Needham and Isaac Schapera, clearly pointed out in their evaluation that the B. Litt. thesis was "based to a minor extent upon his own observations, but much more upon the available literature," though they added that Colin had proven to them that "the existing standard classification of pygmies is inadequate."

From his parent's home in Sussex, Colin wrote Oxford on August 5, 1957, informing them that he was about to depart for at least one year of fieldwork in central Africa. He anticipated completing an acceptable D.Phil. thesis by the end of 1958 but it would, in fact, take much longer than that. In the meantime, Colin must have been corresponding regularly with Newton, who had returned to the United States in 1951 to the Lancaster City public schools, but none of the letters have survived. He and Newton agreed that they would travel together again to the Ituri, and Newton promised to stay for the full year. They met in England at the end of July and prepared their trip.

Colin and Newton sailed for Africa on August 14, 1957, and by September they were in the field. But Colin had neglected to send the anthropology department a final copy of his B. Litt. thesis. "Did you ever think of giving us a copy of your B. Litt.?" the department secretary wrote to him in Africa. Over the next seven years, there would be many more such notes, as his advisors complained, "Where is your thesis?"

When Anne heard about Colin and Newton's plans, she decided to time her own trip to coincide with theirs. She did not plan to reopen the hotel; she said she wanted simply to visit three Mbuti children that she had helped raise during her time there with Patrick. Anne would also use the opportunity to write an article for *National Geographic,* "My Life with Africa's Littlest People," which was published in 1960. She would end up staying the full year with Colin and Newton.

Anne had arrived about three weeks earlier than Newton and Colin because they had decided to go overland again, this time with a motorcycle and sidecar. In another serial for *The Motorcycle,* Colin wrote a detailed account of their experience riding an AJS (the same brand of motorcycle he had taken to Africa in 1951) and Canterbury sidecar outfit. However, on this voyage they avoided the east and started instead in west Africa. Colin entertained the anthropology program at Oxford with letters sent to Phyllis Puckle:

> We unwisely stopped in a thunderstorm in a small village in Nigeria on a Sunday evening. My beard returned, I was mistaken for a Seventh Day Adventist preacher, and it was demanded that I should preach—the Catechist was the only one that spoke any English, and he was not too good at that. I tried to prolong the drumming and dancing, which seemed to be the work-up, as long as possible, but finally could avoid it no longer. I said something rather mildly and quietly, which was received in stony silence. They then demanded again that I should preach, apparently wanting real hell-fire. I agreed to read a juicy bit out of the Old Testament, then found that nobody had one. The Catechist dashed out of the Church and returned in a minute with an English book giving Golden Numbers and explaining all about them, and also a few pages explaining the Epistles and Gospels as they appear in the C of E prayer book. He suggested that I read one verse from this "Bible" while he read the corresponding verse from the Yoruba Bible. I agreed, with faint heart, and he chose Luke 14 for himself and an explanation of one of Paul's Epistles for me. I put my heart and soul into it and really sounded as though I was announcing the Day of Judgement. Unfortunately I didn't know what was in Luke 14—but everyone enjoyed it, and after some more drumming and dancing they took us off and gave us bowls of hot tea.

When they reached Camp Putnam in September, both Anne and the villagers relived their resentment for Colin. Turnbull decided to spend as much time away from Anne and the Bira villagers as possible. There is no way of knowing whether Colin was aware that he responded to Anne and his mother in similar ways; he saw both Anne and his mother as possessive and overbearing, manipulative and cloying, and when in their presence he was often unempathetic and could act blatantly selfish and entitled. The fact that Anne was thirteen years older than he and the widow of the man Colin had imagined as a potential father figure may have added to the stress of their relationship. Interestingly, Anne and Dot met only once, in England when Anne stayed with the Turnbulls on her way home from Africa in 1954. By all accounts they adored one another, in part because Dot never imagined that Anne, being so much older than her son, might be romantically interested in him. Colin's Canadian relatives, who also met Anne, still remember well how alike they seemed; both Anne and Dot wore their passions on their sleeves, and both gushed about how wonderful a man Colin had become.

Colin, for his part, acted more by instinct than insight, recognizing only that he was significantly happier when living away from Anne. In November 1957, he wrote to Phyllis Puckle, saying "I am having a glorious time in the forest, miles away from Camp Putnam or anywhere else." He added that he was surviving on as little as twenty shillings per week, and spending extra money only to gather a small amount of data for a British physical anthropologist named J. S. Weiner who specialized in pigmentation and morphology. Weiner had asked Colin to make anatomical observations, match skin color to shades on a color chart, and make measurements of steatopygia, the large accumulations of fat in the buttocks area so common to many Africans. "An expensive but delightful pastime," Colin wrote to the department, for he paid each of his subjects. "Incidentally do tell [Weiner] I have tentatively pinched a few [buttocks], and will be writing to him shortly." Weiner was pleased and would eventually write to Colin asking only if the skin colors recorded for Mbuti buttocks were from washed or unwashed buttocks. (In his textbook on human biology, Weiner had made it clear that preliminary cleansing of the skin was of utmost importance to a good pigmentation reading.)

It was a strange question. Anthropologists were certainly interested in describing all visible aspects of the body surface, to find out how and why people differed physically throughout the world, but skin color measurements were almost always taken from the inside of the forearm, a part of the body that seldom gets very tan, and therefore gives a good reading of "true" skin color, uninfluenced by the sun. Some biologists like Weiner may have assumed that the buttocks also do not tan, but they generally refrained from having anything to do with the buttocks, if only to avoid offending people's dignity. But, Weiner's intrusiveness aside, it was certainly a sign of Turnbull's close relationship with the Pygmies that he was permitted to make the measurements.

Joan Mark suggests that Colin's desire to live exclusively with the Pygmies may have been partly a reaction to the Bira's anger with him: "The [Bira] villagers correctly understood that they were getting much less from him than they had gotten from Patrick Putnam in his perhaps overtly less-admirable roles of powerful white man and village chief." Colin continued to be called Murefu, a general term meaning a big or tall man. The Pygmies looked up to him, literally and figuratively, and it is hard to imagine that Colin was immune to the pleasures of their deference. As much as Colin decried the ways in which the Pygmies pretended to be servile in the villagers, he did not have the same sensitivities when it came to how they related to him. He represented himself as a friend or as an equal, but one would be hard pressed to believe him. Colin was tall, white, and European, living and working in a colony. Despite his poverty, he was still much better off than most of the local Africans and all of the Pygmies. He could also give minimal medical care and so was seen as both knowledgeable and powerful. Those who did not call him Murefu called him Bwana or "master," the term of respect by which nearly every European scientist at work in Swahili-speaking areas of Africa has been addressed.

Since his childhood, Colin had identified with the weak and vulnerable. In the rain forest, therefore, Colin identified with the Mbuti, searching for ways in which they resisted the Bira. The Mbuti were heroes in Colin's eyes, and as much as the Bira tried to win Colin's favors and convince him that the Mbuti were an inferior people, no Bira was going to teach a lifelong underdog new tricks. Colin knew that the farmers saw him more as a buffoon because he clearly preferred the Pygmies. But perhaps the main reason that Colin was disliked is that he did not respect the villagers. He wanted no part of the Bira because they were ostensibly the dominant community in the area, and yet Colin saw them as vastly inferior, both intellectually and morally, to the Pygmies. One of the reasons Colin wanted to become an anthropologist was to be a legitimate mouthpiece for the oppressed. Despite the occasional criticism that anthropologists were "handmaidens of colonialism"—that their studies facilitated colonial projects—most anthropologists fought hard against colonial officers, usually arguing to deaf ears for the welfare of one or another African community, even when the colonial administrations had funded their research. Colin was no exception. What he did not know then, and perhaps would never fully recognize, was that more than a decade later his own love life would be patterned like the Bira-Mbuti relationship, with one partner seemingly dominant over the other, and that many of his remaining years would involve a struggle to show that the dominant partner was, in fact, inferior.

Colin liked anthropology because it took him to faraway places, away from England, his parents, and the sexual temptations that he believed undermined the lessons of Anandamayi Ma. (There would always remain, in the back of his mind, some regret that in rejecting celibacy and asceticism he was violating Anandamayi Ma's wishes.) But he remained attached to his parents and corresponded with them regularly. He sent film to be developed, boxes of artifacts, and bark cloths. He sent masks and other ritual objects to his nephew David in boarding school at St. Peter's York, which helped make him popular with his classmates as the boy with the intrepid uncle. In November 1957, he sent his father some money so that he and Dot could go out to dinner at his expense and asked for his opinion on future employment. Colin mentioned the possibility of a job in New York at the museum where he had worked with Patrick Putnam's papers, and also suggested that he and his parents might think about moving to Canada one day. Colin had been corresponding regularly with the Anthropology department at the University of Toronto about job prospects there, and though the department appeared to have done their best, the university did not authorize them to make a new hire of any kind. He also reported that he failed to get an offer from the University of the British West Indies in Jamaica.

Colin's father answered on December 21, 1957, "The main point, as I see it, is that you have to establish yourself . . . in the most congenial and promising job and country. You do that first and then let's see whether we can solve the problem of transfer of residence. I think there are far more opportunities within America or Australia for the young than in the U.K. and if I were of the right age I should not wish to remain here where the great desire seems to be something for nothing. Ambition and adventure and the 'joy of the working' seems to be dying out and it's in the younger countries that these qualities still exist. But having reached what I call 'early middle age' I could not hope to earn much for being in a new surrounding. However, we'll see."

The possibility of moving to Toronto must have been entertained seriously enough, since Colin's mother's brother, his Uncle Arthur, sent a long letter on January 18, 1958, giving Colin information about possible houses in new developments outside of Toronto that would be large enough for Colin and his parents to occupy together. He told Colin of one house overlooking a golf course selling for under $15,000 Canadian dollars. He added: "If you were at the University of Toronto I am quite sure your Mum and Dad would never entertain coming out to live anywhere unless you could be with them and have your home with them."

On New Year's Eve 1957, Colin's mother wrote to say that a Mrs. Davies who had passed through the Ituri and had met Colin there called her and Jock upon her return to England and said that Colin had been "badly bitten by skeeters." Dot said she would try to find the best medicine to send him. She also raised the issue of retiring to Toronto in a New Year's wish: "I certainly shall be awake and thinking of you, wondering if you are asleep in your house . . . wherever Darling, my love and wishes will go out to you, wishing so much for you for 1958 and the years to come. How much I think and wonder what we will do, so far no mention from Pops. If he should say 'I can't retire' I think I'll explode. I don't want to be cross. Sometimes here I feel I can't endure it . . .

How much I'd give to be nearer Tor. [Toronto]. Still, I realize how much I have to thank God for . . . So my Colin whatever the New Year holds, 1957 has been one of much joy. All it has meant in your life and all you have accomplished. God Bless you my Darling Colin. Always, always, your loving Mauchka."

On November 26, 1957, three days after Colin's thirty-third birthday, Kumari did not even know where Colin was until he wrote her from the field. She replied immediately, writing a late-night letter in which she explained that without knowing his whereabouts she could not even send him a birthday card. Her letter was affectionate, goading, and playful. She said in jest that she had fallen in love many times and that it was fun. She asked if he had fallen in love and, if so, was she pretty. She teased him, saying that she had grown fat and ugly, and then offered, in a tone that was only half-serious, to come to Africa if he agreed to marry her once and for all.

Several months later, Colin replied, confirming his wish to marry her. Twenty years later, Colin would tell a friend that he had, in fact, broken off the engagement, but that statement is contradicted by a letter Kumari wrote to Colin. After much thought, she gave her broken-hearted answer on June 17, 1958. She said that she loved him and was honored by his love for her, but that she would not marry him. She told Colin that he was not to blame, and that he would have a great life. But if they were to marry, she said, she would hinder his success. Colin's mother, she added, had made her think more fully about interracial issues on the night of their date at Arundel Castle. Kumari also made it clear that her own family had left the matter up to her, having told her they would welcome the marriage even with the complications an interracial marriage might cause. She begged him to forgive her cowardice and to try not to be sad.

In February of 1958, Harry Shapiro of the American Museum of Natural History had written Colin to offer him an appointment as a curator of African ethnology, to begin in September 1959. Colin would no longer be financially dependent on his father, and better yet he would be far from England and his parents. "I suppose they know why they have given me the job," he wrote Evans-Pritchard, "I don't! . . . So that sounds as though I have fallen on my feet again, and it will be my own fault if I don't make something really good out of the opportunity. With any luck I hope to be back in the U.K. at the end of this year, which should give me time at least to write the thesis if not to present it." He wrote about the job flippantly, but he undoubtedly knew it was one of the best jobs in the world for an anthropologist. He would work side by side with some of the most well-known anthropologists in America, including Margaret Mead, and would have plenty of time for research and writing.

Turnbull joked with Evans-Pritchard about American anthropologists. "Do you think that after a few months in the States I shall be opinionating and differentialising? I am thinking of entitling my thesis, after this week's work, 'The Pyramidical nature of Hexeological Structuralisation among the Pygmy-form Population of the Congo.' That's for the American edition . . . the English edition would be more like 'Witches and Bitches.'"

He was now ready to finish his year, gathering as much data as possible. But he still lacked an integrating mechanism, that is, a way to understand how the Pygmies maintained their social solidarity. The remainder of his fieldwork would provide the answer.

The longstanding tensions between Colin and Anne did not lessen because Colin spent so much time away from the camp. In fact, they worsened. She changed her mind about the hotel, now desperately wanting Colin to help her refurbish it, and on top of that she was lonely; Newton's specific whereabouts during most of his year in the Ituri are a mystery. When, during that summer, Colin continued to refuse to help her she became enraged. After all, she had helped Colin get his job at the museum and yet he appeared to be giving nothing back. She wrote him a letter barring him from Camp Putnam. Shortly after sealing the envelope, she stormed out to the roadside on her bicycle, fell, and broke her hip.

Despite the pain, she traveled home alone. Colin and Newton stayed on several more weeks before returning to England. There is nothing in Colin's papers to indicate that he felt any responsibility for Anne's fall. At this point, however, one thing is clear: Colin Turnbull, contrary to the impression left by his early writings on the Pygmies, did not live entirely in the Mbuti forest camps. Like most scientists who have studied the Pygmies, he used a village as a base from which to launch trips into the forest ranging from two days to two weeks in length. There was another problem in Colin's rendering of time spent in the rain forest. Well before he would return to the Ituri forest in 1970, he claimed, and his book jackets claimed, that he "lived among the BaMbuti for three years." He actually spent periods of time with the Pygmies during three different years: two months in 1951, five months in 1954, and one year in 1957-1958, a total of just nineteen months. Newton calculated his own time with the Pygmies as eighteen months, also an exaggeration. Although many anthropologists would likely disapprove of Colin's attempts to overstate his solitude and fieldwork time, few would be surprised. Cultural anthropologists, especially those who are unmarried, have long been expected to work alone, without teams of researchers and usually also without much contact with other "outsiders." For the purposes of Colin's credibility, the less Colin said about Newton the better. Anthropologists habitually exaggerate: the longer the time in the field, the more authenticity the anthropologist believes he or she gains.

Those who shared in Colin's experiences thus went unrecognized. Anne Putnam, Newton Beal, and Francis Chapman were not simply friends in a faraway place; they were active contributors to Colin's research and achievements. There is also the example of Athmananda, the devotee who was responsible for all of Colin's exchanges with of Sri Anandamayi Ma but whose name is mentioned only once in passing in the hundreds of pages Colin wrote about India during his lifetime. When Colin did mention Anne Putnam in his writing, he was not generous and sometimes did not even mention her by name. He named her in footnotes in his more scholarly publications, but made it a point to caution readers that she was not an authority and had collected her materials in Swahili, not in the native language. In 1962, when Colin published *The Forest People,* he wrote in the acknowledgements that "Patrick Putnam deserves special mention, because it was through his friendship and hospitality, and that of his wife, that I first came to know the forest." Anne took Colin's acknowledgment hard for he had, in fact, learned far more from her in his nineteen months in the Ituri than he had from Patrick in two, and yet he did not even distinguish her from Patrick's two previous American wives or his native African wives.

In 1962, he gave Anne a copy of *The Forest People* and inscribed it lovingly: "To Anne and to the memory of Pat, both of you wonderful friends, with sincere thanks for all your help and encouragement. I hope this book will help you recall the days of happiness at Camp Putnam, and the kindness and understanding that Camp Putnam stood for. With much love, Colin, New York, September, 1961." However, he also presented himself as the first person to spend considerable amounts of time with the Pygmies, something Anne believed both she and Patrick had done. In the margins of her own copy of *The Forest People,* next to Colin's statement that "All that we knew of [the Pygmies] to date had been based on observations made either in the villages or in the presence of Negroes," Anne wrote, "This goes too far."

She talked to her friend Eugenia Earle about Colin. "While Anne was hurt that he did not more fully acknowledge her contribution," Earle recalls, "she remained more fond of him and indeed proud of him, in a somewhat possessive way, than he realized. She spoke a number of times in admiration of his having 'taught himself to write' in the process of writing." As for Colin's perspective, Eugenia recognized that "the bottom line is that Colin felt Anne greatly exaggerated the quality and extensiveness of her study of the Pygmies." But Colin did not simply question Anne's authority or knowledge about the Pygmies. There had been tension between them from the first days they met, and if there was a personal attraction or latent affection between them, it was usually hidden well. It would have been easy to write a few generous words in his acknowledgements about her contributions, but it was just as easy to leave them out. His neglect of Anne in print was, like his physical abandonment of her in the field, an act of hostility and resentment against someone who, like his own mother, tried to control him. Anandamayi Ma, to whom Colin expressed his most profound gratitude in the preface of *The Forest People* was a mother too, but she was different from Anne and Dot. Anandamayi Ma was the perfect mother who told Colin that only he had control over his life.

Anne died of cancer in Manhattan on January 28, 1967 at the age of 55. Colin attended the memorial service and gave a eulogy that made no mention of her contributions to his knowledge or the world's knowledge of the Pygmies. He said the right words, but they were perfunctory: "[Anne Eisner] had an intensely inquisitive mind and was forever curious about people. It was a totally inoffensive curiosity, without any attitude or judgment. Anne merely observed that people live their lives in many different ways, and she wanted to know why. Once she knew why she accepted that way without further question as to that person's right to follow it, however much she might disagree with it herself. One of Anne's greatest qualities was her inexhaustible generosity of spirit."

For his part, Newton wrote a children's book about Pygmy music, entitled *Pygmies Are People: Their Folkways, Their Songs, Their Games, Their Dances,* which was published in 1964 with a brief preface by Turnbull. Newton added his own epigram for the book: "Read *Pygmies are People* for enjoyment and don't worry about the facts, for Pygmies are fact, but facts are not Pygmies." The book consists of Pygmy music and lyrics, poems, and a make-believe trip through Africa on a motorcycle and sidecar. It is a tribute to the vocal arts of the Pygmies, and it also contains a good deal of information about the customs and daily lives of the Mbuti. "Can you guess how the Pygmies awaken God?" Newton asked. "They sing, of course." C. Newton Beal died on Christmas Eve, 1966, at the age of 52, in Lancaster, Ohio. He never married and had no children.

Colin spent much of his time during 1957 trying to understand how the Pygmies and farmers maintained their complicated exchange system; the Pygmy-farmer relationship would be the subject of the majority of Colin's academic publications in the 1960s and 1970s, especially *The Forest People* and a revision of his doctoral thesis, a scholarly monograph called *Wayward Servants.* In both publications, Colin would write that the Pygmies and the farmers lived together not because the Pygmies depended upon the farmers but because the economic relationship between them was mutually convenient. He argued that there was no system of inequality and no true oppression, for the Pygmies lived free to do as they pleased. As a result, the Pygmies could be understood apart from the farmers, as a distinct society rather than one that was part of a larger social structure. He went further to suggest that the Pygmies had no formal social organization, legal system, or supernatural belief system, that the Pygmies were a society always in flux. If there was any structure to be found in the Pygmy-Farmer relationship, he believed, it was a kind of voluntary apartheid in which two very different peoples have a relationship based on little more than proximity. If there was a structure to be found among the Pygmies themselves, a structure around which all the Mbuti cohered, Colin believed it was in a spiritual realm, in the beautiful and mysterious rituals called *molimo.*

Of all that Colin wrote, his descriptions of the molimo ritual and the haunting voice of the molimo trumpet remain the most vivid and penetrating. Unlike the nkumbi, which aroused his intellect first and his emotions later, the molimo did the reverse. He first heard the molimo songs in 1954, just before he left for England. It was late at night, and deep in the forest. Here were sounds that moved him so much that he believed they could never have been part of the farmers' culture; he was certain they were authentic Pygmy sounds passed down over hundreds of generations, from well before the Pygmies had any contact with the farmers. He was convinced that these songs could not have originated with the villagers, the recent immigrants to the rain forest, for if they had the Pygmies could not possibly have played them with the depth of feeling he sensed. This was music that belonged to the Pygmies, the rightful inhabitants of the rain forest.

Here was an ancient magic. Here was a music whose power had to be experienced over time. The first time he heard the songs, the Pygmies looked totally relaxed but the music was intense. The second time he heard the molimo songs, the Pygmies' movements were tightly controlled, but the music was relaxed, lazy, and fluid. The third time, he closed his eyes and found himself quickly entering a state of ecstasy. He kept his eyes closed for what seemed, inexplicably, to be a time without time, for he could not tell if it was a moment or an eternity. Late in his life, when Colin was living in India and was immersed in Buddhist philosophy, he would recall that when he finally opened his eyes, "all the others had their eyes open too, their gaze was vacant . . . there were so many bodies sitting around, singing away, but I was the only person there, the only individual consciousness; all the other bodies were empty." Indeed, for much of his life he wondered how seeing with one's eyes affected seeing with one's heart. In his last days of life, Colin found an old diary entry of Joe's in which Joe complained that Colin always kept his eyes open during love-making. "I never understood," Colin wrote in a note he pasted next to the entry, "why we have to close our eyes for ecstasy."

Hearing the molimo was a pivotal moment for Colin. He had liberated himself enough to experience the fullness of the forest. He had also freed himself of some of the constraints of his education, for it was his feeling for music that set him apart from an anthropology focused on kinship relations and political systems. His spiritual methods seemed to yield much more than his scientific ones.

The beauty of the songs and his increasing conviction that the songs conveyed the essence of the rain forest confirmed his decision to live with the Pygmies and not with the villagers. "Then I was sure that I could never rest until I had come out again, free of any obligations to stay in the village, free of any limitations of time, free simply to live and roam the forest with the BaMbuti, its people; and free to let them teach me in their own time what it was that made their life so different from that of other people."

By his return to the Ituri in 1957, Colin had learned enough of the language of the Mbuti and the Bira to conduct some interviews without relying too much on Swahili. But he still needed assistance, and someone was there to help out, a young Pygmy man named Teleabo Kenge. He had helped Colin in 1954 and was ready to help again. As a boy, Kenge had worked for Patrick Putnam and now felt he should be inherited by Patrick's successor. When Kenge's father died, there was no villager who could inherit him as an exchange partner. So Kenge became a general handyman at the hotel, cleaning the hotel grounds, ironing the clothes of hotel guests, and serving food. He spoke Swahili well and wore western-style clothing. He thought a great deal of himself and soon developed a sense for the kind of information Colin was interested in. He would forever be known by Europeans living in the Epulu area as an unusual man—more articulate, vocal, and sensitive than the other Mbuti.

As sophisticated as he might have seemed for a boy of sixteen in 1954, Kenge was still an Mbuti hunter, which meant that he might disappear into the forest at any moment and was unreliable in making appointments. On several occasions when Colin became angry and fired him, he interpreted his dismissals merely as authorized vacations. When Kenge had decided his holiday was over, he would show up for work. There was no question that Kenge would always return to Colin, however. Colin gave him food, money, and clothing, and admired him for his intelligence and his knowledge of the forest. Friends of Kenge say that Kenge felt he had qualities that set him apart from his neighbors, and Colin gave him the recognition that he would never get from his Mbuti peers.

Kenge was there for Colin in 1954, willing to abandon his job as chief bugler at the Epulu animal station, and he was there again in 1957. He and Colin often slept together in the forest. It is impossible to say whether Colin and Kenge had sex together. If they had and it had been discovered, Kenge might have been expelled from his camp, beaten or burned, as had happened with Mbuti men who had committed the crimes of having sexual intercourse with men, children, or goats. For while there is no stigma attached to physical affection between men, the act of sexual intercourse between men is quite another matter. But there is little doubt that Colin loved Kenge, and in the last years of his life he did confess to a friend that he had had a sexual relationship with an Mbuti who was, in all likelihood, Kenge. There is also little doubt that he and Kenge "made love." They made love to each other and to the forest, just as Colin believed he had made love with the spirit when he played the organ in Westminster Abbey. On that one memorable night when Colin saw Kenge dancing under the moonlight, making love with the moon, his view of life fell into place. He saw Kenge move silently and gracefully, his eyes closed as if he was drunk with the spirit of the forest. He saw Kenge's body, his well-defined muscles, and his skin glistening with the palm oil he had applied for good health, and he knew that the world Anandamayi Ma had told him might one day exist, if only he could make it real, was before him. Now he saw that the Mbuti, and not western civilization, would be his reality. The superiority of western civilization was a phantasm, and the line of progress pulling the primitive toward modernity was nothing but a rope of sand.

Colin's love for the forest emerged out of a series of such small revelations about beauty and goodness, and also out of his fascination with the molimo. Colin saw that the molimo was many things—a set of songs, a trumpet, a curing ritual, a festival. It was so central to the Mbuti religious life that if you could comprehend the molimo you were certain to understand the essence of Mbuti society. That essence turned out to be the rain forest itself; for the Mbuti the rain forest was their god, mother, and father. And, like a god or a parent, the forest is basically good. But sometimes, when life gets out of balance from illness, death, an individual's transition from one stage of life to another, or some inexplicable displeasure of the forest, there is noise and disharmony. If a major ritual is about to occur, like the elima, in which a girl's puberty is celebrated by secluding her in a sacred hut for months and fattening her for marriage, the molimo may be played to rid the forest of evil. The molimo is one of the effective ways of restoring quiet. Its songs are sung, indeed they have to be sung, in order to feed the molimo which in turn pleases the forest. The Pygmies place food on a central hearth, replace their village-style clothing with bark cloths, and at various times eat the offered foods together. As the days pass, the molimo trumpets themselves make their appearance. This is a sign that the molimo has been well fed, and that the forest is listening. The forest is the audience that must be awakened to the Pygmy's needs.

The trumpet can be made of different things. It can be a hollowed-out piece of wood or a piece of metal drainpipe. A molimo trumpet does not have a distinctive appearance, so no one trumpet will look exactly the same as another. What matters most is the sound, and the more intense the feeling aroused by its sound, the better the molimo. The Mbuti feed it, give it drink by dipping it in water, and breathe into it to give it life. They rub it with earth and place hot coals in one end. "All the elements are there," Colin wrote, "a glorious dramatic pageant so rich in symbolism that it could easily blind us to its even greater, non-rational, emotional power . . ." As the trumpet is played, and as the men sing their songs, there is a sudden crescendo. If the Mbuti want an echo badly enough, if they truly want to affirm their faith in the forest, the forest will answer. If the forest does not answer, the men say that perhaps not everyone sang, that perhaps someone ate a prohibited food, or perhaps people simply did not want to hear the echo badly enough. But when an answer comes, the Mbuti feel that they have become one with the forest, a oneness that Colin believed was as strong as their separateness from the villages.

Colin had found what he was looking for. The uncomfortable son of a Scottish father and Irish mother, a native of no place in particular, had found a place of acceptance. And the wizard of his childhood stories had found a people who could resist oppression and ridicule the oppressors. Meanwhile, for the sake of his professors and academic discipline, Colin Turnbull the anthropologist had discovered that the Mbuti could not be understood apart from the forest, for the forest itself was the Mbuti logic, the mechanism that kept their society together.

In a forest camp one night, as Colin was about to return to England, an elderly man named Old Moke said to Colin, "When the forest dies, we shall die." And when Colin left, and contemplated his memories of the camp in which he had lived, the magic of the forest was still within reach, and the song remained. ". . . For the song is the soul of the people and the soul of the forest. The molimo trumpet, now infinitely wistful and far away, took up the song and the forest echoed it on with its myriad magic sounds.

"It echoes on and on, and it will still be there when our short lives are silenced . . . until perhaps like us, it comes to rest in the deepest distance of some other world beyond . . . the dream world that is so real to the People of the Forest."

Colin returned to England but spent less than a month there before moving to New York City. But within a few weeks after starting work at the American Museum of Natural History, his euphoria turned to loneliness. He thought about Kumari often and decided that he could not comply with her wishes. From New York, Colin sent a formal letter of proposal to her. Months went by without a word from her. Finally, Colin received a short note from her saying that his letter had only just arrived in Bombay and that she had married two weeks earlier.

Her Indian husband was a rising star in the military, a man who would one day achieve the rank of vice admiral in the Indian navy. By that time, Colin had given up hope on Kumari, and he had already met Joe Towles. But Colin never forgot Kumari. He kept his only portrait of her, an ink drawing, with him until the early 1980s when Joe would destroy it in a jealous rage.

CHAPTER EIGHT

New York City

WHEN COLIN TURNBULL AND JOSEPH TOWLES met in 1959, the overall social environment in the United States may have provided certain freedoms, but popular and scientific sentiment still regarded homosexual sex as pathological, deviant, and immoral. Indeed, when one of Senator Lyndon Johnson's top aides, Walter Jenkins, was arrested for "lewd conduct" in a YMCA basement restroom, just as Johnson declared his interest in the presidency, Johnson demanded his resignation and the *New York Times* editorial page stated, "there can be no place on the White House staff . . . for a person of markedly deviant behavior."

The Jenkins incident took place at roughly the same time that Jim Ford, a well-known archaeologist at the American Museum of Natural History, wrote the museum's president Jim Oliver arguing that the museum had no place for a homosexual like Turnbull, informed the museum's security staff that Joe Towles, Colin's young African American friend and a volunteer at the museum, had been arrested for lewd conduct in a men's room in a West Side subway station, and demanded that Joe's security pass be confiscated.

Although Colin had some exposure to gay social circles and gay clubs during his last few years at Oxford, he never saw himself as a member of a gay community and seldom called himself gay. He found the words "gay," "straight," "queer," "homosexual," and "heterosexual" irrelevant. In England during the 1950s and early 1960s, gay was not a popular synonym for homosexual; in the States the term did not gain popularity until after World War II, and even then it was initially used with some humor. So when a friend sent Colin a postcard of a well-built nude man in January 1953 that read "Have a 'GAY' New Year!," Colin thought it was very funny. In general, he disliked terms such as gay, homosexual, and bisexual because they suggested that sexuality was an inner disposition that could define someone's social identity. He was not interested in being gay anymore than he was interested in being British.

He enjoyed being sexual with people he liked socially and overall he liked men better than women. If there was a difference between sex with women and sex with men it was that, like his parents, Colin always linked sex with women to procreation. He linked sex with men to more simple pleasures, but as he would soon discover, the pleasures he would find with Joe Towles were hardly simple. With the exception of some fantasies about having a family with Kumari, he had little desire to have children. If he was interested in being with someone socially and felt affection for them, sex merely extended the relationship in ways that were pleasurable.

Colin was twenty-four years old when he first had sex with a woman. It was 1949, on the ship to India, with the wife of a British air marshal. She was traveling with her two children to join her husband, already stationed in Pakistan. "She tried to get me into bed with her several times . . . perhaps she thought she was doing a noble service in getting me away from my Indian friends, with whom I spent most of my time. But it was also an older woman proving to other women that she could get a young male. She resorted to bribery, not with money but with good champagne, and all went well until, in the early hours of the morning, I heard, in the same cabin, her children who had woken up and started crying. I had not known they were there, and the realization that she could have sex with someone . . . right in front of her own children, appalled me. I left in a shocked huff, and she promptly disclaimed me to all her upper crust English friends as a nigger-lover."

By the fall of 1959, he was convinced that he should no longer try to have sexual relationships with women. While still at Oxford, Colin began long relationships with two younger men, Michael Elliot and David Quarrell; in fact, he seldom had short-term relationships and complained to his friends that so many homosexual men had hit-and-run liaisons that were purely sexual and emotionally distant.

Michael was a white British drama student who was openly gay. He self-consciously showed it in his mannerisms, gait, voice, and dress. It is hard to know what Colin was attracted to in Michael, for he had little positive to say about him. At the same time that Colin was seeing Michael, he started seeing David, a psychology student who was equally flamboyant, threw tantrums, and tended to exaggerate the intensity of his affections for various men. Although these relationships were put on hold when Colin took his new job at the museum, both men made plans to join Colin in New York. Michael wanted to try his luck acting in the States and Colin promised to help him in whatever way he could. David wanted to attend graduate school at Columbia. Before Colin left England on the *Queen Elizabeth* to sail to New York, David promised to join him. But a few days before the ship was scheduled to depart, David telephoned Colin at his parents' house to complain about his financial situation and tell him that an elderly and fabulously rich investor had asked him to come live with him. Given his precarious finances, David said, he had to accept. Colin actually knew the millionaire. He was an old queen well known to many young gay men at Oxford, and Colin had seen him drive by the campus in his Rolls-Royce. He was the sort of person, Colin wrote, "that made you feel unclean even by shaking hands with you." Colin told Michael about David's situation and Michael promptly stepped in to take David's place, if not on the *Queen Elizabeth* then in Colin's heart. Colin let Michael place a wedding band on his finger, and though Michael agreed to stay in London for the time being, they vowed to live together.

When Colin arrived in New York in August 1959, he found a large ground floor apartment in an old brownstone at 453 West Twenty-first Street, in the Manhattan district known as Chelsea. He had the entire floor with three rooms that offered plenty of space for his keyboards and African art. The front and middle rooms both had marble fireplaces, and there was a small, nine-by-nine-foot back room suitable for a study. By September 1, 1959, his first day of work at the American Museum of Natural History, a Steinway concert grand had been delivered and placed in the front room; he put a harpsichord, clavichord, and spinet in the middle room. As if the room was not crowded enough, he surrounded the instruments with African sculptures, masks, and bark cloths. Above the keyboards, he hung an ink drawing of Kumari. The apartment looked like the home of an eccentric academic, and Colin acted the part even when alone. He recalled in "Lover and Beloved" that "the place was so elegant that sometimes, after cooking my own make-shift dinner at night I would put on my tuxedo and eat in style, at the end of a long dining table. The idea of sharing this with anyone else was the last thing in my head. I had Kumari's portrait high on one wall in the middle room, and that was all the company I needed."

Only one other portrait graced his walls: a black and white photograph of Sri Anandamayi Ma. She was there to remind Colin of the hopes and ideals he had contemplated in India.

Gay people in New York City could meet each other easily at gay bars, but their locations were often secret, and they were constantly subject to police raids and closings. Only as late as 1966 did the New York City Police Department cease using undercover cops to trap homosexuals. New Jersey was no better, taking another year to overturn a longstanding regulation authorizing the police to shut down any commercial enterprise where "apparent homosexuals" congregated. The New York City regulation was enforced through the late sixties, resulting in the famous Stonewall riot of June 17, 1969, when the police raided one of the only places in the city said to be a safe retreat from everyday gay bashing and police harassment.

On a rainy Saturday night, October 24, 1959, Colin decided to go to the Mais Oui. The unmarked bar was small, inconspicuous, hidden in the basement of a hotel on West Seventieth Street between Columbus and Amsterdam Avenues. Turnbull had been in the company of a visiting Turkish archaeologist who, he complained in a note to himself, had a foul body odor and large breasts that she had tried to rub against him. The Mais Oui was a dark place, and with good reason, since few there wanted to be recognized. He moved through an awkward L-shaped room toward the dance floor; the place was mobbed.

Anyone at the Mais Oui or any gay bar in the city knew there were risks. You could be arrested and you could be outed. According to a former customer of the Mais Oui, it was not unusual for the management to turn on a warning light when it was suspected there was an undercover cop in the area. It was a terrifying experience not so much because of the risk of arrest, but because the music would stop, all the lights would go on, and everyone could see everyone else. In a moment, you could be outed, a frightening event even if those who saw you were also outed.

Although Colin had heard about the bar, he had avoided it because its location was too close to the museum. He did not keep his homosexual interests a secret, but he thought it neither appropriate nor in the best interests of his career to risk arrest or an encounter with someone he knew. Colin had been in his job less than two months. This Saturday night was his first visit and he found it intriguing. The crowd was more diverse than he expected. There were plenty of interracial couples, and he could hear a number of different languages being spoken. This was in part because the Mais Oui was on the Upper West Side, not far from Spanish Harlem, and well attended by Puerto Rican men. It was not a bar in which people engaged in sex—that sort of club emerged in the city only in the '70s—but it was distinctive. It was not an East Side bar, which is to say that it was not a quiet, elitist queen bar; it was blue collar, a dancing bar where people could do what was then called "rub-a-crotch" dancing. There was more body contact than one could ever find on the East Side. It was "funky, sexy, cruisy, smoky."

Around 10:30, a young black man was waiting at the Mais Oui for some friends from work. He tried to locate his beer among several opened bottles resting on the shelf in front of a window seat and murmured, "Where's my beer?" Turnbull, still wearing his raincoat—not sure whether he wanted to stay—heard him, pointed toward a bottle and said, "I think it's this one."

In his later years, Colin would recall this man as beautiful and enchanting: "I heard a voice beside me saying 'Has anyone seen my beer?' and my life as an adult began. To say my whole world changed would be no exaggeration, and to this day, over thirty years later, I would not have had it otherwise . . . He was young, well but modestly dressed, and moderately black . . . light chocolate in color . . . with neat, short, crinkly hair . . . Then I saw his eyes and those I *do* remember. They were open and clear and utterly honest. For a moment I thought I was back in Africa."

His name was Joe. Joseph Towles. He was twenty-two years old. In Colin he saw a tall man, handsome with brownish hair who, he believed, was not making a pass at him. When his friends did not show up, Colin invited him down to Greenwich Village for coffee. Joe had not brought a coat so they first went to his place to get one.

Joe was living just one block away from the bar, in a tiny apartment on the third floor of a small house on West Seventy-first Street. There was one bathroom for several tenants who all rented single rooms on the same floor. Joe had hung calico drapes and covered his bed with a delicate pink bedspread. In the middle of the room was a small wooden table and chair. On top of the table he had placed his old Smith Corona, on which he had slowly tapped out his first short story, "The Proper Mother," and had begun a long novel set during the Civil War, entitled "This Vale of Sorrow."

Despite the rain, Colin and Joe walked fifty blocks to Colin's apartment. Colin was stunned by Joe's beauty. Joe wanted to listen to Colin's stories about India and Africa forever. They were both captivated with each other and nervous. Both knew that they would spend the night together.

Joseph Allen Towles was born on August 17, 1937, in Senora, Lancaster County, Virginia to Arcellius Towles and Lucy Blair. He spent most of his early childhood with his grandparents, younger sister, Mary, and older brother, Charles, in Needmore, Tennessee, while his mother, in Virginia, cared for her youngest child, Glenmore. Their grandfather enjoyed telling them stories about the Civil War, especially about the gold said to be hidden in caves across the river from their house. The house sat on a bluff overlooking a wide river, and Joe, Mary, and Charles dreamed of finding the gold, even though they never looked very hard. The Towles children did not feel poor. They had plenty of food, affectionate grandparents, and several aunts and uncles nearby, including their Uncle Robert who had married a part-Cherokee woman. She stimulated Joe's interests in other cultures.

As a child, Joe was always smaller than his peers, at times bullied, at times adored for his cuteness. When he was twelve Joe learned to "play house" with an older, sixteen-year-old-boy, C., who lived next door. At first they made a little house in a barn with hay and old clothing. Fully clothed, C. would lie on top of him, rubbing himself to orgasm. But as time went on, Joe and C. began to sneak out of their houses at night to make love.

When he was fourteen, Joe left Tennessee to live with his parents in Virginia. Away from his doting grandparents, Joe began a period of isolation and insecurity. He told Colin that Glenmore had taken over his mother's love, and that his father seemed to prefer his older brother, Charles. He went to the local public school for blacks, A. T. Wright High School, which was closed after desegregation, where he studied hard as a way to escape his isolation at home. Joe soon distinguished himself as one of the brightest students in the school. He excelled in music, played the piano and organ, and wrote fiction. His class of twenty-four voted him "most likely to succeed." When he graduated in June of 1957, at the age of nineteen, he was valedictorian.

In Virginia, Towles was a famous name, though the ones who boasted about their name were white. The black Towles had the name only by virtue of having been the white Towles's slaves. The extended and wealthy Towles family emigrated from Liverpool in 1652 and settled along the Rappahannock River, where it empties into Chesapeake Bay. There is a small island between the Rappahannock and the Carotoman rivers that is still called Towles Point. The many white Towles families who still live there remember their history well and have kept good genealogical records; although the black Towles families have not kept comparable records, the continued presence of both white and black Towles in the same area serves as a perpetual reminder of their old slave relationship.

Joe did not feel particularly black, inferior, or oppressed in Tennessee. But in Virginia, the Towles legacy made him acutely aware of his blackness and the place of blacks in American society. Joe's few surviving relatives still own five acres of land in Virginia given to them in the nineteenth century when slavery ended. He did not experience much racism firsthand in Tennessee and he was not well informed about racist violence in the United States in general. Joe first saw the frightening white robes of the Ku Klux Klan in Virginia. And it was in Virginia that he first heard about lynchings and burnings and began to read about black history.

During Joe's high school years, his mother told him that he should not resent the white Towles, indeed the white Towles were their kin. Many of the black

Towles assumed that their blood was mixed with the blood of the white Towles. In the 1980s, Colin and Joe would begin a secret project on interbreeding. They searched through old genealogies in Lancaster County with the hopes that they would one day prove what most black people in Lancaster tacitly accepted: that the white and black Towles families were neither white nor black, but a mixture.

A generous and charismatic neighbor of the Towles family, known locally as Miss Queen, encouraged Joe to write fiction and to join her drama club. When he graduated, Miss Queen suggested that he could be a successful writer or actor. So he packed a small bag and headed by bus to New York. He was sure he could live with a distant cousin in Harlem until he got his own place, and that is exactly what he did. He worked at the Bible Mission Society during the day, and at night he attended an actors' center where he met other men with similar dreams. Within the first few weeks of his stay in New York, Joe got his own place on the Upper West Side, quickly made some friends, and realized that he was "something called gay." By the time Joe met Colin in 1959, he had been in New York for nearly two years, was working as a clerk at United Artists, and was expecting a raise and a promotion by the end of the year.

Colin and Joe spent Saturday night and all of Sunday together. They played duets on the piano, read the Sunday *New York Times,* talked, and dozed. For the next thirty years they would repeat the ritual. Every Sunday they would wake up early, get the Sunday paper, read it with breakfast, and fall asleep until the early afternoon. It is hard to imagine that Colin did not see something in Joe that reminded him of Kenge, the companion he had just left in Africa. Just under five-feet-nine, Joe was significantly shorter than Colin, who was six-feet-three, and when they slept together Colin would wrap Joe in his legs just as he had done with Kenge. And like Kenge, Joe came from a different world, about which Colin knew virtually nothing but was anxious to discover. Colin imagined that African American culture contained within it the same untapped brilliance of the Mbuti, that the same potential Kenge had shown Colin could be found in a people who had been subjugated and marginalized. And, by coincidence, both Kenge and Joe were born the same year, 1937.

On the surface, Joe and Colin shared few interests and had dramatically different backgrounds. Joe liked bright music and sunny days; Colin favored bagpipe or organ music played on rainy days. Next to Colin, the Oxford graduate and world traveler, Joe was uneducated, inexperienced, and had never been west of Tennessee. Colin immediately assumed the role of teacher, but not the Oxford tutor engaged in dialogue and verbal dueling—for as Colin was the first to admit, Joe could never win an argument with an Oxonian, let alone engage in one. Despite their differences, and perhaps because of them, Joe was thrilled about Colin. But his friends warned him that by getting involved with a wealthy, educated white, he was only setting himself up for disappointment. Colin loved their differences too. But he also wanted to teach and to nurture, to do for someone else what no one had done for him—not his mother (who was too demanding), his father (who was too distant), or Patrick Putnam (who died too soon). Joe gave Colin that opportunity.

For the first two weeks Joe and Colin knew each other, Joe spent as much time as possible in Colin's apartment, and Colin loved having him there. But after their third weekend together, Colin began to feel that his privacy was at risk. He needed to be in control of his life, his schedule, the objects in his apartment, his diet; he simply did not know how to negotiate his life with another person. The fast pace and intensity of the relationship was mind-boggling, and he feared the relationship was taking possession of him. Nonetheless, he continued to ask Joe to his apartment every weekend. They spent many passionate days together and were exhilarated by each other. In 1992, Colin would recall: "I wondered how I had agreed to let Joe come back again and invade this private place. In point of fact I was scared, because some deep feelings were aroused that I had not felt since I had been in love with Kumari. And I was scared because that reminded me of an obligation I had [to Michael] for whom I had once thought my feelings were just as deep, but which now I realized were not of the same order at all."

It took only a month before Joe told Colin that he was in love with him. And that was when Colin told Joe about Michael. Colin and Joe had known each other only a month, but Joe was devastated. His first question to Colin was whether Michael was black or white. Joe did not think he could compete with a white lover, but then Joe did not know Colin well. In being black, Joe had a decisive advantage over Michael.

Michael was, in effect, the first of many barriers Colin would erect between him and Joe; Michael would actually have little lasting importance to Turnbull or Towles, but he signaled the beginning of a pattern, a series of triangles consisting of Colin, Joe, and a variety of other intruders: Colin's job, Colin's parents, the death row inmates Colin would one day befriend, and Colin's real and imagined lovers.

On New Year's Eve 1959, Colin and Joe joined a large crowd outside the Astor Hotel in Times Square to watch the giant ball come down at the stroke of midnight. As the new year was announced, Colin pulled Joe close to him, trying to hold on as tightly as possible. Colin recalled, "Somehow I knew that this was not just the beginning of a new year, but the beginning of a whole new life. I did not see the symbolism, as it seems now, looking back, when as 1960 was born, the crowd surged so powerfully that Joe lost his footing and was torn out of my arms and disappeared down onto the ground. For a moment I was terrified that he would be crushed. I could hardly see him when I looked down."

A few weeks later, in late January 1960, Joe learned that his father, while walking home along the side of the road, had been accidentally struck and killed by a car driven by a young white man. Although Joe initially assumed the tragedy was racially motivated, he later met the man who hit his father and realized he was truly remorseful. Joe let himself into Colin's apartment with his own key and waited for him. When Colin came in, Joe raced toward him in tears. Colin held Joe in his arms, smoothed and stroked his skin, and told him that he would always protect and take care of him. When Colin was much older, he looked back on that day as a turning point, a moment that signaled a new commitment to Joe. Joe's father's death triggered something in Colin that went beyond empathy or sympathy. Many years later, Colin would recall that when he held Joe on that day, his first thoughts were about his future with Joe. Within a few days, Colin would make up his mind to terminate the relationship with Michael and commit himself completely to Joe. It would be a paternal role, to be sure.

Although Colin told Joe that his feelings for Michael were only of loyalty and obligation, Joe did not believe him. Joe began to write a diary in March 1960, only four months after he and Colin had first met, in part to record his frustrations and jealousy. He wrote the second entry on Tuesday, March 22. "I told him how much I wanted to be with him all the time and he again assured me of what he owed to Michael. I have come to hate this Michael who comes between us even though he is thousands of miles away in England." March 30: "I know there can never be another love for me"; March 31: "I am *with* Colin"; May 24: "I must spend my life with Colin." Later, on June 13, 1960, he wrote, "With Colin I open my heart and share my life—everything, but he never or seldom tells me personal things . . . Yet there seems a closeness between Colin and Michael of which even I am not dared to disturb." Joe promised himself that, if Michael came to the States, he would leave Colin. The same day he wrote: "Could I go on living without my love Colin, my treasure. Not feel his lips on mine, his arms about me? No—I'll be too weak. Everything will have gone from me." Joe did not yet know that the ring on Colin's finger had come from Michael.

That summer, as Joe began to record their relationship, he and Colin visited the Towles family in Virginia, staying one night at his mother's small house along the Rappahannock in Lancaster county. Joe's mother insisted that they come only under cover of darkness for fear that neighbors might notice a white man in her house. Colin made spaghetti for Joe's mother and brother Charles, after which Joe wrote, "They loved my Colin . . . I love Colin so much."

Joe's diary entries during the early 1960s consist almost entirely of passages about Colin, and they fall into two categories: expressions of love and descriptions of trips to concerts and museums. Although Colin did not keep a diary of his own, he wrote of his love for Joe in holiday cards. In fact, Colin and Joe would exchange cards without fail for thirty years, on New Year's Day, Valentine's Day, Easter, their birthdays, the anniversary of the day they met, Thanksgiving, and Christmas. When Joe died in 1988, Colin had filed away nearly 400 cards, and they are included in the Joseph A. Towles archive. Colin usually gave cards to Joe that read "To my wife Josephine," and Joe gave Colin cards addressed "To my husband." Colin's 1962 birthday card to Joe was printed with the words: "Happy Birthday to my Wife. I got wound up over you, the first time we met. And though time has passed, it's true, I haven't run down yet." Joe's 1962 birthday card to Colin said, "Six foot two, Eyes a bright blue, No one has a P.P. like you!"

Joe seldom made any references in his diary to sex, but some letters and cards show that the two were sexually playful and passionate with each other. Once when Colin came home, he found a note written on a piece of scrap paper (a note that was dated 1962 and years later discovered at the bottom of a box containing miscellaneous papers and objects from their New York apartment). It said, "Dear Colin, I.L.U.V.M.I. [I love you very much indeed]. I have felt good all day except an occasional rumbling of the tummy due to constipation in the lower bowel. This bowel will not turn loose no matter how hard I push. How is your bowel? See you shortly, I.L.U."

In Joe's diaries, the entries that concern daily life describe the numerous events they attended together, usually harpsichord concerts, operas, exhibit openings, and movies. These entries state that "Colin took me to . . ." or "Colin says he will take me to . . ." Joe gives the impression that Colin spent much of his time trying to introduce him to "high culture." One of Colin's greatest skills, manifested in nearly all areas of his personal and professional life, was his ability to stay on the acceptable side of the border between paternalism and condescension. He could be pedantic without sounding arrogant, he could guide without being supercilious. He justified his stewardship of Joe as the proper use of privilege and tried to ignore Joe's attempts to subvert their hierarchical relationship: Joe frequently called Colin "father" but Colin saw in that word humor rather than hostility. Colin remained in control of the relationship. He strongly encouraged Joe to pursue a career in modeling or in theater, and by August of 1960 Joe had auditioned unsuccessfully for a number of acting roles under the stage names of Thomas Towles and Glen Wesley (Wesley was an old family name, and Glen was his younger brother Glenmore's nickname).

Colin's spiritual history suggests that he was willing to give way to forces beyond his control and that he enjoyed the idea that his life course was a series of accidents. But the politics of everyday life were a different matter. Joe and Colin were now living together. Colin's privacy was gone; he eventually gave in to Joe's request to end his strict vegetarianism—Joe had refined culinary tastes and did not enjoy a vegetarian diet—but he believed that by changing his diet he had failed Anandamayi Ma. He would lose his temper whenever he felt that Joe was trying to control him. Sometimes their fights became violent.

There were times during the first two years of their relationship when Colin was completely occupied with his book, *The Forest People,* which he had arranged to publish with Simon & Schuster. *The Forest People* (1962) would be the first book his young editor Michael Korda ever published. The son and nephew of two of the most well-respected figures in early motion pictures, and a fellow graduate of Magdalen College, Korda was a rising star in the publishing world. In his memoirs, Korda writes that he got Simon & Schuster to give Colin an advance on royalties of $5,000, a large advance for an unpublished academic author in 1960 and almost equal to Colin's annual salary of $5,400 at the museum. Although the contract states that Colin actually received an advance of only $1,500, the book would have been worth $5,000. It became an immediate best-seller in the early sixties and again in the early seventies, and remains in print after nearly four decades. The book also helped launch Korda's publishing career. He is currently the editor-in-chief of Simon & Schuster.

In April 1960, Colin was at home typing *The Forest People* at his desk, concentrating hard. Joe begged Colin to pay attention to him. Colin tried to ignore him but Joe persisted. Furious, Colin picked up the typewriter and hurled it across the room. Joe calmly picked up the damaged machine, returned it to Colin's desk, and went to the bathroom to cry. One wonders how resentful or humiliated Joe felt when, months later, he patiently typed out the final draft of *The Forest People* at Colin's request on the same typewriter. A month later, Joe was not begging; he was teasing. Colin asked him to stop but Joe continued. He grabbed Colin's waist to pull him closer. As Joe nuzzled his head into Colin's chest, Colin took the half-smoked cigarette in his hand and plunged it into the top of Joe's hand. The burn left a permanent scar.

"I ran into the bedroom and cried," Joe wrote to his diary. "Colin followed and told me he was very temperamental and that I shouldn't have teased him. I said I was sorry and we made up."

Colin remembered the event somewhat defensively in 1993: "Tickling actually makes me physically nauseous and I was trying my best to stop him, both by struggling and by pleading, but with no success. He was too strong and he would not listen. Finally, in desperation, I pushed the burning cigarette I was holding down onto one of his hands, since I could not break his grip any other way. He looked as though I had shot him, and just let go and left me, sitting alone, knowing I had done something wrong, but blaming him for it. We soon made up, as usual, but he never let me forget that incident."

In a June 1960 diary entry, Joe wrote of his concerns about Colin, "My darling frightens me."

Despite the fact that Colin intended to end the relationship with Michael, Joe remained distraught. Colin told Michael about Joe, and Michael responded by writing hurtful letters to Joe but sending them to Colin. Colin could have easily kept the letters to himself, but instead he passed them all on to Joe. In most of them, Michael wrote that Joe was merely a diversion for Colin, that Colin was committed to his much longer and more substantial relationship with him, and that Colin was not someone to abandon his commitments. Michael told Joe about the ring, and Joe promised his diary on July 2 that he would not ask Colin to take it off. Equally disturbing to Joe was that Colin always kept a letter from Michael in his coat pocket. In late July, 1960, Colin and Joe's first summer together, Colin visited his parents in England and, of course, he would see Michael too. Though Colin promised Joe that he would terminate the relationship with Michael, Joe wondered if he would return alone or with Michael.

Colin would be staying a long three weeks and that made it hard to say goodbye to Joe. The mechanics of the departure were also frustrating because Colin and Joe wanted to embrace and kiss and yet, in public in those days, they knew they could only shake hands—not only because they were both men but also because they were not the same race.

On the plane, Colin was discomforted by the thought of all his commitments. Committed to Joe. Committed to his parents. Committed to Michael. Committed to the museum and his career. And when Colin was finally in England, sitting in his parent's comfortable living room in their comfortable neighborhood, he wanted to be committed only to Joe. Irritable and hot, Colin watched with disdain as his father read a politically conservative newspaper, *The Daily Telegraph.* In, "Lover and Beloved," Colin's account of his relationship with Joe, he wrote: "My father rustles *The Daily Telegraph,* which I think he keeps just so that he can lose himself in it when he senses the slightest friction in the household. And the fact that this is the paper he reads openly, whereas he looks at the *Times, Manchester Guardian* or *Observer* whenever he thinks nobody is looking, is a sign that he too is committed. Committed to an ultra right wing conservatism, racist and colonialist, in which he no longer believes but refuses to abandon. And as if to make my homecoming as unhappy as possible, from behind those messy pages he tells us there is a report on those 'blacks' making a nuisance of themselves in London again."

On this trip, Colin was especially sensitive to the house and neighborhood; he found the whole scene, including the street names, to be affected and staged. To get to his parents' house one had to go past mansion-sized faux Tudor and Georgian-styled residences into a private development, then up Silver Lane to Verulam Avenue, down to Rose Walk, and up to Briar Hill. The lawns were manicured; the residents were white. At the house, the chauffeur was washing the car, the housekeeper was cleaning, the gardener was on his way, yet there was no one to talk to. To friends, Colin sometimes called Dot "the blimp," not because she was obese but because she seemed to hover around him without the capacity to engage in meaningful conversation. Colin felt overwhelmed by her. During his stay, she ran the show as she always had, making most of the decisions about Colin's schedule, and despite the fact that she had a chauffeur, she did almost all of the driving herself.

To wile away the time on these tedious visits, Colin liked to play his mother's Beckstein grand piano. "I don't play that well," he wrote about those visits, "but being committed parents they refuse to acknowledge my mediocrity in anything. Even as a nigger lover, they ultimately came to realize, I am far from mediocre." When Colin did play, he almost always played Scottish ballads, not only because he truly loved them and did not know any Irish songs, but because he knew they made his father burst with Scottish pride. If Colin and his father had little in common, at least they shared a profound love for Scotland.

During his second day in England, Colin sat in the living room fuming, annoyed by the preciousness of it all. He fiddled with the gold wedding band Michael had given him to cement their marriage, and waited for something to happen. The phone rang. It was Michael.

Colin's mother and father knew full well about the relationship but they never used the word "homosexual," at least not in Colin's presence. They were convinced that Colin's relationships with men could only be temporary, and they expected that Colin would marry a woman and have children just as much as they expected Colin's male lovers to do the same. Dorothy was ambivalent about Colin's intimate relationships with men, and certainly not happy with Michael's mother. When Michael's mother had learned, only a few weeks earlier, that Colin did not intend to honor his commitment to Michael, she was enraged. She phoned Colin's mother, threatening to sue the Turnbulls for breach of promise and to report to the U.S. immigration authorities that Colin was a homosexual and should be deported. Michael later apologized for his mother's behavior but the damage was done and hard feelings would linger. There was a bright side; Colin's parents supported any move by Colin to break away from Michael.

Colin went to the phone; he found Michael angry. He said he was glad Colin had not brought his "nigger boy" with him. They agreed to meet at Hampstead Heath in the north of London, outside under the sun where they could walk together in the fields. Michael seemed resigned to their break up. Colin was still wearing the ring, though he intended to give it back. Michael was generous in his best wishes to Colin, and confessed that he would not be coming to the States. If the conversation was dull, that was fine with Colin, since from Colin's perspective the entire purpose of the meeting was to end the relationship. And yet, when Colin left Michael and got to Victoria Station, he realized the ring was still on his finger. Michael made a note of that and went home to write a letter to Joe telling him so.

At the train station, Colin tried unsuccessfully to reach Joe by phone so he sent him a telegram instead saying that his relationship with Michael was completely over and instructing Joe to ignore any letters he might receive from Michael. When Colin heard that Michael had written to Joe about the ring, he sent a telegram telling Joe to pay no attention: the Western Union dispatch read, "MJE [Michael J. Elliot] SAYS DISREGARD LETTER ALL WELL MUCH LOVE." The next day Colin sent Joe a birthday card, saying how sorry he was he could not be with him. On the card, he wrote "Happy Birthday" in German, English, Italian, Tibetan, Swahili, French, and Hindi; and then, in Swahili, he wrote "Ninataka kutomba we!" ["I want to have sex with you!"] He added, "My sweet, I am so sorry you must have been terribly worried by Mike's letter. But by now you will have had his second letter and mine . . . I know you will understand that this is a very hard and difficult time for Mike much more than for us, because he faces nothingness . . . We MUST somehow find a way of helping Mike." Four days later, Joe wrote Colin that he was broke and asked for money.

Despite the apparent finality, however, Michael called Colin inviting him to the theater and Colin agreed to accompany him. Perhaps he felt sorry or indebted to him in some way, but Joe remained mystified about the true nature of their relationship. Colin would continue to keep Joe in the dark, and for the rest of their lives he kept much of his personal life and those feelings that ran counter to his idealization of his love for Joe to himself. There could certainly be much more to the story but it died with Colin. That evening at the theater was the last time Colin saw Michael, and there is no record of further correspondence between them. Colin never returned the ring. He stored it with other keepsakes in a small metal box, and its presence never ceased to annoy Joe.

Colin now took on the futile project of convincing his parents that Joe was a dream come true. His father asked a lot of questions about Joe's future earning potential and the breakdown of their food and rent expenses in New York, while his mother stubbornly asked for the names of Joe's girlfriends and which one he was likely to marry. Colin was honest about the nature of his relationship with Joe, and though his parents acknowledged that Colin and Joe were romantically involved, they could not accept that the relationship was enduring or homosexual. It was not only that they feared for Colin's morality. He was now their only son, the only one other than their grandson, David, who could carry on Jock's name into subsequent generations. Colin wrote to himself, "I sensed danger and gave up my attempt to introduce Joe to them by long distance." He naively thought, "They would see for themselves when they came out to visit us the next year. Then how could they fail to love him almost as much as I did?"

On October 23, 1963, Joe pasted to his diary a typed reminder: "Tomorrow is my wedding anniversary." Joe was now twenty-six, Colin thirty-eight. They had been together for four years and lived together in Colin's place on Twenty-first Street. As a couple, Joe and Colin entertained a wide circle of friends. The most common visitors to their apartment included Anne Putnam, Anne's good friend Eugenia Earle, Thubten Norbu (the Dalai Lama's eldest brother, and a colleague from the museum), and the anthropologist Peter, Prince of Greece, to whom Colin had been introduced by Norbu. The prince was the son of the famous psychoanalyst, Marie Bonaparte, who had rescued all of Sigmund Freud's papers from certain destruction by the Nazis and helped settle him in England. The prince's mother was also close to the anthropologist Bronislaw Malinowski and the anthropologist and first president of Kenya, Jomo Kenyatta, with whom she and her son vacationed in St. Moritz. When these famous friends visited and talked of their travels, Joe felt like a bystander. Joe wrote passionately in his diary about Tibet and his desire to see the Himalayas, about anthropological fieldwork and Africa, and his envy of Colin's intellectual relationships with such worldly people.

It was at this time, that Colin and Thubten Norbu began a collaboration on a book about Tibet as seen through Norbu's eyes, as a child and as the reincarnation of the sixteenth-century Tibetan monk and teacher Taktser. For the most part, Norbu dictated the book, and Colin used his writing skills to craft Norbu's narrative into a meaningful whole. The purpose of the book, Colin wrote, was to help Norbu resolve a conflict between his past and present, for Norbu had once been a respected monk and was now an academic at the museum, having renounced his Holy Orders. But though he was physically separate from Tibet and was not available to enlighten monks and build monasteries, he could teach the world about Tibet and thereby fulfill his obligation to carry out the teachings of Taktser, who now inhabited his body. The book, *Tibet,* was published in 1968 by Simon & Schuster with Michael Korda as editor, and it brought Colin and Norbu together in a friendship that would last twenty-five years.

In the early 1960s, Colin's Canadian relatives came to New York with increasing frequency, and Joe and Colin took several trips to Toronto where they stayed with the Gravely family. Joe was unable to sense that any of the cousins were concerned about his race or the nature of his relationship with Colin, and he was right. Nevertheless, the cousins did not like him. They saw him as a spoiled brat, someone sadly insecure and pretentious. Some of them denied the intensity of Joe and Colin's love life, refusing to see it as anything more than sex, and at least one cousin convinced herself that Colin and Joe were not lovers at all but simply good friends.

On one occasion at the Gravelys', Joe woke up late in the morning and saw the remains of Colin's breakfast in the sink. Joe told Colin's aunt, Kitty, that he wanted a soft-boiled egg like Colin's, but that he wanted his egg cooked for twelve minutes. Kitty replied, "Well, I might as well give you a golf ball." Infuriated, Joe stormed out of the house, and Colin and Joe departed for New York the next day on bad terms with Kitty. Pat Gravely remembers that on those visits everyone was "walking on egg shells."

Colin, Pat says, tried to remain always within listening distance to Joe: "If Joe got in over his head, which he often did, or even if we disagreed with his opinion on some political or social matter, Colin would come to the rescue and bail him out somehow." In this respect, Joe resembled Dot. Her siblings, nieces, and nephews remember that Dot, like Joe, would often attempt to say something in conversation about a famous philosopher or painter about whom she had only superficial knowledge, and then when engaged or questioned would find herself on the defensive, feeling angry, hurt, and ridiculed.

Joe was most suspicious of nonrelatives, especially women. In April 1963, Colin invited Anne's friend Eugenia Earle, who had become his harpsichord teacher, out to dinner and to see the new movie *Lawrence of Arabia* with him and his Canadian cousins. Joe stayed at home sick with the flu and fumed about the possibility that Colin and Eugenia might be involved romantically. The whole group came back to the apartment and talked and drank almost until dawn. "I lay in bed," he wrote, "feeling miserable while the party went on.

"Colin came in and I gave him a hard slap, my first. I was really mad that he had a party while I was so sick. But it went on until 4 A.M. at which time he drove Eugenia home. When he finally lay down beside me I was so glad I forgave him. I must try and be more gentle with him. I must make this marriage work. Now almost four years together and I want it to grow stable . . . As always, we made love and everything was fine. I love Colin with all my being and if I lost him I don't know what I would do. He is a wonderful guy, the best! I must be better to him—he deserves more and more than me."

Despite the fact that Joe and Colin's relationship appeared solid to their friends, neither was convinced of the other's commitment. They never would be. Colin had told Joe that he was committed to him for life, but he was not so sure about Joe's commitment to him. Joe in turn wrote in his diary that Colin might leave him at any time. The frequency and intensity of their holiday card exchanges, and their mutual fear that the other would forget to send one, was emblematic of this insecurity.

Out of this uncertainty, both placed great importance on a long trip they planned to make to Europe in 1963. Colin hoped that the trip would prove his love for Joe; Joe thought it would cement the relationship they had been building. Beyond these hopes, and far less often stated, was their longing to be accepted by Colin's family in England. Colin continued to try to persuade himself that his parents were capable of loving Joe as he did.

When they began to make plans for the trip, money became an issue. Colin framed the trip as a gift to Joe, and Colin took secret pleasure in the fact that he had made possible a trip that Joe could never afford. "It was our trip, our honeymoon, but I was the giver," Colin recalled in notes written years later. It is not just that Colin loved the dominant position of the giver; he never trusted Joe with money. Joe liked expensive hotels, elegant restaurants, art and souvenirs. Colin saw himself as someone who lived modestly.

Giving the trip the appearance of equality, Colin and Joe went to the bank together, withdrew money from Colin's account, converted it to travelers' checks, and divided it evenly into two. But Colin would pay for all the transportation. Although he knew he could afford first class accommodations on *The France,* in 1963 one of the most elegant ships at sea (first launched in 1962 and still sailing today under the name *The Norway*), he booked a two-berth room in tourist class (another name for second class), which Colin considered modest but which Joe called "deluxe." Colin knew he would be seasick, that it would annoy Joe, and that it would threaten the total enjoyment of the trip. But he did not seriously consider flying. This is how he wanted it to be, for everyone to see a grand send-off. And it was a spectacular ship, hailed as a marvel at the time, and carrying more than 2,000 passengers.

Colin later recalled, "A number of friends came on board to see us off, but the best was when we were up on the top deck, almost by ourselves, and the ship's horn blasted its warning that we were about to leave. It was as though we were casting ourselves loose, leaving our old lives behind, and if this was how we were to start our new life together, how could it ever be anything less than perfect?"

When they got to the cabin, they found that friends had sent flowers and cards wishing them well. Michael Korda had sent a bottle of champagne. Two friends showed up with a boxed set of "The Alexandra Quartet" for Colin and

Joe to read on the trip. The whole scene was one that resembled more a honeymoon than a trip abroad, and this is exactly what Colin and Joe wanted, and why Colin did not want to fly: a ritualized "bon voyage." On that day, Joe told his diary, "We were going out into the world together, as one."

As *The France* left New York and passed under the Verrazano-Narrows Bridge, it was just Joe and Colin. Thirty years later, Colin would recall that as they passed the Statue of Liberty, he pulled Joe toward him and whispered, "I love you."

In their efforts to make the trip entirely perfect, Eugenia Earle, also a passenger on the same ship, was the only potential thorn in their side: both believed she was in love with Colin; in Spain in 1966 Colin would tell a friend that Eugenia had, in fact, declared her love for him. Certainly Colin was attracted to her music skills. (Eugenia remains a concert level harpsichordist today.) They met at the museum when she enrolled in his African music course. She would also sell Colin a prized flute that he took to Africa and that Eugenia had purchased from the former principal flutist of the New York Philharmonic, Julius Baker. Colin and Joe thought that she had made sure to be on the same boat and Joe, at least, imagined that Eugenia had fantasized that she was Colin's fiancée on a voyage to meet her future in-laws. Eugenia recalls today that she was attracted to Colin, wanted to be intimate with him, knew that the relationship would not happen, and tried to keep her distance. Eugenia, from the Veranda deck, above Colin and Joe, looked down and saw them standing close together in the wind against the backdrop of the Statue of Liberty. "Colin looked like his teacher," she said.

Joe thought he would resent Eugenia being on the ship but he actually found her enjoyable; she kept her distance, chose the second seating for dinner when she found that Joe and Colin had chosen the first, and intended only to make certain that she introduced herself to Colin's parents when the ship docked in England. Colin saw her at one point during the voyage and said, "You disappeared!"

For many people, the pleasure of travel lies less in reaching a single desired end than in reaching the points along the way. That was surely the case here. Before they arrived in Southampton, Colin and Joe luxuriated on the ship. They ate and drank well, Joe tolerated Colin's seasickness with only a few outbursts of anger—he seems to have had a hard time empathizing with Colin's nausea—and, because the trip and meals were prepaid, they delighted in being free of at least one constant public worry: the question of who would pay the bills or even who would get the bills. When they were out at restaurants, the bill would be brought automatically to Colin, a pattern they could only interpret racially—when confronted by a mixed-race couple, waiters assumed the white would pay.

Reality set in on shore. There were Mr. and Mrs. Turnbull (Mr. and Mrs. T, as Joe would call them) and their chauffeur, and to Joe and Colin's surprise, they were as distant and cold to Eugenia Earle as they were to Joe. Eugenia recalls that Colin shook hands with his father in a stiff, formal manner, and that his mother was also distant. She seemed to have no interest in finding out who Eugenia might be. Eugenia did not know much about Dorothy, except that she was a doting mother with whom Colin had fought often and who had always sent Colin homemade marzipan cakes on his birthday, even though Colin hated marzipan. Both Joe and Colin attributed Dot's coldness toward Eugenia to her sex; as a woman, she was more of a threat to Dot's hold on Colin than Joe. Although Dot always hoped Colin would marry a woman and have children, neither Colin nor his relatives could imagine Dot with a daughter-in-law. She was far too possessive to permit it.

Indeed, Dot had become so distressed by the thought of Colin intimately involved with a woman that she began to support his emerging romantic interests in men. Colin and his mother would use the same means for opposite ends: she encouraged him to love men so that she could keep him for herself; he loved men in part to escape from her. She eventually became less worried about whether Colin was homosexual and more concerned about what kind of man he wanted. When Colin brought Joe to England, she complained not about Joe's race but about his lack of success, and once, in exasperation, asked her husband and grandson, "If he was going to bring home someone black, why couldn't it have been someone like Seretse Khama?" The question was pregnant with irony, humor, and foreboding: just after World War II, Seretse Khama, an African prince and heir to the chiefdom of the Tswana, the man who would become the first president of Botswana, had married a white, English woman named Ruth Williams. In response, the British colonial government removed him as chief and exiled both Seretse and Ruth to England.

The chauffeur drove them all to the Turnbull house in Purley, but Dot sat in front and seldom looked back. When they reached the house and were eventually face to face, Dot was irritable. Jock escaped to work and, during the day, Dot spoke mostly to the housekeeper and Colin, making Joe feel excluded and depressed. Colin was angry with his mother, but he was also frustrated by Joe. What could he have expected?, Colin asked himself. Had he not listened to everything Colin had told him on the way over about how stifling the house would feel, that his mother would be overbearing, that Purley was boring, and that he was better off staying in London?

After only two days, Joe agreed to go to London and stay with Dudley Stevens, a good friend of Colin's from Oxford. By the time of their visit, Dudley was making a good living in the theater. He is best known in England for having played the Machiavellian landowner John Sackville in the popular British soap opera "Crossroads," a part that earned him a hard punch in the nose from an angry viewer who saw Dudley on the street and confused him with the evil character he played.

When Colin dropped Joe off at Dudley's house, Joe began to cry. Colin knew he would have to invite Joe back to Purley, and Joe did subsequently return for two short visits. They were unpleasant. Joe slept alone in one of the three bedrooms. Colin stayed in the room in which Jock normally slept and Dot stayed in her own room. Their grandson, David, slept on a cot in the hallway, and Jock slept on a sofa. Dot criticized Joe's clothing and the way he held his knife and fork, and she tested his minimal knowledge of British history. She gave every sign of hating Joe, and Joe hated her in return. Perhaps they knew that, at some level, they resembled each other. Both were seen by their friends and family as snobs and social climbers, and both were possessive of Colin.

They all went sightseeing together. On the grounds of Herstmonceux Castle, Joe noticed a peach tree with ripe fruit on its branches. He picked three—one for Colin, one for Dot, and one for himself. Dot exploded. She said that Joe was rude and ordered him to return the peaches to the base of the tree. Colin defended his mother's attitude, telling Joe that he should have been arrested. The next morning was the day of Martin Luther King's March on Washington. Joe came to the breakfast table wearing a button designed for the march. Dot began to speak about the inappropriateness of political demonstration and asked Joe to remove the button: "You are in England now and people in England do not approve."

Colin took the opportunity to visit with his academic advisor Rodney Needham at Oxford, who was waiting for Colin to make some progress on his thesis. It would take him four more years to finish it and earn his doctorate. *The Forest People* had been published with a lot of fanfare, but it was a popular book, far from what was required for a D.Phil. While Colin was at Oxford, Joe returned to Dudley's place in London, where he met an African student from what was then Southern Rhodesia, and in his diary asked himself, "More and more things are pointing me to Africa, or is this just wishful thinking?"

When they got to Paris, Colin and Joe stayed near the Sorbonne in a small hotel in the Latin Quarter among the bookshops and cafes; Colin had some work to do at the Musée de l'homme and other museums in Europe, trying to secure certain works of African art for the Africa Hall he was designing at the museum in New York. He kept in close contact with Harry Shapiro about the availability and costs of the objects. From there, they went to Amsterdam where they envied the Dutch for their gay bars, which Colin said were "neither covert nor brazen" in contrast to the New York bars. Joe visited Anne Frank's house and it left a strong impression on him. He noted in his diary that her experiences resonated with his own experiences of oppression.

In Heidelberg, they visited Joe's younger brother Glenmore, a tall thin clumsy man stationed there with the U.S. army. Things did not go well. Colin felt that Glenmore acted the older brother, resented Joe's 4F classification as an admitted "homosexual" that permitted him to avoid military service, and could not accept Joe as a gay man in an interracial relationship. They therefore left Heidelberg more than a day early to go on to Austria. As he reflected on Germany, Joe wrote to his diary, "I must say some of the young men here are the most handsome I have ever seen. The boy who served us breakfast on the day we left was a picture of beauty. I wondered what he would have looked like in a Nazi uniform."

At Innsbruck, Joe began to feel the fatigue of the trip and Colin began to sulk. "There is nothing to stop me from going out and enjoying the place by myself" he said in "Lover and Beloved," as if he were writing at that time. "But right now I am just sulking because I know very well that I would enjoy absolutely nothing without Joe enjoying it too. I think back on the good times we have had on this trip, and I can hardly remember what we actually did or saw, all I really remember is the rather smug feeling of self-satisfaction of knowing that Joe was enjoying himself and that somehow I was responsible. Not a very nice feeling, so I am not in a very good mood. Joe says he may feel better after dinner, and perhaps we can go out then and see what is going on. Why am I more concerned about his enjoying himself than I am about his health? He really does have a bad cold! . . . Hell, I just don't know what is right. I know I am wrong, but I also know how right is my love for him, and his for me. And I know that somehow I am letting him down, and he feels it."

CHAPTER NINE

The Museum

COLIN SUSPECTED THAT THE MUSEUM ADMINISTRATION might be racist and homophobic, but he thought that the department of anthropology was different. Colin and Joe attended department parties together, invited all the curators and staff to their own parties, and Joe had a security pass that gave him considerable freedom within the museum. Prior to the events involving an archaeologist named James Ford, there were only two moments that gave them pause, and both involved Joe and Margaret Mead. Once when Joe passed Mead in the hallway, he greeted her with the name Margaret; she replied "It is Dr. Mead." On another occasion, she warned Joe not to attend departmental functions meant for the curators; although she didn't mind homosexuality, she said, others might not be so kind.

In the early 1960s many of the anthropologists at the American Museum of Natural History lived side-by-side in Tarrytown, New York, roughly 40 miles from the museum. Several years before Colin arrived, David Rockefeller offered to sell the curators a large plot of land that they could subdivide to build new homes. Harry Tschopik, Jim Ford, and Gordon Eckholm all built modest homes there. Their relationships with each other were so tense that the development became known as Squabble Hill. When Colin came to the museum in 1959, he could not have imagined the level of childishness he would find. Margaret Mead and Colin Turnbull, neither of whom lived in Tarrytown, seem to have been the only two who absented themselves from all the trickery. Both were polite and distant from their colleagues—according to her biographer, Mead was seen as humorless—and, as a result, both Colin and Margaret were less subject to harassment by the pranksters. Colin's distance, however, made him more subject to rumor and gossip. When he first arrived at the museum, some staff believed that Colin had previously been a successful writer of French pornography and that the many species of parasites called Turnbullensis had been named after him. Much later, a number of anthropologists and philanthropists associated with the museum became convinced that he was the famous novelist Trevanian, who wrote *The Eiger Sanction* and other mysteries; they believed that he was pictured in a full-page photograph of the back of a man's head, published in *New York* magazine during the early 1970s with the caption "Is this man Trevanian?"

Much of the trickery was led by Jim Ford, an icon in American archaeology. When Jim Ford took the claw of a large bear from the museum and made footprints in the snow on some lawns in Tarrytown—a prank originally aimed at Harry Tschopik—residents were alerted, children were kept indoors, and the police and animal control departments were mobilized at great expense. And when Ford and the famous archaeologist Gordon Willey were together in the Viru Valley in Peru, Ford gave him some carefully selected potsherds from an outstanding archaeological site but lied about their location. Ford said the sherds came from a remote part of the valley; as a result Willey spent much time and effort conducting a futile survey on a precarious peak. Knowing that Willey had a fear of heights, Jim intentionally lured Gordon to a slope so steep it would put him in a panic.

Jim Ford was born in Water Valley, Mississippi, in 1911. Although he never did well in school and seemed to like excavation far more than he liked books, he became a powerful innovator in archaeology. It is common knowledge among those who knew Ford well that he was a poor writer and that his wife, Ethel, wrote many of his papers for him without recognition. He made his name directing archaeological work in Louisiana and by excavating a rich site at Poverty Point, Louisiana. (He later provided first framework for the prehistory of native Americans in the eastern United States.) At six foot five, Ford was an imposing presence. He had a big ego and he liked to drink hard. Ford probably did not belong in New York City because he found it difficult to interact with northerners, Jews, and homosexuals. He had few students. He complained often and loudly about the museum, arguing that he was by far the most productive member of the anthropology faculty and that unproductive researchers ought to be fired.

Ford once accidentally discovered conservationists throwing Peruvian botanical artifacts in the trash. It seems an ethnobotanist had died and the museum staff did not know what to do with all the material. Ford was smart enough to know it was wonderful stuff, so he took it and stored it in his office. One of Ford's colleagues was another botanist who worked in Peru. Every week, Ford took a bit of the material, opened the botanist's office when he was not there, and placed it on his desk. He soon began to leave notes along with the specimens telling the botanist that he was an anonymous donor and would be in touch in the near future. The botanist was thrilled and confused. Soon the colleague's office was crammed with botanical specimens, but sadly—at least from Ford's perspective—the botanist died before the denouement.

Ford also had stationery made for a fictitious plantation owner and used it to write letters to another well-known archaeologist named Jimmy Griffin. Griffin had just completed an exhaustive archaeological survey in Mississippi and was certain he had been thorough. Posing as a Mississippi plantation owner from the area in which Griffin had worked, Ford wrote about an enormous quantity of wonderful material that Griffin had missed, and Ford, who knew American archaeology better than anyone, was able to describe the objects in such a way that upset Griffin. Ford told him about artifacts with features that he knew would fit perfectly with Griffin's hypotheses.

In the early 1960s, Junius Bird and Ford together informed the city of New York that emergency salvage archaeology was required in Times Square. They did not intend to do any such thing, but thought it would be great fun to see if they could actually get permission to do it. The city responded by closing off Times Square to all traffic for several hours, during which time Bird and Ford were nowhere to be found. They were celebrating their achievement over a bottle of champagne. They suffered no repercussions.

Ford disliked the new arrival Colin Turnbull intensely. He thought Margaret Mead's popular anthropology and the popular study of the Pygmies Turnbull was in the process of writing were not at all scientific and thus of no use to the museum. And when Colin started a chamber orchestra that practiced at lunchtime on the fifth floor, filling the halls with music, Ford remarked that it was "C-R-A-P." By the summer of 1960, Colin had been working at the museum for less than a year. Yet Ford was already perturbed by the African American man named Joe Towles who kept coming up to the fifth floor to see Colin, and he schemed both to play tricks on Colin and to find a way to prevent Joe from coming to the department.

Ford had a good friend named George Quimby at the Field Museum in Chicago, and together they planned an elaborate, phony correspondence with Colin, the entire purpose of which was simply to harass him, waste his time, and frustrate him. In order to conceal his identity, Ford mailed the letters for Colin to Quimby who, in turn, mailed them to Colin so that they would have a Chicago postmark. Quimby wrote Ford on July 1, 1960, to inform him that the first letter was mailed to "T." with his own residence as the return address. Some days later he wrote Ford another letter to tell him that he had collected wrapping paper with Chicago postmarks and stamps. "You could use this," Quimby wrote, "to fake packages at your end. T. has my sympathy. You are entangling him with a family that would give fits to an Englishman from Oxan [*sic*]."

Ford pretended to be four different people: Mrs. Helen Quigly, Mr. Walter Williams, the Rev. Dr. Alfred Wollensack, and the Rev. Dr. Nicodemus Lovelace. He left only one clue to the hoax. Every one of these people misspelled heathen as "heathern." In the first letter, Helen Quigly wrote Colin to say that she had some "heathern [sic] idols" collected by her recently deceased uncle, Reverend Sam Houston Williams. Houston, she said, was a missionary who had collected the idols in Africa. Now that he was dead, she did not know what to do with them. She said that, since they were "heathern idols," it would probably be best to burn them. She stated that her pastor, Nicodemus Lovelace, of the Fourth Baptist Church in Chicago, had encouraged her to do so.

A photograph of the objects was included in her letter. It showed four outstanding works of art that Ford had discovered in the bowels of the African collection at the museum. Since Colin had been at the museum less than a year, Ford was fairly certain that Colin knew nothing about them, or at least he was certain that Colin would not recognize them.

In the next letter, Walter Williams—Sam's brother, and Helen's uncle—wrote to say that he was taking control of the sale because Helen's son was encouraging her not to sell them, not to burn them, but to keep the objects in their possession.

> As you must have gathered from correspondence, my dear niece Helen is not a business woman. Like many mothers, she listens too readily to her badly spoiled sixteen-year-old son who, I am sorry to say, is very opinionated, a bit of a "beatnick." For these reasons, I have agreed to relieve her of the burden of my late brother's affairs.
>
> Having made certain investigations into the market available, I deem the price of $20.00 (Twenty Dollars) each would be a fair remuneration for these articles. I wish to assure you that my purpose in marketing these idols is to add to the memory and purposes of the dedicated life of my Sainted Brother. The $80 will immediately be contributed in his name to the African Missions of the Southern Baptist Convention.

Williams went on to promise that his son, who worked for United Airlines, would bring the idols to the museum for Colin to see. Colin replied to Quigly.

Mrs. Helen Quigly
5832 Harper Street
Chicago 37, Illinois July 20, 1960

Dear Mrs. Quigly:
Thank you for your letter; I am sorry that you have been having some trouble over the figurines . . . It is not for me to enter into the controversy between your son and his uncle, but I think it would be a great mistake to burn the figures. Whatever significance they had for the people who made and used them, good or bad, they certainly do not have the same significance here, and we would use them for a totally different and, I am sure you will agree, a worthy purpose. Our object is to use such pieces to help us, and the public, to understand peoples of different cultures in different parts of the world. I am sure that if you talk to Dr. Lovelace he will agree that it is in everyone's interest that we should try and understand each other, and particularly that we should understand those to whom we are supposed to bring the benefits of our own way of life.

Colin then answered Williams, stressing that he could do nothing—not even talk about ballpark prices—until he actually saw the idols. Next, Helen wrote back to say that there had been a reversal of opinions. She had changed her mind and was willing to sell the idols. But her Uncle Walter, now under the influence of Lovelace, had changed his mind and wanted to burn them. Colin immediately wrote Walter Williams asking him to desist. In turn, Helen wrote a panicked, undated, letter to Colin.

Dear Mr. Turnbull,
The most dreadful thing has happened. I showed your letter to Uncle Walter but it did not help much. He still feels the same way. Then I took your suggestion and went to Dr. Lovelace and told him about the Idols and showed him your letters. He says his mother took him to New York when he was a small boy. I believe she had a sister in a place called Brooklyn. Well anyway while they were there they went to see the

museum and he remembers a statue showing a Gorilla Carrying a Woman and another of a bear hugging an Indian. They were near a funny restaurant and the food was awful. He has always remembered the Gorilla—used to dream about it and the poor woman.

Well Dr. Lovelace says you are right and I went home to pack up the idols and could not find them anywhere. Uncle Walter was gone and so were they. My neighbor Mrs. Goodman who is a nice pretty young widow who liked your letters says she saw Uncle Walter and Virginia with their suitcase and a package leaving about 3 o'clock. I would go down to Pine Bluff tomorrow only I have a bad foot and cannot travel. Please write Uncle Walter and tell him not to burn those idols.

P.S. Maybe if you quote scripture to him it will help. He kept quoting that part about man shall cast his idols to the moles and Bats. Said it was from Isaih [sic] only I can't find it.

Colin tried to calm Mrs. Quigly.

Dear Mrs. Quigly,

I was very sorry to hear from your letter of all the trouble you are having . . . I think you should ask your lawyer to send us a short note stating who exactly has the right to sell the figures, which is presumably yourself.

I am certainly in no position to say why Mr. Williams has done what he has, but I think it would be best to assume that he has acted from the best of intentions . . . Now I think there is no need for you to get alarmed or to assume the worst . . .

Sincerely yours, Colin Turnbull.

At this point, Colin informed Mrs. Quigly that he was going on vacation for three weeks and she should contact Phil Gifford in collections. Colin, of course, was heading to England to break off his engagement with Michael. Colin left word with Phil to expect a bizarre family to be in contact with him. The pieces, he said, were excellent and should be purchased by the museum for about twenty dollars a piece. At the end of the letter he wrote, "P.S. Phil, for laughs read the Quigly correspondence through from start to finish. I am only sorry that I shall not be here when Uncle Walter's son brings the pieces in."

For the three weeks Colin was on vacation, Gifford received nothing from Quigly, Williams, or Lovelace. When Colin returned from vacation on August 15, he received a letter, dated August 9, written American Baptist Convention letterhead, 482 Lyon Avenue, Chicago 29, Illinois. It was signed "Yours in Christ. Nicodemus Lovelace." Colin was utterly confused by the letter, which suggested that Williams had changed his mind yet again and was now intending to go through with the sale. Lovelace wrote:

> Dear Mr. Turnbull,
> The distressing and disgraceful imbroglio that has transpired in the Quigly family as a result of the possession of the African Idols is the clearest and most manifest example of which I am aware of the machinations of the Great Enemy. My old friend the Rev. Sam Houston Williams would be anguished and mortified did he know that his innocent actions had brought such a curse on this humble God-fearing family.
>
> May God forgive me, but I must confess that I was the unwitting instrument that percipitated [*sic*] the crisis. Last Sunday evening, after delivering a sermon on Brotherly Love, I requested Mr. Walter Williams to lead the congregation in prayer. This he did in a most moving fashion, describing how his love for his deceased brother was being symbolized by substantial contributions to Foreign Missions to be made through him resulting from the sale of Heathern Idols. Most unfortunately, Mrs. Helen Quigly was kneeling beside a heavy bronze vase containing Calla Lillies that had been brought to the Service by Miss Elden Olmstead.
>
> The details of the distressing events that ensued need not be set forth here. Suffice it to say that Mr. Williams is in St. John Memorial Hospital with a serious brain concussion. Mrs. Quigly has a broken leg that will confine her to bed for some weeks to come, and most distressing of all, young Paul Quigly, who has been a Proctor in this church for the last three years is in the hands of the Police. I am afraid that this promising boy will be sent to Evansville Reformatory.
>
> Under the circumstances you will understand that I am assuming the responsibility for the disposal of these Heathern Idols, both to remove this baleful influence from this unfortunate family and to honor the memory of my departed friend. Please forward a certified check made out to my name.

Colin responded to Lovelace on August 23, side-stepping all religious language. He simply stated that the museum needed to know who was legally in possession of the art. That person only was entitled to receive payment. He added, "Please give my very kindest regards to Mrs. Quigly and to Mr. Williams, and my sincere regrets for all the trouble they have had."

At last, Ford sent a letter from Lovelace's assistant pastor that was so outrageous that Colin realized the correspondence was almost certainly a joke.

> Dear Mr. Turnbull,
>
> It becomes my tragic duty to reply to your letter for August 23 directed to my late teacher and superior, the Reverend Dr. Nicodemus Lovelace.
>
> His unexpected demise has been a great shock to the Congregation and it will be a long time before they recover from the distressful event.
>
> Recently, Miss Dovie Bird, charming daughter of a prominent local family, was moved by the Holy Ghost to become a member of our Church and after the Services last Sunday night the Sexton uncovered the Baptistry situated beneath the floor of the pulpit. I attempted to persuade Dr. Lovelace to allow me to officiate in the ceremony of immersion but most unfortunately he insisted on performing this sacrament himself. During the ceremony Dr. Lovelace slipped and by the time the Deacons came to his aid he had drowned.
>
> No I am not a superstitious man, Mr. Turnbull, but one must admit that if the Lord can exert beneficent influences upon human affairs, it is only logical that the Devil can do the reverse. The sum of misfortunes that any logical mind cannot help but attribute to these baneful heathern Idols has become staggering. Mrs. Quigly has had a leg amputated. Mr. Walter Williams lies at death's door and suffers from horrible hallucinations. Paul Quigly is a fugitive from the police and it is not known whether the poor boy was wounded when the Officers shot him as he escaped.
>
> Yours Prayerfully, Dr. Alfred Wollensack.

Wollensack followed the letter immediately with a newspaper clipping that Ford had typeset and printed especially for the prank, and an offer from a Mr. Wallace, the choir leader, to place the idols in a packing box using a long pair of fire tongs. He warned Colin about the terrible risk of receiving the idols, and added "I wouldn't put them off on any man without clear warning. Mrs. Quigly has given up any thought of selling them. She says for me to send them to you at once and may God have mercy on your soul." While the clipping might have validated the whole bizarre story, the language used in the story was almost identical to that used in the various letters. As with all the letters, "heathen" was spelled "heathern." The clipping was attributed to the *Baptist Herald Tribune.*

PROMINENT PREACHER DROWNS
VOODOO SUSPECTED

Last Sunday night while engaged in performing the sacrament of baptism of Miss Dovie Bird, 263 Myrtle St., the Reverend Nicodemus Lovelace, 63, of the Fourth Baptist Church, 482 Lyon Ave, slipped and disappeared into the Bapistry. When he was extracted by the attending Deacons it was discovered that the Rev. Lovelace had met his death by drowning.

Reliable sources attribute this last of a series of near-fatal accidents to the baleful influence of African Heathern Idols, the property of the late Rev. Sam Houston Williams. To date the score is: Mrs. Helen Quigly—right leg amputated; Paul Quigly—fugative [*sic*] from the Police, possibly suffering gunshot wound; Mr. Walter Williams—in serious condition with brain concussion. Parishioners wonder where the curse will strike next.

By now, the hoax was obvious but Colin decided to play along and gather his own information. He wrote Wollensack as if he suspected nothing.

August 26, 1960
Dear Mr. Wollensack:
Thank you for your kind letter of August 24, needless to say I am terribly distressed to hear of the untimely death of the Rev. Pastor Lovelace.

I think the best thing is for you to have the figurines sent here, addressed to me, as soon as possible. I have had some personal experience of these things, and I think you will find they are in safe hands. In any case, I appreciate and accept your warning, and accept these objects on behalf of the museum entirely on my own responsibility.

Sincerely yours, Colin Turnbull.

On this same day, however, Colin sent a letter of inquiry and copies of the whole correspondence with the Quigly family to the director of press relations for the American Baptist Convention, Faith Pomponio. Colin asked her to examine the letters. "I cannot believe," he wrote, "that the letters are genuine, yet if it is some kind of joke it is in the worst possible taste." The letter was probably typed by a secretary or shown to someone in the museum offices who informed Ford behind Colin's back, for the phrase "worst possible taste" would appear in Ford's final letter to Colin.

One day before he heard back from Pomponio, the "idols" were delivered, complete with American Museum of Natural History cataloguing numbers. A letter in a plain envelope without postmark was attached and signed "Your pen-pals."

> August 28, 1960
> Dear Mr. Turnbull,
> The idols will, as you said in your letter of June 30, fill certain gaps in your collection. In the acquisition records you might note that the current market values are as follows: the double figure, $300; the Baluba neck-rest, $75-$150; the other two $80 to $120 each. These are conservative figures.
>
> As you realize, there are hazards in all professions, witness the untimely and sad end of Dr. Lovelace. Similarly there are hazards in the museum business as well, particularly when one has such colleagues as are assembled in your department. I hope you will not continue to think this all "in the worst possible taste."
>
> Your Pen-pals.

Ford did not confess to the prank, but Colin and several others then at the museum were certain that Ford was the culprit. Colin swallowed his pride. He sent a final letter of condolence to the Assistant Pastor Wollensack, knowing, of course, it would end up in Ford's hands. Acknowledging that he had been played for a sucker, Colin signed it "Ethelred the Unready" after the tenth-century King of England who was unprepared for the Danish invasions.

> August 29, 1960
> Dear Pen-pals,
> I was delighted to get your letter, also the Heathern Idols, thoughtfully numbered and catalogued. They will add immeasurably to the value of our collection. The more so as we will now not have to defend a charge to have been brought by the American Baptist Convention against persons unknown for defamation and misrepresentation.

Upon enquiring of a Miss Pomponio (the truth is invariably as hilarious as fiction) last week as to the fate of the Fourth Baptist Church, Chicago, I learned that there was no such Church. We then discussed the possibility of drowning in a Baptistry, and Miss Pomponio, after considerable thought, said that it *was* possible, but that she had never seen it happen. However, she felt that she should contact the police right away and notify them, and she also mentioned taking action against the unlawful users of The American Baptist Convention stationary [*sic*].

At this point, I felt obliged to ask her to refrain from taking any such drastic action until I could ascertain the origin of the hoax, and having allowed the matter to mature over the weekend I was able to call her this morning and assure her that the prank was an internal one, and that in fact no pastor had been drowned in the course of his duties, and no injury had been intended by the use of the letterhead.

Miss Pomponio remarked that I must have some very funny colleagues, to which I agreed, and that I need not despair, not all Americans were so blighted. I imagine that she meant that Baptists were different.

With deep appreciation, and sincere regrets for the untimely decease of so many relatives and friends of the late Rev. Sam Houston Williams.

Your Anglo-Saxon pal, Ethelred the Unready

That was the end of the hoax, but Ford continued to harass Colin. He somehow discovered—the museum curators today believe it was probably through a private investigator—that Joe had been arrested, but not convicted, of "lewd behavior" in the New York City subway. Colin and Joe have both noted in their own papers that there was an arrest. According to Joe's diary, he had diarrhea and had, at the time of a police raid, simply run to the restroom to avoid soiling his pants. At roughly the same time, Ford became aware that the security department at the museum disliked Joe. Most of the security officers were black and resented the fact that Joe was consorting with a white man. Joe had a security badge but the officers were cool to him. Colin wrote in "Lover and Beloved," "I was told by the [white] head of security . . . that I should be ashamed of myself for associating with niggers." Colin believed that surveillance of blacks in the museum was heightened after a high-profile reception for a new exhibition hosted by Joan Crawford, at which Colin displayed large poster-sized photographs of blacks, including Joe, working in the African storage area at the museum. Ford wrote the security office which, in turn, asked Harry Shapiro, then chair of the anthropology department, to confiscate the security badge.

Shapiro told Joe to return the badge, apologized to him but said he had no choice. Joe was not an employee of the museum, Shapiro said.

In "Lover and Beloved" Colin reflected on the pain he and Joe had felt. "And again the bottom fell out of my world, as with that shy smile, not even bothering to try and explain his innocence, but not doing such a good job at concealing his hurt, Joe handed the badge over, and quietly left." Colin was outraged but impotent. He felt his only option was to be quiet about the problem. And when things got worse during the next few months, he kept quiet again.

While in Mexico digging one winter at archaeologist Scotty McNeish's site in Vera Cruz, Ford wrote an angry letter to the museum's director James Oliver, with a copy to Shapiro. The long tirade, nine pages single spaced, written after several drinks, complained about nearly everyone in the department, the museum administration, the trustees, and the volunteers. And toward the end of the letter, Ford wrote that a homosexual like Colin Turnbull had no place in the museum. He mailed it on March 2, 1964, and it would signal the end of a brilliant career.

Ford's letter was ferocious and risky. The museum did not have a tenure system at the time, so Ford did not write from a secure position. Scotty McNeish, now eighty-one and still digging, says that Ford read the letter to him and asked his opinion. McNeish said he agreed with the letter. When asked, "Weren't you concerned the letter might get Jim fired?" McNeish replied, "I couldn't have cared less! Jim could have gotten another job."

Ford was angry that, "for the eighteen years I have been here, the Department of Anthropology has been slowly dying." In the letter, he argued that Shapiro made disastrous hires of unproductive, intellectually dead curators, and he accused Shapiro of all manner of unprofessional behavior. He was also angry because Shapiro reduced his artist budget, limited the time Ford could spend in the field, and gave greater freedoms to his favorites like Mead and Turnbull. In one passage, he complained bitterly that Shapiro was earning significant amounts of money by determining the race of children placed for adoption. Shapiro was a physical anthropologist, and throughout most of the past century many physical anthropologists were employed by the government to identify race when it was not known or was in dispute. (Even today, the Commonwealth of Massachusetts holds that if people wish to change the race identified on their birth certificates, they must obtain an affidavit either from the physician who delivered them or an anthropologist.) Ford wrote to Oliver, "New York law may not be racially intolerant, but it does specify that children up for adoption must go to families of the same race. At least once a week there are nurses with several squalling children in the main anthropology office awaiting the word of Solomon. For these judgements Shapiro collects $25 per head from the welfare agencies."

Shapiro called a faculty meeting of the seven curators in residence, including Colin. Ford was still in Mexico. Shapiro was so shocked by the letter that he could barely read it. By the time of the meeting he had still not finished the letter and had not read the portion about Colin. He passed a single copy of the letter around the room. Robert Carneiro, the museum's expert on South America, read the letter and passed it to Colin. Carneiro watched carefully as Colin got to the final paragraphs and to his surprise saw no reaction. "It was as if he was reading a newspaper," Carneiro said. Colin read that he "had no degrees in anthropology" (a reference to the fact that in 1964 Colin had yet to receive his doctorate), and that he had done no serious fieldwork (an odd charge given that he had lived with the Pygmies and was planning a return trip). But the worst of it was that Colin was also reading about Joe. In a passage accusing Shapiro of misusing museum funds to selectively air condition the department, Ford wrote: "This climatization includes Colin Turnbull, his office harpsichord, the very expensive tape recorder bought by a museum patron at Turnbull's suggestion, and Turnbull's private specimen, Joe."

Ford went on to recommend that Oliver fire Turnbull immediately. "Turnbull is Harry's worst mistake. Judging by all available evidence, he is a practicing homosexual, and most of the Museum personnel as well as many anthropologists are aware of it. His private life might be more easily ignored if he did not insist on bringing his young friend to Departmental parties, to Museum hall openings, and having him work as a volunteer. Joe, the colored boy from Knoxville, Tennessee, was spending most of his time in the Department when I left for this field trip. This, in spite of the fact that he could not qualify as a registered volunteer. Volunteers are fingerprinted. This boy's card was returned to [security] with a record of sexual offences."

Colin was silent during the entire meeting and to say that his calm demeanor in the face of such an outrageous letter earned him respect would be an understatement. His colleagues found his composure truly amazing. Shapiro felt terrible and later apologized to Colin. Carneiro recalls that the department agreed to fire Jim Ford, and Colin's own brief recollection confirms this, but other members of the museum's staff say that the department did not have that authority. They may have recommended dismissal, but it was Oliver's decision. When Ford returned from Mexico two weeks later Oliver called him to his office and said, "This is your letter of resignation, I presume?" Ford answered, "Yes sir, I believe it is."

March 16, 1964 would be Ford's last day in the museum's employ. He ended his career at the Florida State Museum, where he began to theorize about the ancient diffusion of New World Pre-Columbian societies from a single, nuclear, American hearth, probably located somewhere in Ecuador. He even hypothesized that some New World pottery styles had come, by raft, from Japan. In 1968, he died of intestinal cancer.

In 1963, not long after they returned from their trip to Europe on *The France,* Joe began to get restless. Joe, who had been casting about for a professional identity, seemed determined to get a college education and planned to take an admissions test offered by Columbia University in November. But Joe never took the test, or at least he never mentioned it again to Colin. The week after the test was scheduled, President Kennedy was assassinated. For many people at that time, New York seemed at a standstill. Joe gave up his dreams of becoming an actor and for a few months did almost nothing during the day but read, watch television, and wait for Colin to come home from work. As Colin's professional world widened, Joe's world narrowed. But by the early spring of 1964, he had found a renewed sense of vigor: he became an enthusiastic stamp collector, he took piano lessons and practiced for several hours everyday; he also talked more about social problems in America. Colin wrote, "At first it seemed as though our private dream had merely been intensified, the direction of our lives unchanged. But it was not so. Joe was more conscious of his blackness, a term that had not yet quite gained respectability, and I was more conscious that in coming to the States I had not escaped the racism and bigotry and ignorance that I had always associated most with the English and their colonialism. The two of us would have made fine revolutionaries, if only there had been a revolution."

Colin felt, in contrast, that his own career and personal life were stable. *The Forest People* was selling well and receiving critical acclaim. By 1964, he would publish a new book, *The Lonely African,* a collection of vignettes of individual Africans who were experiencing the hardships of postcolonial, urban, capitalist Africa. He proudly told friends that the book had been banned briefly in France. And by 1964, Colin was making plans to conduct fieldwork with a hunter-gatherer group, possibly in Tanzania, Kenya, or in Uganda. There was still fighting in the newly independent Congo and so it would be impossible to return to the Pygmies.

Colin had also embarked on the design and construction of a completely new permanent exhibit in the Hall of Man in Africa at the museum, scheduled to open in 1967, with the Pygmies as a central focus. Colin asked Joe to help. Whereas the old exhibition had presented a view that fit American stereotypes of Africans as timeless remnants of the Stone Age, the renovated hall would show Africans in a dynamic, historical context, including a section on the contribution of African nations to international politics and economics. Colin reached out to embassies, African representatives at the United Nations, and foreign scholars for help in framing the exhibit, still on view at the turn of the millennium. Joe assisted him at every step of the way, and knowing that the exhibition would remain for at least some decades, neither of them underestimated its cultural and political importance to the United States. Both knew that hundreds of thousands of visitors would see the exhibition every year and that, for some, especially schoolchildren, it would be their first and only exposure to African culture.

At the same time, Colin and Joe bought a large plot of land in the northern neck of Virginia, in Lancaster—more than 65 acres, and about 2,000 feet of water frontage along the Rappahannock River. The area meant a lot to Joe. He had grown up in Lancaster and most of his relatives still lived there. They hoped to build a house there one day. But it was rural, old fashioned, and located in a part of Virginia that sometimes feels like the deep South. It was not the sort of place that attracted gay, interracial couples.

The next year, 1965 would be important for another reason. On April 26, Colin became a U.S. citizen.

CHAPTER TEN

The Edge of Humanity

"IN WHAT FOLLOWS, THERE WILL BE MUCH TO SHOCK." When Colin Turnbull wrote these words he could not have been more right. *The Mountain People,* based on Turnbull's fieldwork in Uganda in 1965 and 1966, is a frightening book about the Ik (pronounced "eek"), a group of 2,000 starving and hostile hunters. It remains one of the most controversial and commercially successful books in the history of anthropology. By the time of Colin's second appearance on Dick Cavett's television show in 1973, the book was selling more than one thousand copies a week, and as a result of the publicity, sales of *The Forest People,* which had been a best-seller on and off for more than a decade, jumped to as high as five thousand copies per week. The same year, the purchase of film rights for *The Mountain People* was negotiated and the famous director Peter Brook, then head of the Royal Shakespeare Company, began to adapt the book for the theater.

Graham Greene praised Michael Korda and Colin for their courage; Margaret Mead called it "beautiful"; and reviews in *Life* and the *New York Times* saw the work as a powerful commentary on the human capacity for evil. Others called it "unethical" or "dangerous," and in *The New York Times Book Review* a reviewer called Colin "deranged." A year after publication, one anthropologist called for a professional censure of Colin and his book. Fredrik Barth led the attack and wrote that *The Mountain People* was "dishonest," "grossly irresponsible and harmful," and threatened the "hygiene" of the discipline.

The story of the research behind the book takes us into one of the most harrowing experiences of Colin's life, into a world of human cruelty and despair. The public reception of the book, published much later in 1973, leads us into the troublesome and age-old questions of what makes us human and who has the right to decide who is human.

In Colin's second year in Uganda, as the Ik enjoyed a better harvest and regained some strength, Colin wrote from the field to his boss, Harry Shapiro, at the American Museum of Natural History: "It has been a Hitchcock thriller at its nastiest, watching these poor starving sweet little grey-haired old men and women, on the point of death, having been abandoned by all their children (as indeed was all the case) slowly reacting to the improved food supply. They still look sweet and charming, even as they tear each other to shreds with their new-found strength. Thank heavens they were starving last year, for the unfolding vision of the Ik in full possession of all their faculties is too ghastly to contemplate! There are still a few starving, and likely to starve to death, the very old and the very young. Each have to scavenge for their food as best they can . . . leaves of wild plants, a few figs, and an indigestible elephant fruit. But let them beware if their healthier relatives catch them. There is one slightly mental little old lady . . . wizened and shrunk and terrified. I have seen her chance on a fig and even as she was picking it up be attacked by a gang of youths and have it snatched from her, and the youths far from starving."

Colin would eventually call the Ik "sub-humans" and call for the destruction of their culture. "To enter any village," he wrote in 1966, "is like entering an open graveyard, skeletons crawling about to try to pick up a grain that has fallen from the baskets of their healthy offspring." Colin would never be the same; neither would his readers or the scientific community.

If, instead of doing research in Uganda, Colin had returned to the Ituri rain forest in 1965, as he had planned, he might have been killed. Not even Patrice Lumumba, who believed Colin qualified as "African," would have been able to save him. In the early 1960s, the first republic of the Congo began to collapse, and by 1964 there were violent rebellions throughout the eastern part of the country, especially near Kisangani, not far from Colin's field site. Guerrilla fighters of the Armée Populaire de Libération, popularly known as Simbas (Swahili for lions), formed a corridor of violence along the main north-south road that extended north of the rain forest as far as Isiro. The quarrel was with the African authorities, but there was an enormous amount of anti-white sentiment, and Belgians were not singled out. Europeans fled the country, and many of those who remained or were caught trying to escape were executed.

The Simbas' motivations are not well understood, even by the most knowledgeable historians of central Africa, but we do know that one of the movement's leaders, Nicholas Olenga, was closely tied to Patrice Lumumba. Lumumba was the first prime minister of the newly independent Congo before his execution in 1961 under General Joseph Mobutu's first regime. We also know that the Simbas' anger was directed against wealth and privilege, and against anyone whose political views conflicted with those of Lumumba. He became a martyr after his death, and in Moscow the Soviet government founded Patrice Lumumba University. Lumumba was so well known internationally that he almost made the cover of *Time* magazine. A painting of him was commissioned and slated for the cover, but as the publication deadline neared, the magazine decided, for reasons we do not know, to run instead an image of the secretary of the United Nations, Dag Hammarskjold. The painting of Lumumba was still used, but with a Yousuf Karsh black-and-white portrait of Hammarskjold superimposed on Lumumba's head.

Colin had met Lumumba before the Simba rebellion, when Lumumba was a post office employee, but their friendship would not promise Colin any protection during the period of unrest. Joan Mark, the biographer of Patrick Putnam, interviewed Colin in April 1987, and she wrote about his recollection of his first meeting with Lumumba. "Turnbull had gone into an African bar and ordered a drink. When he was told they could not serve him, someone in the room called out, '*Give* him a drink,' implying that though it was illegal to sell him a drink, it was not illegal to give him one. Glass in hand, Turnbull sat down next to a man playing a mekembi (thumb piano). The African noticed that he was listening intently and asked him in KiNgwana if he could play it. Turnbull replied, 'Yes, but not the way you've tuned it.' The African handed it over, and when Turnbull had retuned it and started playing, he burst into guffaws of laughter. 'That's how the Pygmies play it!' he roared. He took it back and retuned it. 'This is how the Tetela tune it. Now isn't that better?' Turnbull disagreed, and they argued back and forth for a few minutes. Then Patrice Lumumba introduced himself. He had seen Turnbull at the post office in Stanleyville, where he worked as a clerk, and he knew that Turnbull was staying out at Camp Putnam, because that was where his mail was being sent. Lumumba indicated approval and respect for Putnam, implying that he was one of the few Europeans around who cared about Africans."

The relationship between Putnam and Lumumba is unclear, but as Putnam's biographer tells us, a rumor spread widely after Putnam's death that Lumumba might be Putnam's son. There was considerable resemblance between the two, and Lumumba was, like Putnam, an outstanding speaker, an unstable personality, and a genius. Moreover, the name Patrice is the French for Patrick, and Lumumba, some thought, might even be an African variant of Lowell. The story is, of course, not credible since Lumumba was born in July 1925, two and a half years before Patrick arrived in Africa.

The violence in the part of central Africa occupied by the Mbuti was at its peak in 1965. Colin did not know what to do. He wanted to do fieldwork and he planned for Joe to attend school at an African university. Makerere University in Uganda was among the best, in large part because it was closely linked with the University of London. Colin himself had no desire to stay in Uganda; he wanted to return to the Pygmies and was distressed about the news reports coming out of the Congo. The people he loved were in a violent place and, unable to be there, he could only hope that they were safe. He may have wanted to go to the Ituri to be with, protect, or comfort the Mbuti (though he would almost certainly never admit to any capacity to protect the Mbuti). Colin was too intrepid for his own good, and it was hard for him to abandon his plans to return to the Ituri. Consideration of his own safety would have been uncharacteristic, for Colin was confident of his own ability to survive and was unafraid of death. He was so aware of his extraordinary social skills that he believed he could get himself out of almost any scrape.

What did happen to the Pygmies during the uprisings is unclear. There are no accurate figures on how many persons were killed during the Simba rebellion. It is probable that most of the Mbuti fled into the forest and remained safely there, coming to the roadside only occasionally to collect any crops left in the gardens. Many of the farmers with whom the Mbuti lived accompanied them to the forest for protection. The Efe Pygmies, just to the north of the Mbuti, suffered only a few deaths from the Simbas, avoiding the violence by moving continuously in the forest. The Simba rebellion ended in late 1965. By then, the Pygmies and the farmers who had gone with them to live deep in the forest for sanctuary had come back to the roadside. But Colin was already with the Ik, and Joe had enrolled at Makerere.

In 1965, one of Makerere's most eminent faculty members was a visiting professor of anthropology, Phillip Gulliver. He recalls that when Colin arrived in Uganda in 1965, Colin intended to drop Joe off at school and go on to the Ituri. Although Colin intended to be near the Pygmies, he planned to live with the nearby villagers. He had been virtually excluded from their world during his three previous periods of fieldwork and now hoped to look at the Pygmy-villager relationships from the villager's point of view. Gulliver said that Colin had "hatched the plan to enter the Congo from western Uganda and to sneak through the forest back to his area. We were horrified and told him so quite strongly. He was likely to be caught and so might well come to serious harm; he would make things difficult for other anthropologists in Africa in countries where our profession was not altogether popular; he might cause diplomatic conflict for Uganda when it was known that he had entered the Congo from there. And in general, we argued with him, it was a foolish idea. But . . . he appeared to be 'obsessed,' if I may use that term in a non-technical sense and without knowing him well or over a lengthy period, with the Pygmies."

It happened that, years earlier in 1949, when Gulliver was traveling in Uganda, he had come across a group of short-statured hunters who, with the exception of brief mention in an old work by the anthropologist C. G. Seligman, were unknown to any anthropologist. The neighboring Turkana people called them the Teuso. Because the Teuso were fluent in Turkana, Gulliver could communicate with them. Colin would eventually discover that they called themselves the Ik.

At the time Gulliver encountered the Ik, the Ik did not appear to be starving. Women were actively cultivating millet, squashes, and beans; men were hunting over a wide area, including in the Turkana area of northwestern Kenya. They had their own language, which Gulliver briefly studied, but the thing that impressed him most about the Ik was that they were short.

Gulliver recalls: "I got the strong impression that a major factor for [Colin] was the small stature of the Pygmies and almost a disinterest in Africans of usual size." So when Colin came to Uganda, Gulliver thought not only about how foolhardy the clandestine trip to the Ituri would be, but also about the possibility that the short-statured Ik might just be what Colin was looking for. After an initial conversation, Gulliver felt that he "had aroused Turnbull's interest that these people might be something of a substitute for Pygmies." If Colin initially saw the Ik as a substitute, this might explain his extreme disappointment with them. Gulliver said, "As a purely personal opinion, I have always thought that one part of Turnbull's problem was that the Ik were not Pygmies and could not, in his view, meet Pygmy standards."

Gulliver never told any of this to Colin, and Colin seems to have told Joe little about his conversations at Makerere, only that he had found a group in Uganda to study while Joe was in school. At any rate, Joe was preoccupied with his own situation, feeling slighted by the university because, despite having requested a single room, he was assigned a roommate, a Bugandan student named Methuselah Kiberu, with whom he nevertheless became quite friendly. Joe was also disappointed that he was not viewed as African. His diary entries from this time contain descriptions of discussions he engaged in with African students who argued that, despite his dark skin color, Joe was a European. He was also still feeling ill. Only a few months earlier in New York, Joe had spent almost a month in the hospital with hepatitis (in the days when hospital stays were much longer, and women, for example, stayed two weeks after delivering a baby). Still, Africa seemed better than he had expected from his conversations with Anne Putnam. Joe told his diary that Anne had painted "quite a dim view of Africa. I think it was deliberate—she is jealous, hoping I will dislike it." Joe's dean, the well-known anthropologist Raymond Apthorpe, encouraged him to continue with his studies. Joe described him affectionately as "a typically scrawny pinch-faced Englishman with a high-pitched voice." Joe decided to make the most of it, expecting to visit Colin at his field site and to have Colin visit him at the university.

After a few days at Makerere, Colin left to try to secure the proper clearances to live among the Ik. The task was complicated by bureaucratic red tape and his lack of enthusiasm for the project. This lack of enthusiasm was a problem that would stay with Colin for almost two years.

"The Ik," Colin recalled in 1991, "were, at best, a third choice, a last-ditch stand not to lose an opportunity to get into the field." Apart from going back to the Ituri, a second possibility for Colin's fieldwork was a short-statured society called the Onge from the Andaman Islands in the Bay of Bengal off the coast of India. The Onge were sometimes referred to in the scientific literature as Pygmies. The Andamans had been made famous in anthropology by A. R. Radcliffe-Brown, who studied the non-Pygmy Andamans from 1906 to 1908, but almost a century later little is known about the islands or the inhabitants. Colin was without a doubt interested in studying the Onge because of their height. He believed that the Onge resembled the Pygmies both physically and culturally and suspected that they were descendants of the Pygmies. Even two decades later, when Colin went to Samoa, he considered studying a hill community in Samoa known to be short-statured and would stun an audience at the community college in the Samoan capital of Pago Pago by stating his hypothesis that these upland Samoans were, in fact, Pygmies. But whether he was interested in the Onge and the Samoan "Pygmies" simply because they were short or because their shortness was indicative of a possible historical relationship with the African Pygmies is an open question.

By positing that historical relationship Colin was way ahead of his time. By the end of the millennium, scientists trying to prove that humans evolved in Africa and then migrated out of Africa (the so-called Out of Africa theory) were able to extract mitochondrial DNA from hair samples taken by Radcliffe-Brown during his first fieldwork in the Andamans. They found that Andaman islanders' DNA resembled DNA taken from African Pygmies more closely than any other population.

A third potential project was to study nomadic hunters in Kenya, Tanzania, and Uganda, a fourth to study blacksmiths and iron forgers, and a fifth to do a detailed study of the Ik, a hunting group in the mountains separating northern Uganda, Sudan, and Kenya. This last option became the lone choice since Colin was denied permission everywhere else. While Colin himself wasn't disliked, newly independent postcolonial nations were simply not friendly to anthropologists. Anthropologists continued to be linked to colonial administrations since, in the past, such governments funded anthropological research and sometimes designed research projects that would help them dominate communities more effectively.

Colin had no choice but to study the Ik, a small unknown group of about two thousand people. But at least it was fieldwork, and that cannot be underestimated. Fieldwork defines the anthropologist's identity in the same way that a laboratory defines a chemist's. In a letter to Harry Shapiro, written just prior to leaving Makerere for the Ik territory, Colin estimated the cost to the museum to be $13,000, with $1,100 taken up by airfare, $4,600 for a Land Rover to be shipped from London, $700 for an interpreter for twelve months ($60 per month), $750 to pay informants ($15 per week), and remarkably only $1,500 for food (mostly rice and lentils) for twelve months. Colin would eventually need more money because he stayed in Uganda for a total of eighteen months.

What enthusiasm he could muster may have been due to Elizabeth Marshall Thomas's encouragement. In 1961, she had spent a year living with neighbors of the Ik called the Dodos (pronounced doe-DOTH). The Dodos were a tall people, often reaching six feet, and they accentuated their height with tall hairstyles. In the early 1960s, Thomas told Colin that she thought the Ik were a most impressive group of people. "All of the Ik were hard people," Thomas said, "and they lived hard lives." They were also just beginning to suffer from the famine, occasionally attempting to get food from the warring Turkana or Dodos and sometimes working for both sides as spies, scouting out numbers of cattle for future raids. Colin was impressed with Thomas's stories, including one tale about an Ik man who had been caught stealing something from a Dodos family. She recalled, "Nothing seemed to scare [the Ik]. The thief's throat was cut ear to ear and he strolled over to me, blood dripping, and asked me if I could fix him up. Reeling with shock, almost fainting, I took him to the car and drove him to the dispensary. It was in Kaabong, maybe twenty miles away. The Ik man—you wouldn't think anything had happened to him. The Dodos men were laughing at him, ridiculing him. He was laughing with them! When we got to the dispensary he said he didn't want to go. He was scared the dispenser would get the police and they would question him. 'Well,' I said, 'You don't have a choice.' He knew how to speak Dodos so I could talk to him. I said, 'This is where you're going because I can't fix your throat but the dispenser can.' I went in with him to make sure he got there and I left him lying down on a bed. When the dispenser came, the window was open and the man was gone. I was impressed with his courage and I told Colin about it . . . But when I heard Colin give a couple of talks later on about the Ik, he mentioned my own work [in which I write about the Ik] and criticized me for thinking they were better than they actually were."

In Uganda during that first summer of 1965, after he had already made the decision to study the Ik, Colin still went through the motions to obtain clearance from the Indian government for research in the Andaman Islands. He still hoped the Andaman project might work out by December and planned to leave Uganda (and Joe) and go directly to India. Colin wrote Harry Shapiro that he could not be sure how long he would have to be in the field to complete his study: "The trouble is that so little is known of the peoples I am interested in that it is darned difficult to predict how they are going to have to be dealt with."

When Colin departed for the Ik territory, he left Joe standing outside the entrance to Livingston Hall, one of the most elegant halls on an exceptionally beautiful campus. "But all that beauty did not help," Colin recalled. "He was already looking like a Makerere student, with his white trousers and white shirt and red gown, yet I knew his heart had not settled down yet. He stood there and we said goodbye through the window of the Land Rover. I think we even shook hands through the window, both wanting so much more. And as I drove off I was crying so hard it was all I could do to get my hand out of the window again to make some sort of pretence of waving."

The Ik was a group of people seemingly on the brink of extinction. As with other nomadic Africans, colonial and postcolonial governments in Africa had tried to force them to become sedentary, easier to count and easier to tax. So-called nomads are not actually wanderers as the term might imply: nomadic peoples move over a defined territory in order to exploit natural resources. Nomads almost always live in places where movement is a question of survival, and by 1965 when Colin arrived in Uganda, the Ik's movements had changed drastically.

The area in which Colin found the Ik, the eastern edge of Kidepo Valley National Park, lies between the Kenya-Uganda escarpment and Mount Morungole. Before they were forcibly settled by the Ugandan government, they remained at Kidepo for only part of the year; when the heavy rains came and as the large game moved on, the Ik would follow them, first through the Didinga Mountains and into Sudan, then down into northern Kenya along Lake Turkana (called Lake Rudolf in Turnbull's day), collecting honey as they went. At last, they would begin a final journey two thousand feet up into the Kenya-Uganda escarpment and back into Uganda.

. Colin Turnbull and his brother Ian, Southwest Coast of England, 1928. Courtesy of David Turnbull. *Dot and Jock Turnbull each picked a favorite child: Jock chose Ian, the more masculine of the two; Dot chose Colin.*

2. Colin Turnbull with his parents, Oxford, 1947. Courtesy of David Turnbull. *His advisor at Oxford wrote: "Colin Turnbull is tall, fair, handsome, inconsequent, impulsive and elusive; all his screws are loose. . . real communication with him seems impossible. Perhaps one has to belong to one of the 'backward races' in order to get his wavelength."*

3. Colin Turnbull (middle), his brother Ian, and their mother, on vacation in Scotland, 1933. Courtesy of David Turnbull. *Colin had a jeweled soul, a deep, almost melancholic consciousness of the riches that could be found in music, conversation, churches, and the Scottish countryside.*

4 and 5. Mother [Mirra Alfassa] and Sri Aurobindo, with whom Turnbull lived briefly in 1950. Courtesy of the estate of Sri Aurobindo. Photographer unknown. Circa 1940. *"To be with either of them for more than a minute was enough to give me a violent headache."*

6. Sri Anandamayi Ma, 1930s, the Indian saint with whom Turnbull lived from 1949 to 1950. Photographer unknown. Ashram Archive photo. *She taught Colin that something beautiful and pure can emerge from something ordinary or inconspicuous. It might even be found in one person—someone who Colin might one day meet—in whom, deep inside, there was a brilliant light, an inner truth, struggling to blossom.*

7. Frances Chapman and Colin Turnbull, Sussex, England, 1953, preparing to leave for Africa to make their historic recordings of Pygmy music. Photographer unknown. Courtesy of David Turnbull. *Leon Thomas used Pygmy yodel techniques he and John Coltrane heard on Colin and Francis's tapes.*

8. Colin Turnbull and his frequent companion, Newton Beal, in the Ituri Forest, 1957. Photographer unknown. Courtesy of David Turnbull. *The uncomfortable son of a Scottish father and Irish mother, a native of no place in particular, had found a place of acceptance.*

9. The African Queen, the center portion of which was built by Colin Turnbull. Movie still from *The African Queen* courtesy of James W. Hendricks and the National Film Archive, London, Romulus Films Ltd/Horizon Management, Inc., *The African Queen*, Copyright 1951, Copyright renewed 1979, and the estate of Sam Spiegel. *When they arrived at Spiegel's camp with the damaged, dented boiler, Colin and Newton were contrite; to their surprise, Spiegel said, "Actually, it's a nice touch."*

10. A Mbuti camp, 1953. Photo by Colin Turnbull, Courtesy of the Avery Research Center.
Colin Turnbull's life and anthropology were pilgrimages to a beautiful dream world that, in the African rain forest, was inexplicably real.

11. Colin Turnbull with Mbuti children, 1953. Photo by Colin Turnbull, Courtesy of the Avery Research Center.
"What would we lose if we gave our children something different, something of what the Mbuti have to teach us about motherhood?"

12. Patrick Tracy Lowell Putnam, circa 1940. Photographer unknown. Reprinted with the permission of the Harvard College Library. *Patrick became obsessed with power and control as if he were playing out a scene from Joseph Conrad's* The Heart of Darkness.

13. Anne Eisner Putnam, circa 1950. Photographer unknown. Anne Eisner Putnam Papers, by permission of the Houghton Library, Harvard University. *Anne begged Francis to pour cold water over her head to shake her out of the hysteria.*

14. Colin Turnbull recording Mbuti language and music, 1953. Courtesy of the Avery Research Center. *Patrice Lumumba handed the thumb piano to Turnbull, and when Turnbull had retuned it and started playing, Lumumba burst into guffaws of laughter: "That's how the Pygmies play it!"*

15. Colin Turnbull in the Ituri Forest, 1951. Photographer unknown. Courtesy of the Avery Research Center. *"[The song of the forest] echoes on and on, and it will still be there when our short lives are silences . . . until perhaps like us, it comes to rest in the deepest distance of some other world beyond . . . the dream world that is so real to the people of the forest."*

16. Joseph Allen Towles at the American Museum of Natural History. Photographer unknown. Courtesy of the Avery Research Center. *In a letter to the museum director, the archaeologist James Ford wrote: "Judging by all available evidence, Colin Turnbull is a practicing homosexual . . . his private life might be more easily ignored if he did not insist on bringing his young friend to Departmental parties, to Museum hall openings, and having him work as a volunteer . . . Joe, the colored boy from Knoxville, Tennessee."*

17. Colin Turnbull's Pygmy diorama, American Museum of Natural History, Hall of Man in Africa, still on view at the turn of the millennium. Courtesy of the American Museum of Natural History Photo Archives. *The museum did not realize that by permitting Joe and Colin's displays to be included in the Hall of Man in Africa, the exhibition would have greater staying power and political viability than most Africa exhibitions mounted in the United States at that time.*

18 and 19. Head shots of "Thomas Towles," Joe Towles' stage name, 1958. Photos by Samuel Potemkin. Courtesy of the Avery Research Center. *"His eyes were open and clear and utterly honest. For a moment I thought I was back in Africa."*

20. Colin Turnbull at his New York City apartment, 1959. Photographer unknown. Courtesy of the Avery Research Center. *"I wondered how I had agreed to let Joe come back again and invade this private place . . . Deep feelings were aroused that I had not felt since I had been in love with [my fiancé] Kumari."*

21. Joe Towles in front of Colin Turnbull's brownstone, New York City, early 1960s. Photograph by Colin Turnbull. Courtesy of the Avery Research Center. *Joe told his diary, "This was Colin's show not mine . . . I must do something on my own . . . More and more things are pointing me to Africa, or is this just wishful thinking?"*

22. A typical holiday card from Colin Turnbull to Joe Towles, whom he called Josephine. Courtesy of the Avery Research Center. *In 1988, Colin Turnbull wrote to several friends, "I am sure all of you know that we have been what are generally called 'lovers' (a singularly inadequate term for our relationship) for over twenty-nine years."*

23. Colin Turnbull at the American Museum of Natural History, circa 1965. Courtesy of the Avery Research Center. *When Colin came to the museum in 1959 he could not have imagined the level of childishness he would find.*

24. Adupa, 1966, whose death Colin Turnbull described *in The Mountain People*. Photo by Colin Turnbull. Courtesy of the Avery Research Center. *Her parents did not want a starving child in their hut. Finally, when they let her in, she stopped crying, forever.*

25. A starving Ik youth carries his father, Uganda, 1966. Courtesy of the Avery Research Center. *"My suggestion was simple enough. The Ik would have to be rounded up . . . taken to parts of Uganda sufficiently remote for them not to be able to return."*

26. An Ik village, 1966. Photograph by Colin Turnbull. Courtesy of the Avery Research Center. *"To enter any village is like entering an open graveyard."*

27. Peter Brook consulting with his actors, 1974. Photograph by Nicholas Treat. Courtesy of Nicholas Treat. *It was Peter Brook who, remarkably, taught Colin to see the Ik in a new light.*

28. A scene from Peter Brook's *The Ik*, Paris, France, 1974. Photograph by Nicholas Treat. Courtesy of Nicholas Treat. *"The fire was real, the song was real, and they made the sacred real, and suddenly the audience realized the awful truth of just how much these people had lost."*

29. Joe and Colin, Zaire, 1971. Photographer unknown. Courtesy of the Avery Research Center.
"We are both proud of nothing so much as our love for each other."

30. Colin Turnbull's favorite photograph of Joe, Ituri Forest, 1971. Photo by Colin Turnbull. Courtesy of the Avery Research Center. *"Joe's name will be known, and would have been had he not lived in my shadow. Academically, he was far superior . . . I learned so much from him but he always stood back."*

31. Colin Turnbull and his mother, Lancaster, Virginia, 1976. Photographer unknown. Courtesy of the Avery Research Center. *"At the morgue, Colin slipped off his mother's wedding ring and put it on his own finger."*

32. Joe Towles, June, 1988, in St. Croix, just six months before his death from Aids. Photograph by Colin Turnbull. Courtesy of the Avery Research Center. *Colin wanted desperately to die with Joe, and if they could not die together, he wanted at least the same kind of death.*

33. Joe and Colin's gravestone. Photo by Colin Turnbull. *Colin told the friend who presided over the double funeral, "In the part of Africa where we worked, it is said that two people sometimes grow so close together they become one, like single trees with two trunks."*

34. Colin Turnbull's shrine to Joe and Sri Anandamayi Ma in his rented home, Kilmarnock, Virginia, 1993. Photo by Colin Turnbull. Courtesy of the Avery Research Center. *"I was given the opportunity to learn the highest of ideals, in Europe, India, and Africa. I was attempting to live up to them . . . when I met Joe. He has never ceased to remind me of them."*

35. Colin Turnbull [Lobsong Rigdol] holding a friend's baby, Gainesville, Florida, 1993. Photo by Michael Radelet, Courtesy of Michael Radalet. *Colin told Thubten Norbu, the eldest brother of the Dalai Lama, "I want to be free of all my attachments so I can truly be free to help others. That means no less than self-perfection . . . I will be a good monk, I promise."*

Post–World War II political conditions blocked the Ik from passing in and out of Uganda, Kenya, and Sudan, and they were forced to settle and farm on infertile land. Kidepo was named a national park and hunting was outlawed. Some Ik continued to hunt there but at great risk of arrest for poaching. Many Ik were compelled to steal food and cattle from neighboring groups. Having lost the only system of production they knew, Colin argued, they also lost their society. For Colin firmly believed that society and production went hand in hand; a change in one could affect the other profoundly. And so when the Ik lost their hunting and foraging grounds, they found that cooperative and affectionate relationships were maladaptive. Those who shared ended up with little and starved to death while the cutthroat individualist, willing to take food from his own kin, survived. Unfortunately, Colin did not try to reconstruct the lost culture through interviews or oral histories, and he was rightly criticized for this.

Virtues such as generosity, compassion, charity, hospitality, kindness, and honesty, Colin wrote, would not work for the Ik because any Ik who possessed these virtues would die of starvation or be killed off. The Ik showed Colin that the essential qualities of humanity were not these great virtues, as he had previously thought, but rather downright self-interest and greed. "The beautiful human, like the beautiful body, seems to be a myth perpetuated by the game of self-deceit, at which humans are so singularly adept. In fact, after even a few months with the Ik one is tempted to think that if there is such a thing as a basic human quality, self-deception it is . . .

"All this, however, was far from my mind," he later wrote, as his fire-engine red Land Rover carried him north "to the waiting jackals."

There are few places in Africa as different from the Ituri forest as the Morungole mountains. The temperature can be brutally hot despite the altitude, and there are few trees to offer shelter from the sun. Even walking can be difficult because the land has been chiseled and fissured through the ages into deep ravines and treacherous cliffs. Colin nevertheless found something bewitching in the mountains; it was the clarity and dryness of the air and the way the light constantly changed colors, as if the mountains were themselves in perpetual motion, nomadic as the Ik used to be.

To get to the place where Colin eventually lived among the Ik, he had to endure a tedious journey with guides he could barely trust, moving with disappointment from village to village, at times to areas he did not wish to visit. Colin had no idea where he was headed; his guides were taking him higher and higher and he had a terrible fear of heights. As Colin negotiated a treacherous mountain pass, he was certain he would plunge two hundred feet to his death; he noticed his guides jumping up and down with joy, teasing him for being afraid.

Colin found the home of his Ik guide Thomas especially intriguing. The village, like so many in the land of the Ik, was large but empty, with none of the teeming life that can be found in most African villages. The only people Colin could find there were two elderly men. Thomas and Colin's other Ik guide Peter said that everyone had left but declined to say where they had gone. Thomas, schooled at the Catholic Mission in Moroto, had not been back to the village in two years, but seemed uninterested in the disappearances. As it turned out, many had died in this drought-stricken land and many others had left in search of food and water.

Colin wrote, "They said all who were left were the two of them and Thomas's mother, who was in her house, sick. It then struck me as being odd that if Thomas had been away for two years he should not have even inquired after his mother . . . I said goodbye to the two men and got up to leave, but as I did so a strange thing happened. I was shaking hands with the older man and as I moved to take my hand away he tightened his grip so that I found myself actually pulling the old man off the ground. I don't think he could have weighed more than sixty pounds. His haunches were off the ground and then his grip weakened and before I could catch him his hand slipped out of mine and he fell back and collapsed and lay on the ground, all skin and bone, and he was laughing. He held out his hand, still laughing breathlessly, for me to help him back to a sitting position. He apologized for his behavior. 'I haven't eaten for three days,' he said, 'so it's difficult to stand up,' whereupon he and his companion dissolved into laughter again. I felt there was going to be much I had to learn about Ik humor."

As far as Colin could tell, Thomas never did check in on his mother, and the group departed for three more villages. At one village, two teenage girls offered Colin whatever he might want from them in return for the bag of sugar they noticed in the back of his Land-Rover, and much to their surprise he said that what he really wanted was to talk to them about Ik kinship terminology.

At each of these villages, Colin became increasingly frustrated that people begged from him. The Ik greeting seemed not to be something innocuous like "How are you?" or "Have you defeated the day?" but rather "Give me tobacco." Eventually the begging infuriated him and enhanced his hatred of the Ik. Yet this is what most anthropologists experience at some time or another if they work in areas in which people are poorer than they are. Although people throughout the world commonly use the exchange of tobacco as a way to establish social relationships, Colin somehow seemed oblivious to the very act of reciprocity he had once cherished in the rain forest.

At another village, Kalapeto, Colin walked past a stockade and heard a feeble voice giving the standard Ik greeting, "*Brinji lotop*" ("Give me tobacco"). "From inside the stockade one scrawny arm reached out, and automatically I put cigarettes into the waiting hand. Peter came running over and said angrily, 'What are you doing? There's nobody there!' and snatched the cigarettes out of the hand, which withdrew from sight. I began to feel that the Mission had not done a very good job. The boy, sensing an impending flood of abuse, defended himself by explaining, in his most patient and really quite charming way, that I should not be upset, there really was nobody in the village, only that old man and his sick wife. The quavery voice from the other side of the stockade protested, 'She's not sick, she died this morning. Help me dig a hole for her.' 'You see?' asked Thomas, coming to Peter's defense, as though it had been proven. 'You shouldn't have wasted cigarettes in that way.'"

At last Colin found the mountain village of Pirre with a population of about fifty adults, just large enough to sustain a full-scale ethnographic inquiry. Pirre was preferable not only because of its larger population, but because it was near the Police Post, a place that might offer Colin some refuge in the event of a raid for food by a neighboring group. There were, in fact, several villages within some hours' walk from Pirre. The chief, called the Mkungu, ordered a house to be built for Colin. Colin could stay in his Land Rover and at the Police Post for the two months it took to build the house. The Ik, hungry and curious, often huddled outside the Land Rover while Colin tried to conceal what he was doing inside: eating.

"For two months this would be my prison, to which I would be driven, whenever I wanted to eat, by reproachful, sad brown eyes . . . I came to know those eyes only too well. And always there was the same circle of impassive carnivores, waiting for some fatal slip—a chink in a curtain, the too noisy crunch of a dry biscuit, an expression of pain as I scalded my mouth with hot tea, a momentary feeling of compassion. But Peter and Thomas had taught me well. I wondered if the owner of the skinny arm at Kalapeto was now as dead and cold as his wife, and if both were still waiting for someone infinitely kind and stupid to 'dig a hole' for them. With that happy reflection I munched my dry biscuits with a little more assurance, and stepped out into the arena."

Life with the Ik was utterly miserable and Colin would see himself becoming an utterly miserable person. Colin's closest acquaintance was Atum who regularly asked for medicines for his wife who was very ill. As he conveyed the story in *The Mountain People:* "Then Atum's wife died. Atum told me nothing about it, but had stepped up his demands for food and medicine and I felt that if she was really sick I should try to get her to the hospital in Kaabong. He refused the offer and said she was not *that* sick. Then after a while, when I still had not once seen her [his brother-in-law] sidled up to me and said that he supposed I knew that Atum was selling the medicine I was giving him for his wife. I was not unduly surprised and merely remarked that that was too bad for his wife.

'Oh no,' said Lomongin, enjoying the joke enormously, 'she has been dead for weeks. He buried her inside the compound so you wouldn't know.' No wonder he did not want her to go to the hospital; she was worth far more to him dead than alive."

When an Ik died, Colin had little sense that the deceased's relatives grieved. In the past, some Ik said, they cared for the dead in special gravesites, buried them with many of the deceased's personal possessions, and performed complex funerary rituals to mark the passage from the world of the living to the world of the dead. Now the dead were stripped of their possessions and then abandoned. "It was this way," Colin wrote, "with [a man named] Lomeja."

"When I finally left [Lomeja's] body, I had not even reached the door of the hut when the fighting started, the ripping and tearing at the bandages, the cutting of the thongs that laced the leather shin guards around his legs, the wrenching of the little beads that decorated his ear. My last look at Lomeja, from the door, showed me all the bestiality I ever want to see, and the little boy was fighting to tear the ivory lip-plug from his father's dead lip, crying because others were stronger than he."

These experiences among the Ik would shock and change him. He believed he became increasingly like the Ik, and in *The Mountain People* he thanked the Ik for treating him "as one of themselves, which is about as badly as anyone can be treated." In a draft for a British edition of the book published in 1994, Colin wrote, "I think I came closer to losing my humanity than they did."

He once told a journalist: "My first revelation [that I was becoming a nasty person] occurred when a black, American anthropologist and old friend [Joe], who is also writing about the Ik, came to Uganda and was horrified at the way I was treating—or rather, nor treating—the Ik. They were just items for my notebook. I had a bottle of one thousand tablets of enterovioform [*sic*]. Ten tablets cure the worst kind of amoebic dysentery. So I could have safely had one hundred attacks of dysentery in the two-year field trip. My friend took one tablet to give to a child who had dysentery, and I blew my top. 'What, are you wasting that? My medicine! You didn't bring it! That's mine, and there you are, wasting it.' And he just looked at me. At that moment I stopped and suddenly realized I didn't care about these people at all. If they died it was just fodder for my notebook."

From Makerere, Joe wrote letter after letter to Colin, expressing his loneliness and his anger at Colin for ignoring him. Joe berated Colin for not writing to him. Although Colin understood Joe's resentment, he tried to explain that it was hard to write or mail letters from his field site. During much of 1965, Joe made brief entries into his diary noting how much he missed Colin. On October 24, 1965, the anniversary of the day he and Colin met, he wrote: "Today

Colin and I will have been together for six years. It is the first time we have been away from each other in all that time on this day. Oh, dearest Colin, I do love you so much and miss you on this day. However, the time grows short and we will be together shortly."

Joe visited Colin twice at Pirre in the Ik region—for a total of six weeks—during the eighteen months Colin spent in the field, and he was bored there. As Colin continued his difficult work with the Ik, he had little sympathy for Joe's complaints; he urged him to take careful notes during his visits so that he could write a book of his own. The longer Colin lived with the Ik, the more cantankerous he became, and Colin already had a short temper before he got into the field: only a few years earlier, he had stabbed Joe's arm with the lit cigarette. Joe and Colin fought terribly at the field site and even when Colin visited Joe in Makerere they played a cat-and-mouse game, with all the approach and avoidance of a couple uncertain of how to act together.

A photograph of Joe and an elderly Ik man in *The Mountain People* shows them talking intimately. The caption reads: "Lolim used to confer with Joseph Towles as one doctor confers with another." But Joe was able to communicate with the Ik only through an interpreter. Colin, on the other hand, had quickly learned much of the Ik language and his Swahili came back to him easily. In what was undoubtedly an attempt by Colin to give Joe some status, the caption also implies that Joe was a doctor (indeed, in reviews of *The Mountain People,* Joe is often referred to as a medical doctor). Instead of writing his own book, Joe spent most of his visits to the field assisting Colin. Colin had the fantasy that Joe could soon become an intellectual peer, working side by side with him, supporting and contributing to his work rather than impeding it by complaining that Colin loved his work more than he loved him. For the rest of Joe's life, Colin would be annoyed and disheartened by Joe's inability to produce, and after Joe's death Colin spent much of his remaining six years of life trying to piece together Joe's notes and drafts into a book. "Together," Colin wrote about Joe in the preface of *The Mountain People,* "we discovered just how impossible it is, in certain circumstances, to be a beautiful human being. He does not appear in these pages because he has his own story to tell."

In "Lover and Beloved" Colin wrote: "I am not sure that [Joe's] presence made things any easier or not. I certainly would not have had it any other way, just to have him with me was wonderful, and there among the Ik he was more than comforting. But I don't know whether it was the Ik and the hard conditions of living or what, but somehow his presence brought more tension rather than less."

Joe tried his hand at archaeology, beginning with an excavation on a rocky overhang above the villages where he believed there were indications of ancient life. After some days, Joe asked Colin to take a look but Colin was indifferent: "In no way did it excite me, and I must have showed it. He discontinued his work and never told me about any more of his personal projects."

While Colin saw himself becoming mean spirited, he did not see the same in Joe. Joe seemed generous to a fault: moved by the hunger he saw around him, he gave away much of Colin's carefully calculated rations of food. He believed that Joe was threatening his own working relationship with the Ik because from then on the Ik might expect Colin to give food or pay for even the least bit of information or cooperation. "So I got angry at Joe for wasting our precious food and medical supplies. His reply was that it was hardly a waste if it helped save someone's life did not make me any the less angry. For his part, he seemed not to understand that I was trying hard to control our own meager resources and had carefully built up a relationship that he was breaking wide open."

One of their most heated arguments came in late September 1965, a day after Colin had received in the mail the last of a series of tense exchanges with his parents. Colin saw Joe using too much tea in the pot and flew into a rage. Joe never knew about these letters, but they were typical. Colin's parents had written him suggesting that on his way home he could stop in England to see them on holiday in Devonshire. "I had replied that Joe and I would love to come. Their response to that was more than chilly. The idea had been that Joe would be staying in London or go on home; he was not invited. I wrote back to say that in that case neither was I, and I would also either stay in London or go on back home . . . to New York. My mother did not reply to that one. My father wrote to say that they had both been terribly hurt and that it was clear Joe was trying to make trouble, as he had always done, and that he . . . had made my mother seriously ill."

About that event, Joe told his diary: "Colin is blood-mad, he has just come back from one of his walks. At the dinner table, I put in too many tea leaves and from a harangue over that he took on the whole question of our relationship, saying that sometimes he thought it best to be alone. I had give him five years of misery and he could not take it any longer. I am really worried for he really takes on when he gets this way . . . I did not consciously mean to disobey and upset him."

Once they were apart, Colin became more sentimental. On an early morning in September 1965, Colin wrote Joe by candlelight from Pirre: "Still in my pajamas, at the table decorated with flowers, your picture in front of me. The villagers are beginning to stir into life, but I have been alive for six whole years—every minute of them, waking and sleeping . . ." He continued the same letter in the afternoon with an accounting of his evening schedule:

5:30 P.M. Heat soufelir of water. Love Joe.
6:00 P.M. Bathe and change. Love Joe.

6:30 P.M. Peel potatoes. Love Joe.
6:45 P.M. Cook Potatoes, dried peas and lentils in pressure cooker. Adore Joe.
7:10 P.M. Cook bean soup in soufelir. Adore Joe. Fry onions, spices, baked beans and curry. Worship Joe.

At Christmas, Joe visited Colin in this empty land with supplies for a huge dinner. Joe made a corn pudding, minted peas with diced potatoes and onions, cold ham surrounded with sliced eggs and tomatoes, a sweet potato pie, creamed chicken in mushroom sauce, a bottle of Beaujolais, and a small bottle of creme de menthe as an after-dinner drink. Colin came down with an attack of malaria and could barely get out of bed, let alone eat any of the food. "[Joe] was angry with me for that, for spoiling his Christmas, for wasting the dinner he had cooked just to please me. So he took my portion, and anything that was left over, and gave it to Atum, which he knew would really upset me! Yet, he washed my forehead and cared for me."

Six days later, Colin was recovered and happily devoured Joe's New Year's surprise dinner of canned haggis—a Scottish dish of the minced heart, lungs, and liver of a sheep mixed with oatmeal, onions, and kidney fat, and boiled in the animal's stomach.

CHAPTER ELEVEN

Wild Correspondence

In the spring of 1966, Colin decided to go back to the states for a few weeks to inspect the Hall of Man in Africa renovations at the museum. He also planned to attend a high profile conference at the University of Chicago—"Man the Hunter," organized by Irven DeVore and Richard Lee. Everyone who was anyone in hunter-gatherer studies would be there. Even Claude Lévi-Strauss, probably the most well-known intellectual in France, who seldom attended conferences, would be there. On the way back, Colin stopped in Spain to see A., an old Westminster friend. In "Lover and Beloved" Colin says that he told Joe nothing of the trip to Spain or the planned visit to A. for fear that Joe would be suspicious of an affair; perhaps Colin expected he would have one, for he was very disappointed to find that A. had grown ugly.

A. had never found a permanent partner; he had a series of short-term relationships, usually with people in some financial need that he could take under his wing. His current lover was a young man who, prior to meeting A., had been homeless in Madrid. Their relationship had already lasted over a year. But on the night Colin was to stay, A. said that, if Colin wanted, the young man could sleep elsewhere. Colin declined the advance, but A. then arranged for a friend of his lover's to spend the night with Colin. They did sleep together in the same bed that night, but many years later Colin recalled that "that was all there was to it."

Another incident that developed into an affair happened when Colin got to New York. Just before leaving for the conference in Chicago, Colin was staying at the Excelsior Hotel (having sublet his apartment), adjacent to the museum, which has long been home to music teachers. Anyone staying in the rooms next to the teachers has to put up with sounds like those of an entire orchestra and opera company tuning up before a show, but, to some, that is also the hotel's great charm. Colin noticed a good-looking man walking by the front of the hotel carrying a viola; Colin said something to him about his viola, he stopped, they met, and began a passionate affair. When Colin got back from Chicago, this same man, W., was waiting for him, and they stayed together for a full two weeks. In future years, Colin would have brief sexual liaisons with other men, but none touched his heart as W. did. What he had with W. was what Colin called an "affair," and it was the only one that Colin had during thirty years with Joe. All other sexual encounters—those that did not involve the heart—Colin called "incidents."

"[W.] and his friends were good companions, but I knew that even in having a good time by going to a movie, let alone sharing an apartment with another man for a few weeks, I was consciously wanting to hurt Joe for his imagined infidelities at Makerere. In New York, I had heard several stories that he had been sleeping around, but I had never believed them, they were typical of the kinds of stories told by jealous old queens who cannot bear to see people truly in love with and faithful to each other. And although he had plenty of opportunity during those awful weeks of exile in London (when I was with my parents [in 1963]), and I would not have blamed him had he fallen there, the thought never entered my mind . . . However, from the outset I told W. about Joe and when it was all over and I was ready to fly back to Uganda, we had each had all we wanted from the affair."

Colin never saw W. again. But not long after he returned to Uganda, Colin would have yet another ambiguous relationship. Just as he arrived at Pirre to visit Colin, Joe came down with dysentery and Colin took him to a hospital for a few days stay. In the meantime, Colin and an acquaintance, L., went to southern Kigezi to begin filming a documentary about the interethnic relationship between two local groups. Colin complained that L. was spending most of his time trying to find girlfriends, but on the way back he and Colin had to spend the night in Colin's Land Rover and, "as if it were a duty," Colin thought, L. moved over from his side to touch Colin. What precisely transpired is uncertain. But Colin said, "It was not disagreeable, but in no way was it an affair." But the relationship would come back to haunt him.

During the summer of 1966, *The New Yorker* paid Colin a visit while he was in New York. The interviewer opened the piece on the forty-one-year-old anthropologist by noting that although it was the beginning of the summer and Colin's office was hot, Colin was wearing a heavy sweater. In fact, Colin tended to pay little attention either to the clothes he wore or to the temperature of his body. And as he liked to do during all interviews, he probably sipped a glass of Myers dark rum without ice. When he was hot, or when he drank, his face would become flushed, and the initiation marks on his forehead, made during those better days in the rain forest, would become more noticeable.

Colin told *The New Yorker,* "An anthropologist should identify himself with the people he's studying, and I've done that in the past, with the Mbuti Pygmies of the Congo, but I can't do it with the Ik. They are starving to death all around me. I see them getting weaker and weaker. Since they're not allowed to leave Uganda, they can't follow the game. As long as I have enough to eat, I can't identify myself with them. I live on rice and lentils, and I give them what I can, but I can't support two thousand people."

At the end of the interview, he restated his deep interest in going to Little Andaman Island, "which has surf so heavy you can land there only two months of the year, and whose inhabitants are probably Pygmy relics, but the Indian government has refused me permission so far. It may be concerned for my safety. The islanders are alleged to be cannibals, but I don't believe it. They deny it—and they have plenty of food. Even if they are cannibals, it would be an in-group matter. As an outsider, I wouldn't be worth eating. The Turkana raided the Ik while I was around, and killed one of them, but they told me I wasn't worth killing, because I had no cattle. I didn't have any status."

Despite Colin's statements to the contrary in *The New Yorker,* he did identify with the Ik, and he asked his readers to identify with them too. For the fundamental argument of his troubling book, *The Mountain People,* is that the Ik are of interest only to the extent that they teach us about the essence of humanity and inhumanity. For Colin, the Ik were a lens through which he could see the uglier, but perhaps universal, aspects of the human condition. And so too were the Ik a lens through which Colin saw himself and became transformed into a different person. The changes in Colin's personality were probably not simply a bad reaction to a bad situation; Colin could not have lived with the Ik, or struggled to understand them in any depth, if he had not become like them and complied with their ideas and behavior. He had become inured to their suffering and fighting, the smell of the elderly dying inside their huts with neither food or water, the sight of someone eating someone else's vomit. He became filled with hatred. He wished that some of the more despicable Ik would die and that the whole society might one day cease to exist. He felt as if the Ik had infected him with their evil, as if they were parasites eating away at what goodness he had left.

"When the rains failed for the second year running," Colin wrote in *The Mountain People,* "I knew that the Ik as a society were almost certainly finished, and that the monster they had created in its place, that passionless, feelingless association of individuals, would continue, spreading like a fungus, contaminating all it touched. When I left I too had been contaminated, I knew, by the lack of feeling as the house that I had tried to make a home was invaded, the stockade was broken down, and the things I had left to be shared were despoiled by avarice. I was not surprised, nor did it upset me."

The Mountain People stunned the anthropological community. The book and Colin's personal letters described the Ik in terms that went further than most ethnographers would ever go. By the end of his fieldwork, when the famine was lessening due to a decent crop, he would refer to the Ik as "sub-humans," a statement almost unthinkable in the anthropological profession, where a primary rule, usually called cultural relativism, is to refrain from judging people on the basis of one's own standards or norms. In one of his field reports to Harry Shapiro he had written: "All is very well indeed, no more raids, just a steady trickle of refugees limping in from the Sudan, to be pounced upon by these incredible sub-humans I have landed myself amongst . . . And, much to my regret, it is impossible to dislike the Ik because they have no concept of affection anyway. They are merely conscious, as far as I can see, of their stomachs, and of the need to fill them.

"Another twist to this horror story is the fact that I can find no concept of goodness as expressed in action. Goodness only means a full stomach. Someone who gives food without getting as much or more in return is, I am told, merely stupid. I have been told not to give a dying man water, in front of his face, because he was so thirsty he would 'drink like an elephant then there will be none for us, we'll have to go and get more' . . . Laughter is rarely heard, unless someone falls over or hurts themselves . . .

"Lord, I'll be glad when this nightmare ends! And WHAT the hell it will be like when the harvest begins to come in I hate to think! . . . So, Harry, can I have your blessing on my quitting before the final mutual massacre takes place at the end of the harvest . . . ?"

Three months later, Colin was still there, even though he had received Harry's blessing. Colin probably did not want to leave Joe alone in Uganda.

"[The Ik are so weak that] they can not even go outside the compound to relieve themselves, not that there is much to relieve, but it's enough to make the stench pretty nauseating. I know it is not the Museum's function to offer famine relief, but I'll be darned if I can see what else I can do while I'm still working here. I'm not sure which is more depressing . . . feeding those you know darned well will die as soon as you leave, if not before, or fighting off the younger ones who are in no danger at all, barely hungry even, but who will make themselves sick by overeating rather than offer the smallest amount to their relatives. Even the ritual priest, Lolim, with all his power, was abandoned by his children and died just recently. I got the distinct impression that his children were delighted.

"I am going to stick it out to the last, as there is a little individual harvesting (from anyone's fields except your own!) that is anthropologically interesting. And if I can get the few remaining old people to the harvest season they might have a chance. The infants have none, for their mothers just refuse to feed them, and with all my Oxford training I still have not learned how to produce mother's milk."

Twenty days later, he reported a large number of deaths due to starvation, the oldest of the dead being "ten-year-old Adupa, a little mad girl who was quite incapable of defending herself even against the younger children. The rest of the young-dead range from infants to four-year-olds."

Adupa was one of the only Ik about whom Colin nearly cried. She was in some way mentally disabled, though Colin simply called her condition "madness." She was a kind person because of her disability, almost always playful and smiling. But it was because she was kind that she was hungry. When she found food, she would look at it in her hand with delight before eating it, but the other children caught on fast and attacked her for the food. ". . . As she raised her hand to her mouth, they set on her with cries of excitement, fun and laughter, beat her savagely over the head and left her. But that is not how she died. I took to feeding her, which is probably the cruelest thing I could have done, a gross selfishness on my part to try and salve and save, indeed, my own rapidly disappearing conscience. I had to protect her, physically, as I fed her. But the others would beat her anyway."

What killed Adupa was that she needed her parents' love and yet, despite her pleading and crying, they were unwilling to give affection, let alone allow her to live with them. They would not care for a starving and handicapped child while they were starving themselves. Finally, when they let her in the hut she stopped crying, forever. They left her there, hungry and weak, and they promised to bring food back to her. Instead, they locked her in so tightly that she was unable to free herself. When her parents came back a week later, her bloated body was almost beyond recognition, her eyes had been eaten by insects, masses of which were crawling in and out of her mouth, and rodents had begun to gnaw off her fingers, toes, nose, and earlobes.

The central government began to get concerned about the increasing number of deaths and sent a government minister to assess the situation. The minister ordered more maize to be sent, and Colin began "writing a report showing just how the extra ration was distributed."

At Makerere, Colin proposed to the dean, Raymond Apthorpe, that the Ik be relocated to a more fertile area. Apthorpe entertained the idea and sent Joe out to do some initial work; if successfully formulated, Apthorpe would send the plan to the United Nations so that they could consider implementing it. The administrator of Karimoja had also made a personal visit to talk the plan over with Colin and Joe, and Colin thought it seemed likely the Ugandan government would go ahead with some sort of relocation.

To Harry Shapiro, he wrote: "The only tradition that will have to be unlearned will be that of stuffing the individual belly without the slightest regard for any other individual bellies. 'Goodness' is rather horribly defined as having a full stomach . . . A 'good' act is any act that leads to that state of bliss, such as letting that tiresome old witch of a mother die, or that pest of an infant. However, given the area that we have chosen, where the ground is highly fertile and the rainfall pretty even and adequate, this last vestige of their survival culture should, hopefully, fade away. I'll write from the escarpment."

But Colin added that he would not stay to see any changes implemented. He couldn't wait to leave despite knowing that the relocation would make a fascinating study. "It will be a chance to build a new society from scratch and allow it to fit neatly into its new context," he explained to Harry. Colin would gladly let Apthorpe appoint someone else if the plan was realized and someone else could study it too.

Still Colin was not disinterested. He hoped the Ik would be relocated and in the penultimate chapter of *The Mountain People* he advocated a controversial plan that involved rounding up all the Ik and scattering all individuals in new locations. Family members would be separated from each other so there would be no chance of reconstituting Ik society. "My suggestion was simple enough. It recognized that physical coercion would be necessary to relocate them . . . They would have to be rounded up in something approaching a military operation . . . Then they would have to be taken to parts of Uganda sufficiently remote for them not to be able to return to northern Karimoja, for as long as they were within reach they would always try to return . . . Men, women, and children could be rounded up at random and should be dispersed throughout the country, in its mountainous regions, in small units of about ten. Age, sex or kinship was immaterial. Such random grouping would do no violence to the family structure, but would, if anything, be beneficial, for it would complete the fragmentation already complete in all but their continued localization, and would compel their integration into the life of the communities to which they would be allocated . . . I could see no other solution."

Colin could have argued for a quite different solution, that the Ik were so broken and traumatized that instead of being torn apart they needed support, stability, and time to heal. His dispersion plan was never carried out. It sounded preposterous to all who heard it, especially to the Ugandan government and humanitarian organizations working in Africa. But Colin insisted the plan was reasonable, arguing that the concept of cultural relativism was not applicable to a group of people who had lost their culture. He explained clearly why he believed the Ik were acting the way they were. They had effectively been destroyed by outside forces and the horrible behavior that Colin saw was their response to disaster. Individual Ik were struggling to stay alive, and to do so, Colin believed, they had to rely on their most basic instincts, not on any preexisting set of shared values. Ecological and political forces had pared down Ik culture to the core of humanity, and without culture only individuals remained. He interpreted Ik self-interest in the context of his own feelings about western individualism and thus wrote, in an op-ed piece in the *New York Times*, "The Ik have developed individuality to a height matched only by our modern Western Civilization."

Some anthropologists asked him why he continued studying a people who he found to be so depraved. Colin thought the answer was clear: to find out the horrors human beings are capable of. Like Joseph Conrad, he would forever be fascinated by inexplicable horrors; in later years, he would immerse himself in the study of methods of execution, and prison sex and violence. In *The Mountain People,* he hoped, readers would find that it is "oneself one is looking at and questioning; it is a voyage in quest of the basic human and a discovery of his potential for inhumanity, a potential that lies within us all." For Colin believed that the Ik were not always like this; they had deteriorated from prosperity into poverty, from goodness into evil. The Ik was a story of what could happen to any group of people whose society collapsed. And perhaps it had already happened in the West, not through extreme poverty but through extreme affluence, as the morality, cooperation, and love so easy to see among hunter-gatherers such as the Mbuti was subordinated to individualism. Perhaps this is why Ashley Montagu wrote that "the parallel between the Ik and our own society is deadly."

But, as Colin himself noted, any argument about such deterioration depended entirely on a definition of humanity, hardly an easy concept to define. And herein lies the reason why most anthropologists detested the book, and why animal behavior specialists and science writers loved it. These groups saw human beings very differently. Simply put, biological-oriented writers like Ashley Montagu, Robert Ardrey, and ethologists like Konrad Lorenz believed that human behavior was determined by biological imperatives such as hunger and the drives for sex and reproduction. Ardrey, Desmond Morris, Montagu, Lorenz, and the co-authors of a well-known book called *The Imperial Animal,* whose names *really* are Lionel Tiger and Robin Fox, were the predecessors of human sociobiology, a highly problematic field that its founder E. O. Wilson defines as "the systematic study of the biological basis of all social behavior." This school of thought explains complex social and cultural phenomena as the result of individuals acting in their own genetic self-interest. In contrast, culturally oriented writers saw humanity as the capacity for culture, even if that capacity was itself made possible by biological evolution.

While reading *The Mountain People,* Robert Ardrey reflected on the rarity of an anthropologist contemplating the essence of humanity; yet most anthropologists wondered if essences could ever be found, or whether an investigation of essences could ever be done without bias. Certainly, there were political problems entailed in determining who was more or less human than someone else. If one group of so-called experts was empowered to make decisions about culturcide for others, it could be a short step to scientifically justified genocide. Who was Colin Turnbull, and on what basis could he commit such an act of hubris?

The argument was not just between ethologists and *cultural* anthropologists. Biological anthropologists also detested what they claimed were amateurish efforts to reduce culture to biology. In the late 1950s, at the time Colin wrote his first book, *The Forest People,* Elizabeth Marshall Thomas published *The Harmless People,* a popular study of another famous group of hunter-gatherers, the !Kung or Bushmen, of southern Africa. More than a subjective account of a non-violent people, Thomas's book was an elegy to a culture at risk of extinction. Thomas and Turnbull shared a hatred for industrial civilization because they both believed it could sweep over nonindustrial communities, thus destroying what good was left in humanity. This is a perspective still popular today and easily seen in the commercially successful film *The Gods Must Be Crazy.* Most people watched this film with utter pleasure while most anthropologists squirmed. The hunter-gatherers are portrayed as pristine, without aggression or a notion of private property, until a pilot drops a Coke bottle from his airplane, setting into motion the most basic destructive elements of industrial civilization, such as self-interest, violence, possessiveness, and jealousy. Well-known science writers like Robert Ardrey, Desmond Morris, Sir Julian Huxley, and Ashley Montagu were threatened by *The Forest*

People and *The Harmless People* because Turnbull and Thomas both talked about humanity as inherently good and peaceful; these men believed that human beings were inherently aggressive, wired to act in the interests of the self, food, and sex.

But if they had been upset about Colin's previous representation of hunter-gatherers, they embraced the underlying thesis of *The Mountain People.* For in this work they saw humanity as they wanted to see it, as Hobbes's war of all against all. However, it is not entirely clear that Colin shared these views. On the surface, it might have seemed that Ik society, or what was left of it, was determined largely by ecology and instinct, and more generally by the material and biological conditions of Ik life. But whereas these science writers believed Turnbull had found the Ik's true humanity, Turnbull himself believed he had discovered its absence. For him, the Ik were no longer human. The moral of *The Mountain People* was not that human beings are by nature aggressive and territorial, but that under the right conditions Homo sapiens could be stripped of its humanity.

In response to Michael Korda's request for a promotional blurb, Robert Ardrey wrote, "Dr. Turnbull, I am sure, is quite aware that I have few friends in the area of cultural anthropology, and that quoting me may or may not be wise. But my antagonism for cultural anthropology is precisely because it does *not* produce books like *The Mountain People.* Anthropology is the science of man. How often does it obscure, not illuminate, divert us not direct us, delude us not confront us concerning the reality of the human condition?"

By September 1972, two months before publication, there was a huge buzz about *The Mountain People.* Colin wrote to Michael Korda, "Have I written a book? I am getting more reactions from *The Mountain People* before it has even appeared than I might have expected afterwards!" Colin delighted in telling Korda that he was attracting interest from people like Montagu, Ardrey, and Huxley, none of them social anthropologists, all of them ethnologists.

"Wild correspondence from Ardrey . . . And Jake Page from the Smithsonian tried to get the rat man (the name has completely gone from my mind Custer, Cuddles, Calgon . . .) to review the book, since he made such a stir with his rat behavior studies (the stir even reached Zaire!) and C . . . flipped and said NO . . . he couldn't possibly do it but he was sending in right away with a full length article on the book and its implications . . . All these animal behaviorists and psychos are evidently going to take it up . . . so I shall be out of work as an anthropologist for keeps! Except that Virginia Commonwealth University wants me to go there despite it all, and I am sorely tempted."

The "rat man" Colin spoke of was John B. Calhoun, whose studies of aggression in mice were inspired by a short research report on the Ik Turnbull had published in the late sixties. Calhoun starved a population of mice and found that, just as Turnbull's Ik lost their humanity, so too did his mice lose their "mousity," as Calhoun called it. "Though physically they still appeared to be mice, they had no essential capacities for survival and continuation of mouse society . . . It was just such a fading universe Colin Turnbull found in 1965."

If Colin found the way in which Calhoun had used the Ik laughable, he treasured the positive reactions he received from others. One letter that had special meaning for Colin was from Claude Lévi-Strauss, who wrote to him in November 1972, "[*The Mountain People*] is both fascinating and heart-breaking, and will remain as a classic in our field."

The book was an immediate commercial success, selling more than 31,000 copies within the first four months of its publication, but the reviews were mixed. In *Book World,* David Hapgood wrote that *The Mountain People* is "a brilliant, terrifying book—the most compelling chronicle of humanity destroyed that I have read since the concentration camp narratives of the late 40s." In *Time* magazine, Horace Judson wrote in a positive review that "Turnbull compiles the details of the Ik's anti-Arcadia with the obsessive repetitiveness of a man who cannot get his hands clean . . . Turnbull has discovered the reality of evil. The shock has tumbled him from the single Pegalian optimism about man's moral perfectibility that he entertained in his Pygmy days into another error, radical pessimism about man's depravity." Christopher Lehmann-Haupt wrote in the *New York Times* of October 30 that one should question the apocalyptic tone of Turnbull's conclusions and be suspicious of the subjective lens through which Turnbull viewed the Ik. But at the same time, he argued that despite any of these criticisms, the story of the Ik remained profound, shocking, and depressing. He said, "Even alone in its corner of civilization's garden, it is a haunting flower of evil. And Turnbull has described it with hideous power." Lehmann-Haupt predicted that social scientists would not receive the book well, since "it attacks their central assumption: man is by nature, good, or at least neutral, and what vices or aggressions he may demonstrate are distortions in his nature brought on by social forces."

Two weeks later, on November 12, 1972, *The New York Times Book Review* published a review written by Hugh Kenner, a professor and prolific author from California specializing in the work of James Joyce and Ezra Pound. Kenner situated the book in the context of such writers as Samuel Beckett, Jonathan Swift, and Anthony Burgess. He wrote, "[Turnbull] has gazed upon the Ik, upon the worst, and like Gulliver among the Houyhnhms, among what he took for the best, he is somewhat deranged as men tend to be by ultimates." Kenner felt that the comparison between the Ik and "our society" was misplaced, especially specific comparisons between the Ik abandonment of children and the western popularity of nursing homes and preschools. Kenner ended by saying, "What Swift did satirically, Turnbull appears to do blindly."

Michael Korda was incensed and fired off a letter to the editor of the *Times Book Review,* John Leonard, on Thursday, November 9, the same day the early release of the book review section appeared at newsstands and bookstores, but three days before its distribution in the Sunday *Times.* Admitting that for the first time in fourteen years he was breaking his own rule not to express gratitude for good reviews or complain about bad ones, he objected vigorously to Kenner's piece. Korda stated the reasons why the book had received glowing reviews in the *Washington Post, Saturday Review, Life,* and the *New York Times* daily edition and went on to question Leonard's choice of a reviewer. He had nothing personal against the reviewer, just Leonard's choice of reviewer for this particular book.

"No reader or critic has failed to understand the importance of this book except your reviewer.

"And who is your reviewer? By what logic do you assign a major work by a distinguished scientist to the author of a book about Ezra Pound? Had you sent *The Mountain People* to a major figure in the social sciences, somebody worthy of the book and the author, and had he or she disagreed with Dr. Turnbull and argued cogently against him, I should have no complaint to make . . . But you sent a book of the utmost importance to a man who is simply not qualified to criticize Dr. Turnbull's work, and who has further had the outrageous temerity to suggest that Dr. Turnbull is 'deranged.'

"It is impossible to calculate the damage you have done . . . In the past I have kept my feelings about reviews to myself, whether they consisted of pleasure, anger, disappointment or *Schadenfreude.* In this case I cannot."

Korda was receiving a lot of mail as well, including this one from his friend Graham Greene, who, like Kenner, made the comparison to Swift: "I don't know which I admire most—the book or the courage of the author. The Ik could have been conceived by Swift. The only criticism I have to make is of the idealized cover which doesn't at all convey the horror. If you want to quote me of course you can . . . Affectionately, Graham. P.S. if only all anthropologists could write as well as this."

Within a year of its publication, the major international journal of anthropology, *Current Anthropology,* published a series of critical assessments of *The Mountain People,* with a lead article by the anthropologist Fredrik Barth entitled, "On

Responsibility and Humanity: Calling a Colleague to Account." Barth began by saying that *The Mountain People* "deserves both to be sanctioned and to be held up as a warning to us all." Barth made clear that anthropologists have a burden of responsibility to the people they study and that Colin had failed to be responsible to the Ik. For one thing, he noted, Colin had written of the illegal activities of the Ik, such as cattle theft and child neglect, and had published the names and photographs of the Ik who engaged in these activities. He therefore put these Ik at risk of arrest.

Barth and other writers also assailed his methods. Despite Colin's insistence that he abhorred the pretenses of scientific objectivity, especially in a case as extreme as the Ik, anthropologists judged him as if he had tried but failed to write an objective account. Despite the obvious fact that Colin had written a popular book (not withstanding his editor's assertion to John Leonard that Turnbull was a scientist) intended for a general audience that included high school students, anthropologists called his techniques sloppy. He was, after all, a reputable anthropologist. Yet there was no evidence in footnotes or references to oral history he might have collected to suggest what aspects of the culture might have been lost, no statistical information, or even gross estimates about malnutrition, crop yields, and mortality. Much of the book was instead devoted to Colin's own sense of horror, and the reader's glimpses into Ik life are made up primarily of Colin's empathic interpretations of motive.

In doing so, Colin went beyond a mere subjective account and crossed the border into fiction. For example, he imputed thoughts that would be difficult to ascertain and wrote about subtleties that could have been comprehended only by those with skills in the Ik language that far exceeded his own. In writing about the relationship between mothers and infants, Colin wrote that the mother "goes about her business, leaving the child [in the bush], almost hoping that some predator will come along and carry it away." Did he really know that she was hoping for her child to die? In another passage discussed earlier, it is unclear how Colin could have known that his guide Thomas never asked about his own mother since, at that time, Colin could barely speak any of the Ik language. It is highly unlikely that Thomas would have inquired about his mother in Swahili or English, the only other languages spoken in Uganda that Colin knew. Or, take this example about the punishment for adultery, "I do know that Atum enjoyed the vision as he conjured it up, and would doubtless have been first in line to throw his daughter on the fire had I suggested that the custom should be revived."

Think also of the old man sitting in the stockade with his dead wife. Colin saw only a man begging instead of mourning, and noted Peter and Thomas's lack of empathy. What Colin overlooked was the possibility that in begging for tobacco this man may have been trying to initiate a relationship of reciprocity with him or at least a conversation. There are other possibilities. Perhaps Peter and Thomas were not simply cruel like all Ik; both Peter and Thomas may have wanted to keep Colin to themselves, for Colin was enormously wealthy in comparison to them and potentially offered them some wages or social status as the anthropologist's assistants. Possibly the old man and his wife were outcasts and this is why they were alone. Or, all the younger people may have gone in search of food or medicine, leaving the elderly couple at home to rest. Instead, Colin interpreted the situation, one which must have been largely impenetrable to him since he had yet to learn the Ik language, to fit neatly with his early expectation that the Ik were a hostile and unsociable people.

In fairness to Colin, Barth admitted that all anthropologists like some of the people they live with and dislike others, that "There will be many anthropologists who recognize undercurrents from some of their own emotions during less happy fieldworks in the reactions and attitudes which Turnbull gives free play in this book." But, Barth continued, "What is frightening is how they distort his judgment, erode his integrity, and ultimately must have developed into a paranoid hate toward a people he lived among so that all genuine anthropological ballast is lost."

It is safe to say that no anthropologist except Colin believed that Ik culture was nonexistent. Ik associated with one another for the cultivation of fields (so there was social organization and an economy); they tended to live with their blood relatives (so there was kinship or at least enduring social bonds); they possessed sacred caves (so there were religious phenomena); and they were deeply attached to both the mountains and the particular mountain where they lived (they even called themselves *Kwarikik,* the "Ik of the Mountains" or the "people of the mountains," so there was a sense of collective identity). They may have been starving but the Ik laughed a lot—inappropriately, in Colin's view, but then he should not be the judge of Ik humor—so there were social rules and patterns from which the Ik could deviate and about which there were shared understandings.

As it turns out, the Ik still exist, and they have been studied anew by a German anthropologist named Bernd Heine and a Trinidadian student named Curtis Abraham. Their work not only points out some mistakes of translation in Colin's study, but demonstrates the existence of an enduring culture. Although Heine's critique is based on research done almost twenty years after Colin's, the data he provides are potentially devastating. Heine notes that the Ik survived successive droughts as well as a cholera epidemic in 1979-80 during which hundreds of Ik died. Pirre, where Colin lived, had long been abandoned, yet the population of the Ik in 1980 was 50 percent larger than Colin estimated it to be in 1965. Their kinship system was well established and thriving; contrary to what Colin believed, they had a considerable knowledge of the flora and fauna in the area; they were well versed in agriculture, and, most surprising of all, the Ik insisted that they had never been hunter-gatherers. Heine tracked down some of Colin's former informants who told Heine that Colin spent most of his time with non-Ik and that three out of the six villages Colin studied were headed by non-Ik. Heine says Lomeja, a man that Colin called a "true Ik" and who helped Colin learn to speak the Ik language, is not Ik but Diding'a and spoke only broken Ik. Of equal interest is what Heine tells us about the Ik's own reaction to *The Mountain People.* "After they had been informed by the Roman Catholic mission, Kaabong, of the content of Turnbull's publications they were shocked about the way their name had been 'spoilt' in them, and they were reluctant to provide any more information to white researchers. At a meeting I had with the elders of Kamion, Moruatap, Lomoli'j and Nawa'dou on 27 February 1983, I was asked whether it was not possible to take legal action against Turnbull. Should he ever dare to come back to Ik country they would force him 'to eat his own feces.'"

Heine's work is polemical and must be seen in that light. But there are many other anthropologists who have conducted work on distressed communities. Their work shows us that famine-stricken peoples, war-torn communities, refugees, inmates in concentration camps and other kinds of prisons maintain and create shared values and belief systems, however much these values and beliefs may be a product of extreme circumstances. Yet Colin never situated his work within that larger literature and thus missed the opportunity to contribute to our understanding of how societies adapt to crisis.

Still, if Colin is to be criticized for these failures, he can be commended for writing about famine, a subject that, at the time, had received almost no attention in the anthropological literature. One anthropologist writing in 1995 about poverty in Brazil noted that Colin Turnbull is the only contemporary anthropologist to have given a vivid and detailed account of hunger.

Before publishing Barth's charges, the editor of *Current Anthropology,* University of Chicago anthropologist Sol Tax, sent them to Colin. With Tax as go-between, Colin asked Barth to keep the exchange private; Barth refused. Barth recalls that Colin never sent anything directly to him, but confirms that, through Tax, he refused Colin's request for privacy. Barth telephoned Tax and told him, "I am writing for all anthropologists not just to Colin Turnbull." As a result, Colin agreed to write a short statement explaining to the readers that Barth refused to have a private exchange, and that, in turn, he refused to respond to Barth's "personal attack."

"However," Colin wrote, "since Barth, whom I can only assume has been somewhat unhinged by the Ik—by remote control as it were—evidently believes so strongly in his role as Chief Prosecutor, I have sent a copy of his article, and the response I initially made, to each of the five academic institutions with which I am in any way affiliated, together with a letter stating that if they can place any credence in his accusations they are most welcome to my immediate resignation. I shall be intrigued by their replies, which I shall send to the Editor for Barth's information, if not his satisfaction."

In retrospect, Barth thinks that he may have been a bit too harsh, but he was very distressed at the time. He does not recall ever receiving any letters from Colin's employers responding to the essay and offer of resignation.

In the subsequent issue of the journal, six more anthropologists commented on *The Mountain People* (Peter Wilson, Grant McCall, W. R. Geddes, John Pfeiffer, and James Boskey). Colin gave in and published a long reply, in part because, as he put it, enough of his colleagues were "reasonably dissatisfied" with his refusal to reply, and because, while the six were quite critical of *The Mountain People,* they did not share Barth's dogma and did not dismiss the book completely. They at least left room for debate. Colin defended himself vigorously. He argued that he did not write the book for anthropologists (hence, the absence of scientific data); he did not invent the idea of relocating the Ik (the Ugandan government was going to do it anyway so someone who actually cared about the Ik needed to get involved); and he could perceive nothing that warranted the term "social system" (all the evidence of an enduring culture, he said, was beyond his grasp).

He wrote that he was aware of the evidence of a living culture but essentially said that, when it came to the Ik, he was neither an expert nor a scientist! "The evident attachment to the mountains, and to Morungole in particular. The caves. The gregariousness. The villages, however antisocial their design. And . . . I recognize that laughter, as bizarre as it seemed to me, and as incomprehensible as it still is, might in itself hold the seeds of sociality. I am simply not qualified to assess it." Finally, Colin said that he put no one at risk for arrest since the crimes of his Ik informants were well known by the police in the area and, at any rate, more than seven years had passed since the crimes were committed.

Based on comments Colin made in seminars in later years, one suspects that he did not believe the Ik had once been a people who felt kindness and love and that he was unqualified to comment on Ik history. Although he wrote that the Ik behaved as they did as a response to their famine, it is doubtful that Colin would have expected the Pygmies to become evil if they were starving. Despite Turnbull's dedication of the book to the Ik whom he "learned not to hate," he did hate them, and he may have intended the dedication to be ironic. Unlike the Pygmies, the Ik failed to empower Colin. Because he could do little for them the Ik threatened his role as protector or savior. Because they did not seem to respect him or care for him, the Ik never gave him the sense of self-worth he derived from Joe and other underdogs. And because the Ik never gave him someone like Kenge whom he could love and idolize, he grew angry and lonely. The Ik were unlikable to Colin to the end, sadly unyielding to any Pygmalion-like efforts. Joe would undermine him too.

Colin would write little else about the Ik book until nearly twenty years later when he wrote an introduction for the new Pimlico edition. He recalled that the anthropological community had embraced *The Forest People* with the same energy that they had discredited *The Mountain People.* Colin wrote, "I could understand and accept criticism levelled against myself, but I could not understand how people could ignore the very human potential for inhumanity that was the lesson the Ik had to teach us. But that was a truth nobody wanted to listen to; only our potential for goodness were they willing to accept."

In the end, *The Mountain People* and the debates it sparked in journals and in the hallways of academia had been extraordinarily productive. Colin compelled all of his readers and academic peers to confront a conflict inherent in the idea of cultural relativism. Should we tolerate any and all human behaviors, justifying them as "cultural"? And what kinds of writing should we tolerate? (Barth certainly could not tolerate Colin's.) The book is still in print after more than twenty-five years, assigned and debated in social science courses and in law schools where experts in international law and human rights are constantly faced with tough questions about the global implications of human rights. Many anthropologists use a concept of universal rights in their advocacy for immigrants, refugees, and others; many others still cast a suspicious glance on globalizing concepts like human rights or "development."

If the book were published today, it would probably receive reviews similar to those of 1972 and 1973, but there would be three major differences. First, reviewers would ask Colin Turnbull why, if the Ik were in such dire straits, it took him more than five years to document it. Couldn't the international community have done something? Second, reviewers would want to know if all the money Colin made from book sales could have been put back into the Ik community (probably an impossible task but perhaps worth looking into). Colin never told any of his colleagues that he was, in fact, dispensing some of the royalties to charity. Like many anthropologists, he was ambivalent about profiting from the people who had been his hosts, and when he received a large royalty check from Simon & Schuster about a year after the book was published, he wrote a friend, "I am enjoying giving away the Ik's money." Third, reviewers would laud Colin for bringing to light the deleterious effects of state politics but would reject the notion that any culture could be truly defeated. Because anthropologists have in recent years focused much of their attention on the complicated and subtle ways that the powerless deceive, mock, or subvert the powerful, they would want to know how the Ik resisted their domination by the Ugandan state. The Ik must have resisted. They are still living.

In the summer of 1973, Peter Brook, for many years the director of the Royal Shakespeare Company, who also directed such important films as *Marat/Sade, Meetings with Remarkable Men,* and *Lord of the Flies,* asked Michael Korda to locate Colin for him. Brook wrote from his theater in Paris that he had misplaced Colin's address and had "a wild idea that it would be possible to make an interesting theater piece out of *The Mountain People.*" He and Colin had known each other since grade school, and Colin and Joe had visited him in the Caribbean in 1962 when he was filming *Lord of the Flies* (a film produced by Colin's old employer, the director of *The African Queen,* Sam Spiegel). "I have been discussing this with a talented American writer, who has been working with us here, called Colin Higgins [who wrote *Harold and Maude*], and we are proposing to meet together with Colin during the week of June 26-29, in New York, to talk over this totally improbable scheme!"

Brook needed Colin's help. A play about the Ik required something more than a playwright could do since, by Brook's own admission, the idea of making an ethnography about starvation into a play was, even in France, far-fetched. Any playwright would require extensive consultation with the anthropologist.

Thus began a new journey for Colin into the world of international theater, and occasionally into the world of European high society—lunch with Albert Finney, dinners with well-known art collectors. It was a journey that promised to add a new dimension of mutual interest to Joe and Colin's relationship, but which ended up pushing them further apart. Joe dismissed Colin's foray into theater, saying that it was not serious anthropology and that Colin was "playing games." Joe at first used those words innocently but would soon use them to refer to what he came to believe were Colin's sinister attempts to destroy him. Within a decade, a rain would fall on Colin and Joe, and they would seek shelter by retreating into a private, intense world of their own invention, a world that would deteriorate as quickly as it was made.

The theatrical adaptation of *The Mountain People* by perhaps the most important figure in twentieth-century theater would be the highlight of the 1970s for Colin. But much would happen before the play opened in Paris in 1976. For one thing, Colin would resign from the museum and travel with Joe to Zaire to live with the Pygmies again for nearly two years. He would also begin a career as a travelling professor, moving from one job to another, without any real commitment to any institution, and without the job security of tenure. He would spend much of his time trying to build a more secure life with Joe, working late into the night, only after Joe was asleep, to write books and articles. Joe and Colin's marriage would settle into something more stable, even if Joe himself became increasingly unstable emotionally and behaviorally. By the time Colin left the museum in 1969, he had already begun his efforts to shape Joe into a researcher, writer, and teacher in the discipline of anthropology, but Colin would be largely unsuccessful. Colin would repeatedly find himself defeated as Joe's character emerged through the person he thought he had created.

CHAPTER TWELVE

Rain

WHEN COLIN AND JOE RETURNED FROM UGANDA in 1967, they began taking regular trips to Virginia to look over the land they had purchased and to supervise the contractors who were building their house. There would be two residences, a two-bedroom gatehouse near the road that could be rented by the year, and a main brick house with about 4,000 square feet of living space, including a twenty-by-forty-foot music room on the first floor overlooking a creek. The entire construction project cost a little more than $50,000.

The estate, called Chestnut Point, is situated in Lancaster County on the part of eastern Virginia called the northern neck. It overlooks the Rappahannock River near where it empties into Chesapeake Bay, and Colin and Joe designed the house so that they could see the water from their music room. Colin found the northern neck enchanting. It was rural and isolated; it was where Joe had come from; it was where Joe's family still lived; and since most of the residents were African American and most of the whites, he believed, were right-wing Christians, he would not be tempted into befriending people with elite roots. Throughout his more than twenty years in Lancaster County, Turnbull would employ only African Americans to work on his house and property, preferentially shop at black-owned businesses, and, in the end, hire the area's black undertaker to manage his and Joe's remains. At the same time, however, the northern neck reminded Colin of the United Kingdom. There was a lovely town called Kilmarnock, named after the city in Scotland, and with dozens of prerevolutionary churches still standing—most of which are Episcopal even today—the whole eastern shore was a display of British colonial history.

Chestnut Point was not far from Joe's mother's house, and so she came by frequently to watch the construction crews. Others came by to watch, too, and soon the word spread beyond those people who already knew Joe that two gay men were to occupy the new home. Some neighbors complained to the workmen that the house should have been made of wood like all the others in the area, that the two gay men were just trying to do everything differently. Most people blamed "Mr. Turnbull" for the decisions about house materials. For more than twenty years the residents of Lancaster county would call it "Mr. Turnbull's place."

In New York, Colin visited often with Anne Eisner Putnam who, by the close of 1966, was dying of cancer. When she died in January 1967, Colin was surprised to find that Joe was more upset than he was by Anne's death; by his own admission, Colin was not too shaken by her loss. Anne's death was, he wrote years later, "like all deaths . . . an inconvenience and annoyance." Joe wrote sympathetically to his diary about the onset of Anne's illness and described her as "a person who has never known real love." "Poor old Anne," he wrote in 1967, "no more Congo for her." On the night of the funeral, Joe left the museum with Colin and several other members of the Anthropology Department who were also on their way to Anne's funeral service, and walked through Central Park to the funeral home on Eighty-first Street and Madison Avenue. Colin remembered that Joe kept saying to himself, "It is so unfair . . . it is so unfair . . ." "And all I could think in response," Colin said, was "how unrealistic."

The same year, at the age of twenty-nine, Joe started taking courses at Pace University, building on the credits he had already earned at Makerere. He would pass all his courses, but was not a distinguished scholar. He received As in masters of English literature and history of philosophy and Bs in music, western civilization, and architecture. He received Cs in speech, government, and psychology, and Ds in math, economics, logic, and French.

Joe refused to be barred from the museum and dared security to arrest him. When he entered the museum and took the elevator to the fifth floor, security did nothing and, if one judged by his behavior at that time, he was as free as he had ever been. Jim Ford was, of course, long gone, and Harry Shapiro and others had begun to appreciate Joe's efforts. While in Africa he and Colin had together collected a number of objects for the museum, and Joe intended to help Colin on the Hall of the Man in Africa renovations with or without the department's support. Joe worked especially hard developing the portions of the hall that no one really wanted to bother with: a slavery display, a panel on the African experience in the Americas, and a section on Egypt. What the museum did not realize at the time was that by permitting those displays to be included in the Hall, the exhibition would have greater staying power and more political viability than most Africa exhibitions mounted in the United States at the time: thirty years later, the exhibit is still there. It contained portions of a slave ship and manacles; it also showed Egyptian objects at a time when most Africa specialists tended to leave Egypt to the Middle East experts. By the 1980s, Afrocentrist education would embrace Egypt as an integral part of Africa and as the foundation of western civilization. And yet in 1967, when the exhibition opened, all the attention was focused on the more conventional sub–Saharan Africa displays. In fact, most museum curators believe that Colin's Africa Hall was the first exhibition in the United States ever to situate Egypt in Africa.

The museum arranged a candlelight gala to celebrate the opening of the new hall, but while Colin told Joe that friends and family were invited to the opening and mentioned the dinner party, he neglected to tell Joe that the opening and the dinner were two separate events and that Joe was not invited to the dinner, which was for curators, paid staff, and donors. In fact, Colin was excluding Joe from the dinner in order to minimize the museum administration's discomfort with his and Joe's relationship, for Colin could certainly have arranged for Joe and Helena, Joe's sister-in-law, to attend. Joe invited Helena to New York to stay for the week and go to the dinner together; Helena bought a new dress and Joe rented a tuxedo. But on the night of the gala, Colin appeared in the late afternoon dressed in his tuxedo saying that he'd be back after the party. Joe and Helena were speechless. They stayed home and watched television and Helena complained that all white men were the same. When Colin got back he dismissed the gala as a meaningless affair, and told Joe and Helena how he had shocked the audience by saying in his speech that Charles Moore, an African American dancer who performed at the gala, was not African but American.

The next day, Joe, Colin, and Helena attended the formal opening where Joe was disappointed that the museum's director thanked all the volunteers but did not mention him by name. Joe wrote to his diary: "But it was clear, once again, rather like our new house in Virginia, this was Colin's show, not mine, whether we wanted it that way or not. Is that what our life is going to be like? I *must* do something on my own."

He did. Within months after that diary entry, Joe and Colin wrote a joint article for *Natural History* magazine entitled "The White Problem in America." It appeared in the summer of 1968 with Joe listed as first author and it was the only article he would ever publish. They argued that the racial problem in the United

States involved both blacks and whites but that both its cause and solution "lies mainly in the hands of the whites, and in that sense it is finally their problem." Tracing black racism against whites to the slave system, they suggested that slavery continued to cast a shadow of inequality even on the most intimate relationships between blacks and whites in the United States. "Black men kissing white women," they wrote, "is a prime example, whereas white men kissing black women is more easily accepted." They called on white liberals not to be merely outspoken but to act in the service of racial equality; if they did not, Joe and Colin warned, they will be "classed by the bulk of Negroes with the worst of the whites."

But what began as an essay about racism in general became an article focused almost exclusively on explaining black violence. Written in the context of increased racial violence and rioting in America, the article had a particular purpose: to make people aware that black violence was not caused by overcrowding or unemployment in the cities—the conventional explanations given in the media; whites, they contended, were the real cause of black violence. For violence such as rioting and looting was a defiant reaction against deprivation. They wrote: "The Negro youth who runs from a burning store holding a child's doll is clutching far more than fifteen dollars' worth of merchandise: he is clutching a symbol of all that he is deprived of in this anything but equal world. The arsonist who touches off a blaze that will engulf the homes of his fellows, and perhaps only bring a fat insurance payoff to the non-Negro storekeeper, is symbolically destroying the society that pens him in; he is purging himself with fire, for, in biblical thought, the symbolic fire consumes only the evil and leaves the righteous untouched."

Joe wrote the last sentence of the passage. Throughout his adult life, he explained people's ideas and actions in terms of the Bible. He was convinced that violence was useful as a catharsis, and that whatever violence blacks committed was ritualistic in character. Along with Colin, Joe liked to interpret events in terms of their social functions, usually arguing that a ritual or a kinship system was designed specifically for maintaining the social order. So Joe and Colin reasoned that the violence was a safety valve, protecting American society from a much greater disaster and maintaining the stability of the country. Without black violence, they wrote, the country might, in fact, disintegrate into a full-scale war between the races. Blacks, Joe and Colin believed, could completely overthrow American society if they really wanted to. Whites, they implied, should be thankful to blacks for their restraint and for using ritual violence both as a release of racial tension and as a warning of what might happen in the future. Blacks were doing their part, but the burden for ending all violence now rested with whites.

By Christmas 1967, the house in Virginia was almost ready to occupy, and Colin and Joe spent the holidays with Joe's mother and siblings. The architecture and landscaping was just what they had wanted: a simple but large two-story L-shaped brick house nestled among the trees, as if they were living in a forest. On both floors, all the rooms were visible from the foyers. As one entered the house, the large twenty-five-foot-long kitchen was on the right, and then, looking counterclockwise, the dining room, a guest bathroom, the master bedroom, the library, and the music room. There were two guest bedrooms on the second floor, one of which led to a twelve-foot-long balcony.

On that Christmas-time visit they moved a number of their things into the home: a chandelier, a piano, and some furniture for the music room. Joe would forever find the house too dark for his own tastes but Colin loved it. The windows were not well placed for light and the trees blocked direct sunlight. The dining room was the most well-lit place in the house but Colin and Joe would seldom use it. Most of Colin's furniture was heavy and dark as well: large British-made cabinets and tables inherited from his family were placed on dark-stained parquet floors; couches and stuffed chairs were covered in patterned fabrics of brown and maroon. Every window had thick curtains. When it rained, Joe liked to visit friends in the area because the house became gloomy; Colin would smoke a cigarette, play bagpipe records in the music room, and watch the rain from the window.

In the music room where Colin and Joe spent most of their time, there was a large fireplace over which hung an enormous gilt bald eagle. With the exception of the eagle, the room was spare above eye level. In fact, there were few works of art to be found anywhere on the first floor. The most inviting room in the house was the country kitchen with copper pots and pans hanging on the walls. The guest rooms upstairs looked like something one might find in a typical British bed and breakfast: lace bedspreads, delicate vases and picture frames on small night tables, fine linens and, for each guest, sterling silver brushes and combs with ivory handles.

Although they still lived and worked in New York, they began traveling regularly to Lancaster and spent increasingly long periods of time with Joe's family, who seemed comfortable with Colin, especially Joe's sister-in-law Helena. Joe's family also began to visit Colin and Joe more often in New York. Oddly, though Joe expected his brother Charles (Helena's husband) and their mother to come to New York for his graduation from Pace University the next spring, Helena was the only family member to attend. It is not clear why the others did not show up at the graduation at Lincoln Center, but Joe was certainly hurt. As he stood on stage with his graduating class, he looked for them and noticed the two empty seats next to Colin. He also noticed that no one had brought a camera, and after the proceedings, as some of his friends were having their pictures taken with family, he approached Colin with some urgency and said, "Let's go." Colin went into the apartment first and when Joe turned away from him, Colin grabbed the camera, which he had forgotten on the top of a bookshelf, and hid it.

Colin had put champagne on ice and prepared a buffet dinner for friends, and he gave Joe his graduation gift: a complete set of the Encyclopedia of Social Sciences. Joe told his diary, now named "Truthie," "I knew that for what it was, dear Truthie, his way of saying 'Thanks for getting your degree, I know you did it for me, now go for more, don't ever stop!'"

As happy as Joe might have been about graduating and making Colin proud of him, he resented his dependence on Colin. Colin had not encouraged Joe to find work in part because he took such pleasure in supporting Joe financially and because he wanted Joe to study full-time. How else could Joe hope to become a scholar? What is not clear at this time is whether Joe wanted to become a scholar. His diary entries suggest that he imagined himself as a novelist more than anything else. Colin told Joe he wanted to support him in the same way that Jock had supported him through Oxford. At times, Joe would then sarcastically address Colin as "father" and, to Colin's dismay, Joe did not thank him when he began to send monthly amounts of money to a mutual fund in Joe's name. "It became so bad," Colin recalled, "that I was nervous even at going to the movies with [Joe], or out to dinner, for inevitably I had more money in my pocket it seemed (to me) so it was only fair that I should pay . . . And when Joe paid for less costly things like the popcorn, or drinks, or newspapers, I accepted this as casually as he accepted it when I paid for other things . . . [Money was] a constant potential source of friction through which the act of giving, the very act of loving even, came to be seen as acts of manipulation, of possession, of domination." At the same time, Joe took few steps toward becoming financial independent; that he would never look for anything other than occasional academic employment suggests that, to some extent, he and Colin had formed a symbiotic relationship.

In 1968, when Colin and Joe moved to the second floor of their brownstone, Colin bought Joe his own grand piano from Babel Pianos on Twenty-third Street. They made an 8mm film of the movers hoisting it up the front of the building. The short film, lodged with some of Colin's other possessions at the Smithsonian, shows Joe smiling broadly on a sunny day and waving from the second floor, yet Colin and Joe later recalled that day as unpleasant. Joe resented the fact that it was Colin who had unilaterally decided to move—a financial decision he made largely because the second floor could be leased whereas the first floor was only a sub-lease—and Colin tried to buy off Joe's anger with the gift of a piano. On that day, Colin did not think that money was a problem between them: "[The piano] was yours," he recalled many years later, "and you loved it, and I loved you for loving it." Years later, when Colin recalled that day, he was still confused about Joe's dismay, and this is probably the reason he recorded the event. It did not occur to Colin, who operated with a more concrete logic, that Joe might have been afraid of moving, that for him the first-floor apartment meant continuity and stability. It was where they first made love, and where they had lived together for nearly a decade. Joe was so attached to the apartment, the building, and the neighborhood that for the rest of his life he kept a savings account at the bank on the corner of west Twenty-third Street and Eighth Avenue, an account he opened in 1960 on the same day he had moved his things into Colin's place.

Since Joe had studied in Uganda and had spent some time with the Ik, Colin persuaded him that he was capable of teaching anthropology. It was not unusual then for someone to be hired at the university level to teach a course or two or perhaps even be hired in a tenure track position without either a master's or a Ph.D. With Colin's help, Joe received a job offer to teach an introductory course in anthropology at Hofstra University. That day must have been one of the happiest of his life. He wrote to his diary, "Now at last I can do something worthwhile on my own and be worthy of him."

Meanwhile, Colin earned some extra money by consulting for the advertising firm of McCann-Erickson, which had the Camel cigarette account. At the time, they were patterning their overseas ads after the Marlboro Man and wanted Colin to tell them if the Camel models would be appealing in other countries. McCann-Erickson wanted to know how the model should hold the cigarette in ads directed to Asians or Africans, how his legs should be crossed, how he could resonate with Asian or African ideals of masculinity. According to one former employee at McCann-Erickson, Colin's reports, long since shredded, became too sexual, and the agency broke off their relationship with Colin: "It became obvious that Turnbull was more interested in men and sex than in the problem of how to sell cigarettes."

At the museum, Colin tried hard to make two changes. First, he wanted the museum to establish a curatorship for Black America, and if not a curatorship than an assistantship; second, he wanted to establish small storefront exhibitions in Harlem. The museum balked at both proposals. Colin believed that the museum disapproved of the first request because he had suggested hiring a young black scholar and because the administration was reluctant to employ blacks in senior positions. It is hard to imagine that Joe was far from Colin's mind, given the way he framed the request in a memo to Harry Shapiro: "My point about having an extra hand here, at the assistant level, is not merely to take work off my shoulders, but rather to get the work that should be done done more efficiently. A really lively Afro-American, preferably with experience in both

Africa and America, could obviously handle much of the Afro-American side of things, with supervisory guidance from me . . . [he] could work with ghetto communities in such a way as to fill their real needs rather than impose anything upon them."

As for the second request, Colin believed that the museum saw itself as a service to white America and so it made no sense to the administration to reach out to the black community. Besides, one administrator told him, taking valuable objects into Harlem was far too much of a security risk. Colin then pushed the museum to develop an African Center in Harlem, an educational center where there would be exhibits, lectures, and conferences. But he urged the museum to build a center with the full participation and determination of the black community in New York. He wrote Harry: "I feel that we should participate as fully as possible, to ensure that it maintains a high standard . . . However, I feel very strongly that the initiative should come from the black community, not from us, so that they have pride of ownership. It is a technicality, for I am sure that we and other white (primarily!) organizations will be prominent in giving technical and financial assistance, but it is important for the success of the centre among the blacks. I do *not* feel that it will in any way lead to separatism, rather that it will fill the vital need of providing some source of pride for the Afro-American."

Colin was frustrated by the museum's lack of initiative and he planned an act of rebellion. One night Colin secretly removed a number of beautiful African art objects, a heavy-duty glass display case, and a good lock, and took them uptown to Harlem. The exhibition lasted for more than a week and all the items were returned safely to the museum. After the short exhibit had occurred, having been executed without the museum finding out, Colin handed in his resignation and explained what he had done. He could not stay in an institution that, from his perspective, insulted his mission as an anthropologist, his partner, and the larger community to which his partner belonged. This is the reason he gave to his friends and colleagues for his resignation. However, one friend who had worked at the museum as a volunteer for many years and knew Colin well says that the real reason that he quit was because the department of anthropology refused to hire Joe in any capacity. She described Colin in writing as the "best friend and mentor" she ever had and, like many of Colin's friends, could not see why he remained involved with Joe, "a fake," "a phony," someone who was "ruining Colin's life." She added, correctly, that from 1969 on Colin would resign from any institution that refused to hire Joe.

Colin concealed much of what was happening at the museum from Joe for fear that Joe would blame himself. But his secretiveness led Joe to suspect that Colin was having affairs in Harlem, and their relationship suffered. While making love at night, Joe tried to find the marks of a lover on Colin's body, feeling for dried semen, smelling for the scent of another man, and exploring Colin below for any clue that someone else had made love to him earlier that day.

Then, on the heels of one of the best days of his life—getting the job at Hofstra—Joe had one of the worst. Colin was in Uganda for a brief visit, helping film a short documentary. Joe was visiting a senior anthropologist who was a friend and mentor to Joe and who shall remain unnamed; he had a wife and children but was also famous for being promiscuous in the gay academic community. On several occasions he had tried to seduce Joe, and on this day, knowing that Colin was away, he tried again. Joe wrote that he was "quite ugly and physically repulsive to me" but he had not anticipated his meanness. When Joe rebuffed him, the anthropologist said, "Oh, so he's back with his boy friend L. is he?" Joe was silent as his friend continued, "Well, you should know, it was when you were in the hospital, he couldn't wait to go running off with L., they had a wild affair. That's probably just what he's doing right now too."

The next day, the anthropologist found Joe at Hofstra's anthropology department and gave him an envelope containing a photograph of L. and a letter L. had written. In the letter, L. simply asked the anthropologist to send him some money and there was nothing incriminating in it about L. and Colin's relationship. He again asked Joe to go to bed with him. Joe was devastated and briefly contemplated suicide, a plan that he quickly decided was too drastic; instead, he decided to move out, but that plan was also too drastic, and he reminded himself that he had also strayed from Colin, certainly more often, he thought, than Colin had strayed from him. When he met Colin at the airport and they climbed into a taxi, Joe gave the envelope to him. Colin looked at the letter and photo briefly, then handed them back without saying anything. Colin's eyes welled up and he wiped the tears but still said nothing. They would never discuss the matter. Colin's silence and tears were enough for Joe. They were an admission of guilt and a deep hurt, and there was nothing to be gained by talking about it. Colin did not look Joe in the eyes for two days, and neither ever spoke to the other anthropologist again.

To add insult to injury, Hofstra offered Colin a full-time job, eclipsing Joe's achievement. Joe was devastated, concluding that Hofstra had given him the job only to attract Colin. Within a few weeks after starting the Hofstra job, Colin wrote a grant proposal, entitled "Symbiosis and Opposition in Intergroup Relations," for further research in Zaire under the sponsorship of Hofstra with Joe listed as his assistant.

Suddenly Joe felt unimportant. Hofstra showered Colin with attention and did everything they could to arrange media appearances for him. In letters to the *Today Show* at NBC-TV, and other news organizations, the vice president's Office at Hofstra described the forty-five-year-old Turnbull as "an articulate and photogenic bachelor."

Colin's grant application was successful. Effective May 1, 1970, he had $66,900 at his disposal for two years to study how the Pygmies and villagers had changed since he had last studied them in the 1950s. Exactly how Colin intended to spend the money is not clear since the National Science Foundation (NSF) did not keep a copy of the proposal or Colin's record of actual expenditures. Since there was no need for specialized equipment, most of the money must have gone to his and Joe's salaries for Colin and Joe could not possibly have spent it all in the Ituri. These days most single cultural anthropologists without dependants who work in remote regions of the world are able to conduct a year's field research with less than $15,000 a year, in addition to any salary, and in the 1970s could have conducted fieldwork with less than half that amount. It was one of the biggest NSF anthropology grants given out that year and the largest given to a cultural anthropologist.

Even before leaving for Africa, Colin was planning for Joe's career as an anthropologist. He pushed Joe to write and send out for publication articles based on his time with the Ik (Colin himself had yet to even begin writing *The Mountain People*) and together they signed a book contract with Michael Korda at Simon & Schuster for a co-authored study variously entitled *The Black Experience* and *The African Tradition in America* for which Joe would write the black American part and Colin the African part. Though they each received five hundred dollars in advances—a small amount for Simon & Schuster, but a large one for most academics in 1970—nothing ever came of the book, and they were under no obligation to return the advances.

"I don't know what to do," Colin wrote to himself, "Joe has such wonderful ideas and potential, but he just does not seem to have enough interest to push anything through to completion. Is that because he is afraid of failure, of even more rejection? He sure has had more than his share of that, mostly totally unjustified. Or is it because having found that he *can* do something, or *is* needed for something, that knowledge is all he needs so he forgets about whatever it was?"

But then Colin questioned his own criteria. "I publish a book and think that is 'success' . . . How do I know if in fact a publication ever succeeded in doing anything? What if I bothered less about 'succeeding' and a little more about living my dreams, my ideals?" What he did not seem to realize was how much Joe wanted to be like him, and that if Joe did write an article or book, Joe would judge it in comparison to him. Joe's fear of not writing as well as Colin was likely one of the reasons for his inability to complete a written work. Before he met Colin he had completed drafts of several short stories and novels, and though none of them were good enough to publish, they were complete drafts and he was proud of them.

With the grant now funded, Joe and Colin planned to be in Africa from July 1970 until June 1972. It is hard to know exactly how much time Colin actually spent with the Pygmies: in his 1983 book, *The Mbuti Pygmies,* Colin says that he studied with the Pygmies between 1970 and 1973, though there is no evidence of him being in Africa any later than June 1972.

Hofstra gave Colin a leave of absence, and Joe was under no obligation to stay there since he had been hired as an adjunct. As an assistant to Colin, Joe would be able to live in the Ituri and conduct fieldwork, but Colin wanted to maximize their opportunities. If they could spend two years in Africa, Joe could also get a master's at Makerere and even gather data for a future Ph.D. dissertation. Joe wrote to Makerere and was accepted in the anthropology program under the direction of Colin's friend, Peter Rigby. He and Peter agreed that he would take courses at Makerere but travel as often as possible to Zaire to study ritual among a group called the Mbo who, like the Bira villages, practiced the nkumbi ritual and lived in association with Mbuti pygmies.

Leaving Hofstra was not very difficult for either of them. Joe was deflated because he received poor teaching evaluations. By his own admission, he taught in what he called a British style, by which he meant with discipline and authority. He was unable to entertain questions, and certainly not able to withstand *critical* questions. He graded harshly and did not hesitate to fail a student who he believed was not committed to studying the material he had assigned. Though he had taken courses at the college level in anthropology, he had spent only six weeks with the Ik and he was not a trained anthropologist. Colin told his Canadian cousins how proud he was of Joe, but they were astonished that Joe could teach anything and in private talked about Joe as if he were Liza Doolittle claiming at the end of *Pygmalion* that she would teach phonetics since she had obviously learned enough about it from the professor. When, some years later, Colin actually enrolled in Joe's anthropology of religion course at Vassar, Joe gave him a final grade of B.

For his part, Colin not only wanted to revisit the Pygmies, he wanted to escape the increasing turmoil within the university and the escalating conflicts between the university and the anthropology department. Anthropology was booming at Hofstra as it was elsewhere in the country. Many anthropology majors idealized the exotic, wanted to be like American Indians and other nonwestern groups, and saw anthropology as a leftist and humanitarian discipline that supported their antiwar, antimilitary, and antigovernment protests. Sam Leff, a popular anthropology teacher who did research on Yippies and radicals and was friendly with Jerry Rubin and Abbie Hoffman, was himself targeted by campus and federal security personnel for questioning about antiwar protests because the whole university was teeming with activist students, many of whom were anthropology majors. Leff was the faculty advisor for the Students for a Democratic Society (SDS) at Hofstra. He had been arrested at a Grand Central Terminal demonstration for peace in March 1968, which its participants billed as a prelude to the protests that would take place later that year in Chicago at the Democratic National Convention. Leff and Turnbull became good friends and often drove to work together in a Pontiac GTO that Colin had bought to celebrate his resignation from the museum.

Colin and Leff submitted a proposal to the National Science Foundation to establish a graduate program in anthropology, and though they were finalists in the competition, they failed to win the award. Both blamed their failure on the university administration which, they argued, viewed the anthropology department as a collection of radicals and was therefore unwilling to support it strongly enough to win over granting agencies. Leff soon came up for tenure and was denied. Colin supported him strongly and again blamed the university for treating the department as if it were politically dangerous. The reasons for Leff's dismissal must have been more complex: for one thing, Leff did not have a Ph.D., but then—as Leff liked to say—neither did some of the better scholars of the twentieth century, and many of them did not have tenure either.

At roughly the same time, Hofstra administrators began to take seriously the threat of student violence on campus. The president of Hofstra, Clifford Lord, issued a report to the entire university community that began, "In a day when militant black student organizations are disrupting campus after campus, it is appropriate to review the Hofstra record of providing advanced learning for the educationally restricted." That choice of words did little to ease the racial tension, and in those tense days not very long before the Kent State tragedy, Leff believed that the university planned to stimulate a race riot and frame the anthropology department.

In the spring of 1970, as Colin and Joe were preparing to leave for Africa, someone produced and distributed an inflammatory leaflet accusing blacks of attempting to overthrow white rule. Leff and Gerry Rosenfeld, the chair of the department, spent twelve hours with students trying to defuse the problem, and eventually came up with a declaration of student solidarity that brought peace to the campus and prevented a riot. The university launched an investigation into the origins of the pamphlet and determined that it had been written on the anthropology department typewriter. Many in the university suspected that the FBI had broken into the department and had written the leaflet themselves; others believed that a temporary secretary might have been involved. In fact, there was evidence of a break-in. Just before the leaflet appeared, Colin and Sam came into work one morning and discovered that a collection of skulls had been removed from a locked cabinet and placed on the coffee tables in the department. Yet nothing had been stolen. On the heels of this incident, Colin and Joe left for Zaire.

Knowing that Dot and Jock would not want to see Joe, Colin went ahead to England to visit them alone for a few days, while Joe traveled to Virginia to say goodbye to his family. Once they met up in London, Joe and Colin left immediately for Kinshasa. In Kinshasa, they booked passage on a river steamer to Kisangani, the new name of Stanleyville. The university there was still run by American missionaries, and the rector met Joe and Colin at the river with a car. Colin and the rector sat in the back, but the rector asked Joe to sit up front with the chauffeur. When they arrived at the university, Joe was shown his room in a dormitory and Colin was shown his house. Joe told Colin he felt "like a nigger" and refused to stay there; he stayed instead at the most expensive hotel in town. The next day, Colin, unable to arrange any other accommodations for Joe, joined him at the hotel, and they stayed there together until they had bought all their supplies and a truck. After packing up, they were ready to leave for Epulu in the Ituri rain forest, a full day's journey.

Before they left, however, the new government, wanting to establish its power and rule of law, had ordered the residents of Kisangani to watch the execution of two Simba rebels who had refused an offer of amnesty from President Mobutu Sese Seko. Colin and Joe were escorted to the gallows by the governor himself. Joe decided he could not bear to watch it and stayed in the car, but Colin was ushered up to the front. In 1983, Colin recalled the execution: "The trappings were distinctly European: a makeshift gallows, the two nooses dangling at the ready, the hoods waiting to be pulled over the faces of the criminals at the last moment, the governor in full panoply, waiting to read the sentence and give the order . . . When the governor gave the signal, each man in turn was given a bull horn and allowed to address the crowd . . . One of the men, sensing the end was near, collapsed on the floor and from there could barely whisper that he had nothing to say. His companion, however, spoke to us for what seemed like an eternity, in a loud, clear, and almost friendly voice, as though talking to his family."

The man, sitting calmly before the crowd, confessed to having killed innocent people, but recognized that what he was really guilty of, and the reason he had to die, was violating the laws of the new nation. He thanked the crowd, got up, and moved toward the noose. Colin found that perspective almost convincing, despite his opposition to capital punishment. The killer had honored the people he killed by proclaiming their innocence; he had, by his acquiescence, conveyed the power of the new state to enforce a rule of law; and he did it all publicly in a way that helped the community come together and affirm their own unity.

In "Lover and Beloved" he described other aspects of that experience—the feeling of coming alive in the face of a death, and a sense of unity with his companions as they watched death together—echoing his feelings on that terrible day during World War II when he had watched so many of his friends and colleagues die.

"Just before the men themselves were invited to speak, I found Joe standing beside me, shivering with dread. It was the same sort of dread that filled me, I was sure, and I found I was shivering too. It was not a morbid curiosity, but that strange feeling of vitality, that intense awareness of being alive that accompanies any manifestation of death. As though by the death of someone else one is given one more chance at living. I didn't have the strength to say anything to him, but Joe wanted to say something, and just whispered, 'I had to be near you.' As though to reaffirm that the two of us were, indeed, alive. If we could have hugged each other he could not have said it more clearly. When the men were hung and we were still standing there, Joe said 'now it will rain.' And it did. A steady, sad drizzle. 'It always does, we say in the south,' he told me, 'when someone dies.'"

When Colin and Joe got to Epulu, they were given a warm welcome by both the Mbuti and the Bira. Colin was still seen as Putnam's son. Though he was ambivalent about living at Epulu—since there were just too many bad memories of fights with Anne and he always sensed that the villagers were hostile towards him—the Bira and the Mbuti had already made up their minds. They almost automatically began clearing the site where Camp Putnam's buildings had once been and started building a hut on some of the old foundation stones that had survived the demolition of the camp. Many of the Mbuti talked excitedly about taking Colin out to the forest, but he insisted that he was there to study the villagers. He expected them to protest, and when they did not he was hurt because he thought of himself as "Pygmy" and wanted the Mbuti to think of him that way too.

As for Joe, he immediately liked the villagers much better than the Pygmies; he was more comfortable in the larger and drier village dwellings situated along the roadside where there was both pedestrian and commercial traffic, and he could communicate more easily with the villagers since so many of them knew French. In addition, the sedentary villagers appeared more reliable than the peripatetic Pygmies both as informants and language teachers. Colin drove Joe up to Makerere where he stayed only long enough to get Joe settled. After a brief trip to Europe to edit a Viking Fund series of ethnographies, Colin returned to Uganda, just in time to celebrate Joe's thirty-third birthday with him at Chez Joseph. Then one of Kampala's finest restaurants, Chez Joseph was run by a gay couple who, it was rumored, were linked to the last Kabaka, the Bugandan chief. It was common for people to gossip about this or that person as a procurer of young men for the Kabaka. Legend has it that the Kabaka of old tried to mimic the British as much as possible, and one practice that took hold with the last Kabaka's grandfather was homosexuality. The first Catholic martyrs in Uganda were teenage boys who, with the church's support, refused the Kabaka's attempts to seduce them.

Within a few days, Colin made the two-day, three hundred mile drive back to the Ituri and set up residence at the rebuilt Camp Putnam. The Ndaka villagers told him that there would likely be a major nkumbi initiation the next year, and Colin immediately wrote Joe in the hopes he would decide to study it for his Ph.D. dissertation. Colin wanted Joe near him and he was afraid that Joe would decide to go back to the Ik, perhaps risking his life in the hostile feuding between the Ik and the Turkana. Joe wrote back weeks later, sounding desperate and incoherent. He was lonely, he said, running out of money, and losing weight. Colin did not know what to make of it since he had left Joe with plenty of money and had no idea how to get more money to him without making the long journey again from the Ituri to Kampala. After much thought, he decided that Joe had to be treated as an adult and could take care of himself, and even if he could not, his advisor Peter Rigby and Rigby's wife, Zebiya, could. So he simply pretended that he had never received the letter at all, and, in the end, though Joe suspected Colin might have been lying about the letter, he did not go broke and he survived his anxiety and loneliness. He survived by finding lovers.

In 1990, two years after Joe died, Colin typed out a portion of Joe's diary in which Joe recorded his affairs. Unfortunately, Colin lost the original of that same portion from the diaries before he donated them to the Avery Research Center archives, so it is impossible to know how he might have altered it.

According to Colin's transcription, Joe wrote: "I would never have thought it possible, a few years ago, that I would allow so many men to make love to me, yet there is a simple animal attraction to these African men, devoid of love, and I seem no longer able to control it . . . E. [Everest] works at Makerere . . . He has a nice wife and two children, yet he keeps asking me into his room. He introduced me to his cousin, J., since I am lonely . . . J. got me to his studio and tried to make me buy one of his paintings . . . Then he made love to me. I felt really dirty, there was no emotion at all . . . I went to see E. who just wants to have sex with me . . . It is even more clear that it is all physical . . . Sex is so different when you love a person . . . Colin, please come and get me and take me away from here. I never knew I could be so weak. Come and get me, and take me back to the forest with you . . . I like E. too much . . . I met L. in town and we had a drink together. While at the bar a handsome young Ankole youth came in and cut an eye at me . . . Before long we were back at my place and in bed together . . . I gradually met others. C., who was with me at Makerere years ago, and G., supposedly a procurer for the Kabaka, a real queen; he introduced me to S . . . and then to P.'s lover too."

Colin found that in the twelve years since he had been in the Ituri, war had changed things. Many of the people he had worked with had fled to settlements far away from Epulu, and many parts of the forest were now unrecognizable to him. The Mbuti and Bira had both been subject to an array of powerful influences: missionaries, urbanization, wage labor, large-scale agriculture, lumber mills, trading posts, and wildlife activists. For Colin, all of this was what the Mbuti called *akami* or noise. Whereas the Mbuti had once seen the villages as merely a luxury, they increasingly saw them as a necessity. The direction of power had shifted. Colin now felt that the villagers no longer needed the Pygmies in the same way because they had access to goods through other routes, and villagers were now going often into the forest to hunt for their own meat to sell to truckers and traders. Even worse, there were concerted efforts by the government and by local entrepreneurs to "emancipate" the Pygmies from their servitude to the villagers, and this meant discouraging the Pygmies from living as nomadic hunters and encouraging them to become sedentary farmers. During Colin's 1970-72 stay, one such entrepreneur, Ferdinand Lomata, amassed enough money from the government to begin construction of model villages. He carefully selected Mbuti families who he believed were more likely to become sedentary and showered them with new clothes, farming equipment, and money. None of these Pygmies stayed for more than a week or two, but they would be replaced by others so that the villages were always occupied by at least some Pygmies.

Throughout the 1970s and 1980s, there would be many more such failed efforts, with administrators and missionaries making confident predictions that if the Pygmies could only stay in the villages, they would evolve from "savages" into model citizens, and would ride bicycles and hang curtains on the windows of their mud huts. In the early 1980s, the Italian Catholic sisters, living just north of Epulu in a mission funded by the Swiss, devised a rather ingenious plan to free the Pygmies from the villagers. Any Pygmy could bring any kind of handicraft to the mission in return for Swiss Army uniform buttons. The buttons were of varying sizes, with each size corresponding to a different value as determined by the sisters. Only the Pygmies could use the system and exchange their buttons for food and iron at the mission. The sisters were convinced that the Pygmies would now trade with them rather than with the domineering villagers. They never expected that the villagers would accept the buttons from the Pygmies since they were presumably worthless to them. The plan backfired because the villagers realized that if they took the buttons from the Pygmies as payment for food and iron, they could then sell the buttons back to the Pygmies. Instead of disrupting the system of "slavery," they merely fueled the relationship with a new currency, and one that was far more stable than the volatile national Zairean currency.

In the failure of the planned Pygmy villages, Colin saw the triumph of the Pygmies over modernity. While many Mbuti worked as wage laborers, and some were either converted to Christianity or appeared to sincerely embrace village religions, most Mbuti appeared to him to have resisted change. The central message of the book based on the 1970-72 fieldwork, *The Mbuti Pygmies: Change and Adaptation,* was that the Mbuti could themselves adapt to almost any situation, that outside interventions were sure to fail and the Mbuti would continue as a distinctive society of hunters and gatherers. But there were immediate dangers to the Mbuti that frightened Colin. Sanitation in the model villages was poor—there were no outhouses, for example—and Colin believed that mortality rates had climbed and diarrhea was rampant. One young girl died in front of Colin and Joe from what looked like dysentery. Joe suspected it was something worse, and it was. It was cholera, a disease that could spread quickly in the filth of the model villages.

By the fall of 1970, Joe wrote Colin to say that he had moved to a town outside of Makerere. Concerned about where and why Joe had moved, Colin drove up to see him on November 30 to celebrate St. Andrew's Day, the commemoration of the Patron Saint of Scotland. When he arrived in the early afternoon, he found an old man sitting along the roadside who knew the apartment in which Joe lived. He said Joe was not well.

Colin knocked but there was no answer. He opened the door and saw that the room was a mess and Joe was lying face down on an unmade bed. Colin called out to him and Joe opened his eyes, looking at Colin as if he did not recognize him. He lifted himself up from the bed as his eyes filled with tears, and then fell back crying. Colin tried to caress his head but Joe pulled away fast. He had touched his hair long enough to feel the grit and oil of hair that had not been washed for days. He could also smell alcohol in the room.

He decided to leave Joe alone for an hour or two. When he came back, Joe appeared happy and well rested, and had cleaned the room. He said he thought Colin had come earlier but that he was napping and couldn't remember. Colin told Joe he had come in earlier but that he looked so tired he decided to let him sleep. They both accepted the lie, and that night went to dinner with Everest, with whom Joe was having an affair. The next morning they went out to shop and have lunch with Everest, and then Joe and Everest had a drink together at a bar in Kampala called the Grand. The next morning, Colin found a piece of paper and wrote to Joe: "You are asleep in the next room, and I am here at your desk . . . how I love you, and how proud I am of you . . . If you knew how much I loved you, you could not hurt me as you do. How often I have longed to hold your hand in public, to have your arm in mine . . . only twice have you allowed it . . . once in New York when you were almost too drunk to stand and tonight, when it was Everest's hand that yours took first. How much do you think I can stand? I love you so very much, and will never love you less. Until I die I will love you and you alone. But I cannot share you . . . hold your hand on one side while you are holding someone else's on the other. I have failed somewhere, terribly, and now I know it . . . Now I just want to leave Kampala and all its nastiness behind, forever. It has cost me the one and only thing that meant anything to me: you."

On the back side of the paper, was a handwritten note from Joe: "Dearest Colin, Everest and I are gone to the Grand. All my love, your own, Joe."

Colin was elated that, after only a few more days, Joe would leave with him to go to the Ituri. Joe planned to stay about a week before heading off to find a field site among the Mbo. Colin was also delighted that Kenge, who had been living in another part of the forest and who had heard rumors that Colin was in Epulu, came back to Camp Putnam to look for work as Colin's assistant. After all these years, they were back together again and, as it turned out, Colin needed him. Less than a week after getting back to the Ituri and sadly watching Joe drive away to gather more data in the south, Colin developed a hernia. Kenge helped him drive to a large mission hospital, the Centre Médicale Evangelique in Nyankunde, where Colin suffered through not only a painful operation but Protestant missionary attempts to convince him that evolution could never have taken place in God's universe, and that it was merely a trick that God had played on scientists to test their faith. Kenge spent the days sitting by Colin's bed reminiscing and bringing in cigarettes and alcohol for him behind the backs of the missionaries.

When he got back to the Ituri, Luigi Cavalli-Sforza, the famed Stanford geneticist, came by to collect samples of genetic material from Pygmy hair and skin. He brought medicines and good advice about how to prevent cholera from spreading and how to treat leprosy. Cavalli-Sforza also injected as much penicillin as he could into people with yaws, a skin disease that eats away at the flesh, especially on the face, and trained Colin to give more injections after he left. On visits to Colin, Joe took over the medical care, and this gave Joe something of a reputation for being a doctor, a reputation that helped him establish fruitful relationships with the villagers in charge of the ritual aspects of the nkumbi, the subject of Joe's research.

Whenever Joe left, Colin missed him and wallowed in his sadness and his nostalgia for the old days with the Pygmies by immersing himself not in research with the Pygmies but with the painful memories of the Ik. Despite the fact that he had conducted fieldwork with the Ik in 1965 and 1966, until 1970 he had written little about them. During one of Joe's absences, Colin secluded himself within his house at Epulu and began typing *The Mountain People.* This was not neutral ground: while living with the people he loved he would write about the people he hated. It took him only three weeks to finish a complete draft.

One day, Colin and Kenge noticed a villager walking down the road, carrying a long stick in front of him and twirling the outer rim of Joe's straw hat on the end. The man told Kenge he had found it in the forest. Colin was scared, and he even seemed afraid to touch the rim, so Kenge nailed it to the wall of Colin's hut. Kenge was scared of the hat too, as if it were imbued with some sort of ritual power, but he told Colin that if Joe was dead the rim would not have such power. It was only so powerful because Joe was alive, and the rim was calling Joe back to Epulu. And within the next two weeks, Joe appeared, wearing his hat without the rim.

Colin was aware that Joe had become increasingly "native," not only in his behavior but in his appearance. Joe had decided that he was a ritual priest, and he tried to act the part of an other-worldly, spiritual creature by wearing ritual paraphernalia. There was a distance between them that would not be bridged until it was time to leave Africa. Joe managed to gather a lot of details about the Mbo nkumbi, and though he would never publish them during his lifetime, the data would be sufficient to earn him a Ph.D. in sociology and anthropology from Makerere in 1979.

Unfortunately, Colin's two years in Africa yielded few substantial publications and most of the data he gathered, stored today at the Avery Research Center archives, remain unanalyzed. Although he published *Mbuti Pygmies: Change and Adaptation* in 1983, nearly half of the text was a description of the Pygmies at the time of Colin's first fieldwork periods in the 1950s; most of the information had already been published elsewhere. By 1972, at the age of forty-eight, Colin was just beginning to consider his own anthropological work as secondary to the work of loving Joe.

Colin left Africa while Joe finished up his research. In order to prepare the Virginia house for Joe's arrival, Colin bought a tractor and cleared land for planting some crops; he decorated the house and landscaped; he met with an architect to design an addition to the house. And most importantly, as a sign that he was committed to the relationship and to their new life in Virginia, Colin bought a shiny new black Steinway concert grand piano for the music room, the largest piano Steinway made. Joe never found out how Colin got the money to buy a piano that cost $8,500, not much less than his salary at Hofstra. The swimming pool was complete, just in time for Joe's return, and all the pets were well. Colin wrote to himself, "He seems to have no control over money at all, whatever he has he spends. Yet I so want him to have everything. So to hell with the expense, I love him so much. At least he cannot spend the pool or the piano, he can only enjoy them. I just wish there was more I could give him . . . he deserves the best of everything."

At the same time, his exploratory letters and calls to Virginia Commonwealth University (VCU) in Richmond culminated in a job offer. VCU said they had a senior position available for him, and they might even entertain the idea of giving Joe occasional teaching jobs. The possibility of Joe getting a job clinched it for Colin. So he planned to go back to Hofstra for one or two terms, await the publication of *The Mountain People,* go on a publicity tour, and then try to convince Joe to leave New York so that they could live together happily, privately, and forever in Virginia.

CHAPTER THIRTEEN

Peter Brook

IN MARCH 1999, Peter Brook walked to one of his rehearsal spaces near the Place de la Bastille as if he was gliding on ice, his eyes fixed on the horizon. His physical appearance is ordinary but his presence is enigmatic. A visitor seeing him for the first time might be surprised to find that such a gentle and graceful man is a creative genius in the theater, to hear his soft voice with a mild British accent modestly utter phrases that at first sound unworked but a second later seem profound. He is hard to read, since all at a single moment he can look preoccupied or in a daze, worried and confused, completely relaxed, and electrified with creative thoughts. It was late afternoon, the sun was setting on a cloudy day, and he didn't bother to turn on any of the lights. He brought out a bottle of whiskey, drank in the dark, and talked about the Ik and Colin Turnbull.

Brook is suspicious of biographers' intentions, but he knows that Colin wanted his life well known. Not long ago, a biographer asked Brook for his correspondence with a well-known British director, but he was reluctant to make it available.

"But," the biographer protested, "his wife and mistress gave me all *their* letters." "In that case," Brook said decisively, "I am definitely not going to let you see them."

For Brook, it seems, memory is either non-existent, a remnant of experience that you have for a moment and then banish from your mind forever, or it is sacred and private. That a widow or mistress would give up something so precious turned his stomach. His memories of Colin were precious too; even the smallest recollection was a gift he was giving for Colin.

Colin was an inspiration to him, and he believes he was an inspiration to Colin too. For it was Peter Brook who, remarkably, taught Colin to see the Ik in a new light.

The idea for a play based on *The Mountain People* came entirely from Brook, an artistic mastermind widely hailed as *the* intellectual figure of twentieth-century theater. In 1970, at the age of forty-five, Brook left the Royal Shakespeare Company in England, where he had astounded audiences with innovative productions, to establish an experimental theater group in Paris, the International Centre of Theatre Research. Unlike England, where experimentation was nearly always met with suspicion and disapproval, France, he hoped, would embrace something new and daring: a center for workshops, improvisations, and children's events—a place for low-priced, cutting-edge performances. The group would work in Paris and elsewhere, with deaf children, with African Americans in Brooklyn, with Hispanic actors in Mexico, and with Native Americans on a reservation in Minnesota. Brook believed that theater required "more than schools or rehearsal rooms;" it needed an ever-widening expanse of audiences and performances. The critic Albert Hunt wrote in praise of Brook's decision to move to Paris: "That Peter Brook is the most talented individual director, in the conventional sense, to have emerged in our theater for 30 years few people would deny. If he had wanted, he could simply have spent his life turning out one international success after another, as if by magic. But what makes him an important artist is that he's a man possessed by an idea. He's driven by a need to search for ways of exploring the ultimate in human experience in terms of the ultimate in theatrical expression."

Brook and his visionary partner Micheline Rozan had at their disposal a grant of unprecedented size from the Ford Foundation: three million dollars of start-up money for the first three years. Brook had no deadlines and no fixed agenda. But he knew that he wanted the group to break down the barriers that separated actors and audiences from each other, and to expand theater's ability to capture humanity in performance. For the troupe, Brook found a dilapidated theater, damaged long ago by a devastating fire, in an unfashionable part of Paris. He did some minor renovations but left it much as it was. The Bouffes du Nord, as the old theater was called, would be an ideal setting for one of the first plays they would perform, *Les Iks,* based on *The Mountain People.* Theater critic David

Williams wrote that the auditorium itself mirrored "the leprous state of the [Ik] society and the decay of human relationships within the play" and also served in part as a "reflection of the state of our own society."

In 1972, before Brook had even contemplated a play about the Ik, he took his troupe on a long African trek through Algeria, Niger, Nigeria, Dahomey, Togo, and Mali, a remarkable voyage recorded by John Heilpern in his book *Conference of the Birds.* The group consisted of a diverse array of actors, actresses, directors, and artists. It included Brook's wife, Natasha Parry; a well-known French heartthrob named Francois Marthouret; *Life* magazine photographer Mary-Ellen Mark; the soon-to-be Broadway musical sensation Elizabeth Swados; Malick Bowens, a Malian actor who had been introduced to Brook by the theater director Jerzy Grotowski; Helen Mirren, a star of the Royal Shakespeare Company; Michelle Collison, whom Brook describes as "Mother Earth from America"; Katsuhiro Oida, a famous Japanese actor; and a large Greek-American actor named Andreas Katsulas, an extraordinary talent with almost no experience, sent to Brook by Ellen Stewart of New York's La Mama theater. Katsulas would eventually play the part of Colin Turnbull in *Les Iks.*

The central purpose of the trip was simply to travel, to fall into unexpected contexts, especially where there was no tradition of theater. Whereas the actors and audiences in Europe shared similar expectations and understandings of theatrical performance, an awareness of the same kinds of narrative structures, plots, character development, jokes and denouements—not to mention the idea of "theater" and "play"—many African audiences would come to a performance with completely different expectations of what they were about to see. These performances would put Brook's actors at risk of failing theatrically. They would be as free as possible of both the constraints and comforts of European theater.

The troupe did no research or reading about Africa before they left France because, in Brook's view, theatrical experience needs no intellectual background. Take the example of producing Shakespeare. "As in anthropology, there are two schools," Brook told an interviewer in the early seventies. "Certain researchers prefer to go into a far country knowing nothing about it, while others leave only with documentation and after deep study. For me, with Shakespeare, the questions only become strong, hard, interesting when you're inside them. You can approach a Shakespeare text without knowing anything outside."

Brook hoped he could use theater to find something in common with people who knew nothing about him, his group, and their art, and about whom they equally knew nothing. If they could enter a village in Africa, if only for one hour, and perform an improvisational piece for an audience who, by virtue of the absence of a theater tradition in that village, was not even aware of itself as an audience, then perhaps they could all discover together that there was something shared by all humans, an untouchable, perhaps magical, spiritual essence realized in performance. For Brook, the best actor is the one who is totally honest and does not even appear to be acting, for he is simply being human.

Heilpern wrote: "The Hausa language has no word for theatre. Through translators, all Brook could establish was that the troupe would like to 'perform' something. An actor enters, playing an old man. Perhaps he stoops and coughs, playing old. But the audience looks nonplussed, even concerned.

"The audience in the African village didn't see an actor playing an old man. They were receiving a different message. A young actor stoops: there might be something wrong with his back. He coughs: perhaps he's ill. But the African spectator, however sophisticated, doesn't necessarily see an old man. In a sense, he sees a total stranger who isn't pretending to be an old man well enough. Because the actor is relying on his own habits and easy conventions.

"So he must begin again. He must stop 'acting.' And if he can find something fresh and extraordinary within him, he will convince any audience in the world of something very rare: a universal emotional truth. And then theater can become irresistible—a completely truthful, natural event."

Brook and his company entered African nations by car and never by way of the capital city, driving along the countryside until they came upon a group of huts. They would ask to see whoever was in charge—a chief, a commissioner, or an elder—and say simply, "We are trying to see if communication is possible between people from many different parts of the world." They were always welcomed. An actor would lay down a carpet to mark the boundary between audience and performer, wait for a mass of people to arrive, and begin. The plays were, for the most part, purely improvisational. And perhaps they could not even be called plays, for even that category is open to question in Brook's world. In one village, the group placed a cardboard box in the middle of the carpet. "For the spectators, for us, it was the same," Brook recalled. "It was real. An actor got up and went toward it. What was inside? As the actor wanted to know, the audience wanted to know with him, so at once we were on common ground where the imagination can spring to life."

Along the way, the group met some anthropologists who had a hard time understanding Brook's method. By coming to Africa, Brook had opened himself up to suspicion that his project was fundamentally about robbing African culture for European profit, and that he was therefore a colonialist or cultural imperialist in disguise. The anthropologists also scoffed at the brief periods of time Brook stayed in any one place. The anthropologists were interested in how every aspect of behavior, down to the most precise gesture, was an expression of a distinctive culture; they had worked hard for months and sometimes for years to gain even limited access to that culture. And here was a creative genius, speaking a lofty language about bridging cultures in less than an hour. While the anthropologists were exploring cultural differences, Brook was looking at sameness; they were intellectualizing while Brook was feeling his way along. In one sense, Brook was probing the depths of sameness in a way that dissolved cultural differences, that carried the troupe and their spectators away from superficial distinctions into an experiential world of fundamental truths.

"Kissing the lips or rubbing noses may well be conventions rooted in specific environments," Brook once wrote, "but all that matters is the tenderness that they express." He continued: "'What is love? If it has a substance show it to me,' says the skeptical behaviorist. The actor does not need to reply; invisible feelings are what animate his actions all the time. Muslims put the hand on the heart, Hindus bring the two palms together, we shake hands, others bow or touch the ground—any one of these gestures can express the same meaning provided that the actor is capable of finding the necessary quality within his movement. If that quality is not there, every gesture is hollow and carries no meaning. One can enter an African village and smile automatically—and no one will be fooled. If hostility is concealed behind the smile, it will be sensed at once. But if the actor genuinely wishes to convey a deep feeling, if the truth of this feeling is there, it will be felt and understood by everyone, even if the outward sign chosen to express friendship is as unexpected as a clenched fist."

As the African trip progressed, it became clear to Brook that they had to do a play about Africa, and possibly even a play about their own adventures there. But they were too close to that experience to act it honestly without their own egos, ideas, and memories getting in the way. What was needed was what he called a dramatic, creative transposition, something that would touch the actors deeply but which did not really belong to them. And this need led him to his old friend Colin Turnbull, a man who was unlike most other anthropologists and who shared with Brook the view, implied in Brook's film *Lord of the Flies,* that civilization was a fragile social contract, that conditions of extraordinary stress or deprivation could unleash humanity's most aggressive, violent, and self-interested instincts.

After another extended voyage, this time to the United States, Brook and his troupe returned to Paris to perform his first play at the Bouffes du Nord, Shakespeare's *Timon of Athens,* and to begin nine months of work on what eventually became *Les Iks.* At about the same time, Brook was introduced to the playwright Colin Higgins. Higgins was already well known in London and on Broadway for his hit play *Harold and Maude,* and at Brook's request and with Colin Turnbull's blessing, Higgins and a co-author, Denis Cannan, wrote a script based on *The Mountain People.* But Brook almost immediately discarded it. Brook was interested in a performance in which the audience would be unable to discern the author, just as one can never discern Shakespeare himself in his plays. For in Shakespeare's works there are so many voices and points of view, so many dimensions of so many different kinds of characters that his plays were never autobiographical or personal expressions, never subjective. Contemporary authors were, for Brook, much too subjective and thus no good for the theater. Even more damaging, most authors have a distinctive style that threatens the ability of any actor or director to transcend the author's controlling ego.

This desire for freedom was the main reason why Brook favored improvisation over fixed texts. The individual ego of the actor became an issue of control only when he or she improvised in isolation from the group, and this is why Brook favored group improvisational sessions conducted by a group of actors as diverse in background as possible. The group improvised the French language play, *Les Iks,* that was ultimately stitched together by Higgins, Cannan, and a screenwriter, Jean-Claude Carriere, who had written the French version of *Harold and Maude,* but who is perhaps best known for the screenplays of *The Return of Martin Guerre, The Unbearable Lightness of Being, Valmont,* and several Luis Buñuel films.

Brook must have found *The Mountain People* unsatisfying in many ways because Colin did not present the Ik in a way that lent itself to the three-dimensional theater that Brook had in mind. His book was a personal expression about his perceptions, feelings, and reactions to the Ik; it was a book about Colin as much as it was about the Ik. Certainly, a trip to visit the Ik would have been very useful to overcome Colin's authorial presence, but by 1973 the political situation in Uganda made it too dangerous for Brook to travel there. And this is where improvisation helped.

Even if the script eventually consisted of words and actions taken directly from *The Mountain People,* the performance could transfigure simple observations into complex realities. How easy it would have been to portray the Ik as evil. And how much more difficult it would be to portray the complexity of an evil character. For Brook, an actor has to have a script, like those of Shakespeare, that opens up the possibilities for expressing the full complexities of life. "If you're going to act the part of [an evil man]," he said, "you have to defend that character. You have to see how he justifies himself, as hard as that might be."

In Colin's book, the Ik were represented as one-dimensional, and readers could know the Ik only through his eyes. Colin's ego was a controlling presence in nearly all of his works, especially in *The Mountain People* and *The Forest People.* But Brook saw a positive side to Colin's authorial presence in *The Mountain People.* Since most other anthropologists would not have imbued their works with so much sentiment, their works would not have been amenable to theatrical adaptation.

Brook sees the well-known neurologist Oliver Sacks as a contemporary Colin Turnbull, a brilliant observer criticized by his fellow scientists for being a popularizer, or worse a sloppy researcher, who relies on anecdotes and a talent for writing, and who has the ability to touch people deeply. For Brook, Sacks and Turnbull express more about the truths of life than the very best scientists could ever hope to because scientists obscure the realities of life by oversimplifying and reducing the world into laws and axioms. It is no surprise, then, that one of Brook's more successful plays, *The Man Who . . .*, was based on Sacks' study of bizarre neurological phenomena, *The Man Who Mistook His Wife for a Hat.*

Colin embraced the idea of a play about the Ik but was doubtful of the actors' ability to convince an audience that they were Africans. After all, there was only one African in the group, and one woman who was half African and half German; in addition, the most central character of the play, Atum, would be played by the Japanese actor. In one rehearsal, actress Michelle Collison suggested that the group not eat for a few days so that they could all experience something of starvation. The group laughed at her, Brook recalls. "What we *can* do," he said, "is to look at photographs and films taken by Colin to discover the exact bodily positions of the Ik, the weight balance as they walked, the tone of the facial muscles, the way they reached out to find with their fingertips, how they sat, lifted a cup to their lips." This, he thought, would help the actors enter into the feeling of being hungry more successfully than any fast. So they studied the films and replicated the Ik's movements precisely.

When Colin and Joe went to Paris during the summer of 1975 to see *Les Iks* in performance, Colin did not doubt for a moment that the characters were African, indeed, that they were the Ik. At the beginning of a rehearsal he attended, without being told which actor played which character, Colin knew immediately and yelled out at Katsuhiro Oida, "That's Atum!" That recognition was one of the more satisfying moments for Brook. But the most satisfying of all was when Colin told him that through the play he saw the Ik's humanity, a humanity he had been sure was lost forever. In the protected environment of the theater, Brook believed, at a distance, away from the heat and the hunger and the risks of Uganda, Colin rediscovered the Ik as a more complex reality and actually began to like them. It was not that he saw kindness or goodness in Michelle Collison or Katsuhiro Oida, for they did not act kind or good, but these actors were able to convey through the same grotesque behaviors described in *The Mountain People* a sense of the Ik as a people struggling to keep their culture and their families in the face of tragedy. Through the play, he began to respect the Ik, the same people who he had left in disgust and hatred so many years earlier. For Brook, that was successful, transformative theater.

As Colin once told a journalist, he began to see again just how nasty a man he had become among the Ik: "When I saw Peter Brook's play . . . my guts were just churning. I knew exactly what was going to happen. I saw that bastard of an anthropologist up there doing such stupid things, and I knew how mean and selfish he was going to become. I didn't want to see the mother laugh when her child burned its hand in the fire; I didn't want to see the fourteen-year-old retarded girl Adupa get locked in the house by her parents to die of starvation; or Lolim, the last ritual priest, ridiculed by his grandchildren when he was dying. I didn't want to see any of that! And the audience just sat there enthralled!"

But Colin was affected by the play for reasons other than the theatrical skills of Brook and his troupe. Colin was no longer living with the Ik, he knew he would never go back, and his memories of them were eight years old. Lolim and Adupa and Atum were gone, and Colin, the fieldworker of 1966, was gone too. He was able to look at the character of Turnbull partly as a caricature of himself and partly as the kind of person he had become during his fieldwork. He had convinced himself that if he had been as arrogant and mean-spirited as the character Turnbull appeared to be in the play, then it had only been for that one year in Uganda, a terrible episode in a terrible place. Watching Andreas Katsulas play him was like watching a movie of himself as an unhappy child; it was a reality that no longer existed. The play did not, therefore, radically change Colin's character, or make him a better or more tolerant person. It helped him divide his sense of self. Just as he had once divided the good society (the Mbuti) and the bad (the Ik), now he could separate the Colin Turnbull of the present from the bad one of the past. He justified himself in the present by exiling that period of fieldwork in Uganda to history.

One of the most startling aspects of the play for Colin was its simplicity. The troupe had improvised for months, basing almost all their words and actions on *The Mountain People,* and had produced a script that would play longer than nine hours. The actors had devoured every detail Joe and Colin could provide them. Then they deleted, condensed, and boiled down the play to just under two hours, two hours of movement, image, and very few words. The script was less than thirty pages. Katsulas as Turnbull interacted with the Ik but was also set apart from them, occasionally serving as a narrator to impart basic information to the audience, such as "During this two year period, from 1964 to 1966, the population was reduced by one half." Brook made sure that Katsulas never met Colin before the play opened, and never saw any photographs or films of him: he wanted Katsulas to find his own Colin Turnbull from the text and improvisation.

The French version of the play was well received. But even as audiences were packing into the Bouffes du Nord, Turnbull and Brook felt that something was missing. It turned out to be exactly the same thing that was missing from *The Mountain People,* a sense of the Ik's spiritual cohesion and of the sacred, even in the face of horror. In a new European edition of the book, with a new dedication ("For the Ik, whom I learned not to hate; and to Joe, who helped me learn"), Colin wrote of that absence: "The great French anthropologist Claude Lévi-Strauss put his finger on it. He said that for him the play lacked a certain strange beauty that he had found in the book. Peter knew at once where the lack lay, and we set about reintroducing it. It was a brief moment in the book, when a few of the Ik had left their barren homeland and gone into the Sudan, and for a short while lived in a rich valley full of all the food and water that was totally lacking where they had come from. But in the midst of plenty they encountered another absence. Now they had all the material comforts to ensure health and physical survival, but they had lost the sacred. They could no longer even see their sacred mountain, Morungole. And slowly they found that in the Sudan they were dying an even worse death, a spiritual death, so they simply packed up and went back to physical starvation."

To fill this gap, Peter Brook added a scene at the end of the play in which an Ik family leaves Uganda for the Sudan, huddles together at night around a fire, and recalls the sacred in a praise song:

TURNBULL: Atum, I want to see what the Ik are like when they have plenty of food. Will you take me to the Sudan?

ATUM: No. It is too far.

TURNBULL: All right. I'll go by myself. And if I get lost, the government will blame you.
(He takes his rucksack and starts off.)

ATUM Iciebam [friend of the Ik] what do you know about our country?
(Turnbull stops.)

ATUM Come. We go to the Sudan. This way.
(He points in the opposite direction.
He and Turnbull set off. They climb a
Mountain and reach the top.)

ATUM There, that is Sudan.
(We hear singing, the music of flutes. Atum and Turnbull descend.
Losike enters with another Ik.
She lights a fire.
Other Ik enter, including children.
They help themselves to food.

They eat without greed.
They all begin to sing softly.
The children fall asleep.
One Ik bathes his hands in the flames
of the fire, then makes a slow
gesture as though blessing himself and
the others. Others repeat the gesture.
Atum falls asleep.
The song dies away.
Someone puts out the fire.
All leave, in silence.)

Of this scene, Colin wrote: "The fire was real, the song was real, and they made the sacred real, and suddenly the audience realized the awful truth of just how much these people had lost—but ironically, with the sad realization that it had not been lost completely—yet. The crackling of the fire could be heard by the audience, they could see the flames, smell the smoke, and above all feel the beauty of the song. Those were things the book could never do."

At *Les Iks,* audiences saw the actions and words for what they were, and not what the audience wanted the actions to pretend to be. That "unbearable reality," Colin wrote, made the play "a hundred times better than the book."

The French papers called the play groundbreaking, more evidence of Brook's enormous talent and of France's good fortune in giving him a home. African audiences in France were pleasantly surprised that the actors were able to convince the audience of their Africanness. Other French authors wrote about the book in academic jargon. One philosopher described the breakdown of Ik social life not only as "the deconstruction or unravelling of the social contract and signifying code" but also as the deconstruction of the anthropologist's "unifying gaze." In other words, the play showed how fruitless and illusory an anthropologist's pretense of being an objective and privileged scientific observer can be. A German newspaper review found in Colin's possessions when he died argued that the Africanness was made more salient by the fact that the actors were not African, that the stylized, suggestive performances Brook had orchestrated were more precise than any imitation could have been, since any mimicry would have been compared to one's preconceptions about what constitutes reality.

Whereas the book had explicitly asked readers to consider the relationship between the Ik and their own society, some critics suggested that the play drew the audience's attention instead to Turnbull and his problems. The audience saw how Turnbull reacted to the Ik, his struggle with himself over how much to help the Ik and how much to hate them. But in no way was Turnbull a sympathetic character. He appeared naive, a victim of the circumstances. These reviewers felt the onus was on the audience to realize that Turnbull symbolized the West, and that the Ik symbolized what the West might become. Albert Hunt wrote: "How painful it must have been for [Turnbull] to have his water delivered daily from the police bore hole! When all around people were dying because a polluted pool had dried up! How terrible it must have been to realize that your efforts to save one here and there were so futile! No wonder he felt such anger against the universe!"

Reflecting on the way he was portrayed in the play, Colin wrote to the Royal Anthropological Institute Newsletter: "I [am] unhappy with Turnbull as he appears on the stage . . . I recognize myself, my weaknesses, the inherent weaknesses of any fieldworker, my inadequacies, but above all I am unhappy because I am reminded of the change that came over me as I stayed on, month after month, among the Ik." Colin wondered if Brook had inadvertently done an injustice to anthropology and to "Turnbull," and he made a promise to the readers (never fulfilled) that in any rewriting to be done on the American tour, he and Brook would attempt to resolve the problematic depiction of the flawed fieldworker.

In January 1976, the English language version, *The Ik,* played for six weeks at the Royal Shakespeare Company's Round House in London, then in May in Caracas, Venezuela, followed by a six-week tour in the United States, and a shorter Eastern European tour. In England, the reviews were largely positive but the critics were in new territory with little precedent. *The Ik* was unlike anything they had seen before. Reviewers were stunned by the precision of the acting and the degree to which the actors performed their hunger and sickness, including realistic vomiting by at least one actor in each performance. In a review of the play in the *Times Literary Supplement,* the anthropologist Julian Pitt-Rivers encouraged readers to skip the book but to the see play. He tried to acknowledge Colin Turnbull's courage in remaining in a field site many sensible anthropologists would have quickly abandoned, but he had found *The Mountain People* to be "appalling but nothing more." The play, in contrast, gave Pitt-Rivers the sense of the reality and the tragedy of the Ik that was absent from Colin's writing, the sincerity of which he had questioned from the moment he read the dedication page. Although Pitt-Rivers did not address the issue of how successfully either Brook or Turnbull compared Ik and western society, he made one relevant comment: if Brook was able to "make a sacred mountain out of a blank wall and a few guard rails, and turn his fully-clothed, unemaciated cast into naked, starving Ik," then he had perhaps also broken down the communication barrier between cultures. If Brook could achieve this, maybe there was no need to come right out and say explicitly, "This performance is a reflection of what might happen to you."

Not surprisingly there were also those who, like the critics of *The Mountain People,* questioned whether *The Ik* was a reflection of Colin Turnbull's splitting of good and evil, idealizing one society, the Mbuti Pygmies, and then reaffirming that idealization by writing a negative, polarizing account of the Ik. David Williams put it this way: "He is harshly awakened from his post-BaMbuti dream world into a nightmarish reality . . . The positive is implied in the negative; the Ik imply the existence of the BaMbuti Pygmies." Perhaps it was a good thing, then, when Brook decided not to include within *The Ik,* as he had once contemplated, a theatrical adaptation of a small selection from *The Forest People.*

He had written Colin in late 1975: "I am writing now to give you plenty of warning as the more you are with us, the happier we all will be. I am most anxious to include the section from *The Forest People* as we discussed. I think it should be in the form of a 10 min. sequence, like a flash back occurring at some horrendous opportunity to see exactly what the other side of the coin could be . . . What we need is something in which all our actors can reappear as new characters, swiftly and directly established, building an episode in which the positive values of Pygmy (and consequently potential Ik) life can be shown and made dramatically intense."

A smaller number of critics questioned whether the tragedy of the Ik was a legitimate story for the theater. In the *London Times,* Irving Wardle found almost obscene the performance of "human degredation rehearsed in conditions of subsidized security and now imported from Paris as the intellectual treat of the month." Part of Wardle's reaction has to be attributed to the fact that, despite the grim setting of drought-stricken Uganda, the Ik play itself was an aesthetically appealing production. Albert Hunt, who saw the play in Paris, said: "Listening to the applause the other night that burst out in the crowded Bouffes du Nord after the last Ik had vomited up in front of the audience his last sack of relief grain, and then dragged his twisted limbs into a hole at the back of the stage, I couldn't help thinking that Brook, the miracle worker, had pulled it off again. He'd made the Iks enjoyable."

More recently, in a review of Peter Brook's book of recollections, *Threads of Time,* Fintan O'Toole criticizes Brook for failing to address the uneasy relationship between his representation of famine and his position as a European artist. Responding to Brook's claim that his actors "had come to be the Ik and thus to love the Ik," O'Toole writes, "This kind of self-delusion is no less dangerous for being motivated by compassion or implemented by theatrical genius. The belief that some incantatory process of transference can transform well-fed, privileged actors from Europe, America, and Japan into starving African tribesmen is the dark side of Brook's mysticism. To forget the vast difference between playing theatrical games with photographs in a rehearsal room and being a member of a dying, degraded tribe is to lose the sense of proportion that is no less important to great theater than a necessary sense of social mission." The inequality between Brook and his starving subjects does not, O'Toole warns, make projects such as *The Ik* invalid, but the larger issues of cross-cultural communication and representation, of which inequality is unfortunately an inevitable part, should not be ignored.

Brook was unmoved by the criticisms—as perhaps any creative artist must be—convinced that the critics were, by the nature of their business, thinking primarily about mass entertainment, unable to break out of the boundaries of convention.

When it was after 8 P.M. and the interview about Colin Turnbull was over, Brook's rehearsal space was almost completely dark. He rallied himself for a final contribution to Colin's biography.

"In the theater in the twentieth century there are two figures, Gordon Craig and Antonin Artaud, who were totally incapable of any practical work. Each in his own time became landmarks, but in comparison with some like Stanislowski and others, they were impractical. Neither was responsible for more than fifty or sixty evenings of theater in their lives. But their passion made them beacons in the dark. Now, Colin Turnbull. He brought such passion to anthropology, a passion that was almost totally missing in anthropology, a passion that made for an impractical anthropology.

"You know, that passion, it was almost against his nature, the passion in contradiction to his puritanical Scottish background. Here was the Scottish puritan watching the Ik starving and then also the passionate lover feeling hatred, enormous, acute sensitivity. The two united in something that led him out of a conventional career into a different sort of anthropology, the kind of career that would be as likely to end up in a Buddhist monastery as anyplace else. I'm not surprised he became a Buddhist [late in his life] but he needed all those experiences to get him there, to be at the same time free of the world and yet also to exist within a monastery, a place which, in a strange way, had the comforts and closed form of the Scot's puritanism."

CHAPTER FOURTEEN

Virginia

As much as Colin and Joe loved their Virginia estate, it was not easy to live there. At times, Colin felt himself becoming like a southerner, and that transformation was almost like being back with the Ik. Of Lancaster County, Colin said: "Here the county reeks of hatred, ill concealed by that self-satisfied and loudly boasted veneer of Christian morality and southern gentility. There are a few who are genuinely ignorant and just don't know any better, and I feel sorry for them. But the others are consumed by their own hatred, and it is a hard battle not to respond with like hatred."

Neither Colin nor Joe felt safe, especially at night. A group of men that Colin and Joe called "the crew" used to frequent their place. The crew, mostly African American men whom Joe had known since childhood, were often around in the early evening, if not trying to seduce Joe into some nefarious activity, then eating from Joe and Colin's garden or even from inside the house. Joe encouraged them to visit because they made him feel liberated from Colin and less marginalized from the black community; at about this time, he complained to author Elizabeth Marshall Thomas that he was feeling stifled in Virginia and that Colin demanded too much of him. Colin's high expectations were too burdensome for Joe, who over the past ten years had become Colin's symbol of goodness and love. Now Joe was acting as if he wanted to show Colin just how bad he could really be.

Joe was to some extent aware that the crew tolerated his company in order to exploit him but he gave in to them. That was the role he played in other parts of his life—someone who wanted both to achieve status and to be humiliated. Wasn't that the fate, he once asked, of a black man in a racist society, to be humiliated so many times that you start to believe you are inferior?

Joe looked for affirmations of that self-image. Colin gave him plenty of money which he would use to buy drugs, alcohol, prostitutes, and food for the crew. In their company, he put himself at risk for humiliation—for the crew seemed intent on showing him how little his education and his marriage to a white man meant in Lancaster county, that he was still a descendant of slaves—or worse in danger of being arrested or even physically harmed. At one point in the early 1980s, Joe would tell Colin that some of his so-called friends had raped him by the swimming pool. Colin never understood how or why this could have happened, but Joe never reported it to the police and Colin seems to have chalked it up to Joe's paranoia.

Colin did not know what to do when the crew was there; if he tried to get rid of them, Joe would accuse him of racism, and if he tried to warn Joe about them, Joe would feel as if Colin was treating him like a child. One day, Joe won a handgun from someone in the crew during a poker game. Colin hid the gun and ammunition because Joe was getting drunk far too often for Colin to feel comfortable with a gun in the house. Joe begged him for the gun on his hands and knees, both when he was drunk and when he was sober. Colin talked about the gun and the drinking with Joe's family; they all urged Colin to leave Joe alone to learn from his mistakes. Years later, after Joe died, Colin hurled that gun into Payne's Creek, and his mind flashed back in pain to Joe's pathetic face, pleading for the gun.

One way that Joe made himself feel better was to buy cars and drive them fast. Indeed, cars were important to both Joe and Colin. In 1973, when Colin bought a new Datsun sportscar, Joe felt his car, a Pontiac Grand Prix, was overshadowed and decided he wanted a tan Corvette, brand new and loaded. Colin traded in the Datsun 280Z for the Corvette and agreed to drive the Grand Prix until he found something else he liked (it would eventually be a Cadillac Eldorado Biarritz). Joe drove the Corvette to suburban Maryland to visit his sister, Mary Jane, but when he parked it, he mistakenly set off the car alarm. The police, hearing the alarm, stopped Joe, asked for the registration, which was of course in Colin's name, and arrested him for grand theft. Colin had to drive to Maryland to bail him out and tell the police to drop the charges.

Joe would be arrested several more times, usually for driving while intoxicated. It is impossible to know if his long police record was the result of racism, whether a white driver would have been issued a speeding ticket or simply warned while a black driver was given a ticket and a Breath-a-lizer test. But one thing was certain: Joe seemed to look for trouble and, as one friend of his said, "Joe was such a nice guy, but if there was shit on the ground, he'd step in it." Joe drank excessively, but neither Colin nor Joe would ever use the word alcoholism to refer to the drinking. In 1974, Joe decided that, in addition to the Corvette, he and Colin should have a new Grand Prix, but he could not afford it and asked Colin for a loan. They agreed Joe would make monthly payments to Colin, but Joe was either late with his payments or didn't pay at all. They then agreed that if Joe paid off half of the remaining loan, Colin would forgive the rest and the car would be completely Joe's. He loved the car and called it his "pimpmobile"; the local police soon knew the car well. Neither Joe nor Colin would drive at the speed limit and they received large numbers of tickets. They both had to go to driving school on at least two occasions to avoid losing their licenses, and Joe's license was eventually suspended, first for a year and then, in 1975 when he was arrested during a suspension for driving while intoxicated, for ten years. The ten-year suspension would be a major blow to Joe's ego. And unable to act as chauffeur to the crew, his status with them all but disappeared.

Joe and Colin believed that the sheriff had a grudge against Joe for being a black man who lived with a rich white man, and they both hated him. Despite the fact that he disliked guns, Colin bought a shotgun to protect himself from the police and local residents. He fantasized about shooting the county sheriff. Sometimes he would take the gun out to the woods and fire a few shots. The last time he did was on the night of Joe's funeral, a bottle of Scotch in one hand, Joe's gun in the other. During the late 1970s, when Colin became interested in doing anthropological fieldwork in the prison system, he considered committing a crime. He said: "I've been trying to think of what kind of crime I could commit that would get me two years—the legitimate period of fieldwork. It would have to be a crime of passion." He went on: "That damn sheriff—I'd love to get rid of him for one thing. I feel very passionate about the sheriff and his horrid troopers. I think I'd be doing the community a service if I got rid of that sheriff somehow—not by killing him but by proving his fallibility."

When Colin said such things, friends wondered why Colin and Joe wanted to live in Lancaster, for it seemed odd that an interracial, openly gay couple would choose to spend their lives among people they hated and who hated them. It was as if Colin and Joe were punishing themselves. Friends speculated that Joe wanted to live there to show his community what he had done with his life, having gotten an education and having become a Ph.D. candidate, and to have the pleasure of watching the white Towles community seethe with anger when a black Towles moved into a large estate on the northern neck. For Colin, living in Lancaster was certainly an act of resistance against the sort of white people who lived there, but it was also a way to simultaneously affirm his own privileges and suffer from them. Precisely because Colin was so different from everyone else living in Lancaster, he was confronted everyday by the specter of his own whiteness, his British heritage and pedigree, as if he was an anthropologist living with an exotic society, waking up every morning to be reminded of his identity. Lancaster is generally a far more genteel and diverse place than Colin believed it to be. Colin wanted Lancaster to be racist, conservative, and hateful. In that setting, then, if he could make Joe into a professional anthropologist, Joe would have to acknowledge that he was different, that he was a symbol of what a black man in America could become. Then, too, Colin's own identity, as wizard, savior, or Pygmalion, would become more clear.

Colin had shipped many of his things from Zaire, material artifacts that he had collected in the field, too numerous to carry with him. He knew it would take months for them to arrive by sea, but it took longer than expected. Although Joe also shipped his things, oddly he decided to ship his anthropological field notes as well, despite the fact that he had no copies. This is particularly odd as most anthropologists would never let their data out of their hands let alone ship them by sea from Africa. When their bags arrived at the beginning of the summer of 1973 all of Colin's things were intact, but Joe's were not. His field notes and tape recordings were not in his bags. Joe and Colin assumed they had been confiscated or stolen. But was it possible that there were no field notes to begin with? Or could Joe have taken a risk with his notes so that he would not have to produce anything from them?

Distraught, Joe left for Zaire in September 1973, leaving Colin behind to begin teaching at Virginia Commonwealth University (VCU). Joe would work hard over the next several weeks to regather the lost data on Mbo villager rites of passage, in particular, the Mbo version of the nkumbi circumcision ritual.

When Joe returned from Africa at the end of the fall, he was ambivalent about seeing Colin, and sent his arrival dates to his sister Mary Jane only; she called Colin to let him know when Joe would be there. Colin drove up to Maryland to get Joe, who greeted Colin coolly. At home, Joe became a loner, going off by himself, fishing, walking, or gambling with the crew at poker and a game called tonk. Joe now had a bed in his own room, but when he came home drunk, as was often the case, he needed Colin's help to get up the stairs.

Sometimes he didn't make it to bed and Colin would find him passed out the next morning on the kitchen floor. Occasionally, he went into Colin's room late at night to shake him out of his slumber and tell him what he and the crew had done that night. Neither Joe nor Colin recorded those stories, but Colin called them "horrible." He said, "I don't want to hear them, and I don't think I even want to know whether they are true or whether he is just teasing. Even if it is lies, it is a reality he has created, just for me, and I cannot face it."

In the midst of what looked to Colin like a quickly deteriorating marriage, he decided to participate in a conference on "The Child at Psychiatric Risk" in Dakar, Senegal, where he would talk about good parents (the Mbuti) and bad parents (the Ik)—and worry about Joe. On the plane to Africa, after several drinks, he wrote to Joe to beg him for his love. It was a letter he never sent, but it must have been important to Colin. Years later, he would transcribe it into his computer. The letter, written on July 25, 1973, was found on a computer disk twenty-one years later, when Colin died. It is reminiscent of the empty sentimental exchanges Colin had with his mother.

"Sweet love, all I do—even the horrid, hurtful things, are because of my love of you. So even when you know me to be wrong, also know that I love you.

"You have made my whole life, my love, by giving it purpose—and so giving it meaning. Can you believe that? Oh Sweetness, if only you knew how true it is—and how much of a sacrifice you have made for me. I suppose it is because I know it that I go overboard trying to show my gratitude—as well as my love—in ways that so often must seem like parental possessiveness. It is love, darling Joe; the deepest and best.

"I saw you waving at me and just hated to go inside the plane—how little time we have in this life, and I sometimes feel that every minute away from you is the most unutterable stupid waste. Why the hell am I off to Dakar of all God-forsaken places, when I could be with you, my only Joe? I sometimes want to give everything up—everything—and just be . . . Oh sweetness if I could be sure what you wanted for us how I would move heaven to do and be what you want. The only thing I know I am truly good at is loving you.

". . . Buckets of tears—do you know we could buy Tullie Castle for a paltry 40,000 pounds with eight cottages (4 rented) and 125 acres and miles of salmon fishing? You want it? Let's buy it! Oh how I love you. But how the hell does Scotland come together with Africa via two unwilling, unwitting expatriates?

"Joe, Joe, Joe you make the world so rich for me—you give me so much—NEVER be afraid to remind me of how much I owe you—never."

When Colin returned from Africa, Joe continued to drink heavily. But, as he had when Colin found him in a drunken stupor in Kampala in 1972, Joe would always recover after a good sleep and act as if nothing had happened. He pulled himself together for a few weeks while Colin's mother visited in the summer of 1974, but she was not her usual vibrant self. Colin's father Jock was ill in England with complications of diabetes, having had a foot and then a leg amputated. Colin returned to England with his mother and stayed a few weeks with her, long enough to be there for his father's death and help his mother pack her things.

There is no record of how Colin felt about his father's death, no mention of it in letters to friends as there would be when Colin's mother died some years later. But he must have felt sorry for him and regretted the distance between them. Jock had wished for a son who would carry on his business and lineage and Colin, his only hope, did everything possible to avoid both of those duties. Colin's main concern after his father's death was for his mother and he supported her decision to move to Kilmarnock, Virginia, to live near him.

She refused to stay with Joe and Colin for more than a few days while Colin found a house she could buy and move into immediately. She said she "didn't want to be a bother," but in reality she did not want to be around Joe. Kilmarnock is seventeen miles from Colin and Joe's house, and yet Dot wanted to see Colin almost every day. Once she realized that she would never see him enough to suit her, disgusted with Joe and his friends, and feeling lonely in a foreign country and small southern town, Dorothy put the house up for sale and returned to England, after only six months in the United States. But she would not remain in England for very long either.

Meanwhile, Joe was spending even more time with the crew. But at the same time, Joe had been hired to teach courses on the anthropology of Africa, anthropology of religion, and introductory anthropology at VCU. Joe and Colin rented an apartment in Richmond where they could stay on the days they worked late, but Joe and the crew took it over as their headquarters. As a result, Colin found it impossible to stay there. He turned a blind eye to whatever they might have been doing there but was worried about Joe's mental health.

Joe had gotten the job to teach at VCU through Colin. Colin talked to the chairman of the department at the time, John H. McGrath, who recalls that, in order to keep Colin at VCU, the department agreed to bring Joe on board for two academic years, from 1974 to 1976, even though they preferred someone more qualified. "When you have a superstar," McGrath said, "you do what you can do to keep him happy." The students disliked Joe intensely, as they had at Hofstra, because he was autocratic, angry, insecure, and condescending. In addition, he lectured irregularly, canceling class whenever he had gotten too drunk the night before and couldn't manage the drive to Richmond. Students sent numerous letters to the chairman of the department complaining about Joe's absences and tardiness, and asking for their grades to be reviewed by the department. McGrath wrote the personnel committee that "Mr. Towles has been characterized by most students who have visited my office as an embarrassment to the department, as a detriment to the anthropology program, and as a person who is losing potential majors."

The department secretary complained that Joe advertised eight office hours a week but only attended one of them, on Mondays. In an unsigned note, a staff member, probably the department secretary, wrote McGrath on April 24, 1975, to say: "Towles failed to show for his class this morning. No answer at home—no office hours kept. For your info., there are many angry students who can't find him for weeks and weeks. He wouldn't acknowledge any notes left by me or his students. Make-up tests are ignored even when he made appointments with the students. I have to give explanations (lies) to the kids and I have run out."

The anthropologists and sociologists who were employed at VCU at the time recall that Joe seemed overly sensitive to racism, but it is hard to imagine that any African American professional could have worked in Virginia in the 1970s without experiencing some racism. It is likely that Joe was the first black professor, and possibly the first black professional, that many of VCU's anthropology students, black and white, had ever encountered. Joe was indeed sensitive to both explicit and subtle expressions of racism that he believed VCU denied. When the department asked that he include more works specifically on Africa in his course on the cultures of Africa, instead of the more theoretical works he had assigned, he accused the faculty of being racist. McGrath wrote Joe in October 1974 about his poor teaching evaluations and offered some suggestions: "I suspect that what we have here is a cultural difference in terms of American approach versus the British approach to teaching. It is my understanding that your training may be somewhat like the British model which is to give an excellent and comprehensive lecture but to seldom tolerate interruptions. The American model, on the other hand, is to treat the classroom as a dialogue or interchange system . . . I would ask you to consider that this might be part of the problem. I am free to discuss with you at any time whatever you might wish me to do to aid you in your professional efforts."

Over the course of Joe's employment at VCU, McGrath would write many more such letters, recommending that Joe seek teaching advice from the Center for Improvement of Teaching Effectiveness at VCU and urging Joe that it was of primary importance to complete his Ph.D. But in February 1975, when Joe examined the previous semester's poor evaluations, he answered McGrath's October memo: "[Are evaluations] a tool to rid the university of unpopular faculty? Can a white student body be expected to objectively evaluate a black socially conscious faculty member? Are all professors to be coerced to conform to the expectations of students? I demand an investigation and an apology." In his response, Joe also charged the Director of Student Evaluations with "gross negligency" and added, "Any simple checking of registration would have found that I had only seventy students and yet one hundred evaluations were turned in. This is almost one half, surely vengeance-forms."

McGrath responded by saying that he found Joe's remarks "suggesting that a white student body was unable to objectively evaluate a black faculty member as being unworthy of a professor of anthropology."

McGrath told Joe he had received complaints from students about his lack of availability and also from colleagues, who "are complaining that you have no commitment to the department, its programs or its missions." Even more importantly, during the first two weeks of class in September 1975, all thirty-six students enrolled in Joe's introductory class had signed a letter stating: "We, the students . . . believe the present instructor, Dr. Towles is doing an insufficient job teaching this course and he should be replaced. We believe this for the following reasons: 1) disorganized in presentation, 2) he is defensive and overly sensitive (gets angry when student asks a question), 3) has not ordered books (over half of the class does not have textbooks)."

Joe found it even harder to be available to the students during the next semester (fall 1975), when he was no longer able to drive because of his second arrest for driving while intoxicated. Colin wrote numerous letters to the Commonwealth of Virginia attorneys and the Virginia Division of Motor Vehicles in a futile attempt to have the charges against Joe dropped or the ten-year license suspension reevaluated.

Finally, after two semesters, the department faculty decided they would not rehire him, and on October 30, 1975, McGrath sent Joe his letter of termination: "I have been continuously evaluating your performance as an instructor in anthropology . . . I have reluctantly come to the conclusion that your pedagogical talents do not fit with the needs of the students at VCU and thus, you are not helping this department or the university in the quest of their goals. I am recommending . . . that [the dean] notify you that your probationary period with the university end on June 30, 1976."

Joe replied, asking that the university's personnel committee review the matter. He wrote: "I gather, on the basis of a number of complaints from a few disgruntled students in either one of my introductory anthropology classes, Dr. McGrath has taken the student's complaints as wholly justified. Without, seemingly, any consideration for my position, plus the difficulties of maintaining discipline in a huge class of 108 or more people, some of whom seem hostile for various reasons . . .

"I have been charged with being arrogant and the implications of this charge, though really unclear to me, seem to be unworthy of a department chairman. I simply cannot disregard unstudious behavior within the classroom and usually I call this to the attention of the student. I constantly, in these large classes, have to deal with students who sit in the back of the class disrupting the lecture process; reading newspapers, sniggling and giggling at African names, conversing and other forms of rudeness. I consider this unbelievable arrogance . . .

"As an anthropologist, I feel that Black anthropologists often bring a different perspective to comparisons that are made between traditional and modern cultures. I cannot allow the biases of a few students to sway me from this approach."

The personnel committee did review the matter, interviewing Joe twice, as well as three other faculty members and five students, and came to the conclusion that Joe should not be fired. They also noted that Joe had been given no intimation of the gravity of the situation and had not been given enough time to improve his teaching. Despite the fact that Joe's teaching evaluations were "noticeably below the department mean," the committee noted that "there is no policy stating just how bad one has to be in the classroom before termination . . . Therefore, the committee concludes that Mr. Towles should not be terminated because he has not violated any rules or policy insofar as his teaching efforts were concerned."

McGrath disagreed strongly with the committee's recommendation as did the dean, but their hands were tied. They would keep Joe on the faculty until the next semester when they would evaluate Joe again. It was Colin who forced a confrontation that culminated in his and Joe's resignations in the spring of 1976.

Colin had initially tried to stay out of the fray. He wrote to his colleague Lewis Diana, "I think it better if I do not appear before the committee *re* Joseph Towles, though if a full departmental faculty meeting were called I would be prepared to speak then." Friends of Colin and Joe remember that, at the time, Colin pressured the faculty to give Joe a regular position and, when they would not, he tried to use his reputation as leverage. Colin demanded they apologize to Joe for the whole fiasco, destroy the department's biennial reports on Joe, and rehire him in a regular, tenure-track job. McGrath threatened to resign as chair if the department complied with any of the three demands. Colin also began to talk about Joe and VCU in ways that complemented Joe's accusations of racism. He wrote again to Diana, able to put himself in Joe's shoes and describe in a sensible way what seemed, to the department, to be ludicrous. "I wonder if adequate consideration has been given to the large number of outside pressures still weighing on Joseph . . . the loss of his fieldnotes, the lack of clarity of his status with Makerere University . . . his extreme ill health due to a tropical parasite, and the normal amount of police harassment that is the lot of any black who, again, does not conform to the white image. This is all too frequently dismissed as imagination . . . I can testify to it from personal experience."

Colin later wrote that VCU did not like "the company [Joe] was keeping, and were out to get [him] anyway since he refused to be the 'professional' they wanted, a sort of show piece for their phony liberality." He believed that two anthropology professors, Mednick and Knipe, had it out for Colin, that Mednick was envious of Colin's publication record, and therefore wanted to punish him, indirectly, by hurting Joe. Knipe, Colin believed, wanted to fire Joe so that he could use the part-time budget to bring in more highly qualified faculty who had yet to find regular employment. Colin wrote that the whole affair was "one of the most disgusting displays of racism and bigotry" he had ever seen. He wrote a nine-page single-spaced memo detailing the ways in which the department had mistreated Joe and summarily resigned. The bottom line was that both were now jobless.

In October 1976, the U.S. tour of Brook's play *The Ik,* was scheduled to start at Virginia Commonwealth University. But Colin put a stop to it. After resigning from VCU, Colin approached Bob Humphrey, an archaeologist who was then chair of anthropology at George Washington University in Washington, D.C., and Gordon Gibson of the Smithsonian, looking both to find a job and a home for the opening of *The Ik.* "There seems to be some conflict between [the Smithsonian] and the International Center for Theater Research in Paris," Colin wrote to Humphrey. Humphrey immediately tried to find the funds to bring Colin on board and succeeded in having him appointed through the division of experimental programs as a visiting professor of drama and anthropology. But before signing his contract, Colin told Humphrey he wanted it clearly understood by the faculty that he had been romantically involved with a man for more than two decades and asked if that would be a problem. Humphrey told him, emphatically, no, assuming his colleagues would also agree, which they did. Humphrey and Turnbull would soon become intimate friends, sharing a love of beer, wine, and the fiction of Isaac Asimov.

Peter Brook therefore launched his American tour not at VCU, as had been planned, but at George Washington University and then moved on to the universities of Pennsylvania, Chicago, Minnesota, Houston, and California at Berkeley and Los Angeles. In *Newsweek,* Jack Kroll called the tour the most "significant theater event this season." On top of the publicity and accolades, Colin now had a job contract with a salary of $28,000, the most he had ever been paid, beginning in the fall of 1977. George Washington University was very excited about bringing Colin on board because in addition to being a famous name and having made possible a high-profile opening of *The Ik* on campus, Colin had received a letter from the National Endowment for the Humanities expressing serious interest in his developing a program in drama and anthropology at the university, encouraging Colin to apply for as much as a quarter million dollars, over fifty percent of which would be paid to the university in indirect costs.

In the meantime, Colin worked with the Ik production for little money but much professional fulfillment, and in the spring taught courses at West Virginia University in Morgantown. Peter Brook stayed at George Washington University for a week of workshops, rehearsals, and a forum in which audiences, students, and faculty could talk to Colin, Denis Cannan (a co-author of the first draft of the English-language version of *The Ik*) and Joe. Yes, Joe. Colin made sure of it. Brook recalls that "Joe was a very nice man, and was around a lot, but he had nothing at all to do with the play." Yet Joe's name appeared on some programs and on all the workshop memos. In fact, when the play was performed in London, in 1976, at the Royal Shakespeare Company's Round House, Joe was listed in the program as "technical advisor." Joe was seldom asked a question in any of the workshops and he seldom spoke. But whether he was shutting himself out of the production or being shut out by the production, he was always present and was introduced as an anthropologist who had worked with the Ik and knew them better than anyone other than Colin Turnbull. When he did speak, he was able to offer a perspective on the Ik that differed from Colin's. Joe had never detested the Ik as Colin had; he was able to describe the plight of the Ik in more tempered and sympathetic terms that both complemented Colin's grotesque depictions and underscored how extreme Colin's view could be.

At each of the universities Brook, Turnbull, Towles, and Cannan visited, there were several related forums: one on the role of theater as a tool in breaking down class and language barriers; one on the implications of the Ik for American society, with discussion of whether there is an alienated and oppressed people in the United states and whether Americans are producing our own version of an Ik subculture; and a panel of two or more anthropologists, moderated by Colin and Joe, discussing fieldwork as theater and what "act" anthropologists devise when they enter into a new society. There were also three workshops: a master class with Brook, a session with graduate students and Brook's staff on the fieldworker as actor and the actor as interpreter of cultures, and a workshop related to another small production called *The Ridiculous Bag.*

For the University of Chicago forum and workshop, Joe wrote a two-page essay entitled "Reconsidering the Ik," which he distributed to the participants. In the paper, he said that when *The Mountain People* was published, he felt uncomfortable with Colin's interpretation of the Ik. Describing himself as a colleague, friend, and fellow fieldworker of the author, Joe wrote that his own approach was to smooth over interpersonal conflicts with the Ik and to nurture more close personal relationships. He asserted that Colin, as an experienced anthropologist and a white European, tended to distance himself from the Ik, making it clear to the Ik that he would not give them food or medicines. Joe, on the other hand, presented himself as more of a friend to the Ik. "As a Black man," he wrote, "there was also ethnic pressure of a sort to which Colin was not subjected . . . the Ik often came to me knowing I would likely be sympathetic." Joe wrote that his "personal relations with the Ik conflicted with Colin's more academic and scholarly account of the total system. I regarded the Ik's seemingly [word illegible] behavior on an individual basis, giving greater significance to the external influence pressures. It was a temporary phenomenon, I presumed. I was young, inexperienced, idealistic, unacquainted with the darker side of human nature. Enthused with Black consciousness, I was prepared to forgo a critical-negative assessment of the Ik in favor of a more measured view, particularly coming from the gentle and mannerly world of Makerere University at Kampala. We tend to disregard ugliness. Idi Amin's success in Uganda was due to this tendency in man. No one wanted to believe such a benevolent, kind person was capable of such evil. He was always full of laughter and jokes."

Joe went on to say that the biggest problem with *The Mountain People* was that it was intended to jolt a western audience into evaluating their own "Ik-ness," their own abandonment of communal values in favor of self-interest. This is why the book was so controversial, Joe thought. "If it had simply been a book about Africans," he said, "no one would have bothered."

At the workshops, Colin pondered aloud the question of whether theater and theatrical workshops might help students learn that drama can often educate the public about culture more effectively than a "discursive," "written" communication. When Colin defended his book *The Mountain People* from the attacks of anthropologists, he often said that the audiences who watched *The Ik,* the uninformed actors and actresses who performed it, and the workshop participants all understood the reality of starvation in Uganda far better than any anthropologist. Some anthropologists hated the book so much, and were so confused by the avant-garde idea that anthropology and theater could be meaningfully related, that they boycotted the play.

By linking anthropology and performance, and expanding the medium of anthropological representation to include the theater, Colin was ahead of his time. A decade later, anthropologists would begin to write at length about the hegemony of "logocentrism" in the basic and social sciences, the domination of the written word, and especially the conventional forms of scientific writing, over other forms of communication or representation. Colin's name seldom appears in the context of this literature though his work prefigured many postmodern critiques of anthropology as science. Perhaps his greatest professional achievement was to carry on the largely unfulfilled wish of his teacher, E. Edward Evans-Pritchard, that anthropology can be an art as well as a science, at the same time a method both for anthropologists to convey their own personal involvement with another culture *and* for teaching about the diversity of human experience. A few years after the Ik tour, Colin said about anthropological fieldwork: "If you want to convey something of the quality of life in that society or of social forces like love and religious faith at work, then you can't do that by objective study. Your participation has to be internal. When Jerzy Grotowski [Polish avant-garde theater director] talks about acting, he says the actor should be aware of the possibility of becoming someone other than himself. When this happens it is the greatest moment in an actor's life; he makes a total sacrifice of self. For the anthropologist, too! When we bring back what we pretend is an objective study of another society, it's like taking that society and putting it in a museum showcase for everyone to look at as a curiosity. We say, 'How quaint,' but it has nothing to do with us."

By the mid-1980s, few anthropologists would be able to complete their training without learning that the purpose of anthropology is not only to go away but to come back and see one's own world in a new light. Anthropology, for Colin, had become a kind of pilgrimage in search of something good to bring home. And though, at first, he could not see what the Ik had to offer, Brook and his actors convinced him of the Ik's humanity. What a hopeful sign it was that, even when faced with the most dire circumstances, a human being could still go on living.

In December of 1976, just after the Ik tour had been completed, Colin's mother became ill with stomach pains and so she decided to move to Virginia again. Colin put her up at the gatehouse on his and Joe's property and though her health initially improved in January and February, by March her health began to decline rapidly—so rapidly, in fact, that Colin was not with her when she died. On March 13, 1977, after spending a week's spring break with his mother and Joe, Colin left town for two weeks to teach spring semester courses for West Virginia University in Morgantown. He was waiting anxiously for fall to arrive when he would begin teaching at George Washington University; he was happy that during his week home, Dot was making plans for summer outings and seemed at peace with Joe. Her increasing dependence and Colin's absences forced her and Joe into much more frequent contact in what finally ended up as a rapprochement.

While Colin was out of town, Joe became concerned about Dot and decided to spend the night on the floor in the room next to hers. Joe telephoned Colin the next day, on the 14th, to say that Dot seemed very sick, that he was worried and was taking her to the hospital. But when Joe tried to visit her later that day, insisting that he was a relative, the hospital staff asked him to leave. After a lengthy argument, the staff called the police who arrested Joe for disturbing the peace and made him spend the night in jail. Out of jail the next day, he called Colin telling him to come back immediately. Dot Turnbull died the next morning at the age of 75, as Colin was driving home.

Colin would write to his friend, Francie Train, a former volunteer at the museum in New York, that "Joe was just wonderful to [mother], and all last week she was saying how good he had been. You can imagine how happy that makes me. I am going to miss her terribly, but she had a full, rich life . . . We fly her back this week coming, then Joe and I go for a service in London and burial in Scotland."

In the days immediately following Dot's death, Colin complained to the hospital and the police about the way Joe had been treated, and tried to soothe Joe's psychological wounds. It was a traumatic experience for Joe who was simply caring for his "mother-in-law." As for Colin, he mourned his mother's death with some ambivalence.

Colin wrote that, in her old age, his mother was provocative and critical: "Any adult was her prey, and she had an uncanny knack of knowing what was in someone's mind just by squinting at them . . . I would be going through the main gate [in Virginia] and something would make me look around, and there she would be in the window of the gatehouse, peering through the curtains, squinting. Or I would be working in the garden, having left her doing the same in hers, and all of a sudden there she was, leaning on her stick, watching. If I ignored her she just stayed put; immobile, eyes glinting through her spectacles, radiating Irish power, making me wonder what on earth I had done wrong now. That made it easy to blame her when nothing I planted that day ever showed any signs of growing. But if I made a move to go and greet her and find out what she wanted, by the time I had straightened my back she was gone."

Colin often referred to his mother as a "witch." He would actually publish those words in 1983 in a statement that angered his nephew, David Turnbull, and even his Canadian relatives who had never been particularly fond of Dot. No doubt he used the term "witch" to express his hostility (though we cannot know if he did so consciously), but he also used the term liberally to refer to the vital forces in which many people in the world believe. For him, a witch was someone who had special powers.

"She was a witch all right, and many is the time that I cursed her as I hit my thumb with a hammer or swerved into a ditch as she suddenly appeared from nowhere, spectacles ablaze. 'What do you want?' I would ask, testily. 'Nothing, dear!' she would answer, and that made me more angry and accusatory than ever because it was true: she did not want anything. Like other thoroughly good, old people, she just was; but like witches in particular, she was everywhere."

In retrospect, he wrote, "I realize what an extraordinary mother/woman she was; I would like to have thanked her." In his own way, he did. When Colin went to the morgue in Kilmarnock, Virginia, to see his mother for the last time, he noticed that all her jewelry had been removed except her wedding ring. A morgue assistant told Colin that he had tried to remove the ring, but that it was stuck. Colin slipped it off her finger easily and, not knowing what else to do with the ring, he put it on his own finger. It stuck so hard that for the next fourteen years he would take it off only twice, once during an argument with Joe and again at Joe's funeral. In December 1988, Colin would go to the grave dug on his Virginia estate and look at Joe for the last time; he removed the ring, slipped it onto Joe's finger, and said "I love you."

The next year, 1978, Joe submitted a dissertation to Makerere on the nkumbi ritual and to his surprise it was accepted by the three readers without revisions and with no need for an oral examination. The readers were Ed Winter, Aidan Southall, and Colin Turnbull. Winter called it "an excellent piece of work" and a "great contribution to the study of circumcision." Southall praised it for its clarity and completeness, saying of the largely atheoretical ethnography, "It is a highly concrete, descriptive account, yet almost every act or object described is given its array of attributed symbolic meanings, which build into a very elaborate but largely coherent tapestry as the work proceeds." Southall's only substantial objection was Joe's use of the term "tribe," which by 1979 was already becoming outdated for both theoretical and political reasons. Colin said that he had minor disagreements with Joe's interpretations of the Mbuti molimo and elima festivals, but found the dissertation "detailed, methodically written, and an important contribution to ethnography." It was, indeed, a serious doctoral study and one that would be useful to any anthropologist working on similar rituals in central Africa. The dissertation was limited by its failure to integrate data and theory, to show what the various rituals tell us about human ideas and actions more generally. Its strength was the detailed description of a complex ritual process.

Although satisfied with his degree, Joe had become increasingly disdainful of Colin's new work in the theater, calling his "ethnodrama" a "game." And for him it was a game, a game in which Colin and his other white friends and colleagues pretended to be the oppressed and marginalized, convinced that they could understand what subordinated peoples thought and felt. After a pizza party that Colin held in an apartment he rented in Washington, D.C., Joe exploded, saying that he preferred the games he played in Lancaster. He stormed out of the house and took a bus to Virginia where he was arrested for disorderly conduct and jailed for a night. Finally, Colin and Joe became so fed up with their constant bickering that they believed a change of scenery would help. They decided to leave the country for a year and travel around the world. They did not even wait for the announcement of the National Endowment for the Humanities grant for which Colin had applied.

To George Washington University Colin justified the trip as a study of "Tourism and Pilgrimage," in which he and a fellow anthropologist would examine "the dynamics of values in action" as they explored major sites of pilgrimage in the Far East, Polynesia, Southeast Asia, East Africa, India, and the Middle East. Scheduled to begin at the end of the summer 1979, the trip almost did not happen when, after a violent argument, Joe refused to travel. From Washington, Colin wrote a long letter to Joe in which he argued that Joe was wrong about every one of his wild accusations and delusions, that Joe could come along or not, but that if he did not, he would be acting self-destructively.

Colin thought he was fighting back, laying down the law, refusing to accept Joe's behavior any longer, but in fact he was fighting with himself. He complained that Joe treated him as a "sugar daddy" but in the next breath told Joe that if he wanted to break up, he could have the house and alimony payments. He told Joe that his self-destructive behavior was caused by trying to be an "ordinary black man" when he was meant for something greater, yet Colin could not see that Joe was incapable of fulfilling those expectations.

Colin said he could think of only two possible explanations for what Joe was doing: either Joe believed that Colin's love for him had weakened, or Joe's own love for Colin had weakened. With these explanations, Colin reduced the complexities of Joe's experiences to a simple enveloping and forgiving love. Colin could not see that Joe was in trouble and needed help, not money or a trip around the world. He wrote:

> I have burned my bridges [at George Washington University] and will be without a job for a year. So I am going to have to take the year off anyway. I certainly am not going to waste it sitting in a poky D.C. apartment. So I am going to keep to the idea of going around the world, and am going to leave on Sept. 1st. I just want to know whether to get two tickets or one . . .
>
> But come September 1st, since I am the one with the money and the land and the house and its contents, including the Corvette, and since you consistently tell me and everyone else that I try to run your

life, I am going to do that consciously for the first and last time. I am going to give you a clear choice, and I do it with every ounce of all the love I have for you, for all that you have meant to me and always will mean to me regardless of what decision you make. Here it is. Either:

1. On September 1st, you and I set out (provided you are not in jail . . . if that happens, then as soon as you get out) with nothing in our minds but travelling around the world, together, in love, to celebrate our twentieth year together . . .
2. On Sept. 1st., I go alone, leaving you exactly the same amount of money for you to do with as you like in the year. But if you stay you will have to find somewhere else to stay as the house will be occupied [by renters].

I cannot any longer bear having you show your lack of faith in me the way you do at some moments, and show your love for me the way you do at other moments. I believe it is all due to the constant stress you have been under ever since we went to Africa and you began your academic career in earnest . . . It was heightened by all the train of bad luck that dogged you from the start with your fieldwork, then the dirty way you were treated at VCU, and compounded by what I think is the almost impossible problem of returning to live in Virginia, which might be the biggest mistake we ever made. I think that there you were forced to try and be something you have never been and never can be, a country Black that is poor and without any education . . . It is not you Joe . . . You are getting just as heartless, just as conniving, just as self-centred, just as unreliable, just as unresponsive to the needs of others as those who you choose to mix with. And that is not the Joe I gave my life to twenty years ago . . . more and more being suppressed by this gambling, money wasting, totally other kind of Joe. That kind of Joe I just cannot go on living with because it is not the real Joe . . . Have faith in my love and respect for you, whatever you decide. I gave it to you twenty years ago and it is yours forever.

That fight might have heightened Colin's awareness of Joe's personality, what others might have seen as selfish and sadistic, but Colin returned to the old script about the undying love he and Joe had built, the same love that prevented him from developing insight into Joe's character. Never taking his thoughts about their relationship beyond that either/or equation, Colin convinced himself that Joe could never fail, only love could fail; Joe could never be weak, only their love could be weak.

In later years, Colin would not remember the 1970s as a happy or sad time in his life; he would simply remember it as a time in which his love was tested. Happiness was for him a concept akin to love; neither one could be defined in positive or negative terms. Happiness, like love, was fundamentally about joining a lover in his joys and sorrows, about the moments of ecstasy as well as suffering. If you were truly joined together with someone, he thought, then you loved them or hated them only as much as you loved or hated yourself. Colin's nostalgia, then, was not memory without pain. Years later, after Joe died, he would tell his old English friend, the actor Dudley Stevens, "In my perverse way, when I feel utterly miserable . . . actually I am the happiest, because to me that is just evidence of how great and deep was the love that Joe and I had and still have for each other."

Despite jealousy, infidelity, alcoholism, mistrust, and resentment, Colin and Joe would remain married, and it sometimes seemed to them as if the alternative of building new lives without each other was more frightening than staying together. If they were sometimes enemies, at least they were familiar enemies. They justified the costs of their relationship in terms of their faith in love and commitment. The moment their marriage became sacred was the moment it was removed from the realm of debate. Divorce was no more likely than abandoning a lifelong belief in God or science, and the potential pleasures of freedom were nothing in comparison with the idea of love that enveloped Joe and Colin—a halo of clouds that settled over this relationship they had blessed, ensuring their isolation and reaffirming the conviction that straying from that love was a heresy.

CHAPTER FIFTEEN

Withdrawal

THE END OF THE 1970S marked the beginning of Colin's intense interest in death row inmates and the thorny legal and ethical issues surrounding the death penalty in America. Colin had long been fascinated with prisons and prison life. What he saw there resonated with his childhood—his first visit to a prison when he attempted to run away from home, the boarding school society with its emphasis on surveillance, social control, and the body as an instrument of power—and with his experiences among the Ik in the prison-like surroundings of Pirre, Uganda. The prison work was also, at least to some degree, related to Joe; through Joe, Colin became acutely aware of how the justice system affects the daily lives of American minorities, particularly African Americans.

His intellectual interest in prisons coincided with that of scholars within the academic community who had begun to write about the history and structure of western civilization's prison systems. Although Colin Turnbull never mentioned Foucault's name in his prison-related writings and lectures, by 1975 Michel Foucault's *Discipline and Punish: The Birth of the Prison* was being widely read among anthropologists, and it would be unlikely that Colin was unaware of the book and its arguments. Gay scholars were particularly aware of Foucault not only because he was widely known to be gay, but because his historical accounts of how ideas of "normality" were invented in western Europe spoke to political concerns about longstanding popular and legal discrimination against homosexuality as "abnormal."

In 1972 while Foucault was a visiting professor at the State University of New York at Buffalo, he visited the Attica penitentiary and was fascinated by the cultural machinery that had been developed to exclude, eliminate, or shape particular kinds of individuals. Foucault showed how the modern prison emerged, like other institutions such as hospitals, schools, and insane asylums, as a state-sponsored technology for creating docile and "normal" bodies. But Foucault's analysis was more than an analysis of the extraordinary powers of surveillance and discipline. He also showed that prisons were just one aspect of a larger system of power to which everyone, including those who were ostensibly in power, was subjected. In his view, the guards could be just as oppressed as the prisoners. In contrast, when Colin determined to study his prisons, he took as a central goal the analysis of punishment, especially capital punishment, not as an expression of the need to punish or eliminate the abnormal, but as an expression of the loss of humanity in western civilization as a whole.

While Colin was teaching at Virginia Commonwealth University (VCU), he had offered an anthropology course *pro bono* at the local state penitentiary, just across the James River from the VCU campus. He did this as a favor to a friend from VCU named Joy Nachod Humes, a scholar of the turn-of-the-century French poets and playwrights Paul Claudel and Charles Péguy. Humes was deeply involved with teaching creative writing at the prison, and she worked tirelessly to publish a number of poems written by inmates in a large collection entitled "In Celebration." About to leave on a celebratory trip to the Caribbean, she wrote to Colin that the inmates, whom so many of the guards and prison officials referred to as "dumb niggers," had produced a remarkable book, "wrote the poems, and without experience, working with antediluvian equipment, printed it, and are still in the process of collating it, punching holes by hand on a machine which does 5 pages at a time . . . slow, slow work."

Humes inspired Colin to keep working in the prisons, sharing with him her affection and high expectations for what the inmates could achieve. When Colin died, he had in his possession a large stack of poems, many of them by one of Humes's favorite poets at the Virginia prison, Willie J. Williams, who had edited a prison magazine called "The FYSK" (Facts You Should Know). Colin now had his heart set on doing anthropological fieldwork in prisons, especially on the death penalty, a subject he had been interested in for years. He began writing letters to prisons throughout the United States to ask for permission to visit and interview death row inmates. Between 1976 and 1978, he visited Alcatraz and prisons in the mid-Atlantic region, and taught anthropology at the Robert Kennedy Youth Center in West Virginia. He was gearing up for a high profile article on the death penalty to be published in *Natural History* entitled, "Death by Decree." The magazine had solicited the piece when they learned Colin had been teaching anthropology in prisons. They asked Colin to do an anthropological analysis of death row, describing the effects of the death penalty on both prisoners and prison officials. The essay is one of the most well argued and coherent essays Colin ever published, and it is known to nearly every defender of death row inmates working in the United States today.

In 1978, a year before *Natural History* would publish his article on capital punishment, Colin visited the Florida State Penitentiary (FSP), which at the time had as many as 140 condemned men, the largest death row population in the country. Most of the men on death row were housed in solitary cells, barely large enough for one small bed, in a poorly ventilated basement of the prison. But the basement cells, unlike those on the ground or second floors, at least allowed prisoners to see one another across the hallway. Ten cells faced each other in each corridor but cement buttresses prevented an inmate from seeing the man next door, even if his neighbor extended his arm outside the bars. Behind the cell's back walls was the aging electric chair, Old Sparky, as it was called, and along one of the hallways, the prisoners could see the thick black cable that carried electricity to the chair. When a man was put to death, the other death row inmates could smell the burning flesh.

Until very recently, when the state of Florida changed its method of execution from the electric chair to lethal injection, little at FSP had changed since Colin knew it. Once every two weeks, the executioner came to death row to test the electric chair, occasionally talking to prisoners but never looking them in the eye, and when he tested it, all the inmates heard the whine and hum of the generator and thought about the day it would be used for them.

The men on death row at FSP today still get little exercise—two hours, two days a week—and spend as much as twenty-three hours a day in their cells, sleeping, daydreaming, masturbating, watching the walls and the bars, and trying to talk to the other men across the way, or on the floors above or below by "getting into the vents," a phrase that means shouting through the air ducts. There are some prisoners who are so depressed that they are nearly catatonic; others, like the man Colin would eventually call "brother," are inspired through religion and their friends and family to make something of themselves, even under conditions that would break most people's spirits.

Given that Colin quickly made strong attachments, especially with people he believed were oppressed, it is not surprising that he became so involved with the inmates. His files contain hundreds of letters from inmates at various prisons. He sent them gifts of books and magazines and occasionally sent money to their relatives. For some, he badgered their overworked public defenders to pay more attention to their pending appeals. Throughout the late 1970s and early 1980s, Colin corresponded with inmates in Florida and Virginia, most of whom he addressed by their prison nicknames: for example, "Dog," "Monk," "Goldfinger," "Cookie," and "Fast." He wrote to them about his love for Joe, and about his hopes for the dispossessed. He liked them as friends but he also wanted them to help him with his research. Colin was especially interested in hearing about the guards and the wardens. As he wrote one inmate, Willie Williams in the Virginia State penitentiary in 1978, "The weakness of the article [I am writing on the death penalty] as it stands at the moment is that I have not been able to get enough data to show what harm capital punishment does to guards and their families . . . brutalizing them just as it brutalizes prisoners and anyone else the system touches, ultimately the public. That is really one of the strongest arguments against the system. As Joe (remember him?) pointed out to me . . . it works just like slavery worked . . . it corrupts wherever it touches, and brutalizes both sides . . ."

Through these friendships, Colin became a strong advocate for inmates and argued that if Americans ever "expect their criminals to return to society, their conditions of confinement must be consistent with our concept of humanity. This means, at the very least, allowing the prisoner the respect and dignity due all human beings." He also argued that the death penalty is not a deterrent, does not prevent recurrence of murder, is not a moral duty to the law of an eye for an eye, is not more economical than confining prisoners, and is not a more humane punishment than life imprisonment. Furthermore, as Colin and many before and after him have argued, the legal system uses the death penalty unfairly, sentencing black criminals to death far more often than white criminals. Finally, although he did not offer any alternative forms of execution, he argued against the electric chair, hanging, firing squad, and the gas chamber, because he believed that they were all below American technological capabilities, and that each was, in its own way, inhumane. For example, hanging generally rips open the side of the face and if done from too high a platform can cause decapitation—this is why prisoners wear hoods during hanging—and both hanging and electrocution often cause the prisoner to urinate, defecate, and ejaculate as they die; the firing squad disfigures; and the gas chamber is a slow death, coming only after the prisoner hears the cyanide pellets dropped into the acid and listens to the hissing sound as the gas is released.

Colin's closest inmate friend was Wardell Riley, an African American who had been sentenced to die in the electric chair for a double murder. On September 15, 1975, he was working for the Sunset Bottling Company in Hialeah, Florida.

According to the State of Florida, Riley and an unidentified partner got into an argument with his boss, Peter Enea, Jr., about $30 missing from Riley's accounts. At about 6 P.M., Riley and his partner, the prosecutor contended, ordered three men, including Enea's father, Peter Enea Sr., and Robert Lisenby, to lie on the floor where Riley, the state alleged, robbed and shot each of them. Peter Enea Jr., the only survivor, testified that Riley had committed the murders, and in February 1976, a jury convicted Riley of two counts of first-degree murder and one count of assault with intent to commit first-degree murder. The court sentenced Riley to death by electrocution for the murder of Enea Sr., life imprisonment without the possibility of parole for twenty-five years for the murder of Lisenby, and fifteen years for the assault on Enea Jr.

Riley was sent to the Florida State Penitentiary (FSP) in Starke, Florida to begin serving his sentence, await a date for his execution, and work with his lawyers on an appeal. Two years later, he met Colin. Colin had gone to FSP to interview death row inmates for "Death by Decree." FSP allowed him access and ten inmates, including Riley, agreed to meet him to talk about death row. Colin would endeavor to stay in touch with each of them, but with Riley there was something special. After that first meeting, Colin wrote him to say that when they first shook hands and looked at each other, he knew instantly that he wanted to get to know him better. His handshake was strong and warm, in a word, human.

Wardell Riley was born in Calhoun Country, Georgia in 1947. His parents divorced when he was eleven and he moved with his mother to Jacksonville, Florida. He was a good athlete and an excellent photographer, co-editor of the annual yearbook at his high school, and the recipient of a United Negro College Fund photography scholarship to attend Bethune Cookman College. At college, he received poor grades and decided to join the military, but a school counselor advised him against enlistment, encouraging him instead to take a year off from school, get a job, and do some soul searching. During that year, he married and his daughter April was born. At this time Riley got the job at Sunset as a delivery man and had an application pending for training as a police officer. He had no history of criminal activity.

Colin was convinced that Riley was innocent, that Enea had not actually seen Riley and had identified him only by his shoes and pants. In fact, Enea did not see Riley pull the trigger. There was blood found on Riley's shoes, but he had just been hunting, and the lab tests were inconclusive. Riley has, from the beginning, said that he is completely innocent, and that after work on the day of the killing, he left the company and joined his wife and daughter who were waiting outside in their car.

The Miami public defenders who took Riley's case were assisted by Scharlette Holdman of the Florida Clearing House on Criminal Justice, as well as Colin. Colin felt responsible to oversee the public defenders' work, some of whom, he suspected, operated in concert with the prosecutors. Holdman's job was to find good attorneys for death row inmates. Telephoned at her current job in San Francisco, Holdman answers the caller's introduction, "If you are not a convicted murderer or a lawyer ready to defend one, I don't want to talk to you." Journalist David von Drehle described her as a "chain-smoking" workhorse, "hair frizzed, feet bare, body rocking in a cheap swivel chair, face lost in a cloud of smoke." Von Drehle wrote that she spent all day on the phone building a national reputation for her organization, the only institutionalized mechanism in Florida for locating lawyers who will work *pro bono* on behalf of death row inmates. She has worked with some of the best lawyers in the country, including David Kendall, a tireless defender of death row inmates who spent a good deal of his career living in motel rooms near FSP (eventually he became Bill Clinton's attorney during his impeachment hearings). Stories about Holdman in *Newsweek* and *People* magazine have made her well-known and helped her acquire the nickname "The Mistress of Delay."

Holdman claims that Colin Turnbull taught her how to be successful. He told her that to win a new trial or a stay of execution, the prisoner's humanity had to be restored. And the only way to do that, he argued, was to present the court with an enormous amount of detail about the inmate's life—where he came from, what his parents and friends were like, what funny or frightening things happened to him in his life, what pressures had determined his unfortunate life. Arguing a philosophical or ethical issue in the courts, Colin believed, would get them nowhere. The inmates themselves had to be fashioned for the court so that they were seen as victims too. Holdman and her co-workers had to draw the court's attention away from the obvious focus of the crimes committed, to express the humanity that had existed in them long before they murdered anyone, and still existed if anyone really wanted to find it. Colin believed that Holdman could do for the inmates what he had failed to do for the Ik.

The written declarations Holdman's clients make to the courts today are long, detailed life histories, and they are as full of information and context as the best anthropological descriptions. In his essay on capital punishment, Colin argued that the ultimate question about capital punishment is whether the murderer is human or has resigned from the human race and therefore no longer deserves to be treated like a human being. And Colin believed that no one could render an opinion on that question without coming face to face with all the complexities of the death penalty: the grim realities of what goes on in the prisons, in the witness rooms and courts, and in the homes of the guards, wardens, and prisoners' families.

In focusing on the prisoners as victims, Colin echoed his earlier work among the Ik. Colin did not write about the relationship between his studies of prisons and the Ik—probably because, given the ongoing controversy over his Ik project, he wanted to avoid deflecting attention from the prisoners or giving the impression that his prison mission was an act of repentance for having failed to help the Ik. Both projects focused on the humanity of the so-called depraved or inhuman and the Ik were, indeed, something like prisoners, trapped in a drought-stricken land that was foreign to them. The controversial solution Colin proposed had been to save the Ik as humans but abandon all Ik culture, for there was nothing essentially wrong with the Ik as human beings. It was their culture, or lack of culture, combined with an ecological tragedy, that was the problem. Likewise, the prisoners on death row were stripped of their humanity, confined in cages, and treated like animals by a penal system convinced that its own power was right and natural. From the perspective of the prison system, there was nothing wrong with the culture of discipline and punishment. It was the fact that there were animals posing as humans that was the problem, and they had to be eradicated. When Colin looked at the guards he must have seen himself at Pirre, Uganda, dehumanized and unfeeling. Perhaps he could master that horrible experience once and for all, do for the prisoners what he could not do for the Ik, and do it without losing his own compassion.

Colin not only helped Holdman with declarations, he telephoned attorneys to get them to take the cases of the inmates he had met at FSP and berated them when he believed they were doing a poor job. Colin was most involved with the case of Riley, especially after he attached himself to Riley's mother, Minnie. She was the sort of woman Colin wished he had had as a mother: quiet and wise, a woman of sound morals who had endured much in her life without complaining. Colin began to stay with her when he visited Florida. And he also began to call her "mother." This was Colin's forte: within weeks of meeting someone new, it seemed as if he had a new best friend, and yet he was capable of keeping in touch with increasing numbers of "best friends" for years.

Riley was scheduled to die on June 7, 1983. In the days leading up to the execution, there was a mounting campaign to stop the execution from organizations of death penalty opponents, politicians, and the media. Pat Frank, a liberal Democratic state senator from Florida was convinced that Riley was innocent. Then, on June 2, 1983, just five days before Riley's execution, the Florida papers reported that Governor Bob Graham had promised the previous governor, Reuben Askew, not to commute any of the death sentences given during his administration, including Riley's. Furthermore, Riley's lawyers charged that the Department of Corrections, under orders from Graham, transferred an inmate named Anthony Saia (now known as Tshambi Sekou) out of FSP to Connecticut State Prison for reasons connected to the Enea murders. Saia claimed to have heard another inmate confess to the Enea slayings, the *Florida Times-Union* said. The Jacksonville paper also quoted a February 26, 1979 letter from former state Inspector General Richard Williams to the Corrections secretary: "Saia has, in some undetermined manner, gotten possession of an extremely sensitive memo between former Gov. Askew and Bob Graham to the effect that Askew would not commute the death sentence of Spenkelink [John Spenkelink, executed May, 1979], Darden [inmate Willie Darden], Riley, et al. prior to leaving office, thereby assuring his Federal appointment by President Carter, while at the same time Bob would exercise his authority in carrying out those executions based upon party demands."

The same letter asked that Saia be isolated and that charges against him in Florida be dropped so that he could be transferred to his home state of Connecticut. According to Riley's lawyers, Saia heard another inmate, John Ferguson, sentenced to death in 1978 for six murders, confess that someone else had been arrested for a murder he had in fact committed. Court records show that, although Ferguson was incarcerated for much of his life, he was at large when the Sunset murders were committed.

On June 3, 1983, the Florida Supreme Court rejected Riley's plea for a new trial, affirming the life and fifteen year sentences, but remanding the death penalty conviction to a lower court. That court had four days to decide whether Riley lived or died.

In the seven days leading up to an execution, the inmate is shackled and handcuffed at all times. His head is shaven. More deprived of his rights than ever, his emotions run wild. On June 6, the day before the execution was to take place, family and friends started to arrive at the prison to be with Riley, who by that time had converted to Islam and called himself Kamal Hassan. They were allowed short visits with Kamal between 9 A.M. and 1 P.M., to say goodbye. Kamal's mother, sister, and high school principal came, as did his girlfriend, a woman Kamal met through a prison pen-pal program not long after the Enea murders when he and his wife divorced. They all waited with Colin at the prison and took turns visiting with Kamal. Colin reassured Kamal that, as they had arranged previously, he and Michael Radelet, a professor of sociology at the University of Florida and an anti–death penalty advocate, would take possession of Kamal's body, cremate it, and scatter the ashes somewhere in Africa.

At 12:25, Kamal was in the penitentiary superintendent's office when the phone rang. Kamal saw that he was happy, and when the phone call was over, the superintendent told him, "Send your mom home. She's tired. And the media will want to interview you and Dr. Turnbull this afternoon." Kamal left the superintendent's office and told his mother that U.S. District Judge Joe Eaton had stopped the execution order. A small frail woman, she rose from her seat without any assistance and cried, "Thank you, Jesus. Thank you, Jesus." Everyone in the room, including Colin, was crying now. But Kamal did not celebrate. He felt numb and asked Colin why, at a time like this, he would feel so desensitized. "Am I becoming an animal?" Kamal asked. Colin touched him and said, "You've erected a wall to protect yourself. But I want you to go back now to your cell, and talk about this with the people on the row. And write about it too. And, I tell you, the wall will break. And you'll be broken."

"Professor Turnbull," he says, "was the greatest person I ever met. We all liked him. He was inspirational. He was a friend and my brother." He added, "I think, I know, Professor Turnbull liked me too. We just had that kind of connection immediately. I was not into that masculine image of not crying, and I talked about myself and we just connected." As time went on, he said, Colin "prepared me for death, but he also prepared me for how I felt when my death sentence was overturned. Having the death order signed and having your death order thrown out are both pretty emotional experiences."

Kamal talked to the media and to his girlfriend, and he confided in a fellow inmate who was permitted into the visitor's center. As he was talking to his inmate friend, there was a gust of wind from an open door in the reception area, and Kamal said he needed to go back to his cell. He curled into a fetal position on his bed, rocking as he held onto his legs, and wept, thinking "this is what Colin prepared me for." "That experience," Kamal said, "of being that close to death and letting it all out was a passage, elevating me to a higher level. Being in prison is not all bad. You try to rid yourself of the anger. This is a good thing."

But the good news did not last long. By 1986, Kamal was still on death row. It was by now clear to everyone that the Saia evidence had been muffled by the authorities, and that the eyewitness evidence of Enea was not as good as the state needed, but the district court angrily said they would not be coerced into changing the sentence. Another death warrant was signed, and Kamal, now 39 years old, was scheduled to die on November 4, 1986 in a double execution with another death row inmate, a former weightlifter named George Lemon. Colin wrote letters to everyone he could think of, trying hard to get the media involved. He corresponded with ABC's *Prime Time Live,* and with NBC's Tom Brokaw, who had interviewed Colin during the 1970s about both *The Mountain People* and the issue of capital punishment, requesting, to no avail, that the *Today Show* or some other program make the case public.

There was a last minute change. The day before the execution, the Florida Supreme Court granted a stay of execution. Kamal was sent to Miami to the chief circuit judge of Dade County for a new decision about what to do with his case. It might have taken only four to six weeks for the judge to give a ruling, but the appeal dragged on for four years, and from 1988 to 1992, Kamal waited in a Miami prison with no word about the possibility of either a resentencing or a new trial. Finally, in 1992 the state's prosecutor told Kamal and his attorneys that if there were a new trial, the state would fight again for the death penalty, and they urged him to cut a deal. Kamal said, "I didn't want to put my family through any more. I'm innocent, but I gave a guilty plea in return for a life sentence." At the resentencing, Peter Enea, Jr., came to give testimony. Kamal looked at him, but Enea could not meet his eyes. Kamal said, "I don't know if you're certain in your heart, but somewhere in your heart there must be some doubt, and maybe one day you will say to the courts that you're not one hundred percent sure."

Kamal and Michael Radelet wrote to Colin to tell him about the news. Colin felt that he should have been happier that Kamal's life had been spared, but he wanted more for him. He wanted him to be free or at least to be in prison with the promise of freedom in the future. Colin was not certain that either of them would still be alive in 2002 when Kamal was scheduled to come up for parole. Certainly Kamal's mother, already an elderly woman, would never have him with her again.

Today, Kamal lives at the Tomoka Correctional Institution in Daytona Beach, Florida. He was transferred there a few months after his death sentence was overturned. In comparison to FSP, he says, Tomoka is like an idyllic college campus.

In 1979, when Colin's professional life was occupied by death penalty cases, his domestic life was occupied by Joe, with whom he desperately wanted to travel. At the last minute in September 1979, Joe agreed to join Colin on their planned trip around the world. They flew first to Paris where they helped Peter Brook prepare his group of actors for the Australian tour of *The Ik,* and then left for Israel. Joe wrote a detailed account of the trip in his diary, about how much he hated Israel because he believed Israelis were racist (Joe said that Jews spit on him as he walked along the streets), disliked Egypt for its dirt and inefficiency, and resented being with Colin in East Africa. Joe tried his best to ditch Colin in Kenya, hooking up with a Kenyan man named Patrick and his friends, disappearing with them for hours.

The Kenyan group reminded Colin of the crew in Lancaster, and the locals who loitered outside of Colin and Joe's hotel in Nairobi warned Colin that Patrick was a hoodlum. Joe wrote in his diary that Patrick introduced him to the Nairobi gay scene and that he "slept with some handsome men." After several days, Joe finally answered Colin's expressions of frustration and worry by saying that he wanted Colin to go to India alone, that he might or might not meet him there, and that Colin should look at the American Express offices in Bombay and Benares for his letters and itinerary. In the meantime, Joe went to Uganda where he saw his old lover Everest and attended his own graduation alone, without Colin or family. At the age of forty-two, Joe was finally a Doctor of Philosophy. But for the second time, there was no photograph of Joe's graduation.

Joe returned to Nairobi from Uganda and stayed another week until boarding a plane for Bombay. There he met Colin, who had already been in several cities, had revisited old haunts—including the ashram of Anandamayi Ma—and had planned out a trek into the mountains to visit a Tibetan monastery recommended by his Tibetan friend and former colleague from the American Museum of Natural History, Thubten Norbu. Sadly, Colin did not see Anandamayi Ma, who always seemed to be wherever Colin was not.

Together now, Joe and Colin experienced moments of happiness in India, especially in Agra and at the Taj Mahal, where they arrived just at sunset. Colin tried to replicate his visit to the mausoleum three decades earlier on a moonlit night. They traveled to Sri Lanka, Turkey, Japan, Macau, China, Singapore, Bali, Samoa, Tahiti, and the Marquesas Islands. At each stop, they stayed for longer periods of time. Colin was in no rush to get back home. He had heard that the National Endowment for the Humanities decided not to fund the theater project but would entertain a smaller proposal for the next year, one that would eventually be funded for $113,305. They were healthy, and happier than they had expected they would be, but somewhere in the back of Colin's mind he was frightened about returning to Virginia. Within a few years, the manifestations of Joe's alcoholism and mental illness would become more pronounced and debilitating.

Colin returned to work at George Washington University (GW) in September 1980 with the rank of Professor and a new salary of $38,000. He had originally been hired in what is called a non-tenure-accruing visiting status; now, at the age of fifty-five, he was for the first time employed as a professor on a tenure track. But he would have to work for at least three full years before he could apply for tenure, the ultimate career goal in academia: lifetime job security and total academic freedom.

Colin was widely admired at GW. He had a powerful influence on the anthropology students and at the medical school where he and Bob Humphrey jointly taught a popular course called "Evolution of the Biomedical Model." His annual reports from the chair and dean called him "an excellent, captivating lecturer, capable of conveying the broad, humanistic perspectives of anthropology to undergraduates . . . A congenial colleague." In fact, however, Colin seldom went to faculty meetings. He considered academic politics useless and trivial (about fighting with academics, he once said, "It's like wrestling with pigs: you get dirty and they enjoy it") and he was disdainful of the American system of rotating chairmanships that gave the chairs virtually no power over the department. Though his teaching evaluations were excellent, students complained privately that they were never sure what they would be tested on, and that Dr. Turnbull told fantastic stories but wouldn't talk about exams or grades. His written work was progressing well. He had started a project on life stages and rites of passage, originally called "The Dance of Life," later to be changed to *The Human Cycle.*

But perhaps the most notable feature of Colin's time at GW was that he never asked the university to offer a teaching position to Joe. GW faculty dreaded the day they assumed would come, a casual and polite request for Joe to do some part-time teaching leading to a more firm request and an eventual demand they could not fulfill. But it never happened. Joe did apply for a job at Catholic University, and at least two GW professors recommended him highly for it. During his interview at Catholic, Joe talked about the many times he had met Evans-Pritchard but when asked about Evans-Pritchard's work, Joe drew a blank and could not remember a single title of any of the publications he had read. He was not surprised when the rejection letter came. So he stayed in Virginia, spending most of his time on his boat, which he called *The African Queen,* and only occasionally coming up to Washington to stay at Colin's apartment near the university. Joe suspected Colin was having an affair with an African American social work professor named Larry Icard, whom Colin had met at West Virginia University. Colin denied it to Joe and he denied it too in "Lover and Beloved," but according to Icard, they were, in fact, lovers. Colin had helped Larry through a difficult time in his life as he was coming out, dealing with the problem of how to be both black and gay in rural America.

By the fall of 1982, Joe was beginning to be more jealous and paranoid than ever. When the department threw a surprise birthday party for Colin in November, Joe was certain that Colin had known about the party and that he had kept it secret from him. Joe also believed the department of anthropology wanted Colin to break up with him. He so feared a breakup that he decided to move in with Colin in D.C. to keep an eye on him. Some of Colin's colleagues talked privately about what a happy life and successful career he could have without the burden of Joe, but they never dared say anything like that to Colin.

Within a month after Joe moved into Colin's D.C. apartment, they rented a duplex in Rosslyn, Virginia just across the Potomac River from the Watergate complex. Just before Christmas, Colin drove down to Lancaster to help Joe pack his things, but when he arrived, Joe had already gone out with his friends. Late that night, the crew brought Joe back, almost unconscious, and helped him to his bedroom upstairs. Within a few minutes after his friends had left, Joe came down the stairs with an African machete in hand and tried to slash Colin. Colin avoided the knife and wrestled Joe to the ground.

"[Joe] began pulling my rather weak hair out by the roots. Tearing at his hair seemed to have no effect at all. I didn't want to hurt him, but I didn't want to be hurt either, and he was biting and scratching as well as kicking and punching, and though smaller he was a lot tougher than I was. Finally I managed to daze him with a lucky punch, and I rushed out and jumped in my car and drove away as fast as I could. He was close behind me, screaming and hitting at the car."

Colin drove to Washington and en route remembered that once, when he had come to work with scratches and bruises on his face, a colleague had given him the home telephone number of a good friend of his, a psychiatrist who worked in the Georgetown area named Alec Whyte. Colin pulled the number from his wallet and found a pay phone. It was 3 A.M. and many people had already left for Christmas vacations but Whyte picked up the phone. He told Colin to come to his office at seven. At the meeting, Whyte warned Colin not to go back to Virginia, but he went anyway, half expecting to find that Joe had committed suicide. When he got there, everything was picked up in the house, and Joe acted as if nothing had happened. Colin continued to visit Whyte every few weeks, not for his own mental health, he insisted, but in an effort to understand Joe.

They had another fight on February 13, 1983, when Joe asked Colin to cancel his classes so they could be together in Lancaster for Valentine's Day. Part of the argument involved Joe's anger with Colin for leaving him in Africa both in 1972 and in 1979, a charge Colin flatly denied. Colin did not stay with Joe in Lancaster. He went to Washington, taught his class, and returned to his D.C. apartment to write a note about his relationship with Joe, a note that does not seem to be addressed to anyone in particular. At the top of the page, Colin drew a valentine's heart with an arrow through it. The note began: "I love Joe, Joe loves me, we always have, we always will . . ."

He went on: "I feel I must get some simple facts straight, not in self-justification, but because I think they are now major stumbling blocks to his acceptance of my love, making him unnecessarily suspicious and critical. Heaven knows he has reason to be critical, but at least it would help to remove these reasons . . . I did not leave him in Africa in 1972. We were out of NSF money and time, and out of our own . . . I did not leave Joe in Kenya in 1979 . . . he felt a strong need to be on his own, not to have me arranging everything . . . I am terrified of losing Joe, just because I know his love will always be mine, just as mine will always be his. If I were to lose him, the tragedy is that it would be because of no infidelity or loss of love on either side, but because of mutual misunderstanding . . . most likely my own blind stupidity . . . Was Joe's demand that I stay home yesterday to be there for Feb. 14th unreasonable? If I had thought it would have helped us, I would have stayed . . . gladly . . . at any cost . . . if I thought it would help . . . But he had had two rums and wine . . . I still feel he does not really understand the need for me to keep a good job to have the life we want together, in our home, and to ready ourselves for retirement. Does he really know what we would lose if I gave up my job now?

" . . . I also think he does not fully understand that a Professor job is more than just classroom time. Perhaps I should find some other job . . . Perhaps something we could do together. Farm? This is surely worth exploring together."

Colin's work began to suffer. *The Human Cycle* was due out soon, but Colin had few ideas for a next project. In the spring of 1983, Colin wrote Michael Korda at Simon & Schuster to say, finally, "I think I have it!" He submitted two long book proposals. One was entitled "The Anthropologist at Work," the other "The Five Portals: Man's Quest for the Sacred." The latter book, Colin said, would show how people in different cultures seek to enrich their lives with beauty and the divine, and he would advocate more forcefully than ever before for the need of Americans to embrace some aspect of spirituality. The works were quickly rejected by Korda, despite some interest among Simon & Schuster's editors in the book on the sacred. One of Korda's colleagues wrote a memo to him saying, "Michael: Turnbull is turning into [Carlos] Castaneda before our eyes! The book on the anthropologist at work strikes me as hopeless. I think, however . . . there is a market for ruminations on the sacred." Between 1983 and 1992 he would write and rewrite both manuscripts. He entitled the first "The Field Experience," the second "The Flute of Krishna." Despite Colin's best efforts, however, neither would ever be accepted for publication by any publishing house.

After thinking hard about how much Joe needed him, Colin decided to retire from George Washington University. In the spring of 1983, at the age of fifty-eight, Colin told Joe that they had enough money and future royalties to live without his GW salary and that, after one more year at GW, he would resign and return to Virginia to devote himself to their love. Joe was at the same time thrilled and suspicious. In Joe's eyes, Colin was proving his love, and for that gift Joe agreed to visit Dr. Whyte for one session. But he also believed that Colin was playing games. Joe did not believe that Colin would resign for him but for some other unknown reason, and was simply using the resignation to win Joe's favor. He was also suspicious because Colin decided not to tell the university of his plans to retire until the first semester of 1984.

The decision was not an easy one. GW was now paying him $45,000 a year, his highest salary ever, and on May 23, 1983, GW had granted him tenure. He felt GW was his academic home, and he had stayed there longer than he had at any university. Still, Colin's own commitment to GW was in doubt. In fact, he had replied to the Provost of GW, H. F. Bright, three weeks after the notification of tenure, to say that he "did not believe in the tenure system" and preferred "a simple non-tenure appointment that leaves the university free to fire me or ask for my resignation for any reason at any time." Colin wrote that he feared he might one day become a burden to the university or to the Department of Anthropology and wanted GW to have the option of getting rid of him. Bright wrote back that he understood Colin's position on the matter of tenure but added: "The tenure system was established originally to protect academic freedom . . . However, it would seem that academic freedom should permit freedom of choice on the part of an academician as to whether or not he wishes to avail himself of this type of protection." Bright then agreed to make Colin's appointment a continuing, non-tenured one.

Somehow the *Chronicle of Higher Education,* the leading weekly newspaper for universities and colleges in the United States, got wind of Colin's unusual decision, a decision almost unheard of in academia. Colin told the paper that his decision to reject his own tenure was "purely personal" and said that tenure might have given him a reason to "slack off." He also said that his relationship with the anthropology department was one of mutual trust and friendship: "There is something about tenure that smacks of a deal, and I wouldn't want that with a friend." The president of the university, Lloyd H. Elliott, called Colin's decision ironic, because in being so iconoclastic, Colin was doing something that tenure was meant to protect. Still, Elliott continued, sometimes in the absence of tenure, the search for truth "will get someone fired." The chair of the faculty senate at the time, John Morgan, told the paper that while Colin certainly had the right to reject tenure, his decision might encourage other university administrators, many of whom are not academics, to develop negative opinions about tenure. The most outraged was Matthew W. Finkin, chairman of the American Association of University Professors' Committee A on Academic Freedom and Tenure. Finkin dismissed Colin's action as "meaningless" since tenure, he said, is in no way "indentured service; it is a protection of the profession."

Did Colin really dislike the tenure system? Or was he rejecting the offer of tenure because he was secretly planning to retire and thus did not want the university to make a commitment that he could not honor or reciprocate? The answer to both questions is yes. He had long told friends that he didn't need an institution to give him academic freedom; he believed he was inherently free, and that if university administrators didn't like what he was doing, they could fire him. He also took the idea of commitment seriously and was frightened by the prospect of reciprocating the university's large gift of lifetime job security.

At the same time, Colin was beginning to suffer from flu-like symptoms and in the spring semester of 1983, he felt little enthusiasm for teaching. He asked for and received one year's leave without pay. His royalties were quite enough to live on. He would not need the leave, as it turned out, because he would quit entirely. But, not knowing this, the dean wrote to the provost in February 1984, that "Colin Turnbull has been having a series of episodes of illness, which the doctors find it difficult to diagnose, though presumably it all stems from some kind of tropical parasite Colin picked up in his many research journeys." Finally, in the fall of 1984, Colin wrote the chair of anthropology, Ruth Krulfeld, that he would resign and that he and Joe would go to New York where Richard Schechner, in the Department of Performance Studies, had agreed to give him part-time work at New York University. In his resignation letter he said, "Things have not changed and I am afraid that I shall not be returning to full time teaching anywhere. In the Spring I shall be teaching two courses for NYU . . . which I agreed to when I thought I would by then be safely installed in a Chelsea apartment . . . So Joe and I are back [in Lancaster] again . . . I could not have had a happier academic home [at GW] . . . I am truly grateful to all of you.

"The reasons are complex, but they involve both the good of the Department (as I see it) and my own well-being . . . It was not entirely that stupid bug either, it was also just me. The bug I could deal with, it was an allowable excuse I am not! . . . I was not able to give my all at all times, in class and still less out, and this is not acceptable to me."

Throughout 1983, Joe had become increasingly fearful of staying in Lancaster, and so had Colin. There were a number of murders of people both Joe and Colin knew, and one person had been killed in front of their gatehouse. The crew was still around; the police seemed to have it out for Joe and Joe knew just how to provoke them. Someone stole Joe's stamp collection; Joe was ashamed that he could not drive; and Joe feared he might be raped again. Having been granted a leave from GW, seven months before Colin would send in his formal resignation, Joe and Colin decided, together, to move back to Manhattan. They put the house up for sale, though Joe refused to have a For Sale sign posted by the roadside for fear that the crew and his neighbors might think he was fleeing from Lancaster. Colin brought in an antique dealer, put up for sale many of the things his mother had left him—including such heirlooms as his father's war medals—and went up to New York to find an apartment in Chelsea. By October, they had moved into a building on West Eighteenth Street just off Eighth Avenue, only a few blocks from their first home together. They lasted about two months. Joe heard loud noises in the upstairs apartment that would not stop, and one day he took out his anger on the walls and the ceiling. Colin patched up the broken plaster. They returned to Virginia the next day, but Colin was frightened and decided to escape.

While Joe was asleep in their Virginia home, Colin packed some things and drove to his friend Bob Humphrey's townhouse in Falls Church, Virginia, where he would stay for about six months. Bob's mother had passed away and the home was vacant while it was up for sale. Colin never imagined that he would one day leave Joe. But there he was, so improbably fleeing from Joe, the one who had made him feel love for the first time, the one who made him more possessive than he thought he could be, the one who now made him suffer and with whom, he thought, he might never live again.

But rather than stay away completely, Colin started visiting Joe in Lancaster once a week. If he stayed more than a day they would begin to fight. Colin wrote diary entries, something he very rarely did—in fact, he kept the pages loose since he did not have a diary—asking, "Where is Joe? What is he doing? Have I driven him back to the way of life he fought so hard to get away from? What must I do . . . to convince him that his dream, the night of the 23rd [October 23, 1959, when Joe and Colin first met], that we can get back to where we were in New York? Because we can . . . but we have to do it, I believe, by building a new life, from scratch, in our new home in Virginia." Colin planned an addition to the house and he wrote that he hoped this would give them a new chance at building that life. In a July 14, 1983 note to himself, he typed out, "For me, everyday of my life is Valentine's day on which I think of our love and our life, and feel . . . Joe, I love you, I love you, I love you." He then wrote by hand, "*Know* it my love—*please*—it is all in our hands."

While staying at Bob Humphrey's mother's house, Colin lengthened his visits to Lancaster, until finally Dr. Whyte, after listening to Colin's reports but meeting with Joe only once, surmised that it would be safe for Colin to go home. What Colin did not know was that while he was in Falls Church, Joe had seen a physician who told him that he might have been exposed to HIV. But at that time no blood test had been developed, and Joe kept his suspicions to himself.

In late 1983, Joe developed a painful swelling on the side of his neck. He went to the George Washington University medical center, a place he had visited just a few weeks earlier after being mugged near Chinatown. He suspected that Colin had arranged for gangsters to attack him then; now that he had this swelling, he wondered if Colin had poisoned him. It was a swollen lymph node that his physician surgically removed, but while he was in the hospital, he also complained of headaches, blackouts, and strange noises in his head. A number of other tests were done and he was diagnosed with syphilis. Joe had a spinal tap to see if the syphilis had spread to his brain, causing what is called neurosyphilis, but the results of that test are not known. Colin immediately had himself tested for syphilis and was negative. Although Joe was treated for syphilis, his mental state worsened. At Christmastime, after final exams, Colin drove to Virginia and found his study littered with torn pages of his newly published book *The Human Cycle.*

The Human Cycle was a semi-autobiographical book about the process from birth to death with special emphasis on his own childhood, which he described as miserable. Colin drew on his own life as a way to criticize western civilization and praise the way other cultures deal with the various stages of life. He argued that childhood was a time of joy among the Mbuti Pygmies, a time of repression and deceit in England; that Mbuti teenagers practice sex freely and yet rarely have unwanted pregnancies, while in the West sex is always something impure and dirty and without spirituality; that old age in Europe and the United States is "a frightening anteroom to extinction," while in Asia and Africa it is seen as a time of "wisdom, serenity, and power." The entire book is a portrait of human culture in black and white—his society is bad, and others are good. Colin even insisted that childhood among the Mbuti was such a positive experience that children remembered their experiences in the womb, whereas western children cannot remember anything before the age of three or four. The thrust of the book is that western civilization has directed human beings toward the achievement of individual goals at the expense of human values such as cooperation, sharing, and a sense of belonging to nature.

It was not a critical success. In the *New York Times,* for example, Peter Berger wrote: "[*The Human Cycle*] has nothing to do with anthropology as a science. Rather, it is the use of anthropology to legitimate every cliché about Western civilization spouted by its countercultural critics." Even the positive reviews criticized him for making simplistic comparisons across different cultures and historical periods, such as: "The primitive is ahead of us all the way." Were an anthropologist to read *The Human Cycle* with the year of publication unknown, he or she might date it to an earlier period of anthropological history, for the book it resembles most closely is Margaret Mead's *Coming of Age in Samoa,* written in 1927, in which facile comparisons were made between a so-called primitive society and the West, to glorify one and criticize the other.

Despite the criticisms, one could argue in retrospect that there was something positive in the general message of the book, well covered in newspaper stories with headlines such as "Study Raises Question about Who Is Civilized," "Proper Utilization of Aged," and "What Price Freedom?" The book stimulated readers to reflect on the human costs of so-called progress, to rethink the way we treat the elderly, and perhaps to admire varieties of cultural experience so often denigrated by western civilization.

We do not know what Colin's own reactions were to these reviews, with the exception of a short letter he sent to Michael Korda at Simon & Schuster apologizing for letting him down. He wrote, "Dear Mike, I hear that the *NY Times* gave *The Human Cycle* a panning . . . Whatever, I know none of those things is what you would have liked, and I am sorry." In 1983, when he was interviewed by *Omni* magazine, he offered some comment on the view that his depictions of African societies in *The Forest People* and in *The Human Cycle* were romantic or even invented: "I'm delighted to be called a romanticist. It tells me I'm on the right track. They mean I'm reporting only the good and trying to make everything seem perfect; in other words, I'm inventing it. I can respect anthropology only if it is a form of pilgrimage, where we are on a sacred quest to bring back from other societies the good things that can enhance our lives. To hell with people saying, 'Oh, here goes the romantic again!'"

Colin's Canadian relatives, all of whom had first met Colin when he was already grown, were amazed by the book because they had had no inkling that Colin viewed his childhood as so unhappy. Perhaps the angriest was Joe. Despite the fact that the book was autobiographical, Joe and Colin's love was absent, nor did Colin give the reader any clue that he might be gay. Joe found the omissions both hurtful and telling. He had underestimated Colin's narcissism. His own wounds had reopened too, since Colin had published yet another book while he had published nothing.

Throughout 1983, Joe expressed his suspicions in diary entries that chronicled his increasing tendency to link mundane observations to sinister plots against him. He was certain that Colin was reading his diary—if Colin did read it, it must have sent chills down his spine—and felt he had no friends to turn to. Outside of the crew, their friends were mostly Colin's, and though they were very worried about Joe from what little they saw of him, Colin told few people about Joe's paranoia. In fact, Colin tried to keep their relationship as private as possible during the 1980s and had to try hard to resist being pulled into Joe's delusions, a symbolic and well circumscribed world in which everything was meaningfully related to everything else. The meaning would usually be the same, that Colin was trying to destroy him, and there were times when Colin actually believed him. Colin would search for spiritual truths in Joe's delusions, especially after his death. He wondered if Joe had been so deeply in touch with the supernatural forces that he came in contact with when among the Mbo of central Africa that he appeared to be ill when, in fact, he was completely sane.

Jan. 18, 1983
Let me say briefly that it does indeed appear that Colin seeks to interfere in my work . . . I went to a store with him and instead of standing near me, a clerk gave me $4 over limit—not quite sure, I turned around, Colin was gone out as the clerk said he gave me too much. My initiation has implications of theft with the Bakumu-Kumu tree—a knife of circumcision put there to eat the blood of initiates who sleep with the doctor's wife. Also, we had a young man here to estimate [renovation costs] for a room and while in our basement he used the curious expression, "a steal," to describe placing a chimney.

Jan. 21, 1983
Almost constantly, Colin comes into my study and rearranges some of my notes, especially those dealing with witchcraft. Something is wrong with him. Woe is me, for I cry inward, moan and tremble, I look to the past, there is little comfort . . .

Jan 31, 1983
I still get the feeling [Colin] is covering up some dirt, planning to use it up on me. Just the general demeanor of his actions convey this, spending the whole day recording, as though he is manipulating something. Last night when I came to bed, I found an empty mint candy wrapper there—it is these things done while I am out of the house that are so sad. Anne [Eisner Putnam] told me years ago that Colin was intensely selfish, insecure, and now I can see it. If you cannot love and reveal your weaknesses to your lover without fear, then there can be no love.

February 14, 1983
Colin came home as white as a sheet, his hair plastered down on his head, looking as though he was ghost of his real self—making love to him was like putting my member into a great jar—and he smelled of sexual scent—his ass was so big a dump truck could have turned around in it. Even this I overcame, as I know I often went with men. But damn

it, Colin said, in fact, he promised, to keep himself pure in body, as I have since November 24, 1982.

March 30, 1983. 9 A.M.

And now diary, I sit here in wonder and hope. Colin and I had a fight last night . . . While I took a bath, I suddenly saw Colin's shoes under the bureau—the word HOBO was written in them—strange I thought—they were cheap he said . . . He began talking about the dirty old black shoes . . . He still seemed to be acting provocatively, talking about the shoes in double entendre. I felt so bad. This has been going on since November!

Colin bought garlic cheese with herbs. In the myth I am doing, fish is associated with witchcraft and garlic in Europe is anti-witchcraft. To make sure I get the point, Colin kept making Ritz crackers with cheese and popping them in his mouth and eyeing me sideways. Why?

Anyway, I mentioned the shoe episode to Colin as upsetting—all week he has been talking about priests—while we were arguing I turned on the TV and there was a man with a shoe-box and interviewing a priest, I was drinking sherry . . . Colin called me to bed and as I attempted to make love to him, he repulsed me . . . I grabbed Colin on the shoulders and face. He suddenly appeared sitting up in bed, scratches all over his face—under the jaw (he earlier mentioned some pain in the jaw, I told him no young person suddenly just got lock jaw—he protested—no I am sure it was a suggestion—all the matches here are from People's Drug)—in no way could I have caused the fine lined cuts (5) on his face—all over. Under the couch I found a beer cap, was it the scissors? Colin refused to say . . . Colin came to bed and we made love.

He seemed to resent me washing the cuts off. I tried but the substance would not come off—some type of dye? Why? This morning, he came out of the bathroom looking worse. Page A5 of Woodward Lothrop [department store catalog] has a pair of shoes on it—a young man in a suit under it, my house keys were laid on the man's crotch . . . Both of us are frustrated in our love—why. Since Nov. I have been true to him yet I can find little peace of mind. Why does the tea cozy have a cover from my bed in Uganda? I mentioned to him that it had unhappy memories of me sleeping with Everest, yet it is here.

And now I have removed all the symbols of my infidelities, as many as I can find—the couch covers, bottoms and sides—why are they so prominently displayed here? Colin has to be sick.

April 5, 1983
And so, I am here, in bed, wondering, why? Am I so sick, do I live? Why? Oh, Colin, why is this happening. Can you destroy me—of course you can. But really I love you as I said.

May 13, 1983
Colin threatened to walk out on me today. This is the second time in six months . . . A woman called the other night supposedly from Florida, saying her son was moved to Death row—after all this time of nothing but letters, cards and calls from gay prisoners, now comes Death Row. Should I be any more sorrowful than those executed on Robbins I[sland]? I shrugged and he became furious. In my study, I lay on the floor and said "Walk over me, is that what you want?" "No," he flung at me, "You're not worth it."

June 8, 1983
A black paper clip was on my desk yesterday morning—the 7th book of my fieldnotes is missing—a book which I do not remember bringing upstairs lay open on a chair near my bed. Phony owl sounds could be heard in the night—boats turned back to front, encyclopedias, dictionaries, all upside down.

November 9, 1983
On Oct. 31, Halloween Day, Colin's tenants were due to leave the [gate] house . . . The next day we were due to meet the [new] tenant. Colin doubted whether I should come but I told him that I thought it would be a good idea for him to have a witness as the man was leaving the place for the last time . . . The man had left the place filthy . . . He seemed to stumble against Colin. I cannot be sure of this but I am very convinced that I saw Colin pass something to him. Colin had the clipboard in his arm and both of them seemed to know that they should contact one another. The whole while they were going from room to room aimlessly, as though needing some privacy. Parallels . . . the check in the garden, Keys? Leases, a title of my [proposed] book.

On December 23, 1983 Colin bought Joe a bag of Christmas candy and put it on top of an ashtray on Joe's dresser. In the ashtray, Colin had also put four screws from the dresser's mirror, which he was in the process of repairing. When Joe found the candy and screws, he accused Colin of intentionally sending him a thinly veiled message: with the screws, Joe claimed, Colin was telling him he was aware that he was "screwing" around with other men, and with the candy he was reminding Joe of his close friendship with Nate Garner, a theater professor at George Washington University, whose first wife's name was Candy. The mirrors in the house, Joe argued, were strategically placed so that Colin could spy on him, and when, on Christmas day, Colin played a record of Christmas carols, Joe was sure Colin was criticizing him for his failure to believe in Jesus Christ as the Messiah. Colin later remembered: "And when Joe said 'Perhaps I am the Messiah?' he was so cold sober and rational that I found myself stopping to consider it . . . But as with the screws and the candy and the mirror and the noises in his head, I dismissed his question . . . I was dismissing Joe, not even attempting to listen to what he was trying so hard to tell me. But it was like listening to a foreign language."

But what if Colin had listened more carefully? Would he have been able to interpret or find a logic in Joe's delusions? When Colin tried to take seriously Joe's complaints about noises coming from the upstairs apartment in Rosslyn, Virginia, he ended up encouraging Joe's anger at the tenant living above them. And one day when Colin was away at school, Joe became so violent, tearing into the ceiling with whatever objects he could find, that neighbors called the police and Joe was arrested. He seldom let Colin comfort him. For a time, Joe would let his sister Mary Jane come to the apartment to wash his hair and give him a Curly-Q treatment, a hairstyle that was fashionable in those days.

When Mary Jane and Joe's mother visited Lancaster on Christmas night 1983, Joe asked Colin to sleep with him. In the middle of the night Joe started to scratch and bite Colin's face. Colin wrestled himself free but didn't shout for fear of waking up the family. Joe started after him again.

He accused Colin of infidelity and spousal abuse and shouted out that Colin was trying to drive him insane. Colin collapsed to the floor in a fetal position and it was as if Colin, by taking a submissive position, was giving Joe the green light. Joe lunged at Colin, pulled out patches of hair and scratched at his eyes. He tried to pull Colin's head up so that he could see his face, and when he got a glimpse of Colin's cheek, he tried to bite him. Colin waited, hoping that the attack would be over soon, and he comforted himself by touching his mother's wedding ring, still on his finger since his mother had died. He tried to take it off but it wouldn't move. He pulled and pushed at the ring; when it finally came loose, it was stained with blood. Colin had torn the skin off his knuckle. He turned over and with one violent pull at Joe's wrist, he had him on the ground. He unclenched Joe's hand, and pushed the ring onto one of Joe's fingers, yelling,

"I do! I do! I do!" When Joe saw what Colin had done, he stopped his attack. He sat down, touched the ring gently with his lips in a soft kiss, kissed Colin on the forehead, turned over and went to sleep on the floor.

Joe would later give the ring back to Colin for fear of its magical powers.

In the spring of 1985, Joe's violence renewed and Colin decided it was time for another break. He planned to go to the island of Samoa in the South Pacific for several months. He and Joe had loved Samoa when they visited in 1979, and now he had reasons to go back: he needed time away from Joe, there were some fascinating rumors of Samoan Pygmies in the mountains, and he had already involved himself in a controversy over Margaret Mead's famous 1927 study, *Coming of Age in Samoa.* Derek Freeman, an established Australian anthropologist, had written a quite personal attack on Mead, arguing that Mead's depiction of young Samoans as sexually free and unhindered by sexual neuroses or sexual violence was a fiction and that, in fact, the Samoan courts during the 1920s had heard numerous cases of rape and sexual assault. Since Mead's book essentially founded the doctrine of cultural determinism—that is, the idea that culture and not biology determines human behavior—Freeman suggested that all subsequent works of cultural determinism would now be suspect.

In the *New Republic,* Colin called Freeman's work simplistic, misleading, and a male chauvinist attempt to "make a name for himself by unmaking Margaret Mead's reputation." As Colin pointed out, Freeman had not only conducted his fieldwork more than two decades after Mead's, he also studied an island almost 200 miles away from the island where Mead worked. Colin concluded that Freeman's account could potentially harm anthropology and the kind of humanistic anthropology Mead had promoted and might also encourage petty academic rivalries. He was also concerned because Freeman had tried to depict Samoa's darker side, to create an image as simplistic as Freeman believed Mead's had been. Colin quoted one of the many disgruntled Samoans who had been interviewed by *Newsweek* magazine in the context of their own review of the book: "[After Freeman's book] are we Samoans now to be known as a nation of sex-starved, suicidal rapists? I much prefer my previous reputation as a free-loving orgiast . . ."

Why not go to Samoa himself and look into the matter? Two days before Colin was to leave from Baltimore for Samoa, he drove Joe and two neighbors to the grocery store; the neighbors had offered to help chauffeur Joe (since his driver's license was still suspended) while Colin was out of the country. Joe turned on the car's tape player; Colin had put in a cassette of the *Nutcracker*

Suite. "Are you trying to tell me I'm crazy?" Joe cried. He removed the cassette, unraveled the tape from the cassette, opened the car door, and threw the whole mess onto the street. A mile later, Joe heard a ticking noise in the car and, unable to find it or to get anyone else in the car to hear it, he reached under the dashboard and started pulling the plastic that shielded the climate control and other wires. He broke the plastic and tugged at the wires until he fell back in his seat, exhausted. Within a few minutes he was asleep. When they arrived at the grocery store, Joe woke up in a good mood, and the four of them went shopping as if nothing had happened.

Colin's time in Samoa, during the late summer and early fall of 1985, was uneventful. He did not actively pursue any research or engage further in the Freeman-Mead debate. He lived at a small motel with character, with rooms rented by the hour, called Herb and Sia's. Colin paid $250 per month for his room; including food, he spent less than twenty dollars a day. He tried to spend as much time as possible with Samoans but could not avoid being embraced by the small community of white Americans, known in Samoa as "palangi," a word that translates as "sky burster"—that is, the people with airplanes—but is not pejorative. He quickly became friendly with the faculty at the community college in Pago Pago, and established an intimate and enduring friendship with John Enright, the Samoan governor's historical preservation officer, with whom he had long lunches.

Life was pleasant for Colin in American Samoa, mainly because there were few tourists. In contrast to Western Samoa, which has always been poor and has sought revenues through tourism, American Samoa has never fashioned itself for tourists, in part, Samoans say, because the whole idea of "service" is symbolically charged. Who one serves, who one is served by, and how the service is delivered is determined largely by status, and there are many Samoans unwilling to accept jobs in which they might have to serve any person who happens along. Nonetheless, life in American Samoa for visiting Americans is relatively easy. Samoans speak English, use American money, and eat American foods; Colin liked that Samoans smiled and waved but seldom intruded.

On most days, Colin would rise at 4:30 or 5 A.M., have a shower and some tea, write for an hour or two, and go to a corner snack bar or to the Bamboo Room for coffee and an egg sandwich. Forever occupied intellectually with the Pygmies, he spent most of his days in his room writing a book, never published, on his own history of anthropological fieldwork, with the majority of the chapters focused on the Mbuti. Often in the afternoons, he went to a beach park just beyond a hotel called the Rainmaker, where he sat at a table and watched people swim. By 7 P.M. he would be back in his room writing again.

He also collected Samoan folktales for another manuscript, an unpublished collection of stories he would call "Tales of Power," but resisted doing work on the so-called Samoan Pygmies, whom many Samoans claimed still lived in the mountains. Though initially excited by what he might find in the mountains, he wrote Joe that "Stories of Pygmies crop up everywhere, most of all on the island of Ta'u . . . Don't worry, I'm not going . . . if they are there, then good luck to them, and long may they stay 'undiscovered.'"

He spent a lot of time thinking about Joe and kept a photo of him in his doctoral robes, with a full mustache in a frame on his desk next to the typewriter. One day, an elderly Samoan came to his room and noticed the photo. "Your daughter?" he asked. "No," Colin said, "just someone I love very much." He wrote Joe in August, "Dearest Joe, you are so much younger than me, and I am sure that is all part of [our problems]; a natural and inevitable part. But even if you can no longer think of me as a lover, which heaven knows I could understand AND accept, can we not at least be loving friends? There would still be so much ahead; I could never take another lover, and I would never want to . . ."

Throughout the summer of 1985, Colin feared that Joe would enjoy being alone so much that he would decide to split up, and so he wrote Joe numerous letters professing his love. He even wrote to Joe about a thwarted infidelity, a young man he met in Samoa who kissed him on the lips. He told Joe, "For a moment I felt life stirring, but mainly I just felt the good warmth of human affection. He said he would like to spend the night and I could not answer. Of course a physical part of me wanted to say yes, but all the rest of me wanted to say no. So I just showed him your photo, and that was the last I saw of him . . . I felt bad, because it was the closest I have come in years to being unfaithful to you, and even the thought got me so upset that I went down to the beach and just swam out and out, as though I never wanted to come back. Then I got scared . . . I told you I was a coward . . . because the current was carrying me out even further than I thought, and when I turned around I saw what a long way I had to come back, and though I swam as hard as I could I seemed to make no headway. I really thought I was gone, because I could feel myself getting tired, and each time I slowed up to rest I got carried further out. I saw some people on the beach, and waved and shouted . . . it was like a bad movie, they waved and shouted back, watched for a while, waved again then turned and wandered off back through the grove and out of sight . . . I made it; I got onto the reef so I could stand up and rest . . . And you know what, I wondered if I deserved to get back. I came back to the house, had a shower, had my last two eggs, some dry crackers and peanut butter for dinner, and went to bed before 8 o'clock. Your picture looking at me and smiling so lovingly, so full of happiness . . . and I remembered you running back into the house to get it for me, carrying it out, and handing it to me . . . Oh Joe, please love me, just a little, don't let me go out so completely alone. I am so scared of getting back and finding that you hate me as much as ever. Life then would really be over."

He also wrote Joe to tell him that he was getting used to being retired and was now ready to put his own writing on the back-burner and fully support Joe's work, whatever it might be—novels, short stories, African religions, or the history of Christianity and Judaism. He said, "I can face [not living with you anymore] and will do everything I can to help you get the best fresh start in the world . . . I hope that is not how it has to be, because I love you so very much and need you so very much at this time in my life when I seem to be getting older by the minute, with less and less to make life worth while. But it would be even worse if you felt you had to stay with me out of pity . . . No, my love, you are truly free to decide what is best for you . . . So until you tell me otherwise, that is what I am planning on: coming back the first week of October, to a life of living together and of mutual loving and caring, with YOUR life and work as being our guiding principle, just as mine was in the past."

To Colin's delight, Joe wrote back to say that he had never been so lonely and that he wanted Colin back. Most of Joe's activities while Colin was in Samoa remain a mystery, though Lancaster locals say that he spent a lot of time with his mother. But when Colin returned to Virginia in September, Joe said that he needed a vacation and that he had already made plans to visit Scandinavia, Greece, Egypt, East Africa, and India, and had begun to apply for the visas required. It is unclear what Colin thought of such a grand plan, let alone the fact that Joe intended to depart just as Colin returned, because the only response available is a vague and superficial passage in "Lover and Beloved" that reads, "I was a little sad, sad that he wanted to go alone, but happy he was thinking in such positive ways." Ever a master of denial, it seems Colin did not consider the obvious conclusion that Joe was punishing him for having gone to Samoa.

His fears about Joe abandoning him, however, made it hard for Colin to produce any written work. When he returned to Virginia, he wrote Michael Korda to propose a book entitled *Zaire: The Non-Belgian Congo,* and Korda, frustrated that Colin had been unable to come up with any new ideas for a book, asked a new colleague of his at Simon & Schuster, Michael Sagalyn, to generate a list of topics. They included education in Africa, the meaning of tribalism in Africa, American blacks in Africa, the African elite, and biographies of either Jomo Kenyatta or the notorious mercenary Bob Denard; Sagalyn thought the last suggestion was promising and had confidence he could obtain permission for a biography from Clint Eastwood, who owned the rights to Denard's life. Korda told Sagalyn, "[Colin Turnbull] has been floundering for a new idea for a long time now, and I'm just not sure that the fault may not be partly mine . . . Let's discuss. He's someone who really needs help—and is well worth turning in the right direction, since we're still selling *The Forest People* 25 years later!"

Joe left for Paris in early November 1985, less than two months after Colin had returned from Samoa. On the plane he was seated next to a German passenger who gave him a chocolate. When Joe got off the plane, he was disoriented. He got a hotel room but then was somehow taken to the American Hospital in the chic Paris suburb of Neuilly, a hospital that would soon be internationally recognized for its treatment of AIDS patients, including Rock Hudson. Joe told the doctors that a German passenger had poisoned him with candy. "Here I am in the hospital," he told his diary, on November 16, "somewhere in Paris. Yesterday I had an emotional crisis of fear, confusion of the imagination, always flooding in my thoughts . . . I was in the hotel when it began again. Then I prayed for help and understanding of the fear and chills that grip me."

The doctors treated Joe's crisis as an anxiety attack and sent him on his way. Joe was soon in Athens and called Colin to say that he had canceled plans to visit Scandinavia because the weather was too cold there and, at any rate, he had run out of money. Colin was furious because Joe had been in Europe for little more than a week and yet he had already spent two thousand dollars.

Joe left Athens and returned to Paris where he became sick again. In late 1985, the doctors at the American Hospital were just becoming familiar with HIV, the virus that causes AIDS. Scientists had just identified HIV and a blood test was becoming available. It would take some years, however, before physicians understood more fully the variety of forms HIV infection can take, and especially the occurrence of AIDS dementia. Still, when they saw Joe on November 23, the doctors told him they were certain that he had the symptoms of AIDS and gave him the diagnosis without the benefit of the blood test. It does not appear that Joe asked how he had been infected, and he did not ponder the question in his diaries. Comments Colin made years later suggested that both Joe and Colin wanted to believe that he was infected in the early 1970s in Uganda while administering medical care to the Ik.

Joe did not quite understand what was happening. He wrote to his diary, "There was one thing the doctor told me that I was exposed to AIDS and that I might need another spine check. This was such a blow to me for now I have to decide to go home or on with the trip . . . I have been told that I have AIDS exposure if not AIDS! It means I could be affected if I had sex. I shall just not have sex—at least until I know what is implied by 'exposure to it.' I have not been feeling sexy anyway."

The American embassy staff made sure that Joe got on the plane to New York, where he would catch a Greyhound bus to Lancaster. When Colin met him at the bus station, he was startled to find him weak and thin. Joe was wasting away.

They spent Christmas together. Joe's bizarre thoughts had disappeared for a while, but he developed toothaches and a huge abscess in his mouth. By March of 1986, however, Joe was losing touch with reality and often appeared not to know where he was or to whom he was talking. One night, Colin brought him to the emergency room at the Medical College of Virginia, where he was immediately admitted to the psychiatric unit. He stayed for several weeks.

As odd as it might seem, Colin told friends and family that he knew little about why Joe had to be hospitalized. Colin wrote in "Lover and Beloved": "They did not confide in me the details of the case, but said it was a nervous disorder that could be handled perfectly well by medication, and this they would slowly reduce until he was well enough to be released provided I saw he took his pills each day, and brought him back once a week for therapy." Knowing Colin as they did, his remarkable commitment to Joe, and his subsequent demands on Joe's infectious disease specialist for full disclosure of all aspects of Joe's illness, friends say that his ignorance about Joe's psychiatric disorder is hard to believe. But it is also possible that hospital officials were willing to release information only to family—a bureaucratic barrier in medicine that gay men and women know all too well. It is also conceivable that Colin thought mental illness might stain Joe's legacy and so he glossed over it in the same way that he glossed over the fact that Joe's HIV was most likely sexually transmitted, consistently telling friends who asked that if Joe was HIV positive, he must have been infected while giving medical care in Africa.

Colin wrote about that hospitalization in "Lover and Beloved": "Sniggering behind curtains. Joe is behind one of those curtains. Those pathetic imbeciles pretending to be doctors are the ones who are sniggering. I had to fight with them even to get them to look at him. He was almost unconscious so I had to admit him and give all the information. What is wrong with the patient? How the shit should I know, that is your job. Don't swear at me. Fuck you too just do something for him will you? So they take him away from me. On a stretcher . . . I don't want him to be alone but they won't let me go behind the curtain with him . . . Those bastards refuse to say what they have found, what is wrong, treat me as if I am a criminal and Joe is just dirt . . . I think [Joe] smiled. And you dare to ask me if life is unfair?"

Joe was unable to keep a diary at this time, but Colin invented one for him. In 1992, he wrote the following passage in an attempt to describe Joe's experiences: "Oh god help me. Colin my love, where are you? . . . Who are all these people in white coats? Colin, Colin, surely you have not done this to me?

Not even you could do such a terrible thing . . . I just asked you to drive me to the hospital in Richmond because I was feeling so ill again, and thought perhaps that flu was coming back, but you checked me in and as they wheeled me away I saw you talking to them. They sent one doctor after another, and gave me nothing for my headaches. Then they put me on a stretcher and tied me down and I screamed for you . . . I heard a metal door as it clanged shut and keys rattling in the lock. And all those crazies came out to gape at the latest one to be admitted. Oh god, if there is such a thing, I am NOT crazy . . . or if I am, please let me be crazy with Colin . . . Why is it so dark in here, and getting darker?"

CHAPTER SIXTEEN

Death Sentence

WHEN ANNE EISNER PUTNAM DIED, Colin had comforted her family and friends with a Pygmy song about the rain forest that, for him, was like a song about heaven. Even death and darkness can be celebrated in the realm of the sacred.

> There is darkness upon us;
> Darkness is all around,
> There is no light.
> But it is the darkness of the forest,
> So if it really must be,
> Even the darkness is good.

Those words must have comforted Colin, too, as Joe became increasingly ill. Joe's death would come soon, and Colin knew that neither of them could be saved. Colin already knew that his death and Joe's were indistinguishable; with one the other would also go. And with the merging of their lives, the story of Colin Turnbull in the 1980s becomes equally the story of Joe Towles's demise and legacy. The 1980s would be tragic years for Colin and Joe. There would be illness and death, self-doubt and suspicion. There would be Colin's own HIV test and his surprising reaction to the results. Colin and Joe both believed they had built a firm foundation of love that could withstand any momentary crises, but as Joe began to fade away, almost beyond recognition, Colin began to wonder whether their sacred love would survive. That was the question that dominated the remaining years of both Joe's and Colin's existence in this world.

When Joe left the psychiatric unit of the Medical College of Virginia in 1985, he promised Colin he would stop being violent and would take his prescribed doses of Desipramine, an antidepressant. No physician had linked his mental illness and his HIV; even by the end of the millennium, many physicians would remain ignorant about the frequency with which HIV affects the brain.

The medication helped, and when Colin was invited to the College of Charleston to give a series of talks, he asked Joe to come along. Colin and Joe sat up on a stage, speaking in turn about the Mbuti and the Ik, mostly about the philosophical lessons these societies offered western civilization. At the talks, which were videotaped, both men appeared relaxed. Colin was dressed awkwardly in a dark suit and cream colored loafers, Joe in a three-piece blue suit and tie. Colin spoke beautifully as usual but Joe was also articulate, speaking quietly with a slight southern accent about his compassion for the Ik. Colin said that, when he was in Uganda, he refused to give the Ik either food or medicines. "Towles," he said, "takes a different view and is much more skilled at medical work than I am. I say we are not meant to interfere. He says, what kind of a human being are you to sit back and let people suffer?" Turning to Joe, he asked, "So what do you really think when you see me not doing anything?" Joe spoke at length about his inability to stand back from the Ik as if he were a geologist looking at a rock sample, that he could not justify inaction. He wondered aloud whether his race had anything to do with his sense of brotherhood with the Ik.

Joe was energized by the talks and decided to accept a job offer from an old friend of Colin's, Gerry Rosenfeld, who had been chair of the Department of Anthropology at Hofstra back in the late sixties and was now at the State University of New York (SUNY) at Buffalo. Rosenfeld hired Colin as a visiting full professor (without tenure) and Joe as a visiting assistant professor to teach for the 1986-1987 academic year. The department was thrilled to have a big name on board, but they were reluctant to hire Joe. Rosenfeld told his colleagues that Turnbull and Towles came as a package, so they agreed to the double hire.

It was now the summer of 1986 and they planned to move from Virginia, but in some ways, they acted as if they would never leave. Joe spent at least an hour a day in the swimming pool, and they worked harder than ever on the gardens, filled the woodshed in preparation for a winter they would spend hundreds of miles away, and repainted Joe's boat. Joe also tried to spend time with his family and went to the funerals of some of the people of his mother's generation whom he had known since his childhood. He would sit in the back of the church and talk to few of the mourners, but he was there nonetheless, trying to immerse himself in this place that he was so attached to, and that he knew he would soon leave.

Joe and Colin began teaching at SUNY Buffalo, a large department with dozens of full and part-time faculty where there was little oversight and, perhaps because of the size, much less possibility for Joe to interpret the actions of his colleagues as indications of a racist conspiracy brewing in the department. They also lived several hours' drive from campus. Though they rented a small apartment in Buffalo, they bought a wood and brick rambler on Gay Street in Sharon, Connecticut, not far from the large house and farm of an old friend from Colin's museum days, Walter Fairservice. Fairservice was not only an archaeologist but, having been raised in a theatrical family, a producer who staged summer presentations of "East West Fusion Theater" in one his outbuildings. Joe and Colin loved living on Gay Street, which to their even greater delight, ran into another street called Lover's Lane. The house sat on approximately an acre of land that Joe and Colin could view from a large patio adjoining the kitchen. They put the Lancaster house up for sale.

Everything seemed to be going well at school. For the first time, Joe felt that his students liked him. His course evaluations were better than he had ever received, though his lecture notes for his introductory course to anthropology reveal some blatant errors. In his lectures on human evolution, for example, he wrote that Lucy (*Australopithecus afarensis*), the popular name for a skeleton found in Ethiopia, which dated to at least three million years before the present, was the first human tool user, and that by the time Lucy lived, "cultural evolution had come far." In fact, anthropologists are uncertain who the first tool users were, and were just as uncertain back in 1987 when Joe was teaching, but tool users were at least hundreds of thousands of years younger than Lucy. There are no tools associated with Lucy-like creatures, and Lucy's "cultural" achievements, if we even want to use the term to describe early australopithecines like Lucy, were at about the same level as contemporary chimpanzees.

Joe felt healthy and he imagined that Colin would soon retire, making him the sole breadwinner. By the beginning of 1987, Colin had begun to accept more invitations to lecture, and Joe joined him for nearly every one. They gave joint lectures at McGill University in Montreal, the University of

Montana, Notre Dame, the College of Charleston, and Wilfred Laurier University in Canada, receiving between two and three thousand dollars per visit to split between them. Though their hosts were not often surprised that Colin brought his partner along, they were surprised that his partner lectured. This caused some discomfort for the host schools. But Joe and Colin did not care. They were thrilled by the renewed vigor they found in their shared intellectual life.

The most striking absence in Colin and Joe's papers at this time is any discussion of AIDS. Though both mention Joe's bouts of illness, Colin felt Joe was hypochondriacal and Joe wrote to his diary that they were nuisances. Certainly in the back of their minds, they must have recognized Joe's impending death, for by 1987 AIDS was in the news almost every day. Colin never saw any lab results from Joe's blood tests, and Joe never admitted to being infected with HIV or having AIDS. Joe held out a faint belief that he was suffering from the complications of a tropical illness he had picked up while treating people in Uganda or Zaire, and despite his own eventual diagnosis, Colin never fully believed he had AIDS either. Though Colin always considered himself to be an activist, he would never involve himself with campaigns for AIDS awareness, prevention, or treatment.

And so Joe and Colin began to believe that they could grow old together in Connecticut. They had friends nearby; they were close to New York City, not far from Colin's Canadian relatives in Ontario, and Joe's brother Glenmore was still in a Connecticut prison on the other side of the state. They loved the house in Sharon but the kitchen was far too small for them; Joe soon had a builder come out and draw up plans to renovate. They tore out the patio, extended the kitchen into the backyard, enlarged the dining room, and had new hardwood floors installed throughout the house.

The house quickly became a noisy mess, invaded by plumbers, electricians, and contractors for up to twelve hours a day. One reason they liked to lecture was that it got them away from home. The renovations were also more expensive than they had estimated. The area beneath the patio was solid bedrock and had to be blasted, and because the trucks were unable to get to the back of the house, concrete had to be pumped over the roof.

As the renovations proceeded, Joe began to suffer from abscesses in his mouth, ear infections, and headaches. In retrospect, Colin would regret this flurry of lecturing, traveling, and house construction, and wonder if it might have hastened Joe's physical and mental decline. Yet Colin also felt that in those years their relationship began to grow again. From Joe's perspective, however, Colin was increasingly withdrawn and cold. After a long serious talk in February, Joe told his diary, "There seemed very little sympathy in Colin for the illness I suffered, am suffering. But, however, I must be careful. I have done no wrong or wished anyone harm." A few weeks later, he wrote, "Colin was awful today. He came into the room as I was dressing and angrily berated me for leaving the electric plates on the stove, which were red hot, he said. I felt sorry for him, after 28 years together, to value our relationship so little—the kitchen was cold and my dressing took longer."

By the end of the spring semester of 1987, Joe became paranoid about computer invasions and began to isolate himself in the house. He decided to have his own bedroom. He complained that SUNY would not promote him to associate professor and blamed it on departmental jealousies. Colin and Joe were both upset by the continuing problems with their contractors and the fact that the house in Virginia was simply not selling. But at the same time, Vassar offered teaching jobs to both Colin and Joe, with Colin as full professor without tenure, and Joe as associate professor without tenure. They started there in September, one month after Joe's fiftieth birthday, and inaugurated their new jobs and newly renovated home by bringing home a third cat, in addition to the two they already had: Jigme, who had been with Colin and Joe for nearly twenty years, and Gussie.

In the autumn of 1987, Colin declined an invitation to participate in a conference in Paris, organized by Jean Malaurie and sponsored by Jean Duvignaud to celebrate the French publication of a new edition of Peter Brook's play *Les Iks.* He suggested Joe as a substitute speaker despite the fact that Joe was both physically and mentally ill. In early October, the sponsoring organization, Terre Humaine, accepted, and a few weeks later Joe was on his way to Paris.

Colin covered Joe's classes for him, but felt powerless to respond to Terre Humaine when they called from Paris saying that Joe had arrived and then suddenly disappeared. Terre Humaine told Colin there had been a misunderstanding about transportation and that Joe had stormed out, missing the television and radio interviews they had scheduled. Joe was, in fact, angry because there was no car available for him and he was too weak to walk very far, and because he was lodged at a different hotel from the one he had requested. As it turned out, Joe did reappear for his scheduled lecture, but remained aloof. And when Colin picked him up outside customs in New York, he looked sick and in a daze. He recovered slightly in the next few days, but began to complain intensely about his students, their lack of interest, and his own lack of enthusiasm. The only bright side, at this time, was that Joe's ten-year driver's license suspension expired, and he was finally able to drive legally.

But he was arrested yet again. On November 20, 1987, just after 1 P.M., Joe drove onto the prison grounds at Somers Correctional Institute in Somers,

Connecticut, to see his brother Glenmore. Although unconfirmed, in "Lover and Beloved," Colin wrote that he had been incarcerated there for having murdered his girlfriend. Though Glenmore had been in jail since 1981, Joe had never visited him. Since at least the early 1960s, when Glenmore first met Colin in Germany and made it clear that he disapproved of their homosexuality, Glenmore and Joe had had little to do with each other. But knowing he would not live much longer, and regretting his distance from his brother, Joe decided to see him one last time.

It was a terrifying day for Joe, who never did get to see Glenmore. Joe wrote an account of that visit and his arrest by the prison police in his diary. According to Joe, he drove his tan Corvette to the prison visitor's parking lot, walked through the prison metal detector, and registered. After a few minutes wait, Joe was told it might be another half hour until he could see Glenmore since most of the inmates were still at lunch. He left the reception area, got into his car, and began driving around the prison. Joe parked in the middle of a staff parking lot and decided to take a walking tour near the prison water tower. A prison worker yelled out, "Hey, mister, you can't come in this area." Joe wrote, "But I could see no official reason why I should obey the man."

Next, a female prison guard opened a side door and called out something inaudible to Joe. He got back into his car, but as he drove past the other employee parking lots, three police vehicles surrounded him. Three men got out of their cars and aimed their rifles at him. Joe wrote: "This was Connecticut I thought, home of Bridgeport, Middletown, Manchester, and Yale University . . . Now, here in Connecticut, I was face to face with some brutal and potentially violent force familiar only from the TV accounts of Selma, Alabama, Jackson, Mississippi, or Atlanta, Georgia.

"I still felt in possession of my human dignity. Instead of showing anger and fear, not the slightest sign of provocation appeared on my face. I composed myself and was prepared to die remembering all the goodness of the world I had known. I had walked quietly, serenely and politely into the forbidden Golden Temple in Banaras, and was treated wonderfully. Also, in Madras was the gentle goodness of priests and ordinary people life-giving, even so was the memory of sitting on a log deep in the Ituri Forest . . ."

Joe was ordered to drive back to the visitor's area. The police followed him and ordered him to stay in the car. His account continued: "Just moments before, on the other side of the prison, one of the men had yelled at me, 'You smart devil.'

"I was highly startled. It was one of the low points in the volatile atmosphere. The remark was provocative, personal . . .

"Suddenly I lost control of my bowels. Following a slight expelling of gas, I felt the warm fecal matter ooze down inside my thighs. All the horrendous histories of the railroad cars leading to Treblinka came simultaneously. I remained still as the odor wafted outside the car."

Joe was ordered out of the car, frisked and handcuffed, and transported to a local police station where he was read his rights and charged with criminal trespass. Inside the prison, at about 2 P.M., Glenmore stood by a window and watched as a tow truck hauled Joe's Corvette away. The police eventually dropped the charges, and Joe never returned to the prison to see his brother. The dean of Vassar College, H. Patrick Sullivan, a religious historian whom Colin admired immensely, wrote Joe to congratulate him on the outcome of the case. On the other hand, to Joe's dismay, he received no satisfaction from his appeals to the ACLU and to Senator Christopher Dodd. His attorney wrote, "Quite simply, no you do not get a letter of apology from the State of Connecticut." The ACLU did not accept the case, and Senator Dodd's staff wrote back to say they regretted Joe's misfortune but had to respect the courts.

Beginning in January 1988, Joe and Colin jointly taught a course in ethnodrama at Vassar, but as the semester went on, Joe became too weak to stand in class and finally too weak to take part in any discussions. He was admitted to a local hospital, and several students in an anthropology and drama class who had begun to care about Joe asked Colin if they could visit him. They did not visit, and Colin never told them what was wrong with Joe. For their final project, however, the students improvised a curative ritual in which they prayed for Joe's recovery.

At the hospital, Colin told Joe he would get better soon, but Joe sensed something more grave. In "Lover and Beloved," Colin wrote in Joe's voice, "Then why the hell are you crying. Shall we pretend and live a little longer, or die now in peace?" "Funny," Colin wrote in the next passage, "It would be so selfish to die, just yet. Anyway, it might be kind of fun to suffer a little more . . . what difference can it make? What new forms of pain are there? Let's put them all down in our notebook."

Colin continued to write for Joe, blurring the distinction between himself and Joe, between "I" and "we," so that we are not entirely sure in whose voice Colin was writing.

> Let's see if our eminent colleagues have machines that can measure pain, and classify it as animal or human. No they are too ensnared in their own anguish, which they imagine to be pleasure. The pleasure of academic renown. Of a tenured professorship, no less. Of a respectable marriage. Of a solid portfolio. We were snared once weren't we, once, Colin? Oh yes indeed we were. But I broke free, didn't we? And now the final freedom is right around the corner, if only Mama and [Joe's

> brother] Charles would let me go. You sure as hell did your best to make us bankrupt. Then I would have had to live with Mama in that little two room shack, wouldn't we?
>
> Let's hang on to just a little, and then simply throw it all away. All right, throw it in the right direction, if you want to, if you think I know what the right direction is. So let's agree. Keep up the pretence; no stiff upper lips, no spines of steel, no Leonide superman stuff. Let's play the game, because now we know the secret of how to play it. How to find bliss by finding joy in our agony. Come Joe, Colin, let's all get out of this dump and live a little.

Joe taught only a few class periods that spring. He was simply too ill and often too disoriented to teach, so he returned to the still unsold house in Lancaster. Perhaps it was too expensive for most people who lived in that part of Virginia. Or even more likely, prospective buyers were afraid of living in a house whose previous owner had AIDS—the neighbors all knew and could warn them—and of occupying property where, according to Colin's and Joe's wishes, they would both be buried. Colin took the house off the market when it became clear that Joe intended to move back permanently.

Colin initially planned to teach Joe's classes through the end of the semester, resign from Vassar, and then join Joe in Virginia. He traveled down to Lancaster often that spring, sometimes bringing Joe up to Poughkeepsie to teach a class or two. His own enthusiasm for his classes had dwindled to nothing, and he felt himself withdrawing from the whole discipline of anthropology. Perhaps too he felt the discipline moving away from him. Sometime in late 1987, he had received a letter from a man whose book manuscript had been rejected by a university press. It had been reviewed by the famous anthropologist Edmund Leach, whom Colin often called one of the most famously "bitchy" of all anthropologists. Leach had lambasted the man for using such unreliable sources as Colin Turnbull and said that while one of Colin's books "could have been worse," the other was "very bad indeed." Colin had heard these criticisms before and they always convinced him that he had made the right decision to publish for a general rather an academic audience. But during the 1980s, a time when Colin found it difficult to write creatively and produced very little that was publishable, the criticism began to sting.

The spring of 1988 was a period of intense frustration for Colin. In April, he began to acknowledge the possibility that Joe might really have AIDS—after all, every health care professional with whom they had contact referred to Joe's illness as AIDS—and decided to have an HIV test, a test that their doctor felt was long overdue. Colin waited anxiously for the results. When their doctor,

Fred Littleton, called on April 30 to say that Colin's test had come back negative, that he was not infected with HIV, he was despondent. He wanted, more than anything, to be infected, to be positive, to be able to die with Joe. Colin was deeply depressed for four days, in essence mourning the loss of his own death.

On May 5, he received another telephone call from Fred Littleton, who said he had just opened a letter of apology from the Roche laboratory stating that they had made an error—a rare error—and that Colin was, in fact, HIV positive: "The original negative result on this patient," the lab wrote, "was incorrect due to a mix-up between this and another specimen."

Colin immediately wrote a letter to his death row inmate-friend Kamal, rejoicing that he had received his own "death sentence" and saying how frightened he had been when he had received the first report. But at the same time, according to Dr. Littleton, Colin was so angered by the Roche error that he would never fully believe the second result even though he wanted to. Colin refused to pay the fourteen dollars the lab had charged him for the erroneous test, and when the they continued to send a bill to him, he filed a complaint with the Better Business Bureau. Roche ultimately canceled the debt.

Despite the desired results, Colin, a man who almost never lied, would file an application to Blue Cross/Blue Shield in 1990 for insurance coverage, stating that he had neither been exposed to nor suffered from HIV/AIDS. Was he lying? Maybe and maybe not. Even if he was willing to believe that he and Joe had developed antibodies for HIV and were therefore technically HIV-positive, he never fully believed that either one of them had AIDS. Indeed, Colin and Joe seldom uttered the words HIV or AIDS to their friends or their family. Even when Colin sent out a death notice about Joe to more than two hundred friends and colleagues in 1988, he did not mention AIDS, though many suspected.

Certainly for most people, the first HIV test result would have been happy, the second devastating. For Colin, it was the opposite. He wanted desperately to die with Joe, and if they could not die together at the same time, he wanted to die the same kind of death. He had other fears, too: that Joe would die without him present at his bedside, that Joe would fully recover and leave him for another man, that Joe would commit suicide—something Colin would never be able to bring himself to do despite wanting die in the identical manner as Joe. Colin had merged himself so completely with Joe that Joe's impending death was tantamount to a loss of self. The only way to prevent that loss was for him to create his own death, to join Joe in death in an effort not to lose him in life.

On May 6, one day after receiving the news that he was HIV-positive, he wrote about his HIV test to his best friend in Samoa, John Enright, the historic preservation officer: "Short and sweet, more business than anything . . . but first the GOOD news! I GOT IT! The doctors treating Joe thought I should be tested for AIDS also, since it seems that is one of his problems. At first the results came back negative, and I was terribly upset, feeling it to be the ultimate hurt not to be able to share this last thing in our long life together. But then that stupid Hoffman LaRoche company came back with another matter-of-fact note to the doctor saying they had made a mistake and my test was POSITIVE. He thought my pleasure unseemly . . . I am truly happy, for that is what sharing and caring is all about."

Colin hoped John would also be pleased for him. He added that he had a thirty percent chance of dying in the next five years, and his biggest worries were about his finances and his mental health. He wanted to die of AIDS but without dementia. He did not want many people to know, but he did want to tell Kamal. He wrote to Enright: "Of all the capital cases I have come across in that research his has moved me the most, but I was always aware that no matter how close I got to him, and to others, I could never really know what it was like to be under sentence of death. Ha! Now I have a chance! It is really quite intoxicating, it offers so much freedom."

What none of Colin's friends knew (with the exception of John Enright in Samoa) was that he had secret plans to leave Joe in Lancaster once Joe's health improved and travel back to American Samoa. By Valentine's Day 1988, he had a ticket in hand, with the dates left open. This is one reason he kept in such close contact with John Enright.

In March, he wrote to Enright: "I do not think I can move back [to Virginia] . . . For years I have been having a struggle a) to keep alive a deep love that has slowly been gnawed away by drink and nervous disorder, and possibly some underlying brain damage from a childhood injury; and b) to keep that person alive; for when seeing that I am clearly the most immediate and major cause of the drink, and the nerves, though happily not of the childhood injury, the only sensible thing seems to be to remove myself. It is not very complimentary, but I must confess that when I do remove myself, things seem to go better for Joe, for that is his name . . .

"What I need from you . . . is an off the top of the head reaction to whether I could survive, living simply, on my TIAA [retirement plan] income, which is about $800 per month . . . I feel it best to be prepared. I could always bring more cash if necessary, for whatever purposes, but ultimately, if I do leave, I would like to turn over as much as possible into a trust to make sure Joe has ample income, health insurance, and all those other things we dull, dour Scots are given to worrying about!"

Enright answered with the recommendation that Colin house-sit for a Samoan professor on sabbatical from the local college, and Colin wrote back to say he might be able to get away by the end of June. Colin began planning his estate so that he could leave. Upon Joe's death, all the money and property of the estate of Colin Turnbull would go to the United Negro College Fund to establish the Joseph A. Towles scholarship. Joe and Colin had talked about the gift for years, but neither of them expected it would come about so quickly. A gift to the United Negro College fund was the best way, Colin believed, to help other African Americans become educated, just as he had helped Joe. The fund would also help establish Joe's legacy, linking Joe's name in perpetuity with African American education. However, Colin found that planning a gift of a million dollars in cash and property was more difficult than he had imagined, and so he would have to delay his trip to Samoa. He wrote to Enright: "The attorney, a sympathetic soul, is working something out that will get all of it out of my hair except whatever is necessary to get me to Samoa, give Joe the freedom to get himself straight, think things out, and decide what he really wants, without me bugging him with what he thinks I want him to want. Which is what I would inevitably do if I stuck around. Why could I not have been born a mother (preferably with a grown up child) from whom such behavior would have been expected and considered normal?"

Within a week of that letter to Enright, Joe was back in the hospital with pneumocystis carinii pneumonia (an opportunistic infection of AIDS), an infected sinus, rapid onset of amnesia, and intestinal bleeding. While Joe was still in the hospital, Colin wrote Enright that, "I am about to pack my suitcase. Since snow is threatened for today, I think I can safely pack for Samoa without worrying about what I may need here!"

By the end of April, Joe had developed a parasitic infection in his brain, which Joe's doctors said was a common manifestation of AIDS, but Colin wrote to John Enright that, despite the severity of his illnesses, the doctors could not predict how long Joe would live. He told him he could not bear to leave Joe while he was still alive. His trip to Samoa would have to wait, for he could not make Joe suffer any more than he already had.

"How do you say goodbye to your own self?" he asked Enright. "As you see it slipping away piece by piece, and there is not a damned thing you can do about it? As while still alive that old skull begins showing through the flesh and skin, drawn tight in pain, eyes deep and wide in confusion and hurt at dying so young, a living face that knows the very bottom of the pit of misery, yet through that exhausted countenance already the skull begins to grin.

"And the limbs, each day wasting away to nothingness, so tender and sore that even the slightest fluttering love touch of a finger or a lip leaves a scar . . . of both physical and emotional hurt . . . and those sallow eyes, clouded with confusion now silently ask 'You too? Even now you want to hurt me?' . . . I wish

I could say goodbye right now and end it all . . . but not while he is still alive. For then he would suffer all the more."

Colin had often compared his and Joe's love to a full glass of sweet wine, a small taste of which could wash down the dirt and dregs and bitterness of life. It was a glass of wine they indulged in until one day there was only a drop left, and instead of drinking it all and destroying the glass, they clung to the last drop even as it turned sour. Colin did not have the strength to break the glass, even though it looked as if it was nothing but an empty shell. But in staying with Joe, Colin would find that there was sweetness in both life and death and that the emptiness was just an illusion. Though Joe might seem to be disappearing, Colin's love for him was as strong as ever, a vapor easily kindled, a telling silence.

On May 3, 1988, Colin wrote to John, "I still get the occasional howling fit, but am slowly coming to grips with the fact that Joe is going to die, any time from today to two years from today. And, that even if he makes a temporary recovery from the pneumonia, his mind will almost certainly never be the same, and may get progressively and rapidly worse."

On Mother's Day 1988, Joe felt strong enough to take dinner to his mother, but the rest of his family was frightened. Colin wrote that when Joe's younger sister refused to come and visit Joe one day, she asked, "Well, tell me does he have one of these contagious things . . . the way he lives it seems quite possible . . . I mean I have my Mama and my daughter to think about . . ."

"I thanked her for her Christian concern and suggested she go back to her Bible and Prayer Book before she were [*sic*] contaminated by even talking to me . . . gave my best imitation of Deep Throat breathing every germ I could into the mouthpiece and hung up. I got in the car and went down to her Mama's, [Joe's sister] was already on the phone telling her not to go and see her own son, she might 'catch something.' Her Mama hung up and said, 'What am I going to catch son? Are you afraid of catching anything? I'm his Mama and I'm going to touch him and hug him and care for him every way I can, I'm not afraid of nothing . . . if my other children are [scared], they are no children of mine. You and I, we'll look after him won't we son?'"

Those words meant a lot to Colin. The only other person who called him "son" was Kamal's mother.

By the end of May, Joe had gained some strength. Earlier that month, he could not walk and had spent most of his time in bed or in a wheelchair. Abruptly one day, he told Colin he was taking a bus to D.C. to see a movie and a parade and would stay the night at a hotel. But when he did not come back the next day, Colin called the police. Two days later, the police telephoned Colin to say that Joe had been found asleep in a workmen's shed on the grounds of Dulles airport. They said that Joe had no idea who or where he was and that they had identified him from his driver's license. Colin drove up immediately and retrieved him. The next day he wrote John to say that his heart was not simply broken, but "feels as though it is being ripped asunder and trampled on by a herd of elephant, a sensation as physical as it is emotional."

Within the next few days, Joe developed pneumocystis pneumonia again and Colin rushed to get Joe to sign the papers giving everything they owned to the United Negro College Fund. Joe could barely hold the pen, but he was able to sign the documents if Colin held on to his wrist to stabilize it. In a letter to John, Colin estimated the size of the gift at about one million dollars, half in property and half in cash, stocks, and bonds, not counting the donation of future book royalties.

Colin told Enright, "I have the feeling the end is near, and what it will do to me I have no idea. Part of me says I will just die too . . . and indeed part of me will, for he will take it with him . . . But another part of me feels that . . . I might live long enough, at least, to write about him, and us, and to see to the publication of his academic work . . . so that his name WILL be known, as it should have been long before . . . and would have been had he not lived in my shadow . . . Academically, he was far superior . . . I learned so much from him . . . but he always stood back."

When Joe got out of the hospital, the doctors talked to Colin about hospice care but he told them he wanted Joe at home. Joe's physician, Fred Littleton, assured Colin that Joe could do just as well at home if Colin was willing to hire nurses periodically to check for urinary infections that might be caused by the catheter. Colin agreed, but in actuality he seldom allowed nurses into the home. Littleton says that to this day he has never seen anyone give better care to their loved one than Colin did. "Dr. Turnbull," he said, "took care of him 24 hours a day. It was remarkable."

Littleton also told Colin that they could even consider a short vacation, and so Colin and Joe left in June to spend a week at a condominium on the beach in St. Croix in the Virgin Islands. They had such a good time, they ended up staying for five weeks. Colin wrote: "Joe put on weight, he even came in swimming with me a couple of times, though he preferred just to sit in a deck chair and watch. We walked up and down the beach, usually arm in arm, like the lovers we still were . . . It was one of the few times in our life that we have been able to hold onto each other in public, without shame, without being made to feel guilty or unclean . . . We were totally reckless. We drank piña coladas and champagne with every meal."

Though seemingly as content as he had been in a long time, Joe was frail and quiet and in need of almost constant assistance. He continued to have problems with incontinence and diarrhea. The sheets would be soiled in the morning. Once on a street corner, when Joe was aware he was about to lose control of his bowels, he pulled his pants down and squatted at the edge of the road. On several occasions, he sat at the kitchen counter eating breakfast and felt the urge to go to the bathroom, but by the time he got off the stool, he had soiled himself. Colin did not complain about it; he accepted the discomfort as a challenge. Ever the vegetarian, he wrote: "I quickly learned mopping up techniques and found that my hands were the best tools for the clean up job, rather like eating rice and pepper water in South India, and certainly no more repulsive than putting the same hand inside the carcass of a chicken."

But despite these difficulties, Joe laughed with Colin and seemed at ease. Colin began to write Enright with a weekly score along a misery-to-bliss scale, and the St. Croix trip ranked consistently at 8 out of 10. Colin and Joe spoke about the fact that Joe would die soon, but Joe also talked often as if the illness were only temporary. He was now taking a low dose of the antiviral drug AZT, though not regularly, and Colin thought it was helping with everything but Joe's mental state. St. Croix was one of Joe's last happy times.

Perhaps the last happy time was back in Virginia when he was bed-ridden. He was unable to walk because he suffered from AIDS-related myopathy that weakened his ability to control his muscles. But he somehow lifted his spirits and found the energy one day to say that he wanted to go for a drive. "It is my car, you know, I just wanted to feel it was mine once more." So Colin carried him out, and though Joe asked to drive, he must have known it was impossible. He could barely move his legs or feet. With a nostalgia for this car, and all the other cars that had meant so much to him, he relaxed and enjoyed the movement and the roar of the engine.

Colin wrote to Enright about his own health: "Damn, still healthy."

On Labor Day, Joe ran a high fever but refused to go to the hospital. Still feverish the next day, Colin convinced him to go. He wrote, "We drove to the hospital in Kilmarnock, where he did a splendid Protest Pee in his wheelchair, soaking the wheelchair as well as his pants. The bathroom was too small to get the wheelchair in, so I left the chair in the corridor, the door open, and took off his pants and trousers, and with loads of paper towels to mop up the chair sat him back in the chair, emerging naked rear end first, to the shock of some elderly white female Baptists passing by on their missions of mercy. That got action, and rather than let us back in the waiting room the doctor suddenly appeared and had Joe in the examination room and in bed!"

October 24, 1988 was their twenty-ninth anniversary. Colin bought one card for Joe and another for himself, which Joe would sign. Joe took the second card, on which was printed, "Colin, may our love be in bloom always. Happy Anniversary. I never missed a single one!" Joe held the pen and wrote out AAAAAAAAAAA, as if he was trying to write twenty-nine As, each one standing like a birthday candle for an anniversary. At the bottom, Joe wrote the date, the time, and "FROM JOE," followed by "XXXX."

That same month, Colin contemplated asking Joe about assisted suicide. But he never approached Joe about it, keeping his fantasies to himself, wondering what would happen if he stopped feeding Joe.

On November 19, Colin and Joe were watching a rerun of the old television show *Flash Gordon* when Colin welled up with anger and wrote to Enright: "So when with stupid British stiff upper lip, made all the stiffer by that dogged, perverse Scottish obstinacy, I smile when I feel like crying, so that Joe will not feel my hurt. Then I think he may be wondering why the hell I am so happy when he is dying. And when the Irish side of me takes over and I burst into tears, I have to run away and hide them . . . a deceit if not a treachery, because I think they might hurt him. I think . . . I wish. I wish it were all over. Do I wish it had never begun? No . . . for that would be to wish that I had never loved and been loved . . . that like Joe I could look out of the window and see the last few leaves falling from the oaks, the cloudy, cheerless grey sky, the chilly waters of the creek ruffled by an unfeeling breeze. I wish we were away from this god damned mother fucking racist county . . ."

During the last year of his life, Joe increasingly lost the ability to articulate his words, and by the summer of 1988, he was so neurologically impaired that he could barely recognize anyone but his mother and Colin. He had numerous bed sores, a urinary catheter, and an intravenous tube for fluids. During that time, Colin did everything for him, and though Colin welcomed few friends into the house at this time, those few who did visit say that they cannot imagine taking care of their own spouses the way Colin took care to Joe. Heroic: there was no other word for it. Colin bathed him, brushed his teeth, cut his fingernails and toenails, changed the catheter, lifted Joe onto a bedpan, cleaned feces from the bed at least once a day and spoon-fed him both food and medicines on a careful schedule written by Joe's doctor. He held Joe's hand for hours on end, read to him, caressed him, and sat by the bed watching television, just to be together. Joe talked little and had few requests, occasionally asking for a bit of yogurt or some other soft food, and one day asking if he could have his long thin hair parted.

On the cold December night before Joe died, Colin sat on the bed next to him, watching *Murder She Wrote* on the television before getting undressed and climbing under the covers to hold Joe in his arms. Colin couldn't sleep. He stayed up almost the whole night talking to Joe and whispering into his ear, "Satyam, sivam, sundarm" (Truth, goodness, beauty), the mantra he had been given forty years earlier by Anandamayi Ma.

By early morning, Colin could hear only small gasps of air, and he thought about how Joe had suffered during his life. Chinese fortune cookies came to mind: "Why did I always get the best ones?" he asked himself. "If only you knew how I hurt every time something good happened to me and did not happen to you. Even the fortune in the cookies."

Colin listened and looked for signs of life and death.

"Just lie still, Colin," he told himself, his arms wrapped around Joe. "It'll be easier to feel him move.

"That left foot of his, just ever so slightly, is tilting over, reaching out. That is why you mustn't move. Let Joe's foot find its mate. And there it is! A gentle tap. And the foot moves away."

Colin had known loneliness but this was not loneliness. He had once said, "I have seen a solitary nomad in the middle of the desert communing with the heavens—a fisherman with the ocean—and I have seen a hunter in the vastness of the primeval forest dance with the moon. But they were no more alone than is the lover at the side of his beloved, and conversely, when any two human beings meet face to face and open themselves to each other, they have the whole universe in their grasp."

He might have been talking about himself and Joe.

Colin continued to lay next to Joe, supersensitive and wired. The whole room was buzzing.

"A sacred swelling that reaches inside, getting bigger and bigger, as though it wants to burst out, and burst in, to find its twin. Otherwise it is confined, our pettiness has confined it, and unable to escape it has given us pain. It was our hum that pained us, when we would not let it out. Even when we tried to let it out in our music making, our writing, our loving, it hurt, and the physical act of love was a poor substitute for the true mating without which we could only dream of being complete, touching it from afar.

"But when, through some magic beyond even music and poetry and love-making, that coupling happens, then the hum is heard and we lose ourselves in a moment of bliss."

Now, at just after seven o'clock, on the morning of December 19, Colin began to panic. He felt a coldness creeping down Joe's body and begged it to stop. He could not bring himself to look at Joe's face. He just held on tight, listening to the short breaths that kept coming. The sun rose above the horizon with Joe's last gasp, a shallow, tiny burst, a new day.

Colin looked at Joe's face. It was pale, rough, and blue, far from the chocolate brown Colin had found so attractive when they first met. He stared, wanting to convince himself that they were more than simply bodies, that they had a spiritual existence beyond the body. But Joe had soiled himself. He took off Joe's pajamas, and as he was about to wipe him he paused and contemplated this last hint of life. It was small and round and glistened—it was almost a perfect sphere—and he thought it odd that a thing like this, at a time like this, could be beautiful.

He found Joe's favorite pajamas, dressed him, combed his hair, shaved him, and walked to the kitchen to call the undertaker.

The undertaker, a local African American named Barry Waddy, arrived in a clean white uniform that reminded Colin of an astronaut. Waddy had explained to Colin some weeks before that Virginia law required him to wear protective coverings when it was known or presumed that the deceased was HIV positive or had AIDS. Still, Colin was taken aback by the whiteness and by the intrusion. He may have also sensed the undertaker's nervousness, for it was the first death by AIDS that Waddy had ever seen. Waddy's thoughts were focused on the problem of how to drain and dispose of the blood from the cadaver since the state of Virginia prohibited him from using his septic tank for HIV-infected blood.

As Waddy was getting ready to take Joe from the house, Colin tried to get to work, but nearly everything was in order. He scanned his penciled list and crossed everything out. "Thurs.: Bake Pies, Dice Potatoes, Herbal Tea, Coolade [*sic*]. Call AMNH [American Museum of Natural History], get robes ready . . . Friday AM: Mix all salad ingredients . . . turkey, ham, salmon, pot. salad . . ." And finally, "Pies Burned!" He checked Joe's funeral clothes, already packed, a death notice and letters, which he had written on December 1, and which were ready to send to relatives and friends, and a few invitations to the December 23 funeral, to Bob Humphrey and his wife, Johanna; GW theater professor, Nate Garner; Joe's thesis advisor from Makerere, Peter Rigby, his wife, Zebiya, and their daughter Kimule; and Joe's immediate family—his mother, his brother Charles, and his sister, Mary Jane.

Waddy said he was ready to go, so Colin rushed to check on many little things, perhaps even trying to delay Joe's departure. Colin looked at Joe's wrist to make sure that he was wearing the gold Seiko wristwatch that he had given him on his fiftieth birthday, which still chimed every hour and played a few seconds of baroque music every evening at 6. Later, before the burial, Colin would remove his mother's wedding ring from his right little finger and put it on Joe.

Colin reminded Waddy that there were to be two coffins and that he had sent his instructions as well to Bob Humphrey, an ordained minister in the American Fellowship Church and an anthropologist who would perform the service at the gravesite on the grounds of Colin and Joe's estate. Colin fired off a letter to Bob.

"If you want to explain why the two caskets, you can say that in the part of Africa, Zaire, where we two worked, it is said that two people sometimes grow so close together they become one, like single trees with two trunks. When one trunk dies, the other may live on, but is never the same, and so it is with us humans. Joe and Colin both knew that is how it would be with them, and gladly accepted the fact they would each leave this world together, and go on to another life together. The empty casket will occupy a space that will be filled later, according to their mutual wills, which direct that they shall 'ultimately share the same burial place . . . and be buried side by side, as we have lived.'

"Consistent with this, and with the fact that we have lived and worked together for so many years, the survivor will not survive the same person that he was; the best part of him will be buried with his dead companion. For this reason, as a ritual affirmation of our mutual love and trust, of great importance to us, we wish a second casket to be lowered at the same time as that containing the deceased. Both should be adorned with the academic robes and African or other insignia chosen by the respective parties, as determined by the survivor. This second, empty, casket may be removed when the survivor dies and either used for his body or discarded and replaced. At that time there should be NO further service of any kind, and nobody should attend the interment unless Dr. Humphrey should so wish."

The next day he called Bob and John Enright to tell them that Joe had died. During the call, John took notes on a piece of scrap paper: "Joe died yesterday. Funeral on the property. Family and colleagues. Partly African funeral. Died at home. Brain parasite killed him. Couldn't swallow at end. Starved to death—just like the Eek [Ik]."

Colin intended the funeral to have the structure and appearance of a religious ceremony, but at Colin's request, reflecting what he believed would be Joe's wishes as well, Bob never mentioned God. When the funeral rites began, Colin could not stay near the grave. He wandered away to the house and then came back again. Mourners recall not knowing what Colin was up to, as he darted back and forth from the gravesite. He was more an observer than an active participant, in part perhaps because he was being buried as well; since he was in the coffin, at least in spirit, it was only appropriate that he observe the events from a distance. Joe's family was Christian, and Colin wanted to please them by having a minister conduct the service. He walked toward the grave to listen, but when Joe's mother began to wail and struggled to get into the grave, Colin could not control his tears. He turned quickly, walked away, and found a log on which to rest.

He was content to let the mourners have their ritual while he cried alone. Listless, he went back to the house a second time and busied himself by getting things together for the final burial: the doctoral robes they had been so proud to wear together in processions at SUNY and Vassar, a colobus monkey skin, ritual paraphernalia of an Mbo doctor, and a 45 rpm record of a song that they considered "their song," "The Best of Everything." Later, Colin put them in the grave as the mourners looked on.

Joe and Colin's coffins were laid to rest on a beautiful part of their estate, a knoll overlooking Payne's Creek. The grave was topped with crushed stone and surrounded by cinderblocks. Colin attached the Scottish flag to Joe's crabbing pole, a bright yellow flag bordered in red with the image of a griffin, half eagle, half lion, and planted it in the center of the grave. It was a totem of sorts for both of them, since Joe's astrological sign was Leo and Colin was Scottish. He then scattered on top of the grave a variety of objects that had special meanings for both him and Joe. There was a small replica of the Taj Mahal, a stuffed cobra, rocks and seashells they had picked up in St. Croix, pebbles they gathered on a trip to Fire Island, a potted African marigold, and potsherds. He took the blue glass ashtrays they were given on their first voyage to Europe on the *France,* smashed them onto the rocks and shells, and then used the fragments to splash color onto the grave. He threw in two homemade leashes he and Joe had fashioned for two baby leopards they had once cared for in Uganda, the license plates from the Land Rover they used in Africa, and a large metal Japanese garden lantern Bob and Johanna Humphrey had given him as a housewarming gift when Colin and Joe had moved to Sharon.

The cinder blocks formed a square and at each of the four corners Colin inserted a single wooden post, each topped with straw hats Joe had worn, two of them from Africa, one from China, and the fourth from Sri Lanka. One of the hats Joe had worn during their 1970 trip to Zaire, absent the rim that Kenge had nailed to the wall of Colin's house. The largest post had a roll of fishing thread, corn husks, a pig's tooth, a small medicine bag used by Mbo ritual priests, and a piece of bark cloth attached to the pole. On a fourth pole, Colin hung a black and white photograph of Harvard philosopher Kwame

Anthony Appiah as a child of seven or eight whose image was, for Colin, a symbol of racial harmony in the marriage of black and white; for Appiah's mother, Peggy, was the white elite daughter of Sir Stafford Cripps, his father, a black elite Ghanaian politician.

Four years later, Colin would write about that day.

"Oh our two caskets looked so splendid, in their scarlet and purple coverings. That was all I could see. The two of us, side by side, as we always had been and had promised we always would be. Bob said such lovely things and quoted that African proverb . . . He talked about Joe and his accomplishments, and talked about us, and our love.

"You would have cried too, Joe my darling."

The tombstone read:

JOSEPH A. TOWLES		COLIN M. TURNBULL
B. Aug 17, 1937	and	B. Nov. 23, 1924
D. Dec. 19, 1988		D. Dec. 19, 1988

THEIR LIVES CAME TOGETHER ON OCTOBER 24, 1959

TOGETHER WHEREVER THEY WENT, THEY JOINED THEIR MINDS AND HEARTS IN THE SIMPLE JOY FILLED QUEST FOR TRUTH, GOODNESS AND BEAUTY

TOGETHER THEY DISCOVERED THE TRUE MEANING AND RICHNESS OF LOVE

AND TOGETHER THEY REST WELL, BEFORE THEY GO ON AS ONE

Colin asked Bob to place these words in the *New York Times* memorial section the next October 24, which he did, but the newspaper refused to publish Colin's date of death.

On December 25, 1988, a crisp and sunny Christmas day, Colin took his cats, Gussie and Sita, and went outside to set a table he had carried to the foot of his and Joe's grave. He had cooked a turkey, stuffing, and potatoes, blended piña coladas and chilled a bottle of champagne. He covered the table with linen, and set it for two with his best china, crystal, and silver goblets. Sitting out in the sun next to Joe, Colin drank all the rum and all the champagne and pondered his future.

CHAPTER SEVENTEEN

Together at Last

ON DECEMBER 20, 1988, the day after Joe died and three days before the funeral, Colin mailed a letter written in Swahili to Kenge, his old friend from the Ituri forest, asking him to perform a molimo ceremony for Joe, the ritual the Mbuti Pygmies perform at times of crisis. In reply, Kenge asked two ecologists living at Epulu, John and Terese Hart, to write a letter to Colin asking him how much the molimo really mattered to him. For if it did not matter very much, he said, the molimo would be empty and unripe. According to Colin, Kenge dictated, "We have each lost something, someone, who belonged to all of us . . . and for such a death to be a good death, it has to be made to rejoice the forest." A tape was included with a message from the villagers, agreeing with the Mbuti that the molimo should be held "so that the spirit of Yusefu [Joseph] shall rest quietly . . ." Terese Hart, who wrote Kenge's letter in Swahili, believes that Kenge cared for Colin immensely but says that Colin's recollection of the letter was fanciful; the Mbuti simply do not talk in such lofty, abstract, and religious terms. Kenge did not perform the molimo but not because he did not want to. Perhaps it was because he did not know Joe well, or because Colin had failed to send any money for the ceremony, or even because Colin may not have insisted.

On the same day, Colin sent a long letter he had written three weeks earlier to nearly two hundred friends and colleagues. The letterhead gave his address and, in parentheses, a lie: "no telephone." He wrote that Joe's death was also his death, but he assured his friends he had no intention of committing suicide. He was not asking for their sympathy; indeed, he asked that no one try to contact him. Colin did not want pity, just as he did not want to be the mercy for other people's sorrows.

He had committed himself to Joe in life and in death, so all the friends who predicted that Joe's death would liberate Colin to an unburdened life were wrong. In his letter, he did not tell of any regrets, but those who were with him at Joe's funeral know that Colin regretted outliving Joe. He confided in Bob Humphrey that Joe's death had made him think of the others he had loved and outlived, his brother, so tragically killed in his twenties, his mother, whom he had both loved and hated, and his father, whose prized accounting business he had rejected.

He promised to spend his remaining years "putting ourselves quietly and properly to rest." But this letter, he said, was the last his friends or family would hear from him, and with only a few exceptions—Thubten Norbu, Bob Humphrey, Fred Littleton, and John Enright—he kept his word. In the days following Joe's death, Colin occasionally took telephone calls from the few people who had his unlisted number, but only to emphasize the importance of his own impending isolation. There were some who made the mistake of telling Colin that there was a bright side in Joe's death, that he was now liberated from caring for Joe and that he could go on with his life. Colin reacted explosively and no longer considered them his friends.

In his letter, Colin wrote: "I am sure all of you know that we have been what are generally called 'lovers' (a singularly inadequate term for our relationship) for over twenty-nine years . . . since October 24th, to be exact. We have never seen it necessary to allude to the fact publicly, though we have never tried to hide it . . . We are both proud of nothing so much as our love for each other, and our lifelong attempt to deserve each other . . . something in which I know I have failed. And again alas, that is no demonstration of self-pity, it is a simple fact. I was given the opportunity to learn the highest of ideals, in Europe, India, and Africa. I was attempting to live up to them, in a rather half hearted sort of way, when I met Joe. He has never ceased to remind me of those ideals, to tell me when I was falling short, and his own example was the most poignant reminder of all. We both slipped and slid, we know that well enough, but neither of us ever lost sight of those ideals, and each slide backwards was followed by an even greater effort to be worthy."

Colin then gave a brief account of Joe's professional history, writing that "He is now going to undertake the biggest field trip of all, and once again he is leading the way for me, and I cannot wait to follow." He talked about Joe's teaching efforts, and how when he took Joe's advanced course on the anthropology of religion at Vassar the material was so sophisticated and challenging that Joe could not in good conscience have given him a grade higher than B. He said that Joe had been hard at work on a massive and brilliant study of Judeo-Christian history, but offered no details. Joe, he said, was the truly intelligent one in their marriage but that racism had prevented him from achieving greatness. Colin added that Joe contracted during fieldwork a variety of tropical illnesses that "remained undiagnosed, and more than likely caused his ever increasing fits of instability and extreme behavior." Bob Humphrey's eulogy for Joe was attached as well. According to Colin's wishes, Bob said nothing about AIDS. Instead, he said, "It was very likely that in his unselfish concern for the lives of those less fortunate than himself—the starving, the sick, the wounded, the malnourished peoples of tribal Africa—Joe contracted the illnesses that would finally claim his own life."

In his rendering of Joe's life and personal qualities, Colin made Joe the superior one. Colin had become like a Bira villager, who was ostensibly dominant over his shorter, poorer, and less sophisticated partner, but was in fact both intellectually and morally inferior to him. Joe had become like the Mbuti hunter-gatherer who, Colin believed, had the upper hand to exploit his superior's material possessions and use his pretensions against him. Colin celebrated the fact that Joe Towles—the Black Towles from Lancaster County, the descendant of slaves—had become a master, scholar, and professor, living proudly on an estate on Towles Point that was no doubt once occupied by slave owners.

Colin sensed that many of his friends thought of Joe as a spoiled brat who needed immediate gratification, that he was tempestuous and irrational. That is what the villagers always said about the Pygmies. Colin would find the same pleasure in praising Joe as he found in showing that the Pygmies were smarter and better than the villagers. With Joe's death, it became clear that Colin had fashioned his marriage into a metaphor for the Pygmy-villager relationship.

Colin noted that all their possessions would go to the United Negro College Fund, to establish a Joseph A. Towles African Studies Endowment to send African American students to study at an African university. It would be the first time the fund had ever given money for study in Africa. Between 1992 and 1999, twelve students would receive $13,000 each in scholarships. Colin also informed his friends that all of his and Joe's academic and personal papers, films, photographs, recordings, artifacts, and paintings would be lodged at the Avery Research Center for African American History and Culture at the College of Charleston, South Carolina.

The Avery knew the Towles collection would be too unwieldy for their storage space and too expensive to maintain with their limited staff, but they could not turn it down. The Avery was rich in African American archives but needed more materials on Africa; Colin Turnbull was one of the most well-known anthropologists of Africa, his artifacts alone were valuable and he was donating all of his field notes, data, and photographs. Furthermore, Colin had already catalogued nearly all of his 10,000 photographs, saving the archivists weeks of tedious work, and gave the Avery several thousand dollars to support additional cataloguing. In an archive devoted primarily to the history of slavery and civil rights in the middle Atlantic region, it was an unusual collection but one, Colin hoped, that would bring Joe notoriety and the attention of future researchers. If a researcher was going to study Martin Luther King's visits to South Carolina, or explore slave diaries, he would necessarily look at the archive's list of holdings and might easily come across the name Towles. Although Colin donated few of Joe's field notes, the Joseph A. Towles Collection, as it is called, is so large that the inventory is nearly 175 pages long.

There are stacks of Colin's notes, however, and they are remarkable, coming close to what many anthropologists would consider an ideal body of ethnographic data: detailed observations, interviews, linguistic analysis, kinship charts, drawings, maps, myths, and folklore. He was also a skilled artist who, when deep in the forest and without a camera, would draw what he saw: for example, tools, face paintings, huts at various stages of construction. There are drawings of particular body paintings he made from a distant view and then from close up, seen from one side of the body and then from another. He had gathered quantitative data on Mbuti anatomy: measurements of the buttocks, waist, chest, head perimeter, arm, hand, nose and foot length, nose breadth, eye width, weight, and the shape and length of the upper and lower teeth. There are several thousands of pages of data waiting for a scholar to make scholarly use of them. When someone questions the scholarship, research, and knowledge manifest in Colin's published works, he can be sure it was not for lack of data.

The remainder of Colin's papers, mostly anything after 1988 (with the exception of his 1949-1951 India diary and some early photographs, which mysteriously found their way into the collection), would go to the special collections at Boston University. Its director, Robert Gottlieb, took as his mission the development of one of the finest archives of twentieth-century popular American culture, and knew he needed to have at least one anthropologist represented in the collection. He initially tried to secure the papers of Margaret Mead, but they were already at the Library of Congress. The next person he thought of was Colin.

Colin wrote immediately to John Enright to say that he was planning to come to Samoa as soon as he finalized the details of the United Negro College Fund donation. But it took a long time. There were minor problems with Joe's will, which some of Joe's relatives, including his mother, had been led to believe would give them larger blocks of money; Joe had left his mother only a small annuity, and the fund would have to refuse the Towles's demands that they give up some of the money. This created tension between Colin and the Towles family and between the Towles family and the United Negro College Fund, especially much later, in 1991, when Joe's mother died and the fund refused to release money to the Towles family to pay for the funeral. Later, in 1993 when Colin was critically ill in India, the fund refused to even discuss helping pay for him to get back to the United States for treatment. In addition to dealing with family issues, the houses in Virginia and Connecticut required minor renovations and thorough cleanings before they could even go on the market, and there were the cars and all the musical instruments to be sold. The instruments would go to elementary and middle schools, except for Joe's Steinway grand, which was unique. Manufactured with several extra keys, it was purchased by the Viennese-born pianist Anton Kuerti, whom Colin had heard many times and who had spent much of his career in Canada playing with the Toronto Symphony Orchestra.

Colin and Joe seemed to have thrown away very little during their lifetime. They had hundreds of artifacts from Africa and their around-the-world trip. They had several thousand books, record albums, sheet music, furniture, and silver—a Duncan Phyfe sofa, Queen Anne silver candlesticks, an English dinner gong set, Lakewood Royal Porcelain, ivory-handled silver cutlery, and a Royal Worcester dinner service for twenty-six. There was every piece of recording equipment Colin had used in the Ituri forest during the 1950s, their 1978 Corvette, a 1971 Ford Torino station wagon, a 1987 Mazda short-bed pickup, a rowboat, a skiff, two chainsaws, a tractor, two antique barber chairs, and more than twenty leather jackets.

As Colin went through his and Joe's things over the next two months, he found other objects he wanted to add to the surface of the grave: some special champagne glasses, an old milk jug from their New York City days, even some old watermelon seeds Joe had saved to plant in the spring. Colin visited the burial site at least once a day. Going to the grave was almost addictive, like smoking or drinking, or like his nighttime ritual of one rum followed quickly by a glass of champagne.

By all appearances, Colin had always been the leader, and Joe the follower. It was never that simple, of course, but now Joe was clearly in the lead. Colin would spend many of his remaining days shaping the world's memory of Joe

Towles. He chased after Joe, his imagined Joe, in the hope that they would arrive at some final destination where "Colin Turnbull" no longer mattered, where the sun shined only on Joe. But that quest was a curse to Colin, who moved along endlessly in Joe's wake. He would soon isolate himself in Samoa and then in the mountains of India, not for ascetic penitence, as Peter Brook suggested, or to wallow in white liberal guilt, but to withdraw from the world and prepare himself to die. If he was now liberated, as many of his friends hoped, then he was free to follow Joe.

By the end of January 1989, he was already thinking about Buddhism and began corresponding regularly with his old friend and museum colleague Thubten Norbu, now professor of Altaic languages at Indiana University. Though no longer a monk, Norbu was generally called "Rinpoche," a term of respect for teachers in Tibetan Buddhism. As a professor, he was highly regarded by his friends and colleagues, and despite renouncing his vows, he could not renounce his status as the reincarnation of Taktser Rinpoche, a status the thirteenth Dalai Lama had accorded him after a thorough investigation and consultation with the oracles. Colin wrote John Enright, "Any Buddhists in Samoa? Thubten Norbu is still angry with me a) for still being depressed (how does he know, in Bloomington? On the phone I am the epitome of jollity) and b) for going to Samoa where, so far as he knows, there are no civilized people . . . i.e. Tibetans. But any Buddhists would do. Besides, I like Buddhists." A week later, he wrote Enright again, "Any Tibetans on the Samoas?"

Colin had never thought of himself as a Buddhist, but when he was in India with Sri Anandamayi Ma, she had encouraged him to visit the famous Buddhist temples in the north of India—Bodh Gaya, Rajgirh, Nalanda, and Sarnath. In 1949, he had written in his India diary that "Buddha and his teachings have always appealed to me." In fact, many European and American Buddhists begin their spiritual quests in Indian Hindu ashrams and see Buddhism as a natural development, or even a fulfillment, of what they learn from Hinduism. Many find the lifestyles associated with Buddhism more appealing than those of Hinduism, not because of caste issues which bar no one from becoming a yogi or swami, but because of the extraordinary pressures in Hinduism for renunciation and asceticism, celibacy, and vegetarianism: in short, most westerners don't want to totally renounce the world. Colin would not have minded that kind of asceticism or the vegetarianism, indeed he would embrace them as a Buddhist monk, but there were other forces pulling him to Buddhism.

Colin believed that he had always been on a spiritual quest, even as a small child, and that he was always a short step from devoting himself fully to an eastern religious tradition, but he needed to have signs pointing him in the right direction. He hoped the signs would come from Anandamayi Ma. He always remembered how hard he cried when he had to leave her in India in 1951, Anandamayi Ma putting her hand on his head, telling him not to worry, that she would call him back when the time was right. When he visited India in 1979, she was still alive, and he had tried to see her. Yet every time he thought he had found her at one particular place, he was told that she had just left. She was not calling him back.

The call came instead from Thubten Norbu. On the forty-eighth day after Joe's death, a time of special significance for Tibetans, Norbu called Colin to say he had lit butter lamps for Joe's last day in *Bardo.* During Bardo, Tibetan Buddhists prepare themselves for the forty-nine days following death, when the soul, self, or consciousness is free to wander the world at will. It is in its own bodily form, but invisible and inaudible to the living, and it can look for a suitable body to inhabit or, if it is ready, simply merge with pure consciousness. Colin was moved deeply by Norbu's attention to him and Joe, and he wrote to John Enright, "And for Joe to have the Dalai Lama's older brother, a former Abbott, and incarnation of a sixteenth-century Tibetan teacher (even if he is not convinced about it), looking after him . . . what more could one ask for."

Colin now believed that he would die within a matter of one or two years, possibly from AIDS but just as likely from complications of tropical illnesses or an accident, and he wanted to die in Samoa. He had an idealized image of Samoa as a good place to get sick and die. One of Colin's Scottish idols, the writer and fellow anticolonialist Robert Louis Stevenson, had chosen to die in Samoa, living in luxury on a mountaintop like a Scottish laird. As it was for Stevenson, Colin wanted death to take him by surprise, although such a sudden death is unlikely with AIDS. Perhaps, he thought, he might swim out too far in the ocean and be overtaken by an undertow and drown, or perhaps, by some act of magic, he would be taken by island spirits. Maybe he would be able to enjoy a good bottle of something before he died, he thought; that is what Stevenson did, and it is a favorite Scottish way of dying. Stevenson did it with a bottle of old burgundy, though he is also rumored to have had an 1840 Madeira. Colin's great uncle Willy did it with claret. Colin decided that he wanted to die after drinking tea with lots of sugar.

He told his doctor, Fred Littleton, that he did not want to be treated for any illnesses related to HIV or AIDS and he declined Littleton's recommendation to begin taking AZT. He would write Littleton every six months or so to say, "I only wish the darned thing [HIV] would DO something instead of leaving me so healthy and active. I am more than ready to move on." Enright had written to Colin, concerned that Samoa might not offer the best treatment for AIDS. Colin wrote back: "I am serious about not seeking treatment . . . I have seen enough of what that can do, and mostly it is not good . . . Joe hit a happy medium, refusing any medication that was unpalatable and could not successfully be washed down with champagne or piña colada. The only medication he accepted with good grace was for the pain brought on mainly by an attack of shingles somewhere along the line . . . If I detected any signs, knowing approximately how long I would have I would get myself back here while still active and mobile, so that I can thumb my nose at Lancaster County as I die, and be close to where I am to be buried. My Scottish ancestors would revolt at the idea of my body being shipped back first class since it would not be able to benefit from the free liquor . . . And that is one of the good things about AIDS, you are given fair warning and plenty of time to get your act together. And it is a LOT easier the older you are."

He took pleasure in being on the verge of death, and sometimes he loved the idea of dying of AIDS. He enjoyed having the same infection as others who were oppressed and stigmatized. Colin had always been ambivalent about his own privileges and status; he despised the way the upper classes of England treated the rest of society, and in India he despised the way that members of the upper castes in India feared being contaminated by the bodies of the lower castes. He told a friend that, after forty years, he had finally and happily become an untouchable himself.

Colin was in Samoa by May 1989 and he would stay there for about eighteen months. He lived simply on a very comfortable fixed income, from his social security ($923 per month) and retirement fund ($973 per month). He kept a savings account at the Bank of Lancaster with roughly $6,500 and about $15,000 worth of stock certificates in an oil company that had been liquidated and a mutual fund from which he had not received a statement in years. He had no life insurance.

He was happy to be in Samoa, away from the United States mainland. He wrote to his friend Michael Radelet, an anti–death penalty activist, "I certainly feel not one jot of loyalty to this creepy country. I used to. I used to be proud and full of hope. Then along came Nixon, Ford, Reagan, and now the Bush/Quayle era. It is all part of the same thing. The death penalty has now become just an inevitable part of an even larger phenomenon of a growing inhumanity that is not just the new American way, nor is it confined to America's friends such as Thatcher, Shamir, Botha. May Adolph [Hitler] rest in peace, but it is the natural, inevitable, and structurally correct consequence of what we call civilization."

Despite his antipathy to the United States, and despite feeling completely healthy, he wrote Barry and Francine Waddy just after he arrived in Samoa to find out what sort of casket was required for shipping his body from American Samoa to the U.S. mainland. He wanted to make absolutely certain that he would not be cremated and would be buried in Virginia next to Joe. (This was a promise he would keep as a Buddhist monk too, despite the fact that Buddhists favor cremation). Colin told Waddy he had given John Enright about $1,600 on the assumption that the shipment would cost about $4 a pound, and that the casket would weigh two hundred pounds and his corpse another two hundred. Four years later, he would amend his instructions to Waddy and Bob Humphrey to make certain that if, for some reason, his body was destroyed in an accident or could not be shipped back to the United States, then Bob should select some part of him, a piece of clothing or perhaps a letter, to bury next to Joe.

In Samoa, Colin continued to keep up frequent correspondences with a small number of people, such as Bob Humphrey and Michael Radalet with whom Kamal stayed in close contact. Colin also began to write some brief telegraphic descriptions of his thoughts and feelings about his own death in enigmatic computer files. In one unproofread file, entitled, "thesacri.fce" he wrote: "Drifting into another state of being . . . Dying while living . . . you have to think of the future, not just the past . . . as but the past and the future are here and now . . . He HAS to stay alive to keep his love alive, if the one dies so does the other, so that although Colin wants to die and is ready, because he cares for Joe so much he cannot . . . he is condemned to stay alive, and staying alive is his sacrifice. Ref./r>l>s ON WHY HE WERNT TO sAMOA . . . i CAME HERE ONLY TO GROW OLD AND DIE . . . NOT A BAD PLACE FOR SUCH A PUIRPOSE."

At the same time, Colin began corresponding regularly with a young Trinidadian student in New York City named Curtis Abraham. Abraham and Joe had met years earlier when they both took piano lessons from the same teacher, and they met again when Colin and Joe visited the College of Charleston. Abraham now planned to become an anthropologist and to work in Uganda. Colin was impressed with his intelligence and enthusiasm and decided that Abraham should write the biography of Joe Towles. Before leaving for Samoa, he gave Abraham Joe's diaries and correspondences. On several occasions, Colin also supported Abraham's research by sending him money, usually checks of two to three hundred dollars. Abraham replied with specific questions about Joe, and Colin wrote back with detailed descriptions of events, arguments, and love affairs. These letters to Abraham were subsequently included in the Turnbull archive at Boston University. Colin told Abraham much about himself, but the real goal was a biography of Joe so that the world would know about a great but unsung African American scholar who was always working in the shadow of the famous anthropologist Colin Turnbull. Toward this goal, Colin gave Curtis full access to his life, letters, friends, and family, and Abraham eventually interviewed many people; at one time he was introduced to Joe's siblings. Colin also encouraged Abraham to become an anthropologist and hoped that, like Joe, he would go to Makerere University for his graduate degree.

But when Colin went to Samoa after Joe's death, Colin decided he would write his own biography of sorts, the account of his and Joe's extraordinary love for each other that he eventually entitled "Lover and Beloved." He wrote Curtis several times asking him to return the diaries, which he eventually did. By the end of 1990, when Colin left Samoa, Abraham and Colin would correspond only occasionally as Abraham's enthusiasm for writing a biography waned, and Colin became preoccupied with publishing Joe's dissertation, his own writings on Samoa and Africa, "Lover and Beloved," and his account of his 1949-51 stay in India, "The Flute of Krishna." Curtis eventually moved to Uganda to restudy the Ik, and married a Karimojong woman with whom he started a family. He also became a fierce critic of Colin Turnbull. In 1997, he wrote an essay for *The East African* newspaper in Uganda explaining that Colin had thoroughly misunderstood the Ik. According to Abraham, Colin went to Uganda to pursue a romantic vision of primitive man and was unable to reconcile his idealistic expectations with what the Ik really were: a group of people not morally inferior but simply struggling to survive a destructive famine. He also noted that Colin's companion, Joe Towles, had disagreed strongly with Colin's view of the Ik, and had done his best to alleviate the suffering of the Ik. Finally, he quoted an Ik school teacher, who said, "If Dr. Colin was ever to return to our land we will bury him alive!"

Writing "Lover and Beloved" was a mourning process, as Colin painstakingly tried to reconstruct the history of their relationship. He read all the letters they had written to each other, transformed Joe's diaries into a six-hundred-page narrative, and then added another five hundred pages of his own version of the events Joe had described—a version that is, strikingly, almost identical to Joe's. Colin listened to old cassette tapes of Joe, his voice on a birthday greeting in Uganda, a short speech Joe gave in a class at Pace University (a book report on the science fiction book *Starship* by Brian Aldiss), and Joe's awkward piano playing on his first reading of a difficult Chopin waltz.

Colin was doubtful that anyone would be interested in reading the long book, and he was right. Editors and agents saw the lengthy manuscript as dull, repetitive, and unreadable, a rough transcription of Joe's diaries with virtually no interpretation, context, or background. In fact, there is little in the entire story Colin produced of their relationship that could be called insightful, for

Joe's diary was largely a superficial record of events, as many diaries tend to be, and Colin made no effort in his half of the manuscript to explore the motivations, psychological or otherwise, behind their actions and feelings.

An equally noticeable absence is Joe's professional achievements. Although Colin delighted in Joe's Ph.D. from Makerere, he wrote nothing about the topics Joe pursued or what contribution Joe made to anthropology or African studies. Despite writing more than a thousand pages, Colin did not make a case for Joe's heroics, personal or professional. In the end, Joe seems to have achieved little more than a tragic existence. Of course, Joe and Colin did achieve something great together: they managed to remain married for nearly thirty years.

Colin sent everything he wrote to Michael Korda who felt terrible, partly because Colin was clearly not the writer he had once been, and partly because Korda blamed himself for not having given Colin more direction. Colin also sent Korda three other works: "The Flute of Krishna," an account of his two years in India, in which his descriptions of Indian gurus were not put in a context of interest to the general reader; "The Field Experience," an intellectual study of fieldwork practices, interesting for some of the information it provides about the Mbuti but lacking any clear-cut contribution to scholarly literature (in fact, the manuscript contains few reference to any works other than his own); and "Tales of Power," a collection of spiritual, mystical stories from Samoa and central Africa. All were summarily rejected.

Anthropology had changed since the days of *The Forest People* and *The Mountain People* and Colin, now in his late sixties, had not changed with it. He was still accustomed to writing descriptions without theory and arguments, without a body of literature in which to situate them. Although the anthropology of the 1980s was marked by an increasing openness to ethnographic studies in which the anthropologist treated his own personality as an issue relevant to the study of a particular community, in Colin's own self-study, *The Human Cycle,* he offered himself up only as a comparison to other cultures, not as an essential part of his representations of them. The criticisms of this book were precisely that Colin had failed either to see how his own life had influenced his previous work or to use his history as a way to critically reassess his work.

Trying to get Joe's works published was almost as difficult as getting his own works published. It required writing dozens of letters; still neither university presses nor commercial presses were interested in Joe's dissertation or his novels. Colin, blind to the mediocrity of Joe's works, continued to believe in him and hailed him as an undiscovered star of anthropology. Third and fourth tier publishing houses were unwilling to consider the works even with Colin's offers to partially fund publication. Finally, Colin received the happy news that the Royal Museum of the Belgian Congo in Tervuren, Belgium, would publish both

Joe's dissertation, "Nkumbi Initiation: Ritual and Structure among the Mbo of Zaire," and his master's thesis, an account of the rituals of manhood entitled "Asa: Myth of Origin of Blood-Brotherhood among the Mbo, Ituri Forest" in their annual paperback monograph series. Colin ordered several hundred copies, which he sent to the same list of friends and colleagues that had received the 1988 notice of Joe and Colin's funeral. The writing, Colin said, was mostly Joe's, though Colin did edit the manuscripts and wrote two pages that were needed to bridge the sections.

In February 1990, on his way to Japan to serve as a floating ambassador for the Dalai Lama, Norbu telephoned Colin to say that a benefactor had given more than a hundred acres to establish a Tibetan Cultural Center in Bloomington, Indiana. Two years earlier, the Dalai Lama had consecrated the center's shrine or, *stupa* (literally, head of the crown), to commemorate the Tibetans who had lost their lives under foreign aggression and to house valuable relics that had been rescued from Tibet. Bloomington had not seen anything like it before, a large monastery with a golden pinnacle; in town rumors abounded that there were animal sacrifices in the woods and that the Ku Klux Klan was preparing some sort of sabotage. Norbu and his wife, Kunyang, invited Colin to come to Bloomington to relax and write and to serve as a house-sitter and caretaker for the larger property while it was cleared for the construction of the center.

Colin was anxious to leave Samoa, where he felt his isolation was threatened by his increasing closeness to his Samoan and expatriate friends. He had spent most of his time there writing "Lover and Beloved" and socializing with friends from the American Samoa Community College, including John Enright, Jeannette Mageo, a social anthropologist who taught there from 1981 to 1989 and had married a Samoan, and John Kneubohl, a native Samoan playwright and Hollywood screenwriter from the island of Tutuila who died of cancer in 1992. There was an additional temptation to socialize with the community of about a hundred *palangi* (whites), many of whom are called "yacht people," mostly early retirees who sail around the islands. Colin had started to write occasional diary entries in his computer about his discomfort with intimacy in Samoa and his desire for isolation. He wrote that Norbu recommended that he go to a Hawaiian Buddhist retreat, affiliated with the famous Nechung monastery in India, to begin his study of Buddhism: "More than an annoyance, which grows daily, is the fact that the whole island [of American Samoa] is clearly heading in the same direction of the assertion of typical western individual rights and freedoms, while pretending only to loyalty to the traditional system . . . And there is another reason for leaving . . . John E., and John K. have become truly good friends and that is luring me back into the world I want to leave. So my resolve to try again for an ultimate renunciation of worldly goods . . . and give myself full time to the Buddhist path, and so I leave that lovely island and those good people, with my sights set on NDL [Nechung Drayang Ling]."

He wrote to Norbu, "I hope you do not think it silly or needless at my age to start something new like this . . . and of course it IS rather like going back to school, with every chance of flunking! But after all it is something I started when I was in India 40 years ago. And now is the time to pick it up again and put everything into it. It is for that reason as much as any that I seek a teacher and would like to train for Holy Orders, because I need the discipline, and there is so much I need to learn." Colin would go to the retreat center in Hawaii for one month before leaving for Bloomington.

In some ways, he considered himself to be already living the life of a Buddhist monk. He did not work for a living; he had renounced the world and had few possessions; he had returned to being a vegetarian; he tried to make himself pure of body and thought, denying himself occasional opportunities for bodily pleasures and feeling that he was betraying Joe when he sought them out.

In 1990, Colin took two short trips to Hawaii but was dissatisfied. The Nechung retreat in Pahala was far too secular for Colin's needs or tastes. There were few permanent monks there, and Colin found it difficult even to walk around, with one side blocked by a gift shop, the other by an office whose telephone seemed to Colin to ring endlessly. When Colin went to evening prayers, the monk had to stop prayers to answer the phone. The distractions were good training for Colin, who had to work hard to keep his mind on his work but, he wrote Norbu, "I do not feel that the spiritual quest should be a total battle all the way." He wrote to the directors of the retreat, Marya and Miguel Schwabe, voicing all his criticisms and his concerns that their temple had yet to declare itself to any particular Buddhist tradition, such as Gelukpa or Nyingmapa.

Norbu's Bloomington benefactor was Thom Canada, a former student at Indiana who had known Norbu since the sixties. Born and raised in Bloomington, Canada is a wealthy entrepreneur who currently lives next to the Tibetan Cultural Center in a 10,000-square-foot house that he enigmatically describes as "entirely underground and with southern exposure." Canada specializes in locating geothermal fields, especially those that produce dry steam, probably the most clean, pure, and cost-effective form of energy in the world.

Canada, who had been something of a hippie and was an anti-war protester against the Vietnam War, was in the business of building solar houses. He and his wife, Kathy Noyes, an heiress to the Eli Lilly pharmaceutical fortune, delivered their children in their own house, and he spent five years as a stay-at-home father. In October 1983, Canada had gone to southern Utah to drill for hot water to grow sugar beets on a piece of land he had purchased. He took no precautions for the remote possibility that he might find dry steam, especially since, at that time, fewer than six dry steam geothermal fields had been discovered. When the drill entered the pocket, there was an enormous explosion; it took thirty-eight days and more than $2.5 million to cap it. Canada promptly sold it to the Provo Utah Municipal Power Company and began a lucrative full-time career of geothermal exploration. Between 1983 and 1999, he drilled 123 geothermal steam wells.

What is most remarkable about Canada is the way in which he found the wells. Canada is a loner who likes to stay at home and let his brother do the actual fieldwork. Canada claims to have developed the ability to leave his body, entering into the earth to locate wells. He calls it "transchanneling," and with this technique he can see wells anywhere on earth. He had long been interested in spirituality, pacifism, and alternative lifestyles, but the discovery of this new ability led him to a greater commitment to religion, especially Buddhism, which he had studied with Norbu at Indiana. Norbu learned that one of the things Canada was doing with his money was buying up vacant lots near campus. When Norbu approached him for a donation of land for the proposed Tibetan Cultural Center, Canada was happy to give him the lot next to his own house.

By the end of summer, the weather in Bloomington is nearly unbearable. The muggy air seems breathless and the heat radiates so powerfully off the asphalt that it is hard to take a simple walk along the road. The town is quiet, emptied of students and those faculty who manage to find a place to research and write for the summer. On one typically sunny and hot day in August, Canada drove by the land he had donated and noticed a man in the woodland, felling trees and removing weeds.

Neighbors had watched with amazement for the previous two days as this stranger managed to mow all the land in a single day and fight back the constant onslaught of weeds. The man's face was sunburned; he was soaked with sweat, and though the sun was beating down hard, he was not wearing a hat. Canada thought this man must be a vagrant passing through town, doing odd jobs for Norbu, and approached him with the offer of a hat. The man was happy to take the hat and introduced himself as Colin Turnbull, a retired anthropologist.

Thom and Colin quickly became good friends and would see each other frequently enough that Canada today remembers Colin as his "best friend" of that time. Despite their apparent closeness, Colin said little about his past, almost never talked about his career, and spoke of his adventures in the singular. Although Canada remembers hearing about Colin's friend and colleague Joe

Towles, he didn't know about Joe's death from AIDS, that he and Colin had been lovers, or even that Colin was attracted to men. Colin portrayed himself as a Scottish recluse, raised as an outcast in the English school system. He nonetheless enjoyed socializing with a small number of men, including Thom, Jon Brooks, Jeff Ryan, and Michael Schofield, all deeply interested in Buddhism, whose friendships centered around Norbu and the Tibetan Cultural Center. Colin's closest friend was Thom, but there were two important things that he had never told him: that he was HIV-positive and, two years later, why he had a terrible falling out with Norbu and Kunyang.

When Norbu and his wife came back in the fall, Colin stayed on as a caretaker, living on the ground floor while Norbu and Kunyang lived upstairs. He wrote a small number of letters to friends in November 1991 saying that he "holds no official position [at the Tibetan Cultural Center], but is unofficial caretaker/janitor/gardener with his old friends Professor and Mrs. Thubten Norbu." Norbu and Colin began to have long conversations and in the winter Colin told Canada: "Norbu asked if I had the nerve to become a monk. He just sat there like a cat."

In early November 1991, Colin started a diary devoted to Buddhism and begain to ponder questions about becoming Getsul, a particular level of Buddhist monk, for he had already decided to take that path. According to Colin, Norbu told him, "Getsul means taking vows first, any of these monks [in Bloomington] can hear your vows, but I think they are too young. I want you to take them from someone older, more experienced, from who you can receive the proper teachings, the proper lineage. That is most important. How about if we go to India in the spring? I will make arrangements for you to go someplace up in the mountains, you can become Getsul there." The next day, Colin wrote in his diary about Norbu: "He has been and increasingly is my teacher, advisor. At times, I feel so close to him and suspect he knows far more about me than he ever hints at. So I trust him, and of course will do what he says." Colin's love for him grew everyday as Norbu spoke to him about his own life in Tibet, his childhood, how he cried when he was taken from his mother and his hair was cut at Taktser Labrang, and how he could not answer the questions he was asked by the committee investigating the reincarnation of Taktser Rinpoche.

December 1991 was a hard month for Colin. It was the third anniversary of Joe's death and it was Christmas-time, so he felt Joe's absence more keenly. On the nineteenth, the day Joe died, Colin dug out an old bottle of perfume that Joe had cherished. Joe had even, on occasion, poured a few drops of the perfume into his morning coffee. Colin applied the perfume to his body, putting on just enough so that he could use it every day for the next few days, depleting the bottle on the 24th, the same day Joe was buried. Colin wondered if, by finishing the bottle, he would end his mourning. On December 19, he wrote a note to his diary saying that he was having a rough day, but had tried to stay in his room and study Tibetan. It was only when he stopped working that he became sad. "But I know it is partly self regret, regret at not having done all the things I should have done while I could, while Joe was here, while my parents were here, while my brother was here . . . It is partly a desperate longing to be out of this deformed body that is so useless, that has been such a curse and the cause of so much suffering, to me and others. I want to be freed of all these attachments so I can truly be free to help others . . . That means no less than self-perfection."

Colin wrote Norbu in Tokyo in January 1992 of his intention to train for Buddhism in the Dalai Lama's lineage, Gelukpa. "So believe me, my old friend Norbu, alias, Rinpoche, I will not let you down. I am more grateful than I can say for your trust in me, and your willingness to encourage me and help me, as you have done. I will be a good Getsul, I promise." Within three months, he took up the challenge and departed for Dharamsala, the center for Tibetan refugees in India and the site of the Dalai Lama's headquarters and residence. Colin called Bob Humphrey before leaving to make sure that Bob would serve as the executor of his estate, and made it clear that he intended to die in India, and if necessary to be cremated. But he would later change his mind and reaffirm plans to have his body shipped back to the United States for burial next to Joe.

He would study Buddhism at the Nechung Monastery, the representative in Dharamsala of the Tibetan monastery of the same name, and the seat of Nechung, Tibet's State Oracle. The monastery, completed in 1984, sits before the snow-capped Dhauladhar range of the Himalayas, just above the busy bazaars of Dharamsala. Nechung is widely considered to be one of the most traditional monasteries in Dharamsala, and life there is simple. The day, beginning at 5:30 A.M. and ending at 9:45 P.M., consists almost entirely of Buddhist prayer and study, training in chanting, the memorization of religious texts, and preparation of ritual cakes and mandala. Although there is electricity, there is no heat, and Colin would find it difficult to adjust to the cold, especially when he began to wear Buddhist robes. In the summer, the temperature seldom gets higher than 70° F and in the winter, the average temperature is a cool 40° F. The monks housed him in the guest quarters where, in contrast to the monks quarters, there were private baths, but Colin ate all his meals with the rest of the monks and attended all the prayers and study groups conducted in the Tibetan language. He would never become a full member of the monastery—it would require so much study, expertise in the Tibetan language, and the memorization of all the Tibetan sacred texts that it might have taken him more than a decade—but the monks treated him as if he was one of them. He was accorded enormous respect because he was a scholar and professor, because he had been sent there by Taktser

Rinpoche (Thubten Norbu), and because, with the exception of the abbot, Colin was the oldest person in the monastery. The monks remember vividly the first day Colin arrived, brightly dressed in a white sportscoat and black pants, and stunned the monastery with his charisma.

On April 5, 1992, less than a month after arriving in Dharamsala, Colin was ordained a Getsul monk by Lacho Rinpoche Namgyal and given the name Lobsong Rigdol. The name Lobsong, as Colin understood it, means, "He whose way is the way of the heart." Rigdol suggests, "He will find liberation through the mind." Getsul means "novice," and it is an ordination for both monks and nuns, with vows that contain only thirty-six rules or precepts; it does not require a change in appearance, may involve only a temporary vow of celibacy, and can be given to people under the age of twenty. Three months later on July 14, 1992, he received a Gelong ordination, the full ordination, with 253 precepts, including a vow of celibacy. To his great surprise, his Gelong vows were given by the Dalai Lama himself, and Colin Turnbull became a new person. The Dalai Lama, who could have changed Colin's name, accepted him as Lobsong Rigdol.

Within a month at Dharamsala, Colin felt at home. He wrote, "Everything I have ever loved, and every one, far from being lost by the act of renunciation, are with me now more than ever—because it was their 'conventional' existence that was renounced. Now I share my joy with their true essence." He kept a diary of his teachings but only occasionally wrote about his feelings. He was in awe of his teachers and the power of the spirit that filled them. Dharamsala reminded him, gladly, of his own insignificance; once a rising star, privileged and pampered as an elite white Oxford graduate, his wish to be no better than anyone else had come true. He was reminded of Anandamayi Ma's admonition that it might very well be better to be born a worm, a cockroach, or a cricket than a Brahmin.

His activities at the monastery were not remarkable but neither were they ordinary. Lobsang stayed in his room most of the time, studying and meditating and most members of the monastery saw him only for morning prayers. Two monks recall that on Saturdays and Sundays, when many of the approximately seventy monks went into town to the markets, Lobsong stayed at the monastery studying, reading, and writing. He seldom went out except to travel up to the Tibetan library, which taught some classes in English.

We have little information about the vows themselves, in part because they are usually held in confidence. But we do know that Colin took his vows for life with no intention of ever giving them up, something that Buddhists commonly do. (When Robert Thurman, for example, the well-known Buddhist scholar and father of the actress Uma Thurman, took his vows in the 1960s, it was only a short period of time before he gave them back.) Yet whether taken as temporary or permanent, the vows have a powerful influence on one's consciousness. The vows would help Colin prepare for death and maximize his opportunities to reach a different level of realization or awakening at death.

Colin was suspicious of Europeans in Dharamsala. Although he was the only western monk at Nechung, there were many European monks at other monasteries. He doubted their sincerity and commitment, and wondered if they would go back to Europe and make money as pop gurus. He was certainly honest about his own commitment, tempered as it was by his continued devotion to Anandamayi Ma. Even as a Buddhist monk, he kept a shrine to her, and when he got to Dharamsala and began his training, he initially wanted his name to be Premananda rather than Lobsong Rigdol. Remarkably, for a Gelong monk, he would write to an old friend, Panda, living at Anandamayi Ashram, to say that even though he took his Buddhist vows, his allegiance was still to Anandamayi Ma. "Buddhism," he told Panda, "insists that the disciple revere his Guru just as if his Guru was Buddha himself." That is how much he revered Anandamayi Ma. He added, "It did not make me have any less respect for my Buddhist teacher and Spiritual Guide, there was simply no contradiction."

Colin may have had no problem in calling Anandamayi Ma his Buddha, but for a Buddhist it was unusual, and for a fully ordained Buddhist monk it was highly idiosyncratic. Some Buddhists suggest that his continued devotion to Ma was the result of inadequate training; Colin began his Buddhist training at the age of sixty-five and never completed more than four years of study. A typical Gelong monk in the Dalai Lama's lineage might expect to go to school for at least twelve years, if only because it would take that long to perfect his Tibetan language skills.

Colin's reluctance to be exclusively Buddhist is expressed in a short unpublished essay he wrote while in Dharamsala on the relationship between Buddhism and the Mbuti Pygmies. The essay is a reflection on monastic discipline, the spiritual failures of his elite academic training, and the amazingly Buddhist-like lessons he learned from the Pygmies. It suggests that Colin wanted to be an unusual Buddhist, one who would knit together diverse spiritual traditions, from the Pygmies, Sri Anandamayi Ma, and elsewhere. In the text, here quoted at length, Colin wrote about how difficult it was to be both an anthropologist and a monk:

> [A] problem for me as a former anthropologist is the enormous respect many of us develop for the people with whom we live and work. The often repeated reference by Buddhist teachers, whom we also respect, to "barbarians" and "savages" hurts, and smacks of the very ignorance against which we all fight. As anthropologists in the field we often find ourselves in that borderland where the difference between the dharma lived by the people

and Buddha Dharma is both slender and questionable. Does it really matter whether or not they know the name of the Buddha Sakyamuni or any of the other Buddhas? Even Buddhists use different terminologies. Surely what matters most is the coincidence of beliefs and practices.

It is these coincidences that impress me. Let me take the example known to me the best, and on the surface an example that would seem to be the furthest from the most sacred ideals of Buddhism: the Mbuti Pygmies of the Ituri Forest of Central Africa.

To begin with, they are hunters and they live by killing. Yet compassion is central to their lives. They even kill the game that feeds them with compassion, and they have devised a system whereby they never kill more than is absolutely essential to satisfy the immediate needs of the nomadic band. Even more than that, they tell stories of how it is this very act of killing that condemns them and all sentient beings to death. "If only we could learn how to survive without killing," they say, "perhaps we might live forever . . ."

Above all there is an overwhelming respect for motherhood, so much so that women, as the givers of life, are forbidden from taking part in the actual killing of animals, and the father is sometimes referred to as a "kind of mother." And any person in any hunting camp will address all those women old enough to be his mother as "mother" whether there is any biological relationship or not. That may not go as far as recognizing all sentient beings as our mothers, but it is no small step.

Even when it comes to higher flights of Buddhist thought, difficult often for the less well-educated Buddhist laymen, such as the concepts of impermanence and emptiness, these totally non-literate hunter-gatherers, in their frequent contemplative moments, are given to talking and singing and dancing about just these kinds of ideas. Their concern is with the phenomenon of life rather than the actual physical entity, be it a human body or a tree. When a human body dies, it is food for the insects. It is left inside its house, built of sticks and leaves, which is pulled down around it and abandoned. The camp moves on elsewhere, leaving the empty body behind.

The Mbuti do not even consider this quality of life as permanent, as continuing some individual existence in the next world, after death. So they could be said not to believe even in the conventional reality of things. Things are temporary, impermanent appearances. Their language is simple and inadequate for the expression in words of the complexity of their thoughts, so they use other means of communication: sounds, music, gestures, and the natural world around them.

> Water, in this case, is one such alternative to words. "Look at your reflection in the water," they told me. "Then if you still think you are the real 'you', touch your other self with your foot. Next put one foot into the other foot. Then as you walk right down into the water, entering your other body, look upwards. Where has that other body gone? And if you walk completely under the water and come out on the far shore, as you come out some other body, just like yours, comes from somewhere and passes through you back into the water. Now who and where is the real self?"
>
> That was perhaps my first lesson in emptiness, from a non-literate "barbarian" who had never even heard of Buddhism. How can I help but respect him? And indeed, why can't we learn from him and from his uncorrupted wisdom? Just as he has a lot to learn from us, so is the reverse true. I wonder what those people would do, would become, if the Buddha Dharma was translated into their terms. They would certainly recognize it and welcome it with joy . . .
>
> I may have become a monk, and owe an incalculable debt to the Buddhism of Tibet, hence to the Tibetan people. But having had the opportunity as an anthropologist to live among such people as the Mbuti, so much more advanced in many ways than my own, I cannot help but recognize them also as among my foremost teachers, and to make my prostrations equally to them, in all sincere humility and gratitude.

In the fall of 1992, Colin traveled to Hawaii where he tried, once again unsuccessfully, to find peace at the retreat center associated with the Nechung monastery. There were tourists and other "searchers" staying there, and the traffic was at once both intrusive and tempting. In December 1992, Colin returned to Bloomington, where he would stay for less than three months. He tried to keep the friends he had developed at the Tibetan Cultural Center, but he was now a monk and felt a certain distance from them. He had less time to socialize and was now even more private than before. Younger men from the Tibetan Cultural Center, like Michael Schofield and Jeff Ryan, found that Lobsong was able to minister to them, but Thom missed Colin. Lobsong seemed remote, unable to connect in the same way, and he began to look thin and ill. He was technically healthy, but his appetite had diminished and he tired easily.

One day in February, Colin vanished. Thom couldn't find him anywhere. Thom was worried and drove over to Norbu's house. Kunyang met him at the door and said that Colin had packed up and left. She seemed dismissive of his concerns. Thom got into his car and drove down the road where the center and Canada's home are located, until he spotted purple robes billowing in the wind. It was cold, clouds were settling over Bloomington, and a light snow was starting to fall. Thom's first thought was that Colin must be freezing. He pulled up beside Colin who did not stop walking and did not even look at him. Thom pulled ahead and stopped the car. He lowered his window and cried out to him. Colin stopped and turned towards Thom, looking directly at him now, with a face full of anger and hurt. But Colin said nothing. After no more than five seconds, he turned and continued walking down the road. Thom let him be; he never saw him again.

No one but Colin, Thubten, and Kunyang knows what transpired between them. Colin never told a soul, and the Norbus have refused to communicate with me. Despite repeated attempts to contact them, Norbu's assistant said politely in a brief conversation that Norbu "does not grant interviews." The assistant explained his silence by saying that Norbu had never been a good friend of Colin's. When reminded that Colin had co-authored a book on Tibet with Norbu in 1968, the assistant said that Norbu had not, in fact, written any of the book but had simply put his name to it for the purpose of establishing its legitimacy. In fact, Colin wrote it based on Norbu's narration, and Colin's name and not Norbu's was its primary selling point.

Since Colin kept from Thom his "secret" about AIDS as well as the reasons behind his flight from Bloomington, it is likely that the Norbus expelled him from the center because they were afraid of AIDS. Colin's other friends in Bloomington, none of whom know exactly what happened, believe that Norbu was furious when he discovered the true cause of Joe's death and that neither Norbu or his wife were comfortable living with someone they knew to be HIV positive and, they assumed, highly contagious. Colin was not symptomatic at this time; he had lost some weight, but he still looked strong and healthy. Norbu and his wife were simply too afraid. One of Colin's friends, Jeff Ryan, who had his own falling out with the Norbus and is no longer connected with the center, says that although the Norbus were angry with Colin for concealing his HIV infection, it was Colin's decision to leave.

Whatever the reason for Colin's departure, it is clear that, with the exception of Michael Schofield who continues to participate in the center, those who were associated with the building of the Tibetan Cultural Center, and who were friends with Colin, also drew fire from the Norbus. By 1999, Thom Canada had opened his own Tibetan Buddhist Monastery not far from the Tibetan Cultural Center, the Dagom Geden Tensung Ling; it is a monastery for a god named Shugden who, despite being a traditional protector god of the Dalai Lama's Gelukpa order, has now been denounced by the Dalai Lama as malevolent.

When Colin fled Bloomington he went directly to Kilmarnock, Virginia, where he rented a small house not far from where his mother once lived. He stayed there for several months and was a sight to see. In this small and isolated town, he walked down the street proudly in his purple robes and sandals. No one had seen anything like it in Kilmarnock, yet here was Colin Turnbull, a monk, with his head now shaven, going to the bank, the grocery store, and the laundromat. He spent the rest of the winter and spring of 1993 in Kilmarnock but throughout that time he longed for the teachings and Tibetan language training at the Nechung monastery. So he left Kilmarnock, but held on to the lease, arriving in Dharamsala at the beginning of the summer. The monks were thrilled that he was back with them, but they noticed that he had lost weight and also had dark purple patches on his left hand. "It was the strangest reaction to mosquito bites we had ever seen," one monk said. Colin had told them the spots were the result of insect bites; they were, in fact, patches of Kaposi's sarcoma, a cancer associated with AIDS.

Gradually, through the summer and early fall, Colin became increasingly weak. He was almost constantly chilled and so the monks found him two electric heaters. Colin put them on either side of his bed and once brought the heaters so close to his skin that he suffered first degree burns. By December, he had had several bouts of pneumonia and was suffering from tuberculosis. Yet no one at the monastery knew that Colin had AIDS. The monk to whom he was the closest, who asked to be identified only as T., would be shocked and frightened when, after Colin was admitted to the Delek hospital in Dharamsala, the doctors told him Colin's diagnosis. He remembered that when Colin was at the hospital he had bathed him with wet towels and had accidentally removed Colin's IV. Blood spurted from Colin's arm onto his hands. "Thank God," he said, "I didn't have any wounds." Six months later, T. tested negative for HIV. In fact, Colin had not told anyone at the monastery that he had had a male companion or that he had been gay. As T. said about the monks at Nechung, "We never ask such things and also never doubt such things about other people, which maybe is not so wise anymore."

The illness was hard on Colin and hard on the doctors in India, because Colin refused most medications and would not agree to have his blood tested for HIV. At no time in his life had Colin been more irresponsible, for by concealing his infection he put his doctors and nurses, and even a friend like T. at risk. Nonetheless, the doctors recognized the clinical signs and when he was admitted to the hospital that December he was taken immediately to the special ward for AIDS patients and his blood was tested for HIV without his consent. The monks say that this is when both they *and* Colin first learned that he had AIDS. The nurses told T. and the other monks that when Colin was laid on his bed in the AIDS ward he cried silently.

Colin's sole wish now was to get back to the United States to be buried next to Joe. The monks at Nechung Monastery found a business card in Colin's wallet that had been given to him by the owner of a stationery store in Kilmarnock,

Bill Humphreys. Confusing him with Bob Humphrey, a friend Colin often spoke of at the monastery and whose name was listed as Colin's contact in case of emergency, the monks telephoned Bill asking if he could arrange to have Colin flown to a hospital in the United States.

Bill and his wife, Louise, knew Colin because he had shopped at their store, and their daughter Virginia had met Colin on a few occasions in 1993, but they were not prepared for this. Recalling that Colin had once worked at George Washington University, he decided to look there for help and found Bob Humphrey, the man Colin had named as the executor of his literary and financial estate.

Bob was overwhelmed by the task before him, the bureaucracy he would have to deal with to make arrangements for Colin to be evacuated from India and admitted to a hospital in Kilmarnock, and the run-around he would get from insurance companies in the United States only to find out that Colin's insurance would pay for none of his medical care in India and nothing for an evacuation. Bob liquidated Colin's savings account and made dozens of calls asking anyone who knew Colin to make a donation. He pleaded with Visa to increase Colin's credit line and begged the U.S. embassy in India to help find a way to send Colin home. The cost of an emergency evacuation was more than twenty thousand dollars, and Colin had given nearly all of his savings to the United Negro College Fund. Bob called the fund, but they refused to give any money to Colin for fear that it might set a precedent for giving back donations. Bill Humphreys called his U.S. Senator, John Warner, and his congressman, Herb Bateman, but with no results. In the end, Thom Canada gave ten thousand dollars, Bill Humphreys and Bob Humphrey donated hundreds of dollars, and friends and colleagues chipped in the rest.

Meanwhile, in early January 1994, the doctors at Delek hospital told T. and three other monks from Nechung that they would not be able to treat Colin's opportunistic infections successfully. On the doctors' recommendation, the monks then drove Colin eight hours south on terrible roads to a larger and more well-equipped hospital in Chandigarh. On the way, Colin was only half-conscious. Almost every hour, he cried out that he had to urinate, and the monks gave him a bottle. But he never used the bottle, soiling the car instead. When he got to Chandigarh, he was admitted to the AIDS ward, and the monks left to alert the American embassy of Colin's condition.

In late January, an organization called East-West Rescue took Colin from Chandigarh to New Delhi. Of the thousands of miles Colin would travel back to the United States, the trip to New Delhi was the hardest of all. They traveled down mountain passes on a bumpy road, and Colin, who had little muscle control, was thrown against the side of the ambulance and lost two teeth. On

January 25, 1994, he boarded an Air India flight with an Indian nurse, Marianne Johnson-Lucknow, and a physician named Ram Moanohar Pai. Bill Humphreys met the plane at Dulles airport and drove Colin and the medical team to the hospital; Bill had also arranged for an infectious disease specialist, John Deschamps, to care for him since Fred Littleton had moved to North Carolina. Remarkably, it took only three weeks from the time the monastery first telephoned Bill Humphreys to Colin's arrival at Dulles airport. Pai and Johnson-Lucknow spent the next day at the Tyson's Corner shopping mall and returned that evening to New Delhi.

Bill Humphreys was now inexplicably tied to Colin. With the exception of Bob Humphrey and Nate Garner, the only ones who came to see him at the hospital in Virginia were the Humphreys. Bill and Colin became close during those final days. Bill was the chairman of the local branch of Virginia's Republican party, and he and Colin seem to have been the only people in their orbit not surprised that they could be so close. Colin sometimes even called him "Papa," and became close with Bill's daughter Bonnie, who he said was like a sister. Bonnie, the only name that came to mind when Colin saw her for the first time, is really Virginia Humphreys, but the name stuck. She knew Colin perhaps better than her parents because she was interested in Buddhism and had once approached Colin at the grocery store in Kilmarnock after Colin had so precipitously left Bloomington, to tell him that in 1983 when she had $16 to her name she had bought a copy of *The Human Cycle* for $15.99. Bonnie hadn't expected to see him again. When she drove him to the airport for his tragic return to Bloomington the previous year, Colin had looked out of the window while leaving Kilmarnock and said, "This is my home." Bonnie, who grew up on the northern neck, still lives there on a large cruising sailboat, and has often longed to live elsewhere; she marveled that such a worldly man would say such a thing and thought to herself, "*This* place?"

The Humphreys visited him often and listened to him tell stories of his life, especially of that most important day in December 1988 when Colin saw his first life come to a close. He talked to them about his dashing brother Ian, his love for Kumari, and his passionate hatred of western individualism. He told them about Buddhism and how it negated so much of what he learned at Oxford about the Cartesian concept of the self, and the arguments of Locke, Berkeley, Hume, and other British empiricists that existence lies in perception. He talked of how, as a Buddhist, he was using his mind to destroy itself, to free himself from the false illusion of the lesser thinking self.

His mind seemed clear and sharp, but he was physically weak. Though he knew his official diagnosis, he continued to tell Bob and the Humphreys that he might just have a mixture of parasitic illnesses. Colin told one of his doctors that he wanted no medications, especially anything like AZT that might prolong his life, including antibiotics. He did agree to take a drug called Megase, the sole purpose of which is to increase appetite. He meditated and slept, and the hospital staff indulged him often with vegetarian pizza and a bottle of beer.

Once Colin's illnesses were stabilized, the doctors told Colin he might be more comfortable, and potentially more healthy, at the small house he still rented in Kilmarnock. Colin agreed to try it for a few days; Bonnie brought him mueslix on the first day, but on the second day a nurse came by and discovered that Colin had been in the bathroom for more than five hours, either disoriented or asleep. He was immediately moved back to the hospital where he stayed until his death.

Though he told Bob Humphrey that he intended to die within the first week of his return to the United States, he lived for six months. Throughout that year, Bob and Nate Garner drove down to Kilmarnock, three hours each way, once or twice a week to visit him. They were astonished that, despite his illness, Colin still looked strong and tough, and were not surprised that he lived longer than expected. On those trips, Bob would also visit Colin's devoted attorney, Ammon Dunton, and accountant, Charles Duke, who helped prepare and settle the estate. Over the course of their visits, Bob and Nate saw his Scottish persona emerge: the hospital staff were terrified of him and loved him. And, as a testament to the remarkable force of Colin's personality, Kilmarnock locals expressed concern and sympathy for him. Kilmarnock, a place that Colin often professed to hate deeply despite being named after a Scottish city, actually embraced him as their own. He had been accepted in the past by the gold miners in Canada, by Anandamayi Ma's devotees, and the Pygmies, and Kilmarnock would be no different. In retrospect, Bob thinks that the Kilmarnock folks respected Colin because he was, in many ways, an exemplar of the Kilmarnock man: masculine and rugged in appearance, able to drink hard and drive fast. For this reason, Bob would decide to quote Ernest Hemingway at Colin's funeral.

Next to his hospital bed, on his tray, he had a Mexican Toltec figurine that Bob Humphrey had given him as a gift years before, and on the edge of the tray he had taped a colorful drawing of a medicine Buddha that Bonnie had made for him. At the bottom of the page, she had written in purple ink, "Medicine Buddha, King of Lapis Lazuli Light. He holds the begging bowl of life nectar and, with the gesture of giving and compassion, the medicine plant." It was probably the last thing he saw.

CHAPTER EIGHTEEN

Epilogue

Colin Turnbull died on Thursday, July 28, 1994. He was buried next to Joe on their estate, now owned by a middle-aged couple who bought the place from the United Negro College Fund and who agreed to let Colin have his grave there. The undertaker, Barry Waddy, removed the first coffin containing Colin's spirit and replaced it with a new one containing his body. Colin did not want to have a burial service, but Bob Humphrey, Nate Garner, and the Humphreys came anyway, and Bob gave a eulogy. He repeated the joint burial wishes, just as he had at Joe and Colin's funeral in 1988, and told a Bushman story that Colin loved to tell. No other story helps us understand his remarkable life so well.

"A Bushman child drinking from a clear waterhole saw in the shimmering surface the reflection of a beautiful bird—the most beautiful bird—the most beautiful thing he had ever seen . . . But looking upward, he knew that the bird had already gone. The boy decided he had to follow and find it, so off he set. He sought it throughout his adolescence and his youth. Far from being criticized for abandoning his adult role as a hunter, it is recognized by his fellows that the young man is contributing to society by pushing both his faith and belief to the maximum.

"The quest continues throughout adulthood and the hunter who has become a hunter after truth is always one step behind his quarry. Village after village tells him it has just left heading north. In his old age, the hunter reaches the lower slopes of the highest mountain and is told that the bird has been seen high up on the snowy summit. With the last of his strength, the old man—whose quest began as the vision of a child—climbs laboriously up the mountainside. Nowhere does he see any trace of the great bird he devoted his life to finding.

"Finally he reaches the top and he knows that his quest is over, for there in the equatorial snow and ice all his strength is gone, and there is no bird, nothing but emptiness. He lies down to wait for the end, recalling the vision of his childhood, content with a life well spent, for he had been lucky enough to find beauty once, and in his heart he had never lost it.

"He closed his eyes for the last time and as he stretched out his arms in a final gesture, his hand upturned, down from the sky came a solitary feather that settled in one hand. The hand closed slowly, then held it as tightly in death as the vision of beauty had been held during life.

"That, say the Bushmen, was a life well lived."

In January 1995, at Epulu in the Ituri forest, Kenge, now 58, arrived at the home of two American ecologists, John and Terese Hart. The Harts had told Kenge about Colin's death, and now, he said, he was ready to perform a molimo ceremony in Colin's honor. The Harts promised to provide rice, beans, peanuts, and the venue. The molimo would be held in their camp, the same clearing on which both Patrick Putnam and Colin had lived. Over several days, between fifty and two hundred men, women, and children danced and sang the wistful songs Colin knew so well and listened for the trumpet in the night. On the last night, masked dancers playfully abducted two boys who had come from another village to watch the molimo and held them as prisoners for a few minutes; the boys were, perhaps, the symbols of Colin and Joe, the abduction an expression of the Mbuti's longing and regret. Kenge made sure that the molimo was full and ripe, that the good and beautiful forest was pleased, that Colin rested quietly in the spirit world, that his life and his death mattered.

NOTES

ABBREVIATIONS

AMNH	American Museum of Natural History, Archives, New York, New York.
ARC	Avery Research Center, College of Charleston, Charleston, South Carolina.
BU	Boston University, special collections, Boston, Massachusetts.
CT	Colin M. Turnbull
FE	"The Field Experience." Unpublished ms., BU.
FP	*The Forest People.* New York: Simon & Schuster, 1961.
FK	"The Flute of Krishna." Unpublished ms., BU.
HC	*The Human Cycle.* New York: Simon & Schuster, 1983.
JT	Joseph A. Towles
LB	"Lover and Beloved." Unpublished ms., BU.
MP	*The Mountain People.* New York: Simon & Schuster, 1973.
MPYG	*The Mbuti Pygmies: Change and Adaptation.* New York: Holt, Rinehart and Winston, 1983.
NAA/SI	National Anthropological Archives, Smithsonian Institution, Washington, D.C.
RG/IV	Interview with Roy Richard Grinker

Note: All written correspondences are indicated as "____ to ____," for example, "CT to JT, November 23, 1965. ARC."

CHAPTER ONE

3 "There in the tiny clearing": *FP,* 272.

3 "I am back in Africa": LB, 4-5.

4 "That is the point": *MP,* 294-5.

CHAPTER TWO

CT's early life, where not cited directly: Interviews with Colin Turnbull's relatives (George Chapman, Betty Scott, Betty Turnbull, David Turnbull, Francis Chapman, Howard Chapman, Nancy Gravely, Sheila Patterson, Patrick Gravely); *HC.*

9 She named her new son Colin: CT, Informal discussion at Nechung Dorje Drayang Ling, Dharmasala, India, August 28, 1992, computer file, "Rligexp.nce," BU.

9 Dot, as she was called, was born in Bray, Ireland: RG/IV with Betty Scott, December 26, 1998. The invitation to Dorothy Chapman's grandfather, George Chapman, came from Captain William Bourchier. The Chapmans accepted largely because George's wife was ill with what was most likely tuberculosis and her physician recommended a drier climate. Bourchier named his property The Briars. It retains the name today and is a popular vacation resort that the Chapman descendants continue to visit often. Also at "The Briars" were George's brother and sister-in-law. She was the daughter of a biblical scholar, Jacob Hirschfelder, the first Professor of Oriental

Languages at the University of Toronto. Their son, Alfred Hirschfelder Chapman, born in 1879, became one of Toronto's most famous architects, leaving a Beaux-Arts legacy for the city with such landmarks as the Toronto Public Library, Knox College, and the Harbour Commission Building; see Howard Chapman, *Alfred Chapman, Architect, 1879-1949* (Toronto: The Architectural Conservancy of Ontario, 1978). Alfred and his wife Doris had several children, including twin boys, Francis and Christopher ("Kit"), both of whom would have careers in film and television. In 1954, Francis would spend a year with Colin in Africa, making historic recordings of Pygmy music, and films of Pygmy rituals. In 1967, Kit would win the Academy Award for Best Documentary for a film about rural Ontario, entitled "A Place to Stand."

9 But George's son (and Dot's father), Arthur Wellesley Chapman: *Stowe's Clerical Directory,* 1905. Harvard Divinity School. Chapman became a minister with interests in theological theory, in what was known as "high church." After completing coursework at Harvard, in those days the best place in North America to study high church, he stayed in Massachusetts for an additional year to run a parish at Christ Church in Needham. He was still unmarried. Family friends who were wardens at a parish church in Bray, Ireland, wrote to tell George about a family named Figgis, who had a lovely, unmarried daughter for Arthur. Arthur Chapman and Elizabeth Figgis were married in Dublin in 1888.

10 Her family remembers her: RG/IV with Betty Scott (Dot Chapman Turnbull's niece), December 26, 1998, Toronto, Ontario.

10 Two of her nieces: Interviews with Nancy Gravely, Sheila Patterson and Betty Scott, December 26, 1998, Toronto, Ontario.

10 She would never be close with: RG/IV with Betty Scott (Dot Chapman Turnbull's niece), December 26, 1998, Toronto, Ontario.

10 "No matter what anyone talked about": RG/IV with George Chapman, Dot Chapman Turnbull's brother, December 27, 1998, Hamilton, Ontario.

10 The Turnbull family: RG/IV with David Turnbull, CT's nephew, April 1, 1999. London, England.

11 Jock left Scotland: RG/IV with David Turnbull, April 1, 1999, London, England.

11 The Chapmans hoped: RG/IV with Betty Scott, December 26, 1998, Toronto, Ontario.

11 As an adult, Colin would often talk about himself: RG/IV various, with Robert L. Humphrey, Richard Elzay, Francie Train, David Turnbull, Betty Scott.

11 Jock and Dot's marriage: RG/IV with David Turnbull, April 2, 1998, London, England.

11 Colin's mother believed that birth control was a tool: *HC,* p. 59-60.

12 "I would like to think": *HC,* 59-60.

12 Jock could do nothing wrong: RG/IV, various, with Betty Scott, Nancy Gravely, and Patrick Gravely. December 25-6, 1999, Toronto, Ontario.

12 The Turnbulls never forgave: RG/IV with David Turnbull, April 1, 1999, London, England; see also *HC,* p. 59-60.

12 "Phony British accent": RG/IV, various, with Betty Scott; interviews, various, with Nancy Gravely; RG/IV, various, with Patrick Gravely.

12 Colin and his elder brother Ian occupied separate nurseries: *HC,* 63-4.

13 "[Ian was] . . . at times, extremely naughty": J. R. Turnbull. "For David Alexander Turnbull from his Grandfather," September, 1946, unpublished ms. Courtesy of David Turnbull.

13 The nanny system: Jonathan Gathorne-Hardy, *The Unnatural History of the Nanny* (New York: Dial, 1973).

13 "My mother was not allowed": *HC,* 61.

13-14 They would not see his lighter side: RG/IV with Betty Scott, December 26, 1998.

14 "Unfortunately, Irene was a Nazi": *HC,* 61.

14 "[Hans] used to send me": *HC,* 61-2.

14 "To Mom and Dad": Copy of *FP,* ARC.

14 "The feeling of love": *HC,* 62.

14 "Even now, when I am in such trouble": RG/IV with Betty Turnbull, July 24, 1999, by telephone.

15 Colin would always remember: *Der Struwwelpeter.* 1990. Vienna, Austria: Esslinger Verlag J. F. Schreiber.

16 Until he joined the Royal Navy: RG/IV with David Turnbull, April 1, 1999, London, England.

16 On at least one occasion: *HC,* 68.

16 His nanny caught up with him: CT to Curtis Abraham, circa 1993. Undated letter. Miscellaneous computer files. BU.

16-17 "At home my nursery": *HC,* 69.

17 "What would we lose": *HC,* 279.

CHAPTER THREE

CT's early school life, where not quoted directly: Interviews with Colin Turnbull's relatives (George Chapman, Betty Scott, Betty Turnbull, David Turnbull, Francis Chapman, Howard Chapman, Nancy Gravely, Sheila Patterson, Patrick Gravely); *The Human Cycle;* Documents from Cumnor House school, Westminster school, Magdalen College Archives, Oxford; J. R. Turnbull. "For David Alexander Turnbull from his Grandfather," September, 1946, unpublished ms. Courtesy of David Turnbull.

19 "In the very first week": *HC,* 69.

20 Colin was one of five pupils: "History of Cumnor House, Cumnor House Report," 1934. Courtesy of N. Milner-Gulland.

20 Mr. Perry died tragically: Cumnor House Report, 1952. Courtesy of N. Milner-Gulland.

20 Colin's classmates: N. Milner-Gulland to the author, October 20, 1998; John Berkeley to the author, October 30, 1998; G. Van Dulken to Nick Milner-Gulland, November 2, 1998. Colin's classmates included Richard Walker, G. Van Dulken, John Shore, John Berkeley, John Wettern, and Robin Kennard. After sixty years, they remember little about him. The fact that other students did keep in touch suggests that Colin was socially on the margins at Cumnor, or at least that he felt on the margins. In contrast, G. Van Dulken would be John Shore's best man at his wedding, and Van Dulken would marry one of Richard Walker's former girlfriends.

20 "So were others": *HC,* 73.

21 "This was a problem for Ian and Colin": J. R. Turnbull. "For David Alexander Turnbull from his Grandfather," September, 1946, unpublished ms. Courtesy of David Turnbull (courtesy of David Alexander Turnbull).

21 His report cards: *HC,* 73.

21 "Colin is not much good": *HC,* 73.

23 During the plague of 1665: *Great Public Schools,* (London: Edward Arnold, undated, probably 1909).

23 Westminster had knee breeches: In the *Pickwick Papers.* Quoted in John Field *The King's Nurseries* (London: James and James, 1987).

23 "The reason I chose Westminster": *HC,* 113.

24 "With double-thickness soles": *HC,* 100-1.

24 "Unlike other ordeals or punishments": *HC,* 101.

25 Descriptions of boarding schools: Jonathan. Gathorne-Hardy *The Old School Tie: The Phenomenon of the English Public School* (New York: Viking, 1978), 80, 175, 162.

25 Public school could be openly, unabashedly homoerotic: Alisdare Hickson. *The Poisoned Bowl: Sex, Repression and the Public School System* (London: Constable, 1995), 15.

25 "Anyone who has been to an English public school": Evelyn Waugh. *Decline and Fall* (Harmondsworth: Penguin, 1976), 188.

25 "The corporate emotion": Jonathan Gathorne-Hardy *The Old School Tie: The Phenomenon of the English Public School* (New York: Viking, 1978), 112.

26 There is no way to know precisely how common: Though it is unknown exactly what he was referring to, the headmaster of Rugby School remarked in the mid-1800s that "None can pass through a large school without being pretty intimately acquainted with vice; and few, alas! very few, without tasting too largely of that poisoned bowl." Cited in Alisdare Hickson *The Poisoned Bowl: Sex, Repression and the Public School System.* (London: Constable, 1995), 13. Hence, Hickson entitled his study of sex in the public school system, *The Poisoned Bowl.* In that book, he tells us that the very restrictions intended to discourage homosexual sex ended up encouraging it. For sex was deemed illegal by the authorities and, therefore, was also an act of protest and resistance.

26 Senior boys were known to torture their juniors: J. A. Symonds, in Royston Lambert with Spence Millham, *The Hothouse Society* (London: Weidenfeld and Nicolson, 1968), 74.

26-27 "[He] did not yell for help or scream": *HC,* 115.

27 "There were those": *HC,* 117.

28 "My housemaster sat me down in his study": *HC,* 113-4.

29 The weeds were overgrown: John Carleton, *Westminster School* (London: Mars-Davis, 1965), 94-5.

29-30 Excerpts from *College Street Clarion,* 1942, courtesy of Westminster School and Peter Holmes.

30 Letters regarding admission to Magdalen College written by William Millar Mackenzie and John Rutherford Turnbull: Magdalen College Archives, Oxford University.

31 "Turnbull: He's not a bad fellow": Had the headmaster known how Bruce McFarlane felt about Sir Henry Tizard, he might not have mentioned him. When the letter was written, McFarlane had just lost the Magdalen presidential election to Tizard by only one vote and grew to detest him. McFarlane seems not to have been deterred, however, and agreed to interview Colin at Magdalen. Magdalen College Archives, Oxford University.

CHAPTER FOUR

Information on CT's university life and World War II experiences comes largely from the Magdalen College Archives, Oxford; Oxford University Archives; Institute of Social Anthropology, Oxford, Archives; The Joseph A. Towles Collection, ARC; *HC;* "Lover and Beloved;" Royal Navy Volunteer Reserves files, "Colin M. Turnbull."

33 Their conversation began with: *HC,* 156.

34 "I approached the problem": *HC,* 156.

34 Addison's Walk: Named for the famous turn-of-the-seventeenth-century essayist and poet, Joseph Addison.

34 "Alumni wrote about their special love": *Magdalen College Record,* "Magdalen in World War II, 1939-1945, 103.

34 "The ecclesiastical architecture": *HC,* 169.

35 "I spent fourteen months": Edward Gibbon, Memoirs. 1792. Cited in Jan Morris ed., *The Oxford Book of Oxford,* (Oxford: Oxford University Press, 1978), 152; Oscar Wilde, 1877, 279.

35 "At Magdalen the average man": Cited in Jan Morris ed. *The Oxford Book of Oxford* (Oxford: Oxford University Press, 1978), 321-2.

35 The standard of living was generally pretty low: *Magdalen College Record*, 1995, "Magdalen in World War II, 1939-1945," 99. The *Record* states: "Rations of sugar and butter were doled out weekly and were kept in members' rooms, to be carried into Hall for breakfast. These attracted mice and the butter was often imprinted with their toothmarks. Mr. Bond, the awesome and not universally popular Steward of the JCR [Junior Common Room] and the Head Porter were addressed as "Mr." Mr. Kirby, the Head Porter, was another formidable character: The [Porter's] Lodge seemed to be the nucleus of Scout life. Everything flowed through it and the Head Porter ranked only after God and the President of the College.

35-36 Students who were twenty-years-old: M. R. J. Wyllie, *Magdalen College Record*, 1995, "V-E Night at Magdalen," 109.

36 "Nothing personal": A. J. P. Taylor. *Personal History* (New York: Atheneum, 1983), 198-9.

36 "The intimacy of one moment": *HC*, 159.

36 "My tutor interrupted my reading": *HC*, 161.

37 Undergraduates were cared for primarily: At Cambridge, scouts are called "bedders."

37 Scouts cleaned students' rooms: In Turnbull's days, scouts were mostly men, though today they tend to be women; by the 1970s, scouts comprised the cleaning staff and students no longer had the sorts of relationships with scouts that Colin had. See Christopher Platt, *The Most Obliging Man In Europe: Life and Times of the Oxford Scout* (London: George Allen & Unwin, 1986), 15. Porters tended to sort out trouble on campus, knew much of the history of the university, and provided keys and mail service to students. When President Bill Clinton visited University College in 1994, the only person from his old College with whom he wanted to privately converse was the man who had been head porter when he was there.

37 "A relative perhaps?": *HC*, 165.

37 "This ancient seat of higher learning:" Peter Hennessy, *Whitehall* (New York: The Free Press, 1989), 115.

37-38 "If there is one town in this country": A. L. Rowse, *The English Spirit: Essays in History and Literature* (New York: Macmillan, 1945), 261.

38 The hierarchical tone: *The English Spirit: Essays in History and Literature* (New York: Macmillan, 1945), 261-2.

38 "To becoming a socialist": LB, 50.

38 "Oxford did nothing to cure that": LB, 50, BU.

38 "It used to be said that the Oxford Eight": *HC*, 154.

39 "The dean was asleep": *HC*, 167-8.

39 "Approached by a locked door": CT to Johanna Humphrey, July 9, 1993.

39 "All the strain of waiting for good or bad news is over now": From Gerald Harriss ed., *The McFarlane Letters: Letters to Friends, 1940-1966* (Oxford: Magdalen College, 1997), 164.

40 During those years, we do know that Colin strayed as much as possible: LB, 50l, BU.

40 "I found . . . that among the ratings": *HC*, 198.

40 "He felt guilty every time he joined the other": File: "Books. IDS\failures.," BU.

41 "[God Save the King] always brought a lump to my throat": *HC*, 199.

41 "[Getting the name tags] was a disagreeable task for anyone": *HC*, 200.

42 "Oblivious to the other explosive motorboats": *HC*, 201.

42 "I was feeling more alive": *HC*, 201.

42-43 "How proud he was of you when you were born!": J. R. Turnbull. "For David Alexander Turnbull from his Grandfather," September, 1946, unpublished ms. Courtesy of David Turnbull.

43 In September, he wrote a long letter: All World War II correspondence cited here, Magdalen College Archives, Oxford University.

CHAPTER FIVE

CT's voyage to India, 1949-1951: Where not quoted directly, see FK and *HC;* for additional information on Sri Anandamayi Ma, see: Lisa Lassell Hallstrom, *Mother of Bliss: Anandamayi Ma, 1896–1982* (Oxford: Oxford University Press, 1999) and Richard Lannoy, *Anandamayi: Her Life and Wisdom* (Shaftesbury, Dorset: Element, 1996).

47 "Although the number of Indian students peaked": Richard Symonds, *Oxford and Empire* (London: Macmillan, 1986), 260. Those Indians who did go to Oxford usually cohered around a community of students called the Oxford Indian Majlis Society, or Majlis for short *(Majil,* Arabic: meeting or council, used in India with a distinct political connotation). The Majlis society was an organization that was the precedent for subsequent foreign student organizations. However, Indian students were also elected both librarian and president of the well-known Oxford Union, a debating society open to anyone who could afford the steep membership fees. This is not insignificant; the union was the breeding ground for would-be British politicians, there was extraordinary competition for leadership positions, and a glance at the Oxford alumni records of most eminent politicians in Britain would probably show a history of leadership in the union. At Oxford's All Souls College, important figures such as Lord Curzon and Lord Chelmsford spent time with people like Sir Sarvepalli Radhakrishnan, who later became the first president of India, and Lord Radcliffe, who was deeply involved in drawing the line of partition between India and Pakistan. However, the vast majority of overseas students were white, with nearly one third of the total number of foreign students Rhodes scholars. On the Oxford Union, see Brian Harrison, ed. 1994. *The History of the University of Oxford, Volume VIII, The Twentieth Century.* Oxford: Clarendon Press, 615. See also, S. W. R. D. Bandaranaike (Solomon West Ridgeway Dias). *Speeches and Writings.* 1997 [1963]. Colombo, Sri Lanka: Department of Government Printers, 16; and Symonds, Richard. 1986. *Oxford and Empire.* London: Macmillan, 263. Eric Williams of Trinidad, the son of a postal clerk, who attended Oxford in the early forties before going on to become Prime Minister of Trinidad, had little good to say about race relations at Oxford. Knowing full well that Oxford was not hospitable to blacks, his recommender from the Trinidad Department of Education emphasized that "Mr. Williams is not of European descent, but is a coloured boy, though not black."

48 On a Saturday evening in 1948: RG/IV with David Turnbull, April 2, 1999, London, England.

49 "It seems a pretty desperate project": W. M. Mackenzie to CT, March 3, 1948, Magdalen College Archives, Oxford University.

50 "Arriving with empty pockets"; "Colin had an elegant presence": Geeta Mayor to the author, July 25, 1999.

51 He joined two European hikers: William Lyon to the author, December 1, 1998.

51 "So, you didn't want to come": William Lyon to the author, December 1, 1998.

51 "From the narrow main street": FK, 26.

51 She held a Ph.D.: RG/IV with Ingrid Van Mater, Theosophical Society, February 25, 1999.

52 Although one's highest duty: FK, 38.

52 By embracing Hinduism: Colin would later hold Christianity in contempt and seldom spoke about his family's religious traditions. One of Colin's close friends during the 1970s was an Episcopal priest from Atlanta named Austin Ford. The first time Austin heard that Colin's grandfather had

also been an Episcopal priest was when I told him in 1999. RG/IV with Austin Ford, February 7, 1999.

52 "I thought this was really rather a waste of my time": FK, 39.

52 "A little boy came and curled up beside her": FK, 44.

52 Anandamayi Ma then informed Colin: FK, 45.

53 All who knew him during this time: Bittika Mukerji to RRG, June 14, 1999. Mukerji was teaching at Banaras Hindu University and living at the ashram when Colin arrived. She remembers that Anandamayi spent a lot of time with Premananda, that Anandamayi Ma not only advised Colin in great detail, but visited him in his room to help him organize his books and papers.

53 Athmananda had been a devotee: RG/IV with Ram Alexander, April 3, 1999 by telephone. Athmananda's reflections on CT appear courtesy of Ram Alexander, to whom Athmananda bequeathed her diary.

55 "There was once a famous Brahmin saint": FK, 42.

56 In Bengal, the goddess Durga: In central India, the Ramlila festival takes the place of the Bengali Durga festival. There the main subject is not Durga but the King, Ram, whose victory is made possible by worshipping Durga.

57 "In her mild form": CT 1949 Photo-diary, Oct. 2, 1949, BU.

57 '"Primitive? I couldn't even say that"': CT 1949 Photo-diary, October 2, 1949, BU.

57 "They looked beyond the symbol": CT 1949 Photo-diary, October 3, 1949, BU.

58 With a huge explosion: 1949 Photo-diary, October 3, 1949, BU.

59 "The relationship and the conscious effort": *HC*, 241.

60 In 1999, a reporter: Billington, Rachel. "An Englishwoman's Surprise": *The New York Times*, Feb. 28, 1999, 5: 10.

61 "To be with either of them for more than minute": *HC*, 195.

62 "And just as we got to the end of that long reflecting pool": FK, 226-227.

62 "The trail ran along a ridge": FK, 234.

63 Jalal Al-Din Rumi, "Song of the Reed": Colin attributes the translation to Kenneth Cragg. "The Wisdom of the Sufis." Date and publisher unknown.

64 As he prepared to leave India: Athmananda Diary, 1951. Courtesy of Ram Alexander.

65 "The stars shimmered": CT 1949 Photo-diary, early March, 1951, BU; FK, 267-268.

CHAPTER SIX

CT's central African experiences as described in chapters six and seven: *The Forest People, The Mbuti Pygmies, Wayward Servants,* "The Field Experience," notes and correspondences at the Avery Center, documents provided by the American Museum of Natural History, Oxford University and Christie McDonald, executrix of the Putnam Papers, the Houghton Library, Harvard University.

68 "The sound of the voices": *FP*, 13.

69 Newton Beal was an American born in 1914: Graveside Rites held for C. Newton Beal. Lancaster Eagle-Gazette, p. 1 December 27, 1966. Courtesy of the Fairfield County District Library. His trips to Africa were financed by a private benefactor from Lancaster, Ohio named Eva Fulton.

69 Colin carried just one trunk: RG/IV with David Turnbull, April 2, 1999, London, England.

69 When they arrived in Kenya: FE, unpaginated.

70 It was an AJS 500 sport: Thanks to Pete Gagan for identifying the make and model of the motorcycle.

70 "A small boy pointed out": CT, "Land of the Pigmies: How Two Novices Bought a Motor Cycle in Nairobi and Rode it 6,000 Miles Home to England. Part I:" *The Motorcycle,* January 24, 1952, 89-91.

70 The Hollywood producer: FE, unpaginated.

71 Patrick Putnam: biographical information from Joan Mark, *The King of the World in the Land of the Pygmies* (Lincoln: University of Nebraska Press, 1995).

72 Anne Eisner Putnam: biographical details from Christie McDonald, personal communication, 1999; Christie McDonald, "Anne Eisner Putnam: Painting from the Ituri Forest," Annual Meetings of the American Comparative Literature Association, Montreal, Canada, 1999. See also, Joan Mark, *The King of the World in the Land of the Pygmies.* (Lincoln and London: University of Nebraska Press, 1995).

72 "Africa was not a purgatory": J. Mark, 76.

73 Patrice Lumumba: *MPYG,* 77.

74 "The first night out my mind was blown": J. Mark, 165.

74 Filthy and unshaven: RG/IV with David Turnbull, April 1, 1999; CMT, "Journey from Africa: Concluding Article Describing the Trip of Two Novices on a Solo Motor Cycle from Africa to England, Part II," ARC.

75 Colin and Newton were arrested: RG/IV with David Turnbull, April 2, 1999, London, England; see also, LB.

76 The earliest reference to the Pygmies: Authors writing on the Pygmies in the late twentieth century often refer to this ancient encounter. The dust jacket of Louis Sarno's popular book about Pygmies, *Song From the Forest,* reads, "*Song From the Forest* is a window into a vanishing world, and a vivid testament to a form of music so ancient it was sung in the courts of the pharaohs." Louis Sarno. *Song From the Forest: My Life among the Ba-Benjellé Pygmies.* (Boston and New York: Houghton Mifflin, 1993).

76 When Colin died, he still possessed: G. G. di Thiene to CT, December 12, 1956. ARC. Maiuri's analysis was published in "Memorie dell'Accademia dei Lincei 1955—Serie VIII vol. VII fascicolo 2." ARC.

76 "Pigmea is a countree . . .": *Oxford English Dictionary.*

77 In the seventeenth century: R. R. Grinker. *Houses in the Rainforest* (Berkeley: University of California Press, 1994).

77 Colin corresponded with an Italian count: Mario Miniscalchi Erizzo to CT, November 29, 1956. ARC.

77-78 "The curtain rose upon a scene": From Jeffrey Green, *Black Edwardians: Black People in Britain, 1901-1914.* (London: Fank Cass and Company, 1998). Colonel James Jonathan Harrison first contacted and then hosted these Pygmies because he was looking for a profitable theatrical troupe. The trip was at first thwarted because, upon inspection by a British physician at a stopping point in Egypt, only two of the six were deemed healthy enough to go on to England. Although the Foreign Secretary at the time, Lord Lansdowne, objected to the tour—he did not know if the Pygmies were volunteers or captives, and he may have had other moral or ethnical concerns of which we have no knowledge—Harrison claimed that he had received permission from King Leopold to take the Pygmies to England. And despite the increasing opposition in England to Leopold's well-known atrocities in the Congo, *The Times* published a letter from Harrison praising Leopold's regime and casting doubt on reports of Belgian violence. After treatment at a Cairo hospital, the Pygmies arrived in the summer of 1905 and began a demanding tour of England, Scotland, and Germany. After several false starts—the papers continually reported the Pygmies were just about to return to Africa—they toured through the summer of 1907 until they finally set sail in November for Mombasa, Kenya. Harrison unsuccessfully tried to find them again in 1909.

78 On the other side of the Atlantic: P. V. Bradford and H. Blume. *Ota Benga: The Pygmy in a Zoo* (New York: St. Martin's Press, 1992).

79 The Tasaday: Scott A. Bergh, *Lindbergh* (New York: Viking, 1999), 542-3. See also Thomas Headland, "The Tasaday Controversy: Assessing the Evidence." Washington, D.C. Special Publication of the American Anthropological Association, 1992.

79 New evidence suggests: Julio Mercader, personal communication.

82 "A genetically and occupationally segregated segment": Patrick T. Putnam, "The Pygmies of the Ituri Forest." In Carleton S. Coon, ed. *A Reader in General Anthropology,* 322-42. New York: Henry Holt, 1948.

82 "Putnam and Schebesta, who corresponded often but met only once": Anne E. Putnam to CT., April 11, 1957, ARC.

82 "All the Ituri-Bambuti constitute a homogene unity": Father Paul Schebesta to CT., June 17, 1958, ARC.

82 "Pat disagreed violently with": Anne E. Putnam to CT, April 11, 1957. ARC.

CHAPTER SEVEN

85 It had the same fluid prose: Joan Mark, *The King of the World in the Land of the Pygmies.* (Lincoln and London: University of Nebraska Press, 1995), 202-3.

85 "[Racial Unity] has the support": "From Tibet to Toronto Via the Mau Mau Country," *CBC Times,* 1952, 2, ARC.

86 Newspaper articles from the early 1950s: *Daily Telegraph,* February 5, 1952.

86 Colin Turnbull, a student: *Daily Telegraph,* February 5, 1952, 1.

86 "Did you see Racial Unity": Peggy Appiah to CT, May 14, probably 1957. ARC.

86 Her son, Kwame Anthony Appiah, became an: K. A. Appiah, personal communication, December 3, 1999, to Karen Wolny.

86 Beauty contest: Dr. Richard Elzay, RG/IV, March 2, 1999, by telephone.

86 Ball Committee: LB, 47, BU; At a debutante ball: LB, 48, BU; see also, *HC,* 205.

87 A stone wall between the races: *Our Special Speaker,* Canadian Broadcasting Corporation (radio), March 8, 1953, ARC.

87 "Colin loved it there": RG/IV with Patrick Gravely, December 26, 1998, Toronto, Ontario.

88 "We both agreed": RG/IV with Patrick Gravely, December 26, 1998, Toronto.

88 "She was wealthy": Computer File: Curtis. Q&A; 10/27/91, BU.

89 "The most graceful thing": Richard Ellman, *Oscar Wilde* (New York: Vintage, 1984), 193.

90 Joesten: RG/IV with Francis Chapman, August 10, 1999, by telephone.

91 "Anne was worn out": Joan Mark, *The King of the World in the Land of the Pygmies* (Lincoln: University of Nebraska Press, 1995), 197-8.

91 She begged Francis: RG/IV with Francis Chapman, August 10, 1999.

93 "There could be no question": *FP:* 219.

93 "Stealing the Pygmies from her": RG/IV with Francis Chapman, August 10, 1999.

93 "So from the first day to the last": *FP,* 223-4.

94-95 The anthropologist Steven Feld: Steven Feld, personal communication.

95 Anne decided to return: Joan Mark, *The King of the World in the Land of the Pygmies.* (Lincoln and London: University of Nebraska Press, 1995), 201-202.

96 "Kolongo held my head": *FP,* 23-4.

96 "What's the sense, Schebesta's done it": Anne Eisner Putnam to CT, April 11, 1957, ARC.

96 "I was impressed by his energy": P. T. Baxter to the author, October 1, 1998.

97 "Briefly, the point is": CT to E. E. Evans-Pritchard, Feb. 7, 1956, ARC.

98 "There were never more than ten students in any academic year": E. E. Evans-Pritchard, "The Institute of Social Anthropology" *Oxford Magazine,* April 26, 1951.

98 "Someone will be around on Monday": CT to Phyllis Puckle, July 13, 1956, Oxford University Archives.

99 "On Wednesday I was host in Hall to Colin Turnbull"; "This morning while I was out"; "Perhaps one has to belong to one of the 'backward races'": From Gerald Harriss ed., *The McFarlane Letters: Letters to Friends, 1940-1966* (Oxford: Magdalen College, 1997), 141-2, 164.

100 "I hope I can produce something good": CT to E. E. Evans-Pritchard, June 24, 1956, Oxford University Archives.

100 She also gave Colin the folk tales: RG/IV with Christie McDonald. April 14, 1999, by telephone.

100 "Patrick Putnam did not write a great book": Joan Mark, *The King of the World in the Land of the Pygmies.* (Lincoln and London: University of Nebraska Press, 1995), 222.

101 "Schebesta's material": CT, application to the Board of Faculty of Anthropology and Geography for Probationer-Student for the Degree of Bachelor of Letters. December 17, 1956. Courtesy of the Institute of Social Anthropology, Oxford University.

101-102 Tie clip: RG/IV with Virginia Humphries, January 5, 1999. This is a story Colin told on his deathbed to Ginger Humphries, a local Kilmarnock resident who, along with her mother and father, took care of Colin when he returned, dying, from India in 1994. She recalls that he was nostalgic as he thought of that time, delighting in the memory but obviously still feeling its pain.

102 ". . . based to a minor extent upon": Board of the Faculty of Anthropology and Geography, Degree of Bachelor of Letters, Report of the Examiners, July 3, 1957, C. M. Turnbull, Magdalen College. AGR (57)10. Courtesy of the Institute of Social Anthropology, Oxford University.

102 "Did you ever think": Phyllis Puckle to CT, October 16, 1957, Oxford University Archives.

103 "We unwisely stopped": CT to Phyllis Puckle, November 25, 1957, Oxford University Archives.

103 When they reached Camp Putnam: Joan Mark, *The King of the World in the Land of the Pygmies.* (Lincoln and London: University of Nebraska Press, 1995), 206-7.

104 "I am having a glorious time": CT to Phyllis Puckle, November 25, 1957. Oxford University Archives.

104 "An expensive but delightful pastime": CT to Phyllis Puckle, November 25, 1957. Oxford University Archives.

104 Washed or unwashed buttocks: J. S. Weiner to CT., April 17, 1959.

104 In his textbook on human biology . . . : G. A. Harrison, J. S. Weiner, J. M. Tanner, and N. A. Barnicot, *Human Biology: An Introduction to Human Evolution, Variation and Growth* (New York and Oxford: Oxford University Press, 1964), 219. Weiner's former student and successor at Oxford, Geoffrey Harrison, believes that since Weiner was attempting to translate skin color measurements taken on paper swatches into much more precise reflector values, he may have asked Colin to use a portable spectrophotometer. But there is no evidence that Colin used one. It would have been cumbersome. Although the spectrophotometer was portable, it was heavy and required a wet battery source. Geoffrey Harrison to Irven DeVore on behalf of RG, September 15, 1999, courtesy of Irven DeVore.

104 "The [Bira] villagers": Joan Mark, *The King of the World in the Land of the Pygmies.* (Lincoln and London: University of Nebraska Press, 1995), 207.

105 The sexual temptations that he believed undermined the lessons of Anandamayi Ma: Computer File: "Books. IDS\failures.," Disk 5, BU.

106 "The main point": J. R. Turnbull to CT, Dec. 21, 1957. ARC.

106 "If you were at the University of Toronto": A. W. Chapman to CT, January 18, 1958, ARC.

106 "I certainly shall be awake": D. H. Turnbull to CT, December 31, 1957.

107 On November 26, 1957: Kumari Mayor to CT, November 26, 1957, ARC.

107 "I suppose they know why;" "Do you think that after a few months": CT to E. E. Evans-Pritchard, February 7, 1958, ARC.

108 She wrote him a letter: Joan Mark, *The King of the World in the Land of the Pygmies.* (Lincoln and London: University of Nebraska Press, 1995), 208.

108 Newton calculated his own time: C. Newton Beal, "Pygmies Are People Too," unpublished ms., 1-2, ARC.

109 "To Anne and to the memory of Pat": Inscription courtesy of Christie McDonald.

109 "This goes too far": Anne Eisner Putnam, Margin Notes, *The Forest People,* Anne E. Putnam, personal copy. Courtesy of Christie McDonald. Anne also wrote Colin to tell him in detail various disagreements with the particulars of his analyses of the elima ceremony and other rituals.

109 "While Anne was hurt that he did not more fully acknowledge her contribution": RG/IV with Eugenia Earle, January 27, 1999.

110 "[Anne Eisner] had an intensely inquisitive mind": CT, 1967, Eulogy for Anne Eisner Putnam, Houghton Library, Harvard University.

110 Newton wrote a children's book: Newton Beal, "Pygmies Are People Too," unpublished ms., ARC.

110 Graveside Rites held for C. Newton Beal: *Lancaster Eagle-Gazette,* p. 1 December 27, 1966. Courtesy of the Fairfield County District Library.

111 "All the others had their eyes open too": FE, unpaginated; "I never understood" CT, annotations to the diaries of Joseph A. Towles, Misc. computer files, BU.

112 "Then I was sure that I could never rest": *FP,* p. 23.

112 Kenge felt he had qualities that set him apart: Terese Hart to the author. Personal communication.

114 "All the elements are there": *MPYG,* 34.

114 "When the forest dies, we shall die"; "It echoes on and on": *FP,* 278-9.

114 He thought about Kumari often: All information about correspondences with Kumari Mayor, ARC. Kumari Sawhney (née Mayor) declined interviews for this study.

CHAPTER EIGHT

Where not directly cited, information on the relationship between Joseph Towles and Colin Turnbull in this and subsequent chapters derives largely from the diaries of Joseph Towles (Avery Center), "Lover and Beloved" (unpaginated, loose pages), and the notes, papers, and correspondences of Colin Turnbull (ARC and BU).

117 "Lewd conduct" in a YMCA: Cited in Charles Kaiser, *The Gay Metropolis* (New York: Harcourt Brace, 1997), 140-1.

117 Jim Ford . . . wrote the museum's president: James Ford collection, NAA/SI.

118 "She tried to get me into bed with her": LB, 45-6. In the same passage, CT states that this was the first time he had had sexual intercourse with a woman. BU.

118-119 Details on Michael Elliot and David Quarell: LB, 47.

119 "That made you feel unclean": LB, 64, BU.

119 "The place was so elegant": LB, 48. BU.

120 Only as late as 1966 did the New York City Police: Charles Kaiser, *The Gay Metropolis* (New York: Harcourt Brace, 1997), 145-6.

120 The New York City regulation was enforced: Neil Miller, *Out of the Past* (New York: Vintage, 1995), 365.

120 The unmarked bar: Description of the Mais Oui bar, Roy Arrons, RG/IV, November 19, 1998, by telephone. Many thanks to Charles Kaiser for putting me in touch with Arrons.

121 "Where's my beer?": JT diary, January 5, 1960, ARC.

121 "I heard a voice beside me": LB, 53, BU.

121 Joseph Allen Towles was born on August 17, 1937: LB, 55.

122 Glenmore had taken over his mother's love: CT diary, October 29, 1990. Misc. computer files. BU.

122 A. T. Wright High School: Valorie W. Hostinsky, Director of Instruction and Personnel, Lancaster Country Public Schools, to RG, December 3, 1998.

122 "Most likely to succeed": LB, 6, BU.

122 In Virginia, Towles was a famous name: *The Towles Story. Compiled by them.* June 1957. Kansas City, Missouri. Unpublished ms.

123 Miss Queen: LB, 7-8, BU.

124 For the first two weeks: LB, 62, BU.

124 "I wondered how I had agreed": LB, 63, BU.

124 On New Year's Eve 1959: LB, 139, BU.

124-125 "Somehow I knew that this was not just the beginning": LB, 140, BU.

125 Although Joe initially assumed: JT to CT, January 27, 1960, ARC.

127 Korda writes: Michael Korda, *Another Life: Memoirs of Other People* (New York: Random House, 1999), 81.

127 "I ran into the bedroom and cried": JT Diary, April 23, 1960. ARC.

127-128 "Tickling actually makes me physically nauseous": LB, 70-71, BU.

128 Despite the fact that Colin intended to end the relationship, *et seq:* Details of CT's visit to England in 1960, from LB, loose, unpaginated, BU.

128-129 "My father rustles *The Daily Telegraph*": LB, 123-4, BU.

129 "I don't play that well": LB, 124, BU.

130 "MJE [MICHAEL J. ELLIOT] SAYS DISREGARD": Telegram, August 11, 1960. Box 7, folder 2, ARC.

130 "My sweet, I am so sorry": August 12, 1960, birthday card, Box 7, ARC.

131 "I sensed danger": LB, 130, BU.

132 In the early 1960s, Colin's Canadian relatives: RG/IV with Nancy Gravely, (CT's first cousin), September 30, 1999, by telephone.

132 "Well, I might as well give you a golf ball": RG/IV with Betty Scott. December 26, 1998, Toronto, Ontario.

132 "Walking on egg shells": RG/IV with Pat Gravely, September 29, 1999, by telephone.

132 "If Joe got in over his head": RG/IV with Patrick Gravely, December 26, 1999, Toronto, Ontario.

132 "I lay in bed": JT diary, April 14, 1963, ARC.

133 "It was our trip, our honeymoon, but I was the giver": LB, 218, BU.

133 "A number of friends came on board": LB, 220, BU.

134 "Colin looked like his teacher": RG/IV with Eugenia Earle, January 27, 1999, by telephone.

135 "If he was going to bring home": RG/IV with David Turnbull, April 1, 2, 1999.

135 Seretse Khama: Michael Dutfield, *A Marriage of Inconvenience: The Persecution of Ruth and Seretse Khama.* (London: Hyman, 1990).

135 Joe agreed to go to London: Events in London et seq.: LB, unpaginated, BU.

135-136 Dudley Stevens: Stevens died of AIDS in February 1994. Information about Stevens, and correspondence between Stevens and CT, was provided by Richard Chance.

136 Their grandson slept on a cot in the hallway: RG/IV with David Turnbull, April 1, 1999, London, England.

136 "You are in England now": LB, unpaginated, loose pages, BU.

137 Joe visited Anne Frank's house: When Joe died in 1988, he had in his files a number of newspaper clippings about Anne Frank that he had collected over the years.

CHAPTER NINE

Information on Colin Turnbull's employment at the American Museum of Natural History comes from the archives of the American Museum of Natural History and the James Ford collection at the National Anthropological Archives, Smithsonian Institution. Additional materials and information were provided by current and former museum staff.

139 "It is Dr. Mead": RG/IV with Francie Train, January 14, 1999, by telephone.

140 Mead was seen as humorless: Jane Howard, *Margaret Mead: A Life* (New York: Simon & Schuster, 1984), 337.

140 Some staff believed: Trevanian is the pen name of Roger Whittaker.

140 Jim Ford incidents: interviews with anonymous sources, October 1998; RG/IV with Scotty McNeish, March 7 and March 15, 1999; RG/IV with Gordon Willey, March 16, 1999; RG/IV with Stephen Williams, January 28 and March 6, 1999, all by telephone.

140 Jim Ford biographical details: see Michael J. O'Brien and R. Lee Lyman, *James A. Ford and the Growth of Americanist Archaeology* (Columbia: University of Missouri Press, 1998).

142 Quimby wrote Ford on July 1, 1960: George Quimby to Jim Ford, July 1, 1960, NAA/SI.

142 "You could use this,": George Quimby to Jim Ford, undated, probably early July, 1960, NAA/SI.

142 "As you must have gathered from correspondence": "Walter Williams" to CT, July 22, 1960. NAA/SI.

143 "Thank you for your letter": CT to "Helen Quigley", July 20, 1960, NAA/SI.

143 Colin then answered Williams, stressing that he could do nothing: CT to "Walter Williams," July 27, 1960, NAA/SI.

143-144 "The most dreadful thing has happened": "Helen Quigly" to CT undated, NAA/SI.

144 "I was very sorry to hear from your letter of all the trouble you are having": CT to "Mrs. Quigly" undated, NAA/SI.

144 "P.S. Phil, for laughs read the Quigly correspondence": CT to Philip Gifford, undated, NAA/SI.

145 "The distressing and disgraceful imbroglio": "Nicodemus Lovelace" to CT, August 9, 1960, NAA/SI.

146 "Please give my very kindest regards to Mrs. Quigly and to Mr. Williams: CT to "Rev. Lovelace," August 23, 1960, NAA/SI.

146 "It becomes my tragic duty to reply": "Alfred Wollensack" to CT, undated, NAA/SI.

147 "Thank you for your kind letter of August 24, needless to say I am terribly distressed: CT to "Alfred Wollensack" August 26, 1960, NAA/SI.

147-148 "I cannot believe": CT to Miss Faith Pomponio, undated, NAA/SI.

148 "The idols will, as you said in your letter": "Pen-pals" to CT, August 28, 1960. NAA/SI.

148-149 "I was delighted to get your letter, also the Heathern Idols." CT to Pen-pals, August 29, 1960, NAA/SI.

149 "I was told by the [white] head of security": LB, 502, BU.

150 "And again the bottom fell": LB, 504, BU.

150 "For the eighteen years I have been here": Jim Ford to James Oliver, March 2, 1964, NAA/SI. Subsequent quotations concerning CT from the same source. Details of "Jim Ford to James Oliver, March 2, 1964" from the original letter and interviews with Robert Carneiro, October 29, 1998, in New York City and Stephen Williams, January 28, 1999, by telephone.

150 "New York law may not be racially intolerant": Jim Ford to James Oliver, March 2, 1964, NAA/SI.

151 "This climatization": Jim Ford to James Oliver, March 2, 1964, NAA/SI.

151 "Turnbull is Harry's worst mistake": Jim Ford to James Oliver, March 2, 1964, NAA/SI.

151-152 Ancient diffusion of New World Pre-Columbian: Gordon Willey, *Portraits in American Archaeology* (Albuquerque: University of New Mexico Press, 1988), 69.

152 "At first it seemed as though our private dream": LB, 234, BU.

CHAPTER TEN

155 Sales of *The Forest People:* Simon & Schuster, internal memo to sales staff, February 8, 1973, Courtesy of Simon & Schuster.

156 Fredrik Barth led the attack: Fredrik Barth, "On Responsibility and Humanity: Calling a Colleague to Account." *Current Anthropology,* 1974, 15 (1): 100.

156 "It has been a Hitchcock thriller"; "To enter any village": CT to Harry Shapiro, 1966, month and day unknown, AMNH.

156 Guerilla fighters: L.-F. Vanderstraeten, *De la force publique a l'Armée Nationale Congolaise: Histoire d'une mutinerie, juillet 1960* (Bruxelles: Acadamie Royale de Belgique, 1985).

157 "Turnbull had gone into an African bar": Joan Mark, *The King of the World in the Land of the Pygmies* (Lincoln: University of Nebraska Press, 1995),167-8.

158-159 "Hatched the plan to enter the Congo": P. H. Gulliver to the author, November 24, 1998.

159 "I got the strong impression": P. H. Gulliver to the author, November 24, 1998.

160 "Quite a dim view of Africa": JT diary, 1965, day and month unknown, ARC.

160 "A typically scrawny, pinch-faced": JT diary, 1965, day and month unknown, ARC.

160 "The Ik . . . were, at best, a third choice": LB, unpaginated, loose pages, BU.

160 Even two decades later: CT to Michael Korda, undated letter, probably 1985, Simon & Schuster.

161 Colin estimated the cost to the museum: "Field Expenses: Twelve Months (June 1965/June 1966)," AMNH.

161 "All of the Ik were hard people"; "Nothing seemed to scare [the Ik]": RG/IV with Elizabeth Marshall Thomas, February 5, 1999, by telephone.

162 "The trouble is that so little is known": CT to Harry Shapiro, undated letter, AMNH.

162 "But all that beauty did not help": LB, 396, BU.

163 "The beautiful human": *MP,* 33.

163 "All this, however, was far from my mind": *MP,* 33.

164 "They said all who were left were the two of them": *MP,* 49.

164 "From inside the stockade": *MP,* 53.

165 "You shouldn't have wasted cigarettes in that way": *MP,* 53.

165 "For two months this would be my prison": *MP,* 68.

165-166 "Then Atum's wife died": *MP,* 86.

166 "It was this way . . . with [a man named] Lomeja": *MP:* 197-8.

166 "I think I came closer to losing my humanity": Draft for introduction to Pimlico Edition of *The Mountain People,* undated, probably 1992, BU.

166 "My first revelation": CT *Omni,* June, 1983: 87-90; 124; 126-134.

167 "Today Colin and I": JT diary, October 24, 1965, ARC.

167 "Together . . . we discovered": *MP,* 6.

167 "I am not sure that [Joe's] presence": LB, 287, BU.

168 "In no way did it excite me": LB, 287, BU.

168 "So I got angry at Joe": LB, 405, BU.

168 "I had replied that Joe and I would love to come": LB, 408, BU.

168 "Colin is blood-mad": JT diary, 1966, day and month unknown, ARC.

168 "Still in my pajamas": CT to JT, dated September 1966, ARC.

168-169 "5:30 P.M. Heat soufelir": CT to JT, written September 1966, mailed to JT on November 23, 1966, ARC.

169 "He was angry with me for that": LB, 410, BU.

CHAPTER ELEVEN

172 "That was all there was to it": LB, 411, BU.

172 Colin was staying at the Excelsior hotel: LB, 411, BU.

172 "[W.] and his friends were good companions": LB, 412, BU.

172 "It was not disagreeable": LB, 412, BU.

173 Paid Colin a visit: "Outsider," *The New Yorker,* August 20, 1966.

174 "When the rains failed": *MP,* 265.

174 "All is very well indeed": CT to Harry Shapiro, May 28, 1966, AMNH.

174-175 "[The Ik are so weak]": CT to Mrs. Helen Kenyon, undated but certainly late spring or early summer 1966, AMNH.

175 "Ten year old Adupa": CT to Harry Shapiro, August 23, 1966. AMNH.

175 "As she raised her hand to her mouth": *MP,* 132.

175 When her parents came back a week later: My description of the appearance of Adupa's body one week after her death is based on information on body decomposition in the Pirre climate provided by the Smithsonian Institutions' chief forensics investigator, Douglas Ubelaker.

176 "The only tradition": CT to Harry Shapiro, August 23, 1966. AMNH.

176 "It will be a chance to build": CT to Harry Shapiro, August 23, 1966, AMNH.

176 "My suggestion was simple": *MP,* 284.

177 "The Ik have developed individuality": CT, "Dying Laughing," *New York Times,* November 29, 1972.

177 "Oneself one is looking at": *MP,* 11-12.

178 "The parallel between the Ik": Ashley Montagu to Michael Korda, June 8, 1972. Portions were later used as a promotional on the book jacket. Courtesy of Simon & Schuster.

178 "The systematic study": E. O. Wilson, *Sociobiology: The New Synthesis* (Cambridge: Harvard University Press, 1975) 1.

178 While reading *The Mountain People:* Robert Ardrey to Michael Korda, May 21, 1972, courtesy of Simon & Schuster.

179 "Dr. Turnbull, I am sure": Robert Ardrey to Michael Korda, May 21, 1972, courtesy of Simon & Schuster.

179 "Have I written a book?"; "Wild correspondence": CT to Michael Korda, Sept. 2, 1972, courtesy of Michael Korda.

179 "The rat man": John B. Calhoun, *Smithsonian Magazine,* September, 1972, 27-32.

180 "[*The Mountain People*] is both fascinating and heart-breaking": Claude Lévi-Strauss to CT., November 14, 1972. Courtesy of David Turnbull.

180 31,000 copies: *Los Angeles Times* promotion, February 11, 1973 in anticipation of CT book tour.

180 David Hapgood: Simon & Schuster promotional blurb, 1972. Courtesy of David Turnbull.

180 "Turnbull compiles the details": Horace Judson, review of Colin Turnbull's *The Mountain People. Time,* November 20, 1972.

180 "Even alone in its corner": Christopher Lehmann-Haupt, "A Flower of Civilization's Evil," review of Colin Turnbull's *The Mountain People, The New York Times,* October 30, 1972.

181 "[Turnbull] has gazed upon the Ik": Hugh Kenner, "A Hungry Ik is a Mean and Nasty Ik," review of *The Mountain People, New York Times Book Review,* November 12, 1972: 3.

181 "Admitting that for the first time in fourteen years": Michael Korda to John Leonard, November 9, 1972. Courtesy of Michael Korda.

182 "Deserves both to be sanctioned": Fredrik Barth, "On Responsibility and Humanity: Calling a Colleague to Account." *Current Anthropology,* 1974, 15 (1): 100.

182 "Goes about her business": *MP,* 136.

182 "I do know that Atum enjoyed": *MP,* 181.

183 "There will be many anthropologists": Fredrik Barth, "On Responsibility and Humanity: Calling a Colleague to Account." *Current Anthropology,* 1974, 15 (1): 102.

183 They have been studied anew: Bernd Heine, "*The Mountain People:* Some Notes on the Ik of Northeastern Uganda." *Africa* 1985, 55 (1): 3-16.

184 "After they had been informed": Bernd Heine, "*The Mountain People:* Some Notes on the Ik of Northeastern Uganda." *Africa* 1985, 55 (1): 3.

184 One anthropologist writing in 1995: Nancy Scheper-Hughes, *Death Without Weeping* (Los Angeles and Berkeley: University of California Press, 1995).

184 Before publishing Barth's charges: RG/IV with Fredrik Barth, February 2, 1999.

185 "However . . . since Barth, whom I can only assume": CT, "Reply," *Current Anthropology,* 1974, 15 (1): 103.

185 "Reasonably dissatisfied": CT, "Reply", *Current Anthropology,* 1974, 15 (2): 355.

186 "I am enjoying giving away the Ik's money": CT to Frances Train, February 24, 1974.

187 "A wild idea": Peter Brook to Michael Korda, June 14, 1973, Simon & Schuster.

CHAPTER TWELVE

189 "The entire construction project cost a little more than $50,000": LB, loose pages, unpaginated. BU. In 1990, Colin sold the property for a little more than $450,000: Real estate flyer, James W. Luttrell Real Estate, Inc., 1990.

190 "Mr. Turnbull's place": RG/IV with anonymous clerk, General Store, Lancaster, Virginia.

190 "Like all deaths . . . an inconvenience": LB, loose pages, unpaginated, BU.

190 "A person who has never known real love": JT Diary, June 24, 1963, ARC.

190 "Poor old Anne": JT Diary, May 24, 1967, ARC.

190 "It is so unfair": LB, 400. BU.

190 He received As: College transcripts of Joseph A. Towles, Box 7, Folder 6, ARC.

191 Joe worked especially hard: LB, loose pages, unpaginated, BU.

191 In fact, most museum curators believe: Theodore Celenko ed., *Egypt in Africa* (Bloomington: Indiana University Press, 1996), 1; see also, Thomas D. Nicholson, "The Hall of Man in Africa at the American Museum of Natural History." *Curator,* 1973, XV/1, 5-24.

191 "But it was clear, once again": JT diary, 1964, day and month unknown. ARC.

192 "Lies mainly in the hands of the whites": J. A. Towles and C. M. Turnbull. "The White Problem in America." *Natural History,* 1968, LXXVII (6): 6-10; 18.

194 "I knew that for what it was": JT diary, 1967, day and month unknown.

194 "It became so bad": LB, 408. BU.

194-195 "[The piano] was yours, and you loved it": LB, 410. BU.

195 "Now at last I can do something worthwhile": JT diary, May 18, 1968. ARC.

195 "It became obvious": RG/IV with W. O'Barr. January 14, 1999.

195-196 "My point about having an extra hand": CT to Harry Shapiro, undated, probably Winter, 1968. AMNH archives.

196 "I feel that we should participate": CT to Harry Shapiro, undated, probably Winter, 1968. AMNH archives.

196 ". . . a fake": RG/IV with Francie Train. November 28, 1998.

196-197 While making love at night: JT diary, ARC: a number of diary entries from 1968 and 1969 include explicit commentary about CT's body.

197 "Oh, so he's back with his boy friend": LB, loose pages, unpaginated. BU.

198 One of the biggest grants: RG/IV with John Yellen, National Science Foundation, May 15, 1999, by telephone. Only large-scale archaeological or paleobiology projects, like Scotty McNeish's work on the origins of agriculture and Clark Howell's studies of hominid evolution, exceeded the amount of Colin's grant.

198 *The Black Experience:* Colin Turnbull file, Simon & Schuster, courtesy of Simon & Schuster.

198 "I don't know what to do": LB, 428, BU.

198 "I publish a book and think": LB, 429, BU.

199 Colin told his Canadian cousins: RG/IV with Sheila Patterson, Betty Scott, and Patrick Gravely, December 27, 1998, Toronto, Ontario.

199 Joe gave him a final grade of B: LB, loose pages, unpaginated, BU.

200 Leff and Turnbull: RG/IV with Sam Leff, January 22, 1999; February 15, 1999.

200 "In a day when militant black": Clifford Lord to the students, faculty and friends of Hofstra. February 5, 1969, Hofstra University Archives.

200 In the spring of 1970: RG/IV with Sam Leff, January 22, 1999; Febuary 15, 1999, by telephone.

201 "Like a nigger": LB, loose pages, unpaginated, BU.

201 "The trappings were distinctly European": LB, loose pages, unpaginated, also described in *MPYG.*

202 "Just before the men": LB, loose pages, unpaginated, BU, also described in *MPYG.*

202 "Now it will rain": LB, loose pages, unpaginated, BU.

203 "I would never have thought it possible": LB, loose pages, unpaginated, BU.

204 In the early 1980s, the Italian Catholic sisters: Roy Richard Grinker, *Houses in the Rainforest* (Los Angeles and Berkeley: University of California Press, 1994), 67.

206 "You are asleep in the next room": CT to JT, Nov. 30, 1970, "5:45 A.M.," ARC.

206 Kenge spent the days sitting by Colin's bed: Interviews with Fances Train, June 14, 1999, Robert L. Humphrey, various dates.

207 Joe had decided that he was a ritual priest: RG/IV with Frances Train, June 14, 1999, by telephone.

208 "He seems to have no control over money": LB, loose pages, unpaginated, BU.

CHAPTER THIRTEEN

The information conveyed in this chapter comes mainly from the author's interview with Peter Brook in Paris, March 30, 1999.

210 "That Peter Brook is the most talented": Cited in David Williams, ed. *Peter Brook: A Theatrical Casebook* (London: Metheun, 1988), xvii.

211 "The leprous state": David Williams in David Williams, ed. *Peter Brook: A Theatrical Casebook* (London: Metheun, 1988), 242.

211 Heilpern: Some time after the trip, Barbra Streisand and her boyfriend at the time, Don Johnson, approached Heilpern at a party in Manhattan to ask what Peter Brook was really like, and why he had taken such an extraordinary journey through Africa. Heilpern gave them the example of the actor acting like an old man. "Still," said Streisand, "You could have saved yourselves a lot of problems in Africa if you'd flown out an *old* actor!" Heilpern had to admit that she was right, but then Brook's actors would not have learned how to meet the extraordinary challenges and expectations Brook would lay before them. John Heilpern, *Conference of the Birds: The Story of Peter Brook in Africa.* (London: Methuen, 1989), 2.

212 "The Hausa language has no word for theatre": John Heilpern, *Conference of the Birds: The Story of Peter Brook in Africa.* (London: Methuen, 1989), 5.

213 "Kissing the lips": Peter Brook, *Threads of Time* (Woodstock: Counterpoint, 1998), 161.

214 "[an evil man]": Peter Brook's exact words were "an evil man like Slobodan Milosevic," RG/IV, March 30, 1999, Paris.

216 "When I saw Peter Brook's play": CT. *Omni,* June, 1983: 123.

217 "The great French anthropologist": *The Mountain People,* Introduction to the Pimlico Edition, 1993.

217-218 "Turnbull: Atum, I want to see what the Ik are like": Colin Higgins, *The Ik* (Paris: International Centre of Theatre Research, 1974). Quoted by permission of the Dramatic Publishing Company and the Colin Higgins Trust, James Cass Rogers, Trustee.

218 "The fire was real, the song was real"; "unbearable reality": CT, *The Mountain People,* Introduction to the Pimlico Edition, 1993.

218 "The deconstruction": Jean-Marie Benoist, 1976, "A Theatre of Catastrophe," Royal Anthropological Institute Newsletter, 14: 7-8.

219 "How painful it must have been": Albert Hunt, quoted in David Williams, ed. *Peter Brook: A Theatrical Casebook* (London: Metheun, 1988), 238.

219 Reflecting on the way he was portrayed: "Turnbull replies" 1976, Royal Anthropological Institute Newsletter, 16: 4-6.

219 "Appalling but nothing more": Julian Pitt-Rivers, "Review of "The Ik.'" *Times Literary Supplement,* November, 1976.

220 "He is harshly awakened": David Williams, in David Williams, ed. *Peter Brook: A Theatrical Casebook* (London: Metheun, 1988), 232.

220 "I am writing now to give you plenty of warning": Peter Brook to CT, dated only "1975," probably November, courtesy of Peter Brook.

220 "Human degradation rehearsed;" "Listening to the applause": Irving Wardle and Albert Hunt cited in David Williams, ed. *Peter Brook: A Theatrical Casebook* (London: Metheun, 1988), 254.

220-221 "This kind of self-delusion": Fintan O'Toole, review of Peter Brook's *Threads of Time, New York Review of Books,* November 19, 1998, 28-31.

CHAPTER FOURTEEN

Information regarding Colin Turnbull's and Joseph Towles's employment at Virginia Commonwealth University comes mainly from interviews with John McGrath, Joseph Marollo, Ed Knipe, and Robert L. Humphrey, and from correspondence on the subject of Joseph Towles's teaching performance. None of the documents were ever included in a university personnel file. They are quoted here with permission of the authors. I am grateful to Ed Knipe for providing most of the documents.

223 "Here the county reeks of hatred": LB, loose pages, unpaginated, BU.

223 He complained to author Elizabeth Marshall Thomas: RG/IV with E. M. Thomas, October 5, 1999, by telephone.

224 Wasn't that the fate?: JT, "On November 20, 1987", loose diary entry, January 4, 1988, written in Sharon, Connecticut, ARC.

224 Colin hurled that gun: RG/IV with Bob Humphrey, August 6, 1999, Washington, D.C.

225 "Joe was such a nice guy": RG/IV with Bob Humphrey, August 6, 1999, Washington, D.C.

225 "I've been trying to think": *Omni,* June, 1983, 132.

227 "I don't want to hear them": LB, 737, BU.

227 "Sweet love": CT to JT, July 25, 1983, misc. computer files, BU.

228 Colin's father Jock was ill in England: CT to JT, undated, 1973, ARC.

229 "Mr. Towles has been characterized": John McGrath to Lewis Diana, November 12, 1975, courtesy of Ed Knipe.

229 "Towles failed to show": Unidentified author to John McGrath. April 24, 1974, courtesy of Ed Knipe.

229 "I suspect that what we have here": John H. McGrath to JT, October 18, 1974, courtesy of Ed Knipe.

229-230 ". . . a tool to rid the university of unpopular faculty?": JT to John McGrath, February 4, 1975, Courtesy of Ed Knipe.

230 "gross negligency": JT to John McGrath, February 4, 1975, Courtesy of Ed Knipe.

230 "Suggesting that a white student body": McGrath to JT, February 14, 1975, courtesy of Ed Knipe.

230 "We, the students": courtesy of Ed Knipe. September 15, 1975.

230 "I have been continuously evaluating": McGrath to JT, October 30, 1975, courtesy of Ed Knipe.

230 "I gather, on the basis of a number of complaints": JT to All Faculty at VCU, courtesy of Ed Knipe.

231 "Noticeably below the department mean": committee report to John McGrath, undated, Courtesy of Ed Knipe.

231 "I think it better if I do not appear": CT to Lewis Diana, November 17, 1975, courtesy of Ed Knipe.

232 "The company [Joe] was keeping": LB, unpaginated, BU.

232 "One of the most disgusting displays of racism": LB, unpaginated, BU.

232 He wrote a nine-page single-spaced memo: CT to Anthropology Faculty, VCU, March 25, 1976, ARC.

232 "There seems to be some conflict": CT to Bob Humphrey, July 29, 1976, courtesy of Robert L. Humphrey.

232 Colin told Humphrey he wanted it clearly understood: RG/IV with Bob Humphrey, August 10, 1999, Washington, D.C.

232 The fiction of Isaac Asmiov: RG/IV with Bob Humphrey, August 10, 1999.

232 The most "significant theater event this season": Jack Kroll, "Heart of Darkness," *Newsweek,* October 25, 1976, 99.

233 "Technical advisor": Royal Shakespeare Company in the Round House. Program. January 1976. ARC.

235 "If you want to convey something": CT *Omni,* June 1983, 123.

236 "Joe was just wonderful": CT to Frances Train, March 18, 1977, courtesy of Frances Train.

236 Tried to soothe Joe's psychological wounds: CT to JT, March 16, 1977. ARC.

236 "Any adult was her prey"; "I realize": *HC,* 260-2.

237 When Colin went to the morgue in Kilmarnock: RG/IV with Robert L. Humphrey, September 1, 1999, Washington, D.C.; *HC:* 262.

237 Joe submitted a dissertation: The readers were Ed Winter, Aidan Southall, and Colin Turnbull. CT to Aidan Southall, July 16, 1979; Aidan Southall to the Academic Registrar, Makerere University, July 16, 1979. Ed Winter to the Academic Registrar, Makerere University, July 14, 1979.

238 "Tourism and Pilgrimage": CT, George Washington University, Annual Report to the Dean, academic year 1979-1980, quoted with the permission of George Washington University.

238 "I have burned my bridges": CT to JT July 15, 1979, ARC.

240 "In my perverse way, when I feel utterly miserable": CT to Dudley Stevens, November 16, 1990. Courtesy of Richard Chance.

CHAPTER FIFTEEN

In this chapter, descriptions of Kamal Hassan/Wardell Riley are based largely on the author's interview with Kamal Hassan/Wardell Riley, February 11, 1999, at Tomoka Correctional Institution, Daytona Beach, Florida. Additional information comes from legal proceedings, newspaper articles, correspondences between Hassan and Turnbull and CT, "Death by Decree," *Natural History,* 1978, 87 (5), 50-67.

241 Michel Foucault: There is no evidence that Colin ever read the work of Michel Foucault yet, like Foucault, Colin described penal institutions largely in terms of the control of space and surveillance, and he treated both guards and prisoners equally as subjects of power.

242 He did this as a favor to a friend: Joy Nachod Humes is the author of *Two Against Time: A Study of the Very Present Worlds of Paul Claudel and Charles Péguy* (Durham: University of North Carolina Press, 1978).

243 "Death by Decree": CT, "Death by Decree," *Natural History,* 1978, 87 (5), 50-67.

243 Most of the men on death row: CT, "Death by Decree," *Natural History,* 1978, 87 (5), 50-67.

243 Little at FSP had changed: David Von Drehle, *Among the Lowest of the Dead: Inside Death Row* (New York: Mass Market Paperback, 1996).

244 "The weakness of the article": CT to Willie Williams, September, 1978. ARC.

244 ". . . Expect their criminals to return to society": CT, "Death by Decree," *Natural History,* 1978, 87 (5), 66.

245-246 Scharlette Holdman: RG/IV with Scharlette Holdman, May 1, 1999, by telephone.

247 He also began to call her "mother": correspondence between Kamal Hassan and Colin Turnbull, ARC and BU.

248 "Saia has, in some undetermined manner": Letter from former State Inspector General Richard Williams, cited in Andrea Rowland. *The Florida Times-Union,* Thursday June 2, 1983. ARC

249 "Professor Turnbull was the greatest": RG/IV with Kamal Hassan, February 11, 1999, Daytona Beach, Florida.

249 He corresponded with ABC's *Prime Time Live* and with NBC's Tom Brokaw: CT to Tom Brokaw, July 25, 1986, ARC.

251 His annual reports: Information from the teaching and research evaluations of Colin Turnbull at George Washington are cited with permission of the George Washington University.

252 "It's like wrestling with pigs": RG/IV with Robert L. Humphrey, September 1, 1999.

252 Colin had helped Larry through a difficult time: RG/IV with Larry Icard. March 14, 1999, by telephone.

253 "[Joe] began pulling my rather weak hair": LB, 930, BU.

253 They had another fight on February 13, 1983; "I love Joe, Joe loves me;" "I feel I must get some simple facts straight": Miscellaneous note, February 14, 1983, ARC.

254 "I think I have it!": CT to Michael Korda, undated, probably March, 1983. Simon & Schuster files.

254 "Michael: Turnbull is turning into [Carlos] Castaneda": Memo, from "J." to Michael Korda, undated, courtesy of Simon & Schuster.

255 "Did not believe in the tenure system": CT to H. F. Bright, June 14, 1983, courtesy of George Washington University.

255 "The tenure system was established": H. F. Bright to CT, July 29, 1983. ARC.

255 "There is something about tenure": CT, "'In' Box": *Chronicle of Higher Education,* November 30, 1983.

255 "Will get someone fired": "'In' Box": *Chronicle of Higher Education,* November 30, 1983.

255 "Meaningless": "'In' Box": *Chronicle of Higher Education,* November 30, 1983.

256 "Colin Turnbull has been having a series of episodes": C. D. Linton, memorandum to the Provost, February 7, 1984, courtesy of George Washington University.

256 "Things have not changed": CT to Ruth Krulfeld, September 28, 1984, courtesy of George Washington University and Robert L. Humphrey.

257 While Joe was asleep in their Virginia home: LB, unpaginated, BU.

257 "Where is Joe?"; "For me, everyday of my life is Valentine's day": CT to JT, July 14, 1983, ARC.

258 "[*The Human Cycle*] has nothing to do with anthropology": Peter Berger, "Western Complaints," review of Colin M. Turnbull's *The Human Cycle, The New York Times Book Review,* April 10, 1983.

258 "Study Raises Question": Margaret Gray, review of *HC, The Sacramento Bee,* Sunday, July 3.1983.

259 "Proper Utilization of Aged": "Editorial: Properly Utilization of Aged," *Erie Pennsylvania Times,* June 1, 1983.

259 "What Price Freedom?": Barbara Liss, review of *HC, The Houston Post,* May 15, 1983.

259 "Dear Mike, I hear that the *NY Times*": CT to Michael Korda, April 16, 1983, courtesy of Michael Korda.

259 "I'm delighted to be called a romanticist": CT, *Omni,* June 1983, 124.

259 Joe found the omissions: LB, unpaginated, BU; RG/IV with R.L. Humphrey, May 14, 1999.

259 On December 23, 1983: JT diary, December 23, 1983, ARC.

259-260 "And when Joe said, 'Perhaps I am the Messiah'": LB, 930, BU.

260 Colin collapsed to the floor: LB, 937, BU.

264 Colin quoted one of the many disgruntled: CT, "Trouble in Paradise, *New Republic,* March 28, 1983: 32-34.

265 "Are you trying to tell me I'm crazy?: LB, loose pages, BU.

266 "Stories of Pygmies pop up everywhere": CT to JT, August 28, 1985, misc. computer files, BU.

266 "Your daughter?": CT to JT, August 14, 1985, misc, computer files, BU.

266 "Dearest Joe, you are so much younger than me": CT to JT, August 22, 1985. misc. computer files, BU.

266 "For a moment I felt life stirring": CT to JT, August 28, 1985, misc. computer files, BU.

267 "I can face [not living with you anymore]": CT to JT, September 9, 1985, misc. computer files, BU.

267 Sagalyn thought the last suggestion: Michael Sagalyn to Michael Korda, December 3, 1985, courtesy of Simon & Schuster.

267-268 "[Colin Turnbull] has been floundering": Michael Korda to Michael Sagalyn, August 28, 1985, courtesy of Michael Korda.

268 "There was one thing the doctor told me": JT diary, November 23, 1985, ARC.

269 "They did not confide in me": LB, 1052, BU.

269 "Sniggering behind curtains": LB, 950, BU.

269-270 "Oh god help me": LB, 924, BU.

CHAPTER SIXTEEN

Information on Joseph Towles's illness and the funeral for Joseph Towles and Colin Turnbull comes primarily from "Lover and Beloved," some pages of which are numbered, interviews with their physicians, their undertaker and friends, and letters and documents provided by John Enright and Robert L. Humphrey.

271 When Anne Eisner Putnam died: CT, eulogy, "For Anne, and her parents," New York City, 1967. Courtesy of Christie McDonald.

272 Rosenfeld told his colleagues: RG/IV with Gerry Rosenfeld, July 6, 1999, by telephone.

273 Lover's Lane: CT to John Enright, July 22, 1986, courtesy of John Enright.

274 Though their hosts were not often surprised: RG/IV with Mathias Guenther, Horst Jarka, and Gerry Rosenfeld, July 6, 1999, by telephone.

274-275 "There seemed very little sympathy in Colin": JT Diary, February 24, 1987, ARC.

275 "Colin was awful today": JT Diary, March 6, 1987, ARC.

275 Colin covered Joe's classes for him, but felt powerless: LB, loose pages, BU.

275 On November 20, 1987: untitled, JT loose diary entry, January 4, 1988, written in Sharon, Connecticut. ARC.

276 Though Glenmore was in jail since 1981: Despite an extensive search, I was unable to locate Glenmore or obtain any information about his incarceration.

277 Inside the prison: Glenmore Towles to JT, November 27, 1987. ARC.

277 The dean of Vassar College: CT to John Enright, October 17, 1989, courtesy of John Enright.

278 While one of Colin's books "could have been worse": CT to John Enright, June 11, 1987, courtesy of John Enright.

279 "The original negative result": Philip A. Foster (Roche Laboratory) to Fred Littleton, May 11, 1988. Courtesy of Fred Littleton, M.D. and the Estate of Colin M. Turnbull.

279 File an application to Blue Cross/Blue Shield: Application for medical insurance, June, 1990, BU.

279-280 "Short and sweet": CT to John Enright, May 6, 1988, courtesy of John Enright.

280 "For years I have been having a struggle": CT to John Enright, March 21, 1988, courtesy of John Enright.

281 "The attorney, a sympathetic soul": CT to John Enright, April 6, 1988, courtesy of John Enright.

281 "I am about to pack my suitcase": CT to John Enright, April 15, 1988, courtesy of John Enright.

281 "How do you say goodbye?": CT to John Enright, April 28, 1988, courtesy of John Enright.

282 "I still get the occasional howling fit": CT to John Enright, May 3, 1988, courtesy of John Enright.

283 "Feels as though it is being ripped asunder": CT to John Enright, May 1, 1988, courtesy of John Enright.

283 "I have the feeling the end is near": CT to John Enright, May 23, 1988, courtesy of John Enright.

283 "Dr. Turnbull," he said, "took care of him": RG/IV with Dr. Fred Littleton, June 29, 1999, by telephone.

283 "Joe put on weight": LB, 1085.

284 On several occasions, he sat at the kitchen: CT to John Enright, September 11, 1988, courtesy of John Enright.

284 "I quickly learned mopping up techniques": CT to John Enright, September 11, 1988, courtesy of John Enright.

284 The St. Croix trip ranked consistently at 8: CT to John Enright, September 11, 1988, courtesy of John Enright.

284 Taking a low dose: RG/IV with Fred Littleton, June 29, 1999, by telephone.

284 "We drove to the hospital in Kilmarnock": CT to John Enright, September 11, 1988, courtesy of John Enright.

285 Colin contemplated asking Joe about assisted suicide: CT to John Enright, October 11, 1988, courtesy of John Enright.

285 "So when with stupid British stiff upper lip": CT to John Enright, November 19, 1988, courtesy of John Enright.

286 "Just lie still, Colin": and subsequent detailed description of Joe's death, LB, 1100-1119. BU.

286 "I have seen a solitary nomad": Graduation Exercises, George Washington University, May 24, 1983.

287 Waddy's thoughts were focused on the problem of how to drain: RG/IV with Barry Waddy, Colin Turnbull and Joe Towles's undertaker, August 6, 1999, by telephone.

288 "If you want to explain why the two caskets": CT to RLH, Dec. 20, 1988. Courtesy of Bob Humphrey.

288 "Consistent with this": CT to RLH, Dec. 20, 1988. Courtesy of Bob Humphrey.

288 "Joe died yesterday. Funeral on the property": John Enright notes, courtesy of John Enright.

290 "Oh our two caskets looked so splendid": LB, 1118, BU.

CHAPTER SEVENTEEN

293 "We have each lost something": CT, Introduction to *FP,* Pimlico, New Edition, 1992.

293 Terese Hart, who wrote Kenge's letter in Swahili: RG/IV with Terese Hart, October 8, 1999.

293 . . . or because Colin had failed to send any money: John Hart and Terese Hart, "Colin Turnbull's Last Molimo," *Anthropology Newsletter,* November 1995: 39.

294 Colin reacted explosively: RG/IV with Francie Train, January 27, 1999.

294 "I am sure all of you know": CT, Letter to Friends. December 1, 1988. courtesy of Robert L. Humphrey.

297 . . . it was purchased by the Viennese-born pianist Anton Kuerti: CT to Harold Gibbard, August 8, 1991, misc. computer files, BU.

297 As Colin went through his and Joe's things; Going to the grave was almost addictive: RG/IV with Robert L. Humphrey, May 25, 1999, Washington, D.C.

298 "Any Buddhists in Samoa?": CT to John Enright, January 30, 1989, courtesy of John Enright.

298 "Any Tibetans on the Samoas?": CT to John Enright, February 7, 1989, courtesy of John Enright.

298 "Buddha and his teachings have always appealed to me": CT, India photo-diary, 1949-51. BU.

299 Stevenson did it with a bottle of old burgundy: Gavan Daws, *A Dream of Islands* (New York: Norton, 1988).

299 Colin's great uncle Willy: CT to Johanna Humphrey, July 9, 1983. Courtesy of Johanna Humphrey.

299 He declined Littleton's recommendation: Frederick C. N. Littleton to CT, September 18, 1991, courtesy of F. Littleton.

299-300 "I only wish the darned thing [HIV] would DO something": CT to Fred Littleton, September 25, 1991, misc. computer files, BU.

300 "I am serious about not seeking treatment": CT to John Enright, February 13, 1989, courtesy of John Enright.

300 "I certainly feel not one jot of loyalty": CT to Michael Radelet, February 3, 1989, courtesy of Michael Radelet.

301 Colin told Waddy he had given John Enright about $1,600: CT to Francine and Barry Waddy, 1989, undated, BU.

301 Four years later, he would amend his instructions to Waddy: CT to Bob Humphrey, April 3, 1993, courtesy of Bob Humphrey.

302 "If Dr. Colin was ever to return to our land": Curtis Abraham. "A Book the Ik Community 'Could do Without'" In *The East African,* Part 2: IV. June 30-July 6, 1997.

303 Anthropology had changed since the days of *The Forest People* and *The Mountain People*: George E. Marcus and Michael M.J. Fischer. *Anthropology as Cultural Critique: An Experimental Moment in the Human Sciences* (Chicago: University of Chicago Press, 1986), 160.

304 "More than an annoyance, which grows daily": CT, March 1, 1991, misc. computer files, BU.

305 "I hope you do not think it silly or needless": CT to Thubten Norbu, February 25, 1990, misc. computer files, BU.

305 "I do not feel that the spiritual quest": CT to Thubten Norbu, June 7, 1990, misc. computer files, BU.

305 He wrote to the directors of the retreat: CT to Marya and Miguel Schwabe, June 14, 1990, file: NECHDRJ.J14. Disk 28, BU.

307 "Holds no official position": CT to Bob Humphrey, November 2, 1991.

307 "Norbu asked if I had the nerve": RG/IV with Thom Canada, March 28, 1999.

307 "Getsul means taking vows first": CT diary, November 4, 1991, BU.

308 "But I know it is partly self regret": CT diary, December 19, 1991, BU.

308 "So believe me, my old friend Norbu": CT to Thubten Norbu, January 12, 1992. misc. computer files, BU.

309 "He whose way is the way of the heart": CT to Harold Gibbard, October 19, 1992, misc. computer files, BU.

309 "Everything I have ever loved": CT Dharamsala diary, undated, probably April 5, 1992.

309 His activities at the monastery were not remarkable but neither were they ordinary: Ven. Thupten Sherap Sangye to the author. August 28, 1999. Unfortunately, I was never able to reach the man with whom he spent the most time at the monastery, Sangye Tendar Naga, who was the librarian.

310 Colin was suspicious of Europeans: CT Dharamsala diary, March 28, 1992, 4. BU.

310 "Buddhism" he told Panda, "insists that the disciple revere his Guru": Letter to Panda, Anandamayi Ashram, April 4, 1993, entitled "How a Devotee of Anandamayi Ma Becomes a Buddhist Monk," signed, Premananda/Lobsong Rigdol, misc. computer Files, BU.

313 No one but Colin, Thubten, and Kunyang: I subsequently sent Norbu a summary of my conversation with his assistant, asking him to make any corrections he thought were necessary, and I never heard back from him.

313 "It is a monastery for a god named Shugden": Jason Vest. "Bickering Buddhists," *The Village Voice,* July 27, 1999, 44-5.

314 He spent the rest of the winter and spring of 1993 in Kilmarnock: RG/IV with Ginger Humphrey, April 1, 1999; RG/IV with Robert L. Humphrey, April 22, 1999; RG/IV with Richard Elzay, April 1, 1999, Kilmarnock, Virginia.

314 Blood spurted from Colin's arm: "T." to the author, September 20, 1999; RRG/IV with "T.", October 18, 1999, by telephone.

316 "This is my home": RG/IV with Ginger Humphrey, April 22, 1999, Kilmarnock, Virginia.

316-317 Colin told one of his doctors that he wanted no medications: RG/IV with John Deschamps, M.D., September 5, 1999, by telephone.

CHAPTER EIGHTEEN

319 "A Bushman child drinking": Robert L. Humphrey, eulogy for Colin Turnbull, August 1, 1994. Quoted with the permission of Robert L. Humphrey.

320 In January 1995, at Epulu: John Hart and Terese Hart, "Colin Turnbull's Last Molimo," *Anthropology Newsletter,* November 1995, 39.

BOOKS BY COLIN TURNBULL

1961. *The Forest People.* New York: Simon & Schuster.
1962. *The Lonely African.* New York: Simon & Schuster.
1962. *The Peoples of Africa* (Illustrated by Richard M. Powers). Cleveland, Ohio: World Publishing Company.
1965. *The Mbuti Pygmies: An Ethnographic Survey. Anthropological Papers of the American Museum of Natural History,* 50 (3): 139-282.
1965. *Wayward Servants: The Two Worlds of the African Pygmies.* Garden City, New Jersey: Natural History Press.
1966. *Tradition and Change in African Tribal Life.* Cleveland, Ohio: World Publishing Company.
1968. *Tibet.* Thubten Jigme Norbu, first author. New York: Simon & Schuster.
1973. (editor) *Africa and Change.* New York: Alfred A. Knopf.
1973. *The Mountain People.* New York: Simon & Schuster.
1976. *Man in Africa.* Garden City, New Jersey: Anchor Press/Doubleday.
1983. *The Human Cycle.* New York: Simon & Schuster.
1983. *The Mbuti Pygmies: Change and Adaptation.* New York: Holt, Rinehart, and Winston.

INDEX